T0367984

Marketing Management in Geographically Remote Industrial Clusters

Implications for
Business-to-Consumer Marketing

Marketing Management in Geographically Remote Industrial Clusters

Implications for Business-to-Consumer Marketing

George Tesar
Umeå University, Sweden &
University of Wisconsin-Whitewater, USA

Jan Bodin
Umeå University, Sweden

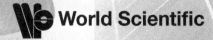

World Scientific

NEW JERSEY • LONDON • SINGAPORE • BEIJING • SHANGHAI • HONG KONG • TAIPEI • CHENNAI

Published by

World Scientific Publishing Co. Pte. Ltd.

5 Toh Tuck Link, Singapore 596224

USA office: 27 Warren Street, Suite 401-402, Hackensack, NJ 07601

UK office: 57 Shelton Street, Covent Garden, London WC2H 9HE

British Library Cataloguing-in-Publication Data
A catalogue record for this book is available from the British Library.

MARKETING MANAGEMENT IN GEOGRAPHICALLY REMOTE INDUSTRIAL CLUSTERS
Implications for Business-to-Consumer Marketing

ISBN 978-981-4383-05-9

In-house Editor: Wanda Tan

Typeset by Stallion Press
Email: enquiries@stallionpress.com

Printed in Singapore.

*This book is dedicated to
my Sluníčko,
my family*

Preface

This book is a result of many coffee (*fika*) conversations at the Umeå School of Business and Economics with our colleagues and friends. The Umeå School of Business and Economics is located in northern Sweden, in an area populated by entrepreneurs, small manufacturing enterprises, and even large international corporations, and a short distance away from geographically remote industrial clusters. For example, a short distance from campus is one of the largest forest industry clusters, an industrial cluster that serves "forest companies" in northern Sweden. There is also a cluster that serves automobile companies in testing automotive products. And not far away is one of the world's largest clusters for building products from wood (e.g., stages for performing arts, custom-designed staircases, and large wooden interior structures). During our discussions, we wondered why smaller enterprises in northern Sweden are so willing to cooperate. We also learned that some of our colleagues have managed research projects whose objective was to learn how to form even more industrial clusters to bring more productive enterprises together.

Forming industrial clusters, especially in geographically remote areas such as northern Sweden, is not a simple process. There are economic, social, and even environmental conditions that very much influence this process. Although similar conditions may exist in other parts of the world, few, if any, industrial clusters exist. In discussions with our North American colleagues, we learned that the individual competitive drive combined with a strong will to succeed tends not to tolerate cooperation. From our African doctoral students, we learned that cooperative action outside of the extended family is not possible due to the strength of family ties. We wanted to explore these perceptions, observations, and generalizations.

Since both of us have had academic and professional experiences with foreign universities in several countries, we decided to compare notes and ideas concerning geographically remote industrial clusters abroad. We learned that some universities, mostly in rural areas, have attempted to form industrial clusters by first building incubators or industrial parks. They have targeted small and medium enterprises in their service areas to come and be part of a value chain designed by academics and implemented with the help of university administrators, local business leaders, and government officials. Sometimes it has worked and sometimes it has not. However, economic and regional developers today are eager to form industrial clusters in geographically remote areas because they believe that they will create jobs.

We wanted to explore some of these issues. We solicited for cases that would help us dig deeper into these issues and help students, and perhaps some of our interested colleagues, to better understand the relationship between marketing management and geographically remote industrial clusters that attempt to market their products or services both in business-to-business and business-to-consumer markets. We thank you all!

George Tesar
Jan Bodin

Contents

Case Contributors

Andrew Arbuthnott was, up until the summer of 2012, a Lecturer at the Umeå School of Business and Economics, Umeå University, Sweden. He was part of the Entrepreneurship teaching team at the Umeå School of Business and Economics, where he lectured at the undergraduate and postgraduate levels. His teaching and research expertise is in the fields of business administration, entrepreneurship, and regional cluster development. Email: arbuthnott.andrew@gmail.com

David Ballantyne is an Associate Professor of Marketing at the University of Otago School of Business, New Zealand, and an International Fellow at the Centre for Relationship Marketing and Service Management, Hanken School of Economics, in Helsinki, Finland. He is a co-author of *Relationship Marketing: Bringing Quality, Customer Service and Marketing Together* (1991), the first international text published in this field of inquiry. He is a member of the editorial review boards of the *European Journal of Marketing, Journal of Business-to-Business Marketing, Industrial Marketing Management, Journal of Business Market Management,* and *International Marketing Review*. His current research interests are the service-dominant logic of marketing, relationship marketing, internal marketing, and

dialogue as a co-creative knowledge-generating mode in marketing.
Email: david.ballantyne@otago.ac.nz

Tomas Blomquist, PhD, is a Professor at the Umeå School of
Business and Economics, Umeå University, Sweden. He is head of the
"Projects, Innovations and Networks" research profile at the business
school, and Director of the Erasmus Mundus joint Master's Program
in Strategic Project Management with Heriot-Watt University and
Politecnico di Milano. In recent years, he has worked on research
concerning projectified firms and how they organize, manage, and
control their projects, as well as studies in product development and
customer projects. His work has been published in several journals
including *Business Strategy and the Environment, Industrial Marketing
Management,* and *International Journal of Project Management.*
Email: tomas.blomquist@usbe.umu.se

Jan Bodin is a Lecturer and Head of Marketing Section at the Umeå
School of Business and Economics, Umeå University, Sweden, where
he also previously earned a doctorate in business administration
(marketing). He has a long history of cooperation with the Umeå
Institute of Design, where he also previously held a position. He
also lectured at the ICN Business School in Nancy, France, during
a period of two years; first as a Visiting Chair in Marketing and
Design sponsored by the region of Lorraine, and afterwards as an
Associate Professor in Marketing. His research is focused on product
development in general, and the interaction between marketing,
design, engineering, and production in particular. Other research
interests are wine marketing and artists' entrepreneurial ventures.
Email: jan.bodin@usbe.umu.se

Gert-Olof Boström is an Assistant Professor of Marketing at the
Umeå School of Business and Economics, Umeå University, Sweden.
His research interest is in the business-to-business context, where he
has done several studies. One of his focuses is on the adoption of
new technology. He is currently conducting an international project

in order to study geographical differences in factors affecting the adoption of IT applications. Email: gert-olof.bostrom@usbe.umu.se

Håkan Boter is a Professor at the Umeå School of Business and Economics, Umeå University, Sweden. He is also active at the Centre for Inter-Organizational Innovation Research (CiiR), focusing on innovation processes in non-metropolitan regions. Besides innovation aspects, his main fields of research are entrepreneurship, business development, internationalization, and emerging markets/developing countries. Email: hakan.boter@usbe.umu.se

Tom Bramorski is a Professor of Management at the University of Wisconsin-Whitewater, USA. He received his MBA and PhD degrees from The University of Iowa, USA. He has published four books and numerous papers in academic journals, and has presented papers at national and international conferences. He also serves on the editorial boards of several academic journals in the areas of operations, supply chain, operations strategy, and quality management. Dr. Bramorski has consulted with companies and government agencies in the United States and Central Europe in the areas of quality management, operations management, technology management, and Central European privatization issues. He frequently conducts guest lectures at several universities and training institutions in Europe. He is a former Fulbright Senior Lecturer in Oman and in Poland.

Thommie Burström received his doctorate from the Umeå School of Business and Economics, Umeå University, Sweden. He started his career as a military officer in the Swedish army, after which he became a sales manager in the home electronics industry and in the advertisement industry. From 1999 to 2003, he studied at the Umeå School of Business and Economics, and then worked as a business consultant and university teacher. He has dedicated his work efforts to the academy since being accepted to the doctoral program. He typically performs research through a practice approach, aiming to understand what is actually "going on" in new product development projects. His specialty is in the field of platform studies. Email: thommie.burstrom@usbe.umu.se

Sue Caple is an Assistant Lecturer at the University of La Verne, USA. She received her PhD from the University of Otago, New Zealand, in 2011. Her research interests are collaboration, networks, and place branding. Email: scaple5555@gmail.com

Arnim Decker is an Assistant Professor at the Centre for International Business, Aalborg University, Denmark. He received his doctoral degree from Universidad Complutense de Madrid in Spain. Dr. Decker also studied Business Economics and Finance at the University of Cologne in Germany. Between his undergraduate and his doctoral studies, he visited at the Universidad de Chile. He also spent some time as a trainee at Deutsche Bank AG in Cologne. Dr. Decker entered his doctoral studies with a broad international financial background, which he extended by focusing on environmental management and risk control for his thesis research. Dr. Decker also has an entrepreneurial and consulting background; he established an IT firm that specialized in web server management, which he eventually sold. His consulting experience ranges from gathering market intelligence to using applications of electronic commerce. Email: decker@business.aau.dk

Jens Graff is an Associate Professor and Chair of International Business Management at the SolBridge International School of Business, Woosong University, South Korea. He received his PhD from the Umeå School of Business and Economics, Umeå University, Sweden, where he also lectured. Before that, he lectured at the Copenhagen Business College, Denmark, for more than two decades in most business administration disciplines. His business career has included, but has not been limited to, marketing consulting and business advisory assignments. Email: jensgraff@outlook.com

Sofia Isberg, PhD, is an Assistant Professor at the Umeå School of Business and Economics, Umeå University, Sweden. She is responsible for educational matters within the Marketing Section at the business school, and is also the program director for an undergraduate program with a focus on service management. Her research interests include service management, service logic, service innovation, and branding. In recent years, much of her focus has been on studying organizations from a sustainability perspective, including the use of corporate social responsibility as part of branding. Email: sofia.isberg@usbe.umu.se

Mattias Jacobsson, PhD, is a Lecturer at the Umeå School of Business and Economics, Umeå University, Sweden. He currently holds a two-year post-doctoral position in the "Projects, Innovations and Networks" research profile. He mainly teaches in the fields of organizational behavior, project management, and leadership. In addition to his PhD, Dr. Jacobsson has a Degree of Licentiate of Philosophy, a Bachelor and a Master of Social Science with a major in Business Administration, a Master's degree in Information Technology in Business Development, and a University diploma in Law. Since 2008, he has also been a member of the Business Advisory Board of RedQ. Email: mattias.jacobsson@usbe.umu.se

Johan Jansson, PhD, is a Senior Lecturer and Assistant Professor at the Umeå School of Business and Economics, Umeå University, Sweden. His research mainly concerns consumer choices with environmental and social impacts, corporate and consumer responsibility, and consumer decision making related to eco-innovations. Jansson has published in journals such as *Journal of Consumer Marketing*, *Journal of Consumer Behaviour*, and *Business Strategy and the Environment*. He is currently the Director of the Research Institute for Sustainability and Ethics in Business (RiseB) at the Umeå School of Business and Economics, where he teaches primarily in marketing ethics and consumer behavior. Since 2008, he has also been a member of the Business Advisory Board of RedQ. Email: johan.jansson@usbe.umu.se

Catherine Lions is currently an Assistant Professor at the Umeå School of Business and Economics, Umeå University, Sweden. She was previously an Associate Professor at Euromed Management, France. She received her PhD from the University of Grenoble in 1987. She became a CPA in 1993 and worked for several years in an auditing firm. Her research interests include value-based management and intellectual capital. She teaches management accounting, operations management, and risk management. Email: catherine.lions@usbe.umu.se

Hamid Moini is a Professor of Finance at the University of Wisconsin-Whitewater, USA, and a resource person specializing in corporate finance and globalization of small- and medium-sized enterprises. Over the past 25 years, Dr. Moini has focused on the development of global market entry strategies for smaller firms and strategic planning for minority-owned banks. In his practice, Dr. Moini offers a range of services including planning for foreign direct investments, capital budgeting, and financial structuring, along with cross-cultural training for managers. He has published many articles in leading journals in finance and international business. Email: moinia@uww.edu

Britta Näsman is a Research Assistant in Marketing at the Umeå School of Business and Economics, Umeå University, Sweden. Her research interest is in the role of market information and the impact of this information. She is especially interested in the process of formulating the marketing strategy for a company. Her studies are focused on the business-to-business marketing environment. Email: Britta.nasman@gmail.com

Daniel W. Ndyetabula is currently a PhD fellow at the Centre for International Business, Aalborg University, Denmark. Email: dwn@business.aau.dk

Carl Patrik Nilsson is the Director of the Stockholm Institute of Communication Science (STICS), working as a lecturer and consultant in marketing and marketing communication. He was previously associated to the Center for Digital Business at Umeå University, Sweden. He holds a PhD in Marketing from the Umeå School of Business and Economics at Umeå University. Email: patrik@stics.se

Francisco Puig is an Associate Professor at the Department of Management, University of Valencia, Spain. He holds a PhD in Economics and Business (Extraordinary Award) from the University of Valencia. He was previously a visiting researcher at the HEC Montreal, Canada, and at the Manchester Business School, UK. He specializes in strategy, turnaround, and clusters/industrial districts, and has published articles in leading journals as well as co-authored books and chapters in collective volumes. Email: francisco.puig@uv.es

Helena Renström is an Assistant Professor at the Umeå School of Business and Economics, Umeå University, Sweden. She has a PhD from the Hanken School of Economics, Helsinki, Finland. Her research interests include service marketing, relationship marketing, service innovation, and consumer behavior and attitudes. She has been studying the role of dynamics in customer relationships and the management of customer relationships in different service industries. Her work has been published in *Managing Service Quality*. Since the fall of 2012, she has been the Marketing Manager at Skellefteå Municipality. Email: helena.renstrom@usbe.umu.se

Marcelo Royo-Vela is a Full Professor of Marketing in the Department of Commercialization and Market Research at the Economics School, University of Valencia, Spain. He holds a PhD in Business Sciences from the University of Valencia. He has been a visiting scholar and researcher at UNC-Chapel Hill, Erasmus University, University of Pittsburgh, and University of Girona. From 2005 to 2009, he was the Director of the International Master in Business Administration at the University of Valencia, focusing on global marketing strategies and international marketing communications.

He has authored books, chapters in collective volumes, and research papers published in the *European Journal of Marketing, Journal of Current Issues and Research in Advertising, Journal of Tourism Management, Sex Roles, Journal of Air Transport Management, Online Information Review,* and other well-known Spanish refereed journals. At the same time, he has presented papers at the EMAC, AM, and AMS Conferences. Email: marcelo.royo@uv.es

George Tesar holds the title of Professor Emeritus from the Umeå School of Business and Economics, Umeå University, Sweden, and from the University of Wisconsin-Whitewater, USA. He serves as the Chief Scientific Officer for Social Marketing at the Institute for Lifestyle Options and Longevity (ILOL) in Prague, and is also an Adjunct Professor at Aalborg University in Denmark. His research focus is on the internationalization of smaller high-technology manufacturing enterprises and the technology transfer of new products and ideas. Email: tesarg@uww.edu

Maree Thyne is an Associate Professor at the University of Otago, New Zealand. Her research interests are research methodology, consumer behavior, and tourism marketing. She is especially interested in tourist behavior, cruise tourism, and environmental values. Email: maree.thyne@otago.ac.nz

Romeo V. Turcan is an Associate Professor of International Business and Entrepreneurship at the Department of Business and Management, Aalborg University, Denmark. His research interests are in the areas of internationalization of knowledge-intensive ventures, international entrepreneurship, sociology of markets, and theory building. He received his PhD in International Entrepreneurship at the Hunter Centre for Entrepreneurship, University of Strathclyde, Glasgow, and his MSc in International Marketing at the Department of Marketing, University of Strathclyde, Glasgow. Email: rvt@business.aau.dk

Zsuzsanna Vincze is an Associate Professor at the Umeå School of Business and Economics, Umeå University, Sweden, and a Docent at the Turku School of Economics, University of Turku, Finland. Her present research focus is on coordination mechanisms in transforming clusters, within a project financed by the Academy of Finland. Besides this project, her research interests include the internationalization process of smaller manufacturing enterprises as well as the creation and change of business models in various industries. She teaches entrepreneurship courses at the Master's level, and supervises doctoral theses about entrepreneurial growth in developing countries. Email: zsuzsanna.vincze@usbe.umu.se

Introduction

In the evolution of various concepts in marketing and related disciplines, there is a time when some of the theories, concepts, and even practices begin to merge and their synergy creates a new approach or new way of thinking. This creative process generates a new field of study that potentially may contribute to the solution of economic or social problems. The material discussed in this case book focuses on two such approaches — marketing management and industrial clusters; more specifically, the contemporary approach to marketing management with its role as the dominant managerial function in modern enterprises, especially smaller manufacturing enterprises, and geographically remote industrial clusters. When these two concepts are linked, they produce a powerful tool for economic development in areas or regions of the world considered as remote by many governmental agencies.

Interest in marketing management and geographically remote industrial clusters (GRICs) is relatively recent, although economic and regional development specialists have discussed the possibility of introducing marketing management as a useful framework for economic and regional development. Several university programs in North America and Europe have conducted seminars to examine

1

the feasibility of combining marketing management and industrial cluster development as a viable economic and regional development tool. Some of these seminars have produced research papers and some have even reached academic publications. More recently, some marketing programs have introduced basic seminars and workshops on the topic.

The objective of this case book is to present a broad theoretical and conceptual framework, a series of original cases, and an integration of topics. It is intended to be used as a primary textbook in courses, seminars, and training workshops focusing on marketing management activities in GRICs. The textbook might also be useful in examining GRICs and the potential role that they might play in international operations, especially in exports. Most of the cases include international dimensions or problems that need to be examined from an international perspective.

GRICs are perceived today as important tools in economic and regional development because they create jobs, stabilize local economies, increase the tax base, and in general stabilize the social climate in geographically remote areas and regions. Most GRICs are made up of smaller manufacturing enterprises (SMEs) that are still growing or evolving into major international competitors. Many of them started as fledgling high-technology shops and grew into stable SMEs as they gained market recognition. Others started out as machine shops, fabrication shops, or some other craftsman-based entities that found productive roles in GRICs. Within GRICs, SMEs have the potential to grow and expand their operations collectively or individually and eventually become job-creating entities within their geographic area or region.

The concept of GRICs and their formation is not a new phenomenon in economic or regional development; however, with the new emphasis on local entrepreneurship, local value creation, and regional development, many regional and local governments now place great emphasis on establishing local incubators, technology and industrial parks, and other infrastructural components to stimulate economic development and growth. Numerous examples can be found in North and South America, Australia, and Europe. GRICs have several characteristics in common such as transportation, communication, specialized labor, and resource management issues, among others. Marketing management specialists suggest that if GRICs are managed with clear marketing management perspectives, they will succeed.

Economic and regional development specialists have been writing about industrial clusters since the early 1980s, and have managed to convince governments in several countries to encourage and support their formation. Formation of industrial clusters initially was considered to be a process that occurred naturally. Today, most economic and regional development specialists believe that industrial clusters can be formed and serve as a useful development tool, especially in geographically remote areas or regions where they combine the activities of various enterprises in basic agricultural production, high-technology mining operations, manufacturing products, or specialized service offerings.

What is also new about GRICs is the use of theories and concepts of marketing management as their main operational and strategic philosophy. Marketing management is used to formulate GRICs' missions, harvest available resources (financial, physical, or human), identify market opportunities, and build productive value chains. Marketing management is also used to bring together SMEs, local fabrication and machine shops, local service shops, and entrepreneurs to collectively produce products and services that deliver lasting market value for their consumers and end users.

To a certain degree, GRICs are based on the fundamental notion of cooperation. Although this notion may not necessarily be fully accepted in mainstream marketing in large, internationally competitive markets, it seems to be acceptable among GRICs' member enterprises. Marketing managers generally do not think in collective, non-competitive terms; they prefer market conditions where they can gain strong competitive advantage and are able to manage a significant and well-defined market share. When enterprises join together to form a new value chain or simply work together for the benefit of their consumers or end users and simultaneously create value for the local community, they need to cooperate by sharing marketing ideas, concepts, approaches, and strategies.

Some entrepreneurs, startup enterprises, or successful SMEs find the notion of cooperation in GRICs restrictive, and attempt to expand their operations outside of GRICs by participating in other value chains or by simply developing their own market presence without the involvement of the entire GRIC. Some technologically innovative enterprises simply outgrow their role in a GRIC and venture outside of it. Yet, a small number of enterprises that started their operations in a GRIC have become major international competitors and are very proud of the fact that they started in a GRIC.

The case study approach was selected to examine the recent interest in using marketing management as the primary operational and strategic philosophy in GRICs. To examine the various aspects of how marketing management is embedded into GRICs' operational and strategic philosophies, specific original cases were collected. They represent four major GRIC areas: (1) formation, (2) internal and external information needs, (3) marketing management operations and strategies, and (4) information technology issues. The cases have been written to stimulate discussions among students concerning their views on the formation, development, and operations of GRICs as a major economic development tool.

The text and the cases are presented in a sequential process to familiarize students with the complexities of how a GRIC is formed and how marketing management is embedded into its operational and strategic processes. Some of the material is based on research experiences, while some has been collected over several years of consulting experience with SMEs in remote areas in North America and Europe. The combination of our experiences gives this case book a broad international perspective.

Chapter 1

An Introduction to Geographically Remote Industrial Clusters

There are two types of industrial clusters that can be found among commercial activities today: industrial clusters that historically developed in many areas around the world, and more recently modern industrial clusters that were formed or initiated by entrepreneurial individuals. Most industrial clusters that evolved over time were based on an abundance of natural resources, concentration of knowledge, or uniqueness of the area. Examples can be found in mining ore or drilling for oil, transferring university research into industries such as electronics or biotechnology, and growing feed corn for livestock or conversion to ethanol. More recent industrial clusters formed or initiated by entrepreneurial action systematically sought some common dimensions, generally in remote areas, and their objective was to establish profitable enterprises, create jobs, and contribute to the economic and social stability of the area. Modern industrial clusters represent a new and innovative tool of management; and their formation, growth, strategies, and operations are emphasized in the content that is to follow.

Industrial Clusters

Geographically remote industrial clusters (GRICs) can be found in areas where industrial enterprises concentrate in order to produce

7

goods or services or to perform complementary, supplementary, or support activities for other enterprises in or out of the cluster. GRICs tend to create conditions in which industrial enterprises coexist and grow symbiotically, in spite of many infrastructural challenges and frequently adverse environmental conditions. GRICs also evolved because local conditions were transformed into favorable market demand for special goods or services such as natural resources, forest products, or agricultural commodities.

Predisposed social, economic, or technological conditions for the eventual development of GRICs frequently may have existed for a long time, but GRICs are often the result of individual initiatives by professionals who returned to the area, or by others who had the abilities to foster local financial, physical, or human resources, and initiated cooperative efforts intended to create a series of commercial activities that resulted in an industrial cluster. Some of these clusters represent a complete value chain. In addition to the conditions described above, physical conditions such as extreme temperatures combined with seasonal area accessibility and a limited labor force may also bring locally concerned individuals together to facilitate the initiation of activities that create a favorable platform for a potential industrial cluster.

Recent perspectives offered by economic and regional development specialists concerning GRICs suggest that in addition to natural resources such as minerals, petroleum, forests, or even wind power which historically provided platforms for development, environmental conditions combined with land use suitable for harvesting resources such as fast-growing trees for paper, grapes to make wine, or corn to produce ethanol tend to stimulate the formation and development of GRICs. Some industrial cluster specialists also believe that knowledge generated at rural or regional universities provides an excellent platform for formation and growth of GRICs, because the historical underpinnings of each university represent unique core knowledge on which GRICs can be established.

There are many examples of modern GRICs that meet the new perspectives of economic and development specialists. Medical centers, automotive assembly facilities, hand-crafted furniture, or cultivation of fruit and vegetables are only a few examples. The economic and development specialists also point out that in all of these examples there is generally an individual who recognizes an opportunity, takes the initiative, and pursues the opportunity. Both academic and professional literature show, for example, that in ventures such as rural medical centers with a network of local providers of support services, subcontractors to oil drilling operations, or establishment of agricultural operations in areas where manual harvesting is required, there is an abundance of labor. These represent new approaches to GRIC development.

Unusual environmental conditions frequently provide platforms for creating GRICs. Environmentally adverse temperature climates at both extremes provide interesting opportunities for individuals with entrepreneurial abilities to create settings sought after by enterprises producing consumer goods. Product-testing facilities for automobiles and related products such as tires or batteries in northern Sweden or Alaska require an infrastructure of service facilities suitable for low-temperature climates. The opposite facilities are needed to test products in high-temperature climates in places such as Equatorial Africa. Due to recent climate changes, manufacturers of consumer products are even more interested in on-location environmental testing. These newly created opportunities for local entrepreneurs to develop suitable infrastructures and support networks may also lead to new GRICs.

In the past, a number of GRICs were formed because of singular conditions in which economic or technologically accessible natural resources facilitated their formation and growth. Recent socio-economic and managerial perspectives indicate that GRICs are formed or initiated from singular ideas presented by individuals with missions and visions. These include establishing wind power farms, harvesting fish in coastal areas, or converting petroleum from shale deposits. Close cooperation with researchers and scientists at a rural university also presents opportunities for individuals to form unique GRICs. However, some managers view many of these perspectives and approaches as still relatively new and requiring a major shift in managerial thinking.

From a historical perspective, clusters are internationally pervasive. Early in the history of the United States, industrial clusters appeared in geographic areas where natural resources were readily available even if transportation access or local infrastructure had to be developed. New clusters offered employment opportunities and motivated the creation of population bases surrounding the clusters. Some examples of early industrial clusters in the United States include the establishment and growth of the steel industry around Pittsburgh in Pennsylvania and Gary in northern Indiana, glass manufacturing in upper New York State, and the early lumber industry in northern Michigan, Minnesota, and Wisconsin, all of which were based on access to vast natural resources. Similar examples of early clusters can be found in northern Sweden in Kiruna where iron ore is mined, around Lycksele where extensive forest harvesting operations are located, or in Skellefteå where large prefabricated wooden structures are produced. Additional examples include crude oil production in the Middle East, steel production in Argentina, and wool processing in New Zealand, among others.

From a historical point of view, many resource-based industrial clusters are transitory and temporal, and have a predictable life cycle. Their long-term stability is very much dependent on changes in economic and technological climates — changes in the economic climate that relate to long-term economic recessions or expansions, and changes that introduce long-term technological innovations. The combination of these changes has a negative impact on the stability of resource-based industrial clusters. Looking into the future, recent economic and technological changes and the predominant environmental conditions will have a dramatic impact on the future of resource-based industrial clusters.

Although researchers, academics, and public policy decision makers who are currently developing theoretical and conceptual foundations for GRICs are also reinterpreting the traditional definition of industrial clusters, including GRICs, differently, they agree that the concept of industrial clusters is not a new phenomenon. Developmental economists and regional planners have discussed the existence and future potential of industrial clusters, and more recently GRICs, for over the past 40 years. Researchers such as Michael Porter, Peter Drucker, and others have described the existence of industrial clusters extensively in their writings. For example, Porter (1998) mapped over 30 major clusters in the United States and offered insights into their birth, evolution, and decline. Kukalis (2010) pointed out that the evolution of clusters is a natural phenomenon and that some smaller enterprises naturally gravitate toward industrial clusters.

The notion that some industrial clusters evolve naturally while others are formed, or initiated, by some interested entity or by entrepreneurial action is important. Developmental economists interested in the historical evolution of industrial clusters reason that they tend to emerge over time in locations where the conditions are favorable from the perspective of natural resources, factors of labor, and know-how. Accordingly, it is a natural process that is nurtured and managed by industrial cluster participants. This is primarily because symbiotic relationships are forged within the industrial cluster over time. However, the more traditional perspectives presented by developmental economists tend to consider only the external and apparent dynamics of industrial clusters, and do not generally probe the internal managerial practices and strategies from the point of view of individual cluster members.

More recently, some regional planners and developers have introduced a new set of theories and conceptual frameworks in which they suggest that industrial clusters can be formed or initiated by interested private or public entities, or by entrepreneurs. This is particularly relevant to regions that appear to be somewhat remote from main administrative centers (capital cities) or major metropolitan areas (industrial centers). A number of universities in the United States and Europe are located in rural areas that could be characterized as geographically remote regions. Some regional planners and developers perceive some of these geographically remote regions as ideal platforms in which industrial clusters could be formed or initiated. A substantial number of them offer extensive plans and programs designed to stimulate formation of industrial clusters in geographically remote regions.

The Concept of Remoteness

The notion of remoteness is highly subjective. There is an ongoing discussion among rural economists, sociologists, and developmental specialists, including public policy decision makers, concerning the definition and interpretation of the concept of "remoteness." The contemporary interpretation of remoteness suggests that there are several determinants or measures of remoteness. Typically, remoteness is defined by linking it to the notion of geographic distances by many economists, sociologists, and even development specialists; however, some of them propose that in addition to the notion of a geographic distance, there are also social and psychological (psychic) determinants or measures of remoteness.

These additional definitions point out, along with the geographic notion of remoteness, that enterprise managers may perceive remoteness in various ways. In geographic terms, remoteness, or a remote location, may be too far for a manager living in the center of a large metropolitan city. Conversely, a manager living in a rural part of the country may perceive a certain distance, let us say 100 kilometers, as a nearby location.

Social remoteness is perceived in terms of social distance between social classes or social groups that are dominant in specified geographic areas or regions. A group of individuals living in rural areas dependent on occasional employment opportunities and preoccupied with activities that provide day-to-day livelihood may represent substantial social remoteness for a manager who is attempting to build an assembly plant in a socially stable location. The concept of social remoteness may exist between neighborhoods of a large city as much as across populated areas or regions. The extent of social remoteness is defined by individuals and is based on their social backgrounds and experiences. The concept of social remoteness became important in the 1980s and early 1990s in locating automotive assembly plants in various emerging markets in Asia, Europe, and the United States; it was particularly highlighted by early experiences of Japanese and European automobile manufacturers in the southern parts of the United States and later in Central and Eastern Europe.

The concept of psychological remoteness is even more complex. The notion of psychological remoteness is based on attitudinal, perceptual, and preferential behavioral factors of individuals. From an attitudinal standpoint of an enterprise manager, psychological determination of remoteness may exist between two locations that are equidistant, in geographically measurable terms, but one location is perceived as being farther away because of its unfavorable surrounding or older industrial infrastructure. The notion of psychological or psychic distance is based on the nature of individuals' psychological filters that are built around educational background, upbringing, or psychological conditioning. What individual managers perceive is unique. Preferential psychological or psychic remoteness can be partly explained in the following way: Because of their unique filtering mechanism, each manager develops his or her own portfolio of preferences which is factored into the manager's decision-making process. For example, a manager who attended a prestigious university in a well-established academic community may be reluctant to participate in the formation of an industrial cluster around a second-tier state university in a rural community far away from an administrative center and a major city.

Geographic remoteness is also important in marketing management, not only for opportunity and market assessment but also for decisions concerning logistical support. Geographic distances between markets may be very short, but they may be very long from the perspectives of marketing managers and consumers because of ethnic, cultural, or other differences.

Regions in South America are separated by distinct landmarks such as valleys, rivers, and forests. Each valley, river bank, or part of a forest may have a totally different cultural make-up with virtually no direct social or economic interactions between them. Both the social and psychological distances between them are significant.

Similar conditions exist in parts of Central and Eastern Europe, where ethnically or culturally homogeneous groups perceive substantial differences between themselves and the other groups. These perceptions of social and psychological distances also lead to their own definitions of geographic remoteness. The social and cultural interpretations of differences between agriculture and industry — or more specifically between agricultural and industrial land where there are large concentrations of heavy industry (e.g., steel mills in the center of agricultural land farmed by small local farmers, such as is the case around Košice in Slovakia or Katowice in Poland) — are perceived by both sides as a form of remoteness. Other countries in Europe also perceive social or psychological separation concerning the notion of remoteness; for example, when Swedes from southern Sweden point out that life in northern Sweden is substantially different, this may also be interpreted as social or psychological remoteness.

In large metropolitan areas in North America, the notion of remoteness takes on an even more complex dimension. Individuals who live in New York, Los Angeles, or Toronto and leave their cities tend to feel that they have ventured into geographically remote areas. Although the actual distances from the cities are relatively short, measured in kilometers or miles, the individuals from the cities nevertheless believe that the distances are significant in social or psychological terms.

All three notions of remoteness — geographic, social, and psychological — are important information for the initiation of GRICs. The notion of geographic remoteness is perhaps the most important; nevertheless, remote areas or regions may also have social and psychological dimensions which, from a managerial perspective, may be rational and may be used in managerial decision making. Geographic remoteness, measured in specific terms such as kilometers or miles, may also be highly subjective for many managers.

Formation of Industrial Clusters

As mentioned previously, there are two fundamental views in the literature describing how industrial clusters form. The traditional view represents a theoretical and conceptual framework that industrial clusters evolved naturally because of local conditions and some concentration of entrepreneurial drive. At a given point in time, the local conditions represented the optimal combination of physical, financial, and human resources that were activated by some arbitrary entrepreneurial initiative. Accordingly, such entrepreneurial initiative created the core set of activities which, in turn, stimulated infrastructural growth and facilitated the process of bringing a core set of activities profitably into the marketplace. Examples can be found in mining, forestry, automobile manufacturing, and steel making worldwide. In the literature, this view is known as the historical approach to the development of industrial clusters.

According to several recent studies conducted in Europe and in the United States, traditional industrial clusters initially formed around a combination of natural resources. The resources typically were located in rural areas, but their economic value was high enough to attract development of the necessary infrastructure and labor to harvest the resources. Coal mining, steel making, forest harvesting, and even agriculture initially stimulated the growth of clusters. As industrialization progressed and manufacturing processes evolved on a large scale, some industrial and commercial goods required larger facilities where suitable infrastructural components such as roads or railways could be built to deliver the goods to markets. Automotive manufacturing, steel fabrication, and rubber manufacturing historically clustered in relatively rural areas. Later, when markets expanded and consumers demanded better services from manufacturers, a need for infrastructural intermediaries emerged. Railroad centers, warehousing facilities, and distribution facilities had to be built in strategic areas to better serve consumers. Many of these infrastructural intermediaries were also located in rural areas to serve manufacturing and transportation interests.

Traditional industrial clusters also emerged because the core idea for the industrial cluster required safe environmental conditions with vast open spaces. The small aircraft industry that developed around Wichita, Kansas, is an excellent example. The small aircraft industry needed an airport and space to test their planes. In the middle of the previous century, the emerging space industry required similar conditions. Other examples from the industrial histories of Europe, the United States, and other parts of the world also illustrate this phenomenon.

The accumulation of knowledge, scientific and managerial, has also provided platforms on which very successful industrial clusters were formed. In the United States, for example, universities such as the University of Wisconsin-Madison initiated an internationally known industrial cluster in biotechnology, while Stanford University was instrumental in forming an early industrial cluster emphasizing the development and production of electrical and electronic equipment. Some universities also contributed to the development of pharmaceutical and health care-related industrial clusters. In Europe, similar examples can be found especially among universities in the United Kingdom, Sweden, and Italy. All of these efforts were related to the formation of traditional industry clusters and were, more or less, natural extensions of scientific research and managerial thinking.

The notion of innovative industrial clusters has evolved more recently and is a byproduct of greater involvement of developmental economists, regional development specialists, regional planners, government administrators, and academics. Some researchers refer to this approach of forming industrial clusters in the literature as the modern or innovative approach. Its theoretical and conceptual framework was mostly developed by developmental economists and regional planners.

Academics such as scientific researchers, individuals interested in entrepreneurship, and management specialists were instrumental in implementing the theoretical and conceptual frameworks developed by developmental economists and regional planners. Although many of the ideas presented at the theoretical and conceptual levels were substantial, their implementation had to be adjusted frequently to meet the conditions under which an industrial cluster could be formed. In other words, the theoretical and conceptual frameworks had to be modified to reflect market reality.

The developmental economists and regional planners perceived ideal situations and ideal conditions under which industrial clusters could be formed, and did not allow for the variety of behavioral tendencies characteristic of entrepreneurs and enterprise managers. Entrepreneurs have a strong tendency to act as individuals and have difficulty conforming to strict theoretical or conceptual models. Managers generally also do not believe in collective action. They are competitive and strive for a unique market position. Both entrepreneurs and managers tend to participate in collective actions, such as industrial clusters, only if they perceive profitable benefits.

The more innovative view of how industrial clusters are formed presumes that they can be formed or initiated by various public or private entities such as municipalities, rural administrative units, university administrators, and occasionally individual enterprises or entrepreneurs. This view is not necessarily based on availability of natural resources; it suggests that a single public or private entity may opt to initiate the formation of an industrial cluster. That is, anyone who has sufficient entrepreneurial drive and takes the initiative to form an industrial cluster may succeed in actually forming an industrial cluster. Various motives may lead to initiating an industrial cluster, including public motivations to develop rural regions of the country, utilize the local knowledge base, or combine local interests in economic, social, and technological activities to create a productive local enterprise in order to create jobs and stabilize the local economy.

Innovative approaches leading to the formation of industrial clusters continue to be especially attractive to university administrators and academics interested in putting into practice the results of scientific research and disseminating new knowledge. An increasing number of rural and regional universities are building facilities such as incubators, technology parks, and science parks as the initial infrastructural components required to provide platforms for the growth of anticipated industrial clusters. The platforms are designed to stimulate researchers, scientists, academics, and even students to start new enterprises and potentially participate in a cluster. Some of these attempts have produced successful industrial clusters that became internationally efficient in transferring knowledge generated within the universities.

Examples in the United States include the research park at the University of Idaho in Post Falls and a new incubator at the University of Wisconsin-Whitewater. Similar efforts can be found in Europe. A recently built incubator at Aalborg University in Denmark is attracting a great deal of interest not only among the academics currently employed, but also from the local industrial sector. The incubator at Aalborg University potentially has the ability to change the nature of the manufacturing and service sectors in Aalborg and its vicinity. A new incubator combined with a science park at the Brno University of Technology in the Czech Republic operates as a series of laboratories available to students, scientists, and other entrepreneurial academics, and has been successful in attracting smaller enterprises to form a cluster around scientific developments in the electronic and computer software industries.

In the formation or initiation of industrial clusters, especially GRICs, it is important to understand that any theoretical and conceptual foundations must realistically reflect the actual preferences and practices of entrepreneurs and managers who intend to participate in an industrial cluster, including their potential preferences and willingness for collective and cooperative activities. It is important to realize that some industrial clusters may only be loosely organized, whereby each participating entity operates under its own business model and follows its own unique marketing strategy. The other extreme is industrial clusters where all the participants manage toward a common goal. They all operate within one value chain and each participating entity has a clearly specified function to perform within the value chain. There are also various management styles between the two extremes.

Industrial clusters can range from loosely organized enterprises producing products or offering services in totally unrelated markets and only sharing some infrastructural elements and support services in a given industrial cluster to highly structured and organized industrial clusters representing a single value chain designed to service a specific market segment. However, entrepreneurs and enterprise managers also look for industrial clusters in between these two extremes, where they can rely on the infrastructural elements and services they need to manage their own day-to-day operations and formulate their own strategies for getting their products into the marketplace. They are not necessarily interested in cooperating or coordinating managerial activities within the industrial cluster.

Industrial Cluster Participation and Administration

Most entities that operate in industrial clusters, including in GRICs, generally prefer to operate independently. They may share some infrastructural elements and use some support services, such as administrative offices, manufacturing space, warehousing facilities, and research laboratories, but they are reluctant to share their know-how, skills, or any proprietary assets or technical information they may have. Other entities may utilize selected specialized services such as marketing research, participate in promotion of the industrial cluster itself, or assist in overall economic or technological improvements in the internal or external operations of the cluster. All of these anomalies require special operations and management styles from the entire industrial cluster.

In general, most participants in industrial clusters are interested in improving the internal and external operations of the entire industrial cluster that lead to more effective and efficient connections with the marketplace. This is particularly apparent in GRICs. Improvements in information technology, in road, rail, and air transportation capabilities, as well as in the availability of new production technologies typically represent major improvements in an industrial cluster's performance and market accessibility. Even if individual managers are reluctant to cooperate and coordinate with other members, they generally tend to be willing to improve the cluster's performance, reputation, and visibility.

Industrial clusters that were formed on the basis of cooperation and coordination and represent a single value chain function differently. Each entity's role in the value chain is determined by their ability to contribute a set of unique competencies that have a singular purpose in the goods or services produced by the industrial cluster. In other words, each participating enterprise has its own clearly defined purpose and shares that purpose with all the other members.

On a higher level, industrial clusters, such as GRICs, need to be administered by professionals who understand their mission and understand the needs of the individual members. Regardless of how much individual members are expected to participate in the overall mission of their industrial cluster, its administrators need to be able to support and facilitate the individual missions of each member enterprise.

Bibliography

Feser, Edward J. and Edward M. Bergman (2000). "National Industry Cluster Templates: A Framework for Applied Regional Cluster Analysis." *Regional Studies*, 34(1), February, 1–19.

Feser, Edward J., Kyojun Koo, Henry C. Renski, and Stewart H. Sweeney (2001). "Incorporating Spatial Analysis in Applied Industry Cluster Studies." Document prepared for *Economic Development Quarterly*, Department of City and Regional Planning, University of North Carolina, Chapel Hill, North Carolina, March.

Kukalis, Sal (2010). "Agglomeration Economies and Firm Performance: The Case of Industry Clusters." *Journal of Management*, 36(2), March, 453–481.

Porter, Michael (1998). "Clusters and the New Economics of Competition." *Harvard Business Review*, November–December, 77–90.

Schiele, Holger (2008). "Location, Location: The Geography of Industry Clusters." *Journal of Business Strategy*, 29(3), 29–36.

Tesar, George, Hamid Moini, John Kuada, and Olav Jull Sørensen (2010). *Smaller Manufacturing Enterprises in an International Context: A Longitudinal Exploration*. London: Imperial College Press.

Chapter 2

Formation and Growth of Geographically Remote Industrial Clusters

Geographically remote industrial clusters (GRICs) represent an important economic development tool. Both the research literature and actual experiences of economic and regional development specialists suggest that there are two distinctly different types of GRICs: those that formed or evolved naturally over time, and those that were initiated administratively with the purpose of contributing to economic development in the region. The concept of naturally formed GRICs was first recognized in the late 1940s and quickly spread to industrialized regions of the world. The systematic initiation of GRICs as a means to local economic development emerged approximately in the late 1960s and also became a tool of economic development in economically challenged countries around the world.

Although GRICs that formed over time are very important concepts in the overall field of local and regional development, they do not have the flexibility of forming in a relatively short time period with a specific mission and a resource base. The GRICs that evolved over time and are specific industry-related may be subject to economic and technological fluctuations. Many of these GRICs have transitional or temporal characteristics. Their productivity and prosperity fluctuates with the demands of the entire industry they represent.

Initiated GRICs may also fluctuate and change over time; but because they are frequently managed as an economic unit with a single mission and set operational and strategic objectives, they generally have a better probability of adjusting to adverse market conditions. In addition, initiated GRICs tend to have an organizational and structural ability to adjust to market conditions. The focus of this chapter is on GRICs formed or initiated by individual or collective action for the purpose of local or regional development.

Formation of Initiated GRICs

Interest in GRICs is growing internationally. Developmental specialists in many parts of the world consider the formation of GRICs by local initiatives as a viable means for stimulating industrial or agricultural development. They emphasize that GRICs represent employment opportunities, introduce efficient use of natural resources, utilize environmentally friendly green technology, improve the local tax base, and stabilize the local economy. Both developmental economists and regional planners also point out that GRICs create an economic and social bond between individual enterprises, public and private institutions, and the local or regional administrative units.

This bonding process is especially apparent in rural towns and regions where universities are located. In many parts of the world, numerous public and private entities are creating programs specifically designed to initiate the formation of GRICs based on local universities and their scientific specializations. Other public and private alliances are developing innovative cooperative programs that potentially have the ability to operate and manage highly specialized GRICs based on cooperation between small startup enterprises, parts of universities, and public administrators.

Large domestic and international industrial enterprises are also interested in cooperating with GRICs. They are starting relationships and forging alliances with universities in rural and regional areas to create more favorable conditions for the formation of high-technology GRICs. These efforts frequently focus on the development of new technologies, testing of capabilities under less visible and competitive surveillance, or small-scale production of specialized products. Many of the large domestic and international industrial enterprises locate their research laboratories in GRICs.

A review of recent literature in areas of economic development and regional planning suggests that the formation of high-technology GRICs by local initiatives is a global phenomenon, and the underlying assumption is that these attempts are designed to create favorable conditions for small high-technology enterprises. However, in reality not every GRIC needs to focus on high-technology activities; in some remote regions, low- and medium-technology GRICs are just as desirable for economic development as are high-technology GRICs.

Virtually every country, including countries with highly developed industrial sectors, has regions where the population considers itself to be geographically, socially, or psychologically remote and subject to development. The concept of remoteness is important in the formation of GRICs. It is not where GRICs are physically located that needs to be understood, but rather what is important are the general perceptions of the individual participants in GRICs' initiation and formation. For many entrepreneurs and enterprise managers, any form of remoteness today can be overcome by improvements in communication, information technology, and logistics, among other socio-economic or psychological factors.

Attempts to deliberately initiate the formation of GRICs by individuals, public or private entities, or government officials for whatever reason came about in North America and Europe in the early 1980s during the period of fast technological growth when enterprises, commercial research laboratories, and university administrators in particular looked for ways to connect with each other and exchange available knowledge in order to speed up economic growth and expand their presence in the marketplace. A number of rural universities changed their image, sought partnerships with major enterprises, and developed unique educational programs with a focus on the local or regional business climate.

The idea of forming GRICs by initiatives attracted individual and corporate entrepreneurs along with public entrepreneurs employed by governmental agencies, universities, and quasi-public entities. GRICs also started to evolve through various entrepreneurial activities within enterprises such as technological diversification, new product development, or new business development ventures. Entrepreneurs were involved with introducing new high-technology products in biotechnology, software development, and many other activities serving new emerging markets and industries. Entrepreneurs working within economic development agencies at various levels (local, regional, or national) side by side with regional planners were more interested in bringing together small- and medium-sized enterprises and public entities in order to facilitate the formation of GRICs. Rural and regional university administrators were interested in providing the skills and know-how needed to form a successful, well-integrated GRIC to transfer the knowledge that was being developed within the university walls. It quickly became apparent that each entity involved in the formation of GRICs had different market interests and objectives, resulting in the need for a clear mission statement that would integrate all of the conflicting expectations.

Several theoretical and conceptual models leading to the formation of GRICs can be found in the literature. The literature represents two major constituencies interested in the initiation of forming GRICs: private and public entrepreneurs, and economic and regional development specialists. The difference between the two constituencies is clearly defined by their fundamental expectations. Private and public entrepreneurs are interested in creating a profitable environment in which they can prosper. Many public entrepreneurs cross over to the private sector after a GRIC has been established. On the other hand, economic and regional development specialists are interested in creating an environment in which private enterprises can prosper and the region can benefit from various entrepreneurial actions by strong economic growth, higher employment, and increased tax revenues. The theoretical and conceptual models presented by the entrepreneurial participants lack the public perspective of the economic and regional developmental specialists, and vice versa.

Some of the theoretical and conceptual models have, in the past, been proposed by marketing and management specialists, mostly academics, based on scientific studies among entrepreneurs and managers of smaller enterprises. Additional models have been designed by economists, regional planners, and developmental specialists, who at times have worked together. More recently, models intended to assist with the formation of GRICs have been introduced by consulting agencies and are generally based on the experiences of management consultants for smaller manufacturing enterprises. All sources of the theoretical and conceptual models have some merit and are useful in initiating formation of GRICs. Typically, they all need to be adjusted or modified to meet the needs of unique local or regional conditions. Past experience gained in forming GRICs has quickly demonstrated that a universal model does not exist; this means that every situation leading to the initiated formation of a GRIC is different and needs careful analysis.

Both practice and research indicate that there are usually three groups interested in forming a GRIC: public entities, rural and regional universities, and individuals. Public entities consist primarily of local or regional economic development agencies, governmental planning commissions, government agencies concerned with export development or technology transfer including natural resources, and governmental agencies concerned with transportation policies. Economic development agencies often cooperate with technology councils and agencies responsible for the transportation policies on formation of GRICs' infrastructure as well as the solicitation of enterprises and individuals expected to operate within the infrastructure. The infrastructure may be an incubator providing research, production, or management facilities, or providing assistance with technical, marketing, and management activities. This is particularly common in high-technology GRICs in the United States. In these instances, governmental agencies together are likely to offer a variety of incentives ranging from financial loans or grants, tax holidays, to training grants, or even space for research or production.

Rural or regional universities tend to follow public entities in the process of initiating the formation of GRICs. More specifically, centers for small business development, technology transfer or innovation centers, and productivity centers commonly found within universities perceive GRICs as within their realm of responsibilities. University extension specialists are also likely to initiate the formation of GRICs because, from an applied perspective, they have the capabilities to assist in GRICs' management and growth. In addition, faculty members who have strong entrepreneurial interests and access to results of scientific research or other developments resulting from academic experiences also have the potential to form GRICs. It is relatively common today for rural universities to participate in the ownership of incubators. Many recent GRICs formed by rural universities' initiatives actually started inside incubators.

Finally, initiatives to form GRICs also come from individuals. Although these initiatives are few, there appear to be three types of individuals potentially interested in forming GRICs. The first type includes investors with capital interested in building the necessary infrastructural elements within which participants of GRICs can operate, such as incubators, science parks, and manufacturing facilities. The second type are individuals who have entrepreneurial tendencies, understand markets, and are willing to function collectively with other individuals or enterprises to satisfy market demand for specific products or services. The third type consists of managers of industrial or agricultural enterprises who, in order to grow, perceive a need to increase their market presence by developing an efficient and effective value chain.

Individuals with capital interested in forming GRICs are relatively common in the United States and Europe, especially in the United Kingdom. Most of these investors look for opportunities to develop GRICs that are connected with rural universities. Individuals who have strong entrepreneurial skills and understand markets are more likely to be found in economically challenged countries or emerging markets. Managers of enterprises who perceive the need to participate in a value chain generally operate in rural areas where a number of enterprises have different sets of skills and managerial know-how that potentially offer synergistic action evolving into a strong value chain. Several wine-growing areas in Australia, Chile, and Argentina represent such initiatives. Also, GRICs formed in small rural towns in the United States and Canada, typically with the cooperation of local leaders and university administrators, represent the efforts of individual enterprise managers to expand and grow by using more modern technology and cooperating with others.

There are interesting examples where low-technology fabrication, machine, and even welding shops making custom-designed machinery have moved up the technology curve by working with information technology specialists at the local university to learn how to automate their equipment by integrating computer electronics. Many such shops working in a GRIC have been able to progress from simple low-technology machine shops to high-technology providers of computer-operated production equipment.

In assessing overall efforts to form GRICs, it appears that public initiatives remain the principal drivers of forming GRICs. In many rural areas in countries worldwide, public initiatives address the needs of the rural population and assist with the development of local resources. Economic and regional development specialists point out that the main motive under which governmental bodies seek to form GRICs is the general public good. The expected return from GRICs is job creation, increased tax revenue, and economic and social stability.

High-technology GRICs, stimulated by public initiatives, have a tendency to draw a highly educated and skilled labor force that demands higher salaries and quality of life. Many have extensive personal and professional networks, and are interested in the communities in which they live and want to contribute to their social and economic development.

There are also closer relationships between skilled manual labor and engineers, technicians, and scientists in the smaller rural areas, where GRICs tend to be located, and these closer relationships generally make rural communities more socially stable and economically more viable. Economic development specialists have documented several rural areas where GRICs are functioning and where startup and smaller enterprises have benefited from interaction with the individual members of GRICs. At the same time, they also concluded that the rural areas, in terms of their socio-economic dynamics, have improved substantially over time.

The primary problem that the government agencies face in attempting to form GRICs, aside from a range of financial issues, is the reluctance of managers of smaller manufacturing enterprises, and frequently owner-managers, to join and actively participate in the formation of GRICs regardless of what the incentives are. The results of internationally based studies among smaller manufacturing enterprises indicate that managers perceive the initiatives by governmental agencies to form GRICs as unproductive and lacking any systematic approaches to markets.

These anomalies may explain why GRICs in some countries are organized and managed as complete value chains, while in other countries GRICs' participants tend to operate individually. The tendency in Europe, especially in Scandinavian countries, is to cooperate within a formal infrastructure, while the tendency in the

United States is to be more individualistic and not cooperate. Many smaller manufacturing enterprises in the United States are willing to join a value chain, but at the same time pursue their own specialized market opportunities.

Because GRICs represent workable entities, in order for them to operate and grow, they need to be managed. The management of GRICs is a complex undertaking that requires specialized knowledge of organizational behavior and managerial action. GRICs' management needs to be able to identify and access markets defined under its mission, and must be able to negotiate with the individual participants to assure their full cooperation. In reality, GRICs' management must understand the overall market that each GRIC attempts to serve as well as the potential markets of each participant because potential markets represent the singular capabilities of each participating enterprise.

Each participant in a GRIC also needs to understand the mission of the GRIC and needs to agree with it. Managers of individual enterprises participating in GRICs need to understand their own capabilities and what contributions they can make. In other words, managers must be skilled and understand their markets.

The common dimension that brings GRICs' managers and managers of the participating member enterprises together is their knowledge of markets, and both need to be skilled at identifying market opportunities. The one managerial function that is able to improve operational and strategic market opportunities for GRICs and their enterprises is marketing management.

Marketing Management in GRICs

The key success function of private and public entities today is marketing management. In order to succeed, private enterprises need to understand their markets and, more specifically, their consumers to respond to their needs for goods and services. Public entities need to know their constituencies and their economic and social expectations. Both of these tasks require the ability to collect the necessary data, information, and intelligence to generate sufficient understanding of customers and constituents.

Marketing management and marketing activities in general are typically missing from the overall managerial styles of GRICs. In fact, the lack of well-developed plans for marketing activities on both operational and managerial levels needs to be rectified, for they should be systematically developed and introduced early in a GRIC's activities. Managers responsible for GRICs' marketing operations and strategies are responsible for developing marketing activities on two levels: communicating with the public, and assisting in identifying market opportunities for the participating members.

Participating enterprises on their part are responsible for their own operational and strategic marketing activities, in addition to participating in the collective activities of the other participating members. Their own marketing management activities are related to the development and maintenance of their differential advantages, which strengthen their own market position within the GRIC. It is also important for participating members to strengthen their own internal position in a cooperative way and contribute to the overall efficiency and effectiveness of the entire GRIC.

In terms of marketing management, private enterprises are interested in maximizing relationships with their consumers or users, whereas public entities press for optimal relationships with their constituents. Although the two entities differ in their fundamental objectives, they both need to forge relationships with those they serve. Both entities need a strong marketing focus that is capable of creating value for their consumers or constituents. This is a dilemma faced by GRICs' management. From an external perspective, GRICs' management is expected to provide employment for their communities, improve their economic climate, and even create better cultural conditions. Internally, however, they need to assist the development and implementation of operational and strategic options for each GRIC participant. Both the external and internal responsibilities of GRICs' management require systematic marketing approaches.

Marketing management responds to both fundamental private and public objectives. In general terms, marketing management is accountable for designing and directing a total system of marketing action to achieve predetermined objectives. For most marketing-oriented entities, private or public, their objectives are finalized based on optimal information derived from systematic analysis of data collected via large-scale studies. Once reliable information is available, it needs to be converted to management intelligence produced by combining managerial knowledge and skills with available resources and operational and strategic initiatives.

In applying marketing management as a tool for GRICs, their managers need to understand that the operations and strategies that promote GRICs as social institutions differ significantly from those that assist participating enterprises in gaining markets and favorable competitive advantages. Promoting GRICs as social institutions intended to improve the economic and social well-being of a remote region requires close coordination and communication with local constituencies, which include local communities, governments, universities, and organizations that represent local collective initiatives such as chambers of commerce or even volunteer organizations. The objective of these groups is to develop a suitable understanding of how well GRICs are doing in improving the local economic and social conditions.

In dealing with internal considerations, GRICs' management must clearly understand the needs of each participating enterprise and provide sufficient knowledge and resources needed to reach the collectively defined markets. When an entire GRIC is structured as a single value chain, each participating enterprise must clearly understand what exact role it plays in the entire value chain. This is the responsibility of the GRIC's top management. If the participating enterprises are not integrated into a single value chain, top management's responsibility is only to be well-informed about the internal dynamics of each participating enterprise, but not necessarily about their operational and strategic activities.

Both management practices and available literature suggest that in order for GRICs to function successfully on all levels, regardless of the actual organizational structure of each individual GRIC, their management needs to develop a strong commitment to marketing and introduce marketing management practices early in a GRIC's development. Equally important is the introduction of marketing management practices among the smaller participating enterprises, since many of them tend to be either startup enterprises or enterprises that are in transition from relatively low-technology into more high-technology ventures. Smaller manufacturing enterprises in particular need to understand the importance of marketing management activities in their short- and long-term plans.

SMEs and GRICs

As stated above, the main role of GRICs today is to construct new and innovative environments, which in turn will stimulate jobs and improve the economic and social climates in the remote regions. Both practice and research results clearly suggest that the most expedient way to meet these objectives is to focus on the smaller manufacturing enterprises (SMEs). GRICs' management worldwide has developed programs designed to attract SMEs in various stages of their development. GRICs greatly benefit from focusing on SMEs because of their inherent innovative tendencies and operational flexibility; however, they are frequently reluctant to participate in GRICs' formation and thus hesitate to cooperate. Given that SMEs are excellent generators of new technologies and flexible approaches to marketing innovations, these challenges need to be resolved.

Many GRICs built by public entities are in areas where the ongoing emergence of new ventures is leading to the establishment of SMEs. For example, some GRICs originated as infrastructural components for rural agriculture when farmers and growers perceived a need to include value-added services to their products or commodities for their consumers. Many were started by university extension services. Some of the value-added services included convenient packaging or preconception processing that required the services of local SMEs to develop suitable technology. A similar example can be found in the expanding oil shale industry, where SMEs were asked to develop methods designed to support day-to-day operations of the oil shale industry. These efforts were typically initiated by local economic development agencies. In all of these examples, SMEs possessed the skills, know-how, and flexibility to introduce and support the innovative techniques that were needed.

Traditionally, there are three different types of SMEs. The first type are SMEs that simply respond to some challenge or local need that is clearly apparent and does not require a great deal of technical knowledge, large investment capital, or significant labor force. For example, in the highly automated agricultural GRICs in Kansas and South Dakota, there was an opportunity for local individuals to set up computer monitoring stations to follow the operating conditions of automated agricultural equipment and provide instantaneous feedback for their operators, especially during planting and harvesting. A number of individuals established SMEs that now provide fast local monitoring services.

The second type are SMEs that have moved up the technology curve. They usually begin as fabrication shops, machine shops, or millwright and repair services — they frequently fabricate and maintain custom-designed production equipment. Over time, these SMEs gain knowledge and experience in operating large-scale production equipment and start to offer design options to their clients.

When such SMEs become successful in offering design options and integrating them into clients' production facilities, they may opt to design their own proprietary production line components. As they move along the technology curve, they may also provide automation consulting services to further integrate equipment of their own design into the clients' key production processes. This SME type has a tendency to expand from a provider of low-technology hands-on services to a provider of high-technology production automation. Examples can be found in the forest industry in northern Sweden and Finland, in automobile assembly operations in the southeastern part of the United States, and in the emerging wine-producing GRICs in Central and Eastern Europe.

The third SME type reflects strong entrepreneurial initiatives. These SMEs range from, on one end of the spectrum, purely entrepreneurial operations offered by individuals with ideas who are willing to promote their ideas at all costs to, on the other end of the spectrum, individuals who have invented or discovered new products and processes or offered solutions to scientifically based problems. This spectrum contains a variety of entrepreneurial activities that provide viable foundations for SMEs' operations and growth. It is frequently the developments in science and high-technology potential that attract them to GRICs. Many high-technology entrepreneurs have established spinoff ventures from university laboratories or other related research operations.

Some SMEs are started by individuals who offer services necessary to operate and maintain production equipment, automation services, or services that require special tools or equipment such as laser metal cutting services. All of these services represent relatively low entrepreneurial drive and tend to respond to well-established requirements within GRICs. It is the high-technology entrepreneurial efforts that face substantial risks. High-technology startups frequently represent scientifically and technologically sophisticated ventures that may not be well understood by others, particularly by venture capitalists who may perceive the venture as uncertain. The lack of managerial, and especially marketing, know-how among high-technology scientists frequently encourages them to cooperate with others, and many of them form new ventures connected with GRICs whereby they can rely on managerial and marketing support services.

All three types of SMEs have a strong potential for growth, especially within organized and structured infrastructural environments such as GRICs. It is possible to construct a model of how they grow based on results of research studies, observations, and consulting experiences. They all start out with some level of innovative activity which, from a technological point of view, may range from low to high. Innovative activities generally lead to new ways of doing things, that is, new technology. A new technology provides opportunities for developing new products and services. New products and services, in turn, need new developmental strategies that need to be introduced internally. As new developmental strategies focus on new products or services, marketing strategies are needed to reach external markets and potential consumers or users. Marketing operations need to be implemented throughout the entire marketing system. When marketing operations are in place, they must be monitored for market and consumer feedback.

The above set of marketing management activities is rapidly becoming a framework for SMEs operating within GRICs. GRICs' management has the responsibility to ensure that individual participants have the reasonable potential to progress along these stages and systematically implement outcomes of the previous stages. For most SMEs, these stages are also accompanied by marketing tools managers use to make rational decisions. These tools include: (1) technical and managerial descriptions of a product or service concept; (2) technology briefs; (3) detailed business analysis of potential breakeven points, rate of return on investment, payback periods, and other financial calculations; (4) comprehensive business plans; and (5) proposals for integration of new technology into the GRIC's infrastructural framework.

Some startup ventures that anticipate joining a GRIC may need considerable managerial expertise in developing the essential stages and drafting the necessary managerial decision-making tools. Almost all GRICs that are linked with high-technology environments maintain a staff of qualified management specialists who offer these services. Under these conditions, most GRICs require some formal agreement or contract from which the GRIC will benefit in the future if the potential venture grows into a profitable SME.

An increasing number of high-technology GRICs have developed models describing the growth path of new high-technology ventures. These models, given a specifiable set of conditions, are able to assign probability estimates indicating the likelihood that the venture will proceed through the standard stages of typical growth: establishment, growth, expansion, consolidation, stagnation, decline, and liquidation. The future success of a new high-technology-based venture can be predicted based on these estimates, but the GRIC's management should be able to decide the future of individual ventures within its infrastructure and what contributions the new venture will make in the future.

Bibliography

Bilkey, Warren J. (1970). *Industrial Stimulation.* Lexington, MA: Heath Lexington Books.

Blair, John M. (1972). *Economic Concentration: Structure, Behavior, and Public Policy.* New York: Harcourt Brace Jovanovich, Inc., pp. 85–133.

Cortright, Joseph (2006). "Making Sense of Clusters: Regional Competitiveness and Economic Development." A discussion paper prepared for the Brookings Institution Metropolitan Policy Program, Washington, D.C., March.

Feldman, Maryann P., Johanna Francis, and Janet Bercovitz (2005). "Creating a Cluster While Building a Firm: Entrepreneurs and the Formation of Industrial Clusters." *Regional Studies*, 39(1), February, 129–141.

Galbraith, John Kenneth (1964). *Economic Development.* Boston: Houghton Mifflin Company, Sentry Edition.

Kotter, John P. (1996). *Leading Change.* Boston: Harvard Business School Press.

Meier, Gerald M. and Robert E. Baldwin (1957). *Economic Development: Theory, History, and Policy.* New York: John Wiley & Sons, Inc.

Mytelka, Lynn and Fulvia Farinelli (2000). "Local Clusters, Innovation Systems and Sustained Competitiveness." Discussion Paper Series #2005, United Nations University–Institute for New Technologies, Maastricht, The Netherlands, October.

Niu, Kuei-Hsien (2010). "Organizational Trust and Knowledge Obtaining in Industrial Clusters." *Journal of Knowledge Management*, 14(1), 141–155.

Tesar, George, Steven W. Anderson, Sibdas Ghosh, and Tom Bramorski (2008). *Strategic Technology Management: Building Bridges between Sciences, Engineering and Business Management,* 2nd ed. London: Imperial College Press.

Ulrich, Dave and Norm Smallwood (2007). *Leadership Brand: Developing Customer-Focused Leaders to Drive Performance and Build Lasting Value.* Boston: Harvard Business School Press.

Chapter 3

Smaller Manufacturing Enterprises in Geographically Remote Industrial Clusters

Most regional development specialists believe that high-technology smaller manufacturing enterprises (SMEs) are the basic building blocks of geographically remote industrial clusters (GRICs). Experience with a variety of GRICs furthermore suggests that small- and medium-sized enterprises also provide strong foundations. Some GRICs were formed by bringing together a number of startup SMEs, while others also included those in the early stages of their manufacturing and marketing operations. These preferences for forming GRICs are well documented in the economic and regional development literature. The theoretical foundation for these practices is based on the idea that dynamic, high-technology SMEs provide the entrepreneurial drive and innovative flexibility necessary for GRICs to be profitable and endure in the future.

High-technology SMEs have the ability to enter the global marketplace very early in their life cycles. It is this global dimension combined with a synergistic effect among a GRIC's members that stimulates their overall market dynamics and makes them competitive. SMEs have to be fully internationalized in order to successfully enter the global marketplace. It is the responsibility of their managers to integrate their domestic and international operations into one comprehensive marketing management strategy.

In the age of information technology and digital marketing, integration of domestic and international operations into one comprehensive managerial strategy is becoming almost a standard mode of operations. This is apparent among SMEs because for the most recently educated managers, who are responsible for the operations and strategies of SMEs, international perspectives were integral components of their managerial education. SMEs' managers employ the drive and flexibility of their enterprises as a means to enter into professional relationships, form strategic alliances, and participate in GRICs with extensive reliance on innovative contemporary managerial practices in the international marketplace.

Not all GRICs are formed with a focus on high-technology SMEs. There are numerous low- and medium-technology SMEs that are capable of providing the necessary products and services needed to form and operate successful GRICs. In many instances, successful GRICs deploy older technology but utilize effective and efficient managerial techniques and marketing strategies to service competitive market niches. In order to understand the advantages and disadvantages that SMEs represent in the formation of GRICs, it is important to examine their operational and strategic dynamics.

Smaller Manufacturing Enterprises

Smaller manufacturing enterprises differ significantly not only in terms of their size, management styles, or financial strength, but also in terms of their technical knowledge and skills, marketing abilities, and profitability. Some SMEs start out as low-technology fabrication shops and then progress to high-technology service centers that supply a range of automation solutions for high-speed manufacturing processes. Low-technology SMEs generally fabricate parts, components, and custom-designed production equipment to clients' specifications, which generally do not require extensive technical expertise. However, high-technology SMEs tend to utilize their technological expertise and skills to their fullest potential. Those SMEs that typically progress along a learning curve, or a technology curve, have a tendency to consistently acquire new technical knowledge and skills and, as they move higher on the learning curve, their products and services become more technologically complex.

As the technological climate advances worldwide, the number of high-technology SMEs is also increasing. The reasons for this development vary. Some SMEs start out as spinoffs from universities, private and public research laboratories, manufacturing operations, or even government agencies; while others start out as individual entrepreneurial initiatives based on discoveries, inventions, or process improvements. At the same time, lower-technology SMEs have taken account of their technical knowledge and skills and refocused their resources and capabilities towards higher technological levels of activities, and have proceeded to move towards the development and marketing of high-technology products and services.

Systematic improvements in SMEs' technological capabilities are frequently related to changes in their marketing operations and strategies. Their market focus changes as improvements in their technological capabilities appear. They become much more aware of their customers' requirements and adjust their relationships to meet customers' expectations for a given level of technology. That is, high-technology products and services demand a higher level of marketing support. There is a point in SMEs' life cycle when they begin to experience systematic improvements in their technical knowledge and skills and marketing management becomes important for their future.

Many SMEs begin as fabricators of custom-designed equipment for clients. They perform valuable services by fabricating equipment designed by the clients' engineering staff and intended for use in manufacturing or production processes. Their skill set consists of cutting and welding metal, machining necessary parts, assembling the final equipment, and testing. These types of SMEs tend to serve a rather narrow but necessary niche in the marketplace. Some fabrication shops progress from low to high technology, and expand their market niche to fabricate and market equipment designed internally by them as a result of their learning experiences. Fabrication shops tend to serve an important function in GRICs' operations and growth.

The low-to-high technology continuum includes a large variety and combination of SMEs that offer intermediate products or services for their customers. In a typical GRIC, the participating enterprises tend to be located along the entire continuum and can be classified into several categories of activities necessary to create and contribute value for others. These activities include engineering, manufacturing or production, automation, packaging, logistics, and technical support services. Each set of services is clearly defined and integrated into the overall operations of each GRIC. Depending on how an individual GRIC is organized and managed, the above activities may be organized within a complete value chain or may be offered individually to a variety of customers. A number of SMEs maintain two types of market activities: within the GRIC, and independently outside the GRIC.

The willingness and ability of SMEs to advance and move along the technology curve is very much a function of their entrepreneurial drive, managerial creativity, understanding of market opportunities, and ability to communicate directly with customers and consumers or users. The entrepreneurial drive depends on top management, or more specifically, on the primary decision maker responsible for the SME's marketing activities. Managerial creativity is related to an SME's ability to communicate internally, gather new ideas, solicit consensus, and make profitable decisions that benefit the ultimate consumer or user. This may be a challenge for some SMEs. In order for SMEs to understand market opportunities, their top management must be proactive in gathering information about market trends and market potential, including the latest technological developments in their areas of expertise.

SMEs that are successful candidates for GRICs need to understand that there is a delicate balance between SMEs' technical expertise and marketing abilities. When the technical expertise and marketing abilities are properly managed and an SME exhibits signs of creativity, market growth, and strong competitive position, the entire GRIC tends to benefit.

There is also a negative side to SMEs that are successful, grow, and enjoy increased market visibility. Successful SMEs tend to become acquisition targets for competitors, investors, and other entities, and are acquired for their scientific know-how, technological capabilities, new product concepts, or markets, among many other reasons. One of the negative aspects of SMEs' membership in GRICs is that they are likely to be acquisition targets, and the acquisition of participating members changes a GRIC's dynamics. Changes in a GRIC's dynamics also occur when a participating enterprise becomes too successful within a GRIC and wants to expand outside through diversification, acquisition, or investments. Such external activities by participating enterprises may, at times, overwhelm a GRIC's entire operations and even change its operational and strategic objectives.

Management of SMEs

The management of SMEs is very much dependent on the top decision maker, since most SMEs have a single manager. The manager may be a scientist, engineer, former executive, or other entrepreneur who initially started the venture. It may be an individual with limited technical skills and managerial abilities. The managerial styles of SMEs very much reflect the technical and marketing approaches of the top decision maker. The SMEs' managerial styles are also influenced by the original initiative or basis on which the SMEs were organized. For example, studies have documented that scientists and engineers are motivated by different incentives than former executives or academics and tend to have different management styles. Traditional entrepreneurs are motivated by financial rewards much more than scientists or engineers and exhibit completely different management styles.

Recent studies show that SMEs have three different types of managers. The first type includes individuals who are interested in the products they produce, and the equipment and processes needed to produce them. For purposes of convenience, they are called craftsmen simply because their managerial interests are closely aligned with the internal technical capabilities of their enterprises. The second managerial type is interested in promoting their enterprises and their products or services as being outstanding without actual market- or competition-verified performance. These managers are called promoters because they generally have a minimal understanding of the technical or marketing side of their enterprises, but nevertheless they believe that their enterprises excel in overall performance. They promote their products and their enterprises. Promoters as managers tend to have very strong entrepreneurial tendencies and a high propensity to face risk. The third managerial type is interested in rational allocation of financial, physical, and human resources, and therefore is typically labeled a rational manager. Rational managers make decisions based on their technical competence combined with substantial market information and assessment of their competitive position. Such a decision-making approach requires that decisions are based on factual information and objective determination of market options facing their enterprises.

SMEs that tend to move along the technology curve and expand their marketing capabilities occasionally need changes in leadership. As an SME moves up the technology curve, there comes a time when the managerial leadership may no longer make operationally and strategically relevant decisions. In order for the enterprise to continue to grow, its leadership and managerial style has to change. Craftsmen are replaced by either promoters or rational managers, and promoters can only be replaced by rational managers.

The initial professional focus of top managers is another characteristic that describes SMEs' management types. Craftsmen who manage low- or high-technology SMEs most likely have a scientific, technological, or technical professional background as research scientists, engineers, or information technology specialists, among other backgrounds. Promoters tend to have only a marginal interest in the scientific, technological, or technical side of the enterprises and are more likely skilled in marketing management, especially advertising, promotion, or sales. Many promoter-type managers have a professional background in sales and marketing, but more likely in sales. Rational managers tend to have extensive managerial experience with a combination of technical and marketing backgrounds. Some recent studies suggest that rational managers tend to have advanced degrees in sciences or engineering as well as in marketing or financial management, and they tend to make quantitative rather than qualitative decisions.

It is important for GRICs' management to recognize that the managerial styles of their participating members will change over time. The participating member enterprises are likely to pass through several stages of growth and be managed by different management types. At the same time, it is also important to understand that SMEs' overall technical and marketing profiles change over time as well. SMEs that start as low-technology product- or process-focused enterprises may evolve into efficient high-technology enterprises with substantial marketing capabilities and strong rational management.

SMEs' rather complex management styles are also apparent in the growth and expansion paths of individual enterprises. Several studies suggest that SMEs managed by craftsmen and promoter-type managers are much more likely to be sold, acquired, or even liquidated by competition than those managed by rational managers. In other words, the life expectancy of SMEs managed by craftsmen or promoters is shorter than that of those managed by rational managers. In addition, if SMEs managed by rational managers are sold or acquired, their value is generally higher than those managed by craftsmen or promoters. All of these factors have a direct impact on GRICs' operations and growth patterns. GRICs may be justified in developing replacement plans for future contingencies of attrition and replacement of enterprises.

Growth and Expansion

Growth and expansion among SMEs are important factors in their life cycle as well as in the lives of entire GRICs. SMEs participating in GRICs have two sources of growth and expansion: internal and external. SMEs internally driven by scientific or technological advancements, or by managerial potential, are likely to outperform the entire GRIC. Similarly, SMEs driven by external market demand, in which the demand outside of the GRIC is greater than the overall demand within the GRIC, may also outperform their GRICs and eventually leave them.

Thus, it is important to understand the natural growth and expansion process of SMEs. It is also important to recognize conceptual differences between growth and expansion. The literature presents several models of growth whereby individual stages are clearly defined and articulated. Research studies, however, suggest that as academic and professional researchers gain a better understanding of SMEs, they are able to more accurately identify stages of their growth. The commonly accepted description of SMEs' growth stages, regardless of their technological sophistication, is as follows: foundation, growth, expansion, consolidation, stagnation, decline, and liquidation.

In this description of SMEs' growth pattern, expansion is considered one of the stages of growth. In fact, expansion seems to be a highly volatile stage in SMEs' life cycle. The expansion stage may reveal how an SME manages its success. If an SME is profitable and has accumulated large cash reserves, it is likely to diversify into new products or product lines, new markets, or other unrelated ventures. In all of these instances, there is the likelihood that a given SME will separate from the original GRIC and function independently. In a few instances, an SME will stay and assist the GRIC with further development and possible internal and external adjustments.

Based on practical experience, it is presumed that the first critical time for new startups is in the foundation stage. Regardless of who manages a startup, there are many unforeseen obstacles and challenges that need to be overcome. These obstacles and challenges are naturally embedded in new technologies, tentative market analyses, or larger-than-expected capital requirements. For some managers of startups, these obstacles and challenges may be so overwhelming that the stage is never completed. However, some options may be left open for them. They may be able to sell the technology, idea, or product concept and terminate their involvement completely. Such occurrences may take on different perspectives if the startups are carefully managed within a GRIC.

From a marketing management point of view, the growth, expansion, and consolidation stages are generally positive experiences for most SMEs. In these stages, SMEs gain market share through product development as well as aggressive marketing and sales strategies, and their profit margins increase. SMEs' managers carefully synchronize their technical and marketing expertise, and develop their operations and strategies to facilitate growth. In the expansion stage, they look for new products and markets, and they aggressively seek various diversification options. In the consolidation stage, SMEs assess their technological and market position and value their assets and resources in light of increasing competition. Skillful managers, especially rational managers, are capable of maximizing the impact of each of these three stages on the technological as well as the marketing side of their enterprises.

The stagnation, decline, and liquidation stages clearly represent negative experiences for SMEs and their managers. The tentative expectation among SMEs' managers is that a given SME will remain in one of the positive stages forever. However, in a highly competitive global marketplace, this notion is not realistic. When an SME ceases to be competitive in the marketplace and its profit starts to drop, it most likely has entered the stagnation stage. Management may attempt to remedy its market position, but it often does not have sufficient resources to do so and is forced into the decline stage by depletion of resources. An SME in the decline stage becomes even more vulnerable because its market position quickly deteriorates. Once an SME enters the decline stage, it is very difficult to reverse the situation and liquidation tends to follow shortly thereafter.

According to organizational specialists, the above model and several similar models describe a natural phenomenon of managerial behavior. Every enterprise proceeds through a similar life cycle in the long run. For some SMEs, this cycle may be long and profitable, while for others it may be very short-lived. The highly competitive scientific community that provides the impetus for numerous high-technology startups today also tends to contribute to the shortening of their life cycles. There is frequently a major incongruence between the scientific offerings and the ability of the marketplace to absorb them. This is the main reason why the formation of GRICs is very dependent on the expected life cycle of the participating enterprises, especially high-technology SMEs.

Mergers and Acquisitions

At any point along SMEs' life cycle, mergers and acquisitions represent both positive and negative challenges. What may be a positive challenge for a member may be a negative challenge for the entire GRIC, depending on how important that SME is to the GRIC's overall success. For example, if an SME is the key principal innovator that has significantly contributed to the market success of the entire GRIC and it chooses to merge with an outside entity that perceives little value in collaborating with the other GRIC members, the GRIC may lose its favorable market position. On the other hand, if a GRIC's participating enterprise agrees to merge with an outside entity which, from a marketing management perspective, is technologically much stronger and this strength is brought back into the GRIC, all the members stand to benefit.

Although mergers and acquisitions are common in all stages of SMEs' life cycle, they are particularly visible in the expansion stage. For highly prosperous SMEs, the expansion stage opens up an entire portfolio of internal and external options. Internal options may include a minor merger to fill gaps in technology or to create auto-mated processes necessary to expand production, or the acquisition of service entities to provide after-sales services for end consumers or users. Internal options may also include adjustments in physical and human resources. This typically involves larger and better facilities or manufacturing processes through outright purchases or long-term leasing plans. Many SMEs in their expansion stage also opt for education and training for their managers and technical staff. Exposing employees to additional education and training helps SMEs strengthen their market and competitive positions.

External mergers and acquisitions by SMEs are more apparent, and are frequently perceived by their competitors as aggressive moves in the market. It is generally the successful enterprises that initiate a merger or acquisition with a specific goal or objective such as technological advancement, better market access and greater possibil-ities for market penetration, innovative approaches to new products or product lines, and availability of better service delivery; or, on the negative side, competitive pressures. Additional motivations to merge or acquire may include higher-than-normal accumulated assets, surplus of innovative technology, underutilized managerial expertise, or spin-off or auxiliary services.

51

Academic and professional studies, especially in management consulting, clearly illustrate some of the positive and negative consequences that mergers and acquisitions have on SMEs; nevertheless, SMEs merge, acquire, and are acquired. If enterprises participating in a GRIC are going through periods of mergers or acquisitions, internally or externally, they need to communicate closely with the other participating enterprises and the GRIC's management because these events may have a positive or negative impact on the entire GRIC. The experiences of a variety of GRICs' managers suggest that some of them attempt to intervene in merger or acquisition processes in order to preserve a sense of continuity and survival for the entire GRIC.

Internationalization

Efforts to internationalize GRICs and their participating enterprises are essential for their survival. Recent studies of GRICs suggest that a majority of them begin their operations in international markets and thereby introduce their participating enterprises to manage on an international level. There are also examples where a dominant enterprise within a GRIC becomes active on an international level and, by this action, internationalizes the marketing operations and strategies for the entire GRIC. Although internationalization of SMEs has a long history in academic and professional literature, it is not well understood.

There are two approaches to internationalization of SMEs: the systematic stages of internationalization approach, and the internationalization portfolio approach. The first approach suggests that SMEs proceed through a series of steps deemed necessary for management to become comfortable with unfamiliar and unusual marketing transactions, economic and cultural environments, and foreign consumer habits, among other obstacles perceived by SMEs' managers. The second approach assumes that there are options for internationalization, which change the mode of SMEs' operations in foreign markets.

SMEs typically start out as indirect or direct exporters in one market and then move to another one as they become familiar with a given foreign market. Exporting is subsequently followed by joint ventures, cross-marketing agreements, mergers, and acquisitions, among other approaches. The traditional understanding was that SMEs begin to export, form joint ventures, merge, and/or invest directly, depending on their level of risk tolerance and financial strength. The traditional understanding of how SMEs internationalize was based on a series of studies among manufacturing enterprises before the onset of information technology, when international communication was cumbersome and necessitated extensive travel and other inconveniences related to management of international marketing operations.

With the introduction of information technology, especially the Internet, international marketing operations became simplified. Many SMEs began to participate in digital technology and viewed international marketing operations and strategies as portfolios of options from which to select, depending on the needs of individual foreign markets. In some foreign markets, the local conditions required SMEs to be closer to their customers, consumers, or users. The SMEs established operations such as cross-marketing agreements or directly invested in those markets, among other approaches, to accomplish their objectives. The typical portfolio of approaches to internationalization includes export operations, joint ventures, licensing arrangements, contractual agreements, and direct investment options. Among high-technology SMEs, the process of matching the needs of international markets with the suitable mode of market entry has become the preferred approach to internationalization.

There is also discussion in the internationalization literature that questions whether or not some SMEs are "born global," i.e., fully international from the moment they start operating. The managerial response to this approach suggests that for many SMEs, particularly those that are extensively dependent on information technology and the use of the Internet, this concept is merely a natural response to the Internet's global capabilities.

There is agreement among SMEs' managers that they have to internationalize their operations and strategies in order to survive. There is also agreement that many GRICs today are formed with high expectations regarding entry into foreign markets. By combining technological and marketing advantages internationally, SMEs can gain strong competitive positions in the global market.

Bibliography

Ante, Spencer E. (2008). *Creative Capital: Georges Doriot and the Birth of Venture Capital.* Boston: Harvard Business Press.

Bilkey, Warren J. and George Tesar (1977). "The Export Behavior of Smaller-Sized Wisconsin Manufacturing Firms." *Journal of International Business Studies,* 8(1), Spring/Summer, 93–98.

McCraw, Thomas K. (2007). *Prophet of Innovation: Joseph Schumpeter and Creative Destruction.* Cambridge, MA: The Belknap Press of Harvard University Press.

Morosini, Piero (2004). "Industrial Clusters, Knowledge Integration and Performance." *World Development,* 32(2), 305–326.

Smith, Madeline and Ross Brown (2009). "Exploratory Techniques for Examining Cluster Dynamics: A Systems Thinking Approach." *Local Economy,* 24(4), June, 283–298.

Snow, C.P. (1963). *Two Cultures: And a Second Look.* New York: A Mentor Book.

Tesar, George, Hamid Moini, John Kuada, and Olav Jull Sørensen (2010). *Smaller Manufacturing Enterprises in an International Context: A Longitudinal Exploration.* London: Imperial College Press.

Chapter 4

Business-to-Consumer Marketing Management

Business-to-consumer marketing management spans the entire process of value creation for consumers or end users from the incipiency of new product ideas or services to the point where the economic, social, or psychological values are reduced to their minimum and the products have left the entire consumption process. It involves the constant generation and management of information throughout the entire value chain with a direct focus on the ultimate consumer in the consumer marketing sector, or the end user in the business-to-business marketing sector. Equally, business-to-consumer marketing management represents the entire integrated process of creating and delivering product or service value on all market levels in either business-to-consumer or business-to-business marketing, but ending specifically at the point where, for whatever reason, a product or service has been discarded by the consumer or user.

In this context, which combines both market and technological dimensions, marketing management can be defined as a series of professional and scientific activities that guide the creation, delivery, and consumption of products or services in rapidly changing consumer- and technology-driven markets. From a managerial point of view, marketing management begins when potentially profitable market opportunities are defined and formulated into a value-generating product or service. Marketing management terminates when the consumer or user fails to perceive any real or imaginary value in a product or service and, subsequently, any remaining residuals have been removed from the entire value chain.

In high-technology markets, marketing management not only necessitates highly developed marketing skills, but also requires a fundamental understanding of the relevant technology underpinning the current value-creating products or services. In other words, marketing managers need to be rational decision makers and capable technologists. The necessary preconditions for rational decision making are an appropriate understanding of marketing theories and concepts, market-specific know-how, the ability to understand appropriate technology, refined operational skills, and the fortitude to challenge the future by shaping dynamic strategies.

Technologically competitive markets require that marketing managers acquire two fundamental attributes: (1) the ability to activate and manage all corporate resources of an enterprise — financial, physical, and human — and maximize socially beneficial present and future market opportunities by creating economic, social, or psychological value for its consumers or users; and (2) the ability to empower the entire enterprise with the notion that its overriding mission is to serve the consumer or end user by delivering the best possible value they may obtain in a competitive market. The focus on the consumer or end user is fundamental to the marketing concept.

Functions of Marketing Management

Marketing managers are responsible for implementing the fundamental marketing management functions. Typically, marketing management functions are described in the context of specific strategies and operations that need to be accomplished in order for the enterprise to deploy a value creation process. In this context of marketing management, these strategies and operations, frequently somewhat overlapping and interrelated depending on how technologically sophisticated the enterprise is, are outlined as follows:

1. Clearly delineate, examine, and define markets with respect to their potential and technological sophistication, along with both quantitative and qualitative recovery estimates in terms of profits and market positions. This course of action also needs to include an assessment of markets' propensity to accept innovation.

2. Understand consumers' purchase behavior along with a determination of consumers' ability to purchase economically, socially, and psychologically significant products or services. Employ marketing research studies to generate the data and information necessary to obtain sufficient insight into consumers' purchase decision.

3. Develop new products based on research and development efforts within or outside of the enterprise; engineer new products for manufacturing and ready them for consumers and end users. This process involves cooperation between marketing managers and the technical side of the enterprise, and financial analysis of the entire new product development process should be the platform for cooperation. At the same time, existing products need to be monitored for their performance and a predetermined replacement routine needs to be managed in the case of non-performing products.

4. Manage the entire value chain with respect to incoming raw materials, supplies, components, accessories, or any necessary items needed to manufacture a final product, along with the entire distribution system necessary to deliver the finished product to consumers or users. Design and put into action an integrated logistical system with its external and internal components for the unique use of the individual enterprise. These activities include decisions and considerations concerning off-site manufacturing or product assembly.

5. Design and implement communication channels between the enterprise and its consumers or users as a reciprocal-flow channel, and use it as a basis for relationship development in marketing management. Communication channels in marketing management need to have the ability to allow bidirectional flow of unrestricted information — to the market and from the market.

6. Closely monitor consumers' and users' satisfaction in today's socially, environmentally, and technologically sensitive societies. Marketing managers are responsible for the consumption and post-consumption behavior of their consumers and end users, and need to understand the residual impact that their products leave on society. Comprehensive feedback is needed from consumers and users, combined with quantitative and qualitative measures of performance, leading to clear measures of consumer and user satisfaction and enterprise profitability frequently provided by independent and unbiased auditors.

In the overall context of marketing management, market delineation simply means a clear specification of the market that each enterprise is prepared to serve with a specific product or service. For example, for many startup enterprises, this is the first step in marketing management. Market delineation is followed by an examination of potential purchase decisions or buying decisions in business-to-business marketing. Not only do marketing managers need to have a clear understanding of their markets, but they also need to understand what motivates their potential consumers or business-to-business customers to purchase their particular products or services. These tasks require a great deal of information that is precise to the marketing and technological focus of each enterprise.

The new product development process is highly integrated and structured within the marketing management needs of each enterprise. It typically begins with an idea, discovery, market innovation, or other technological advancement. Startup enterprises, new products and product lines, or even new enterprise divisions evolve from such occurrences. More advanced enterprises operating in high-technology markets typically manage effective research and development facilities to stimulate new product development efforts. The new product development process requires up-to-date scientific input from research and development efforts combined with strong marketing management knowledge of how to develop a new product and bring it profitably into the markets. Various types of research efforts are involved, ranging from pure scientific discovery research to applied scientific research and engineering followed by marketing and consumer behavior research.

In order to deliver an optimal product or service to consumers or end users, marketing managers need to identify relevant and efficient sources of the required inputs, which necessitate a strong input assessment process. In the age of information technology, the input assessment may take several forms, including Internet actions offered by individual enterprises for potential suppliers. Marketing managers also need to deal with manufacturing options — in-house, domestic, or foreign. Depending on the manufacturing options, direct or indirect logistical options need to be developed and implemented in order to reach consumers or end users. The process of delivering products or services to consumers or end users is a dynamic process that constantly changes in light of evolving logistical options.

In this age of information technology, communication channels connecting marketing managers and their consumers or users reflect the complex realities of direct and indirect communication options and personal and impersonal contacts via print and social media. The nature of communication as well as the nature of advertising are rapidly changing. Advertising has become much more targeted and personal because of social media. This phenomenon is combined with consumer or user satisfaction.

The level of satisfaction in today's society is tempered by social, environmental, and technological dynamics, since consumers and users consider not only how satisfied they are with a specific product or service, but also how it impacts their social and the physical environment and whether or not it represents an appropriate technology for a given product or service. Consumers and users today are very much concerned with how discarded products are removed from the post-consumption process. These are new dimensions that face marketing managers and need to be considered in the overall context of the entire consumption and post-consumption processes.

For new, emerging, or existing enterprises, marketing management functions can be formulated and articulated as five separate functions that require the same level of enterprise attention but different sets of marketing management skills and specializations. These functions are derived from the above discussion and reflect the impact of information technology on contemporary marketing management practices.

The first marketing management function is the entire process of assessing market opportunities for a given enterprise. This marketing management function begins with an incipient notion for a product or service that may originate anywhere in the scientific or commercial domain. In the scientific domain, a research scientist may discover a process, identify a solution to an existing social problem, or discover a new pharmaceutical product. Once such events are scientifically verified, they need to be tied to market reality; the scientists need to interact with marketing managers in delineating the market and estimating the market's potential. In this function, marketing managers must be able to communicate with the scientists, and vice versa. More specifically, marketing managers must be able to understand the fundamental scientific and engineering underpinnings of potential products and markets under assessment. Conversely, if the new product idea originates in the commercial domain, the marketing manager must be able to explain its market ramifications to the scientists. This function is considered to be comparatively external to the enterprise.

The second marketing management function is the responsibility to plan out specific courses of action and program them for eventual product or service opportunities. When specific courses are planned, each course of action needs to be systematically programmed. A product or service may have several potential market options for its implementation. Each option needs to be carefully considered with respect to market penetration success and potential profitability. The optimal course of action needs to be planned subject to the amount of available resources allocated. After the plan for an optimal option has been prepared, individual tasks or activities need to be programmed in an overall marketing strategy and its implementation. Individual products or services may require a unique plan and implementation program. At this point, marketing managers need to focus more on the entire scope of each opportunity rather than on the end result that the opportunity may generate. Marketing managers need to be innovative and resourceful in creating additional potential market options for a given opportunity. This function focuses primarily on internal resources and the expertise of the entire enterprise.

In order to implement the planning and programming function, a well-structured and operational marketing organization needs to be developed. This is the third function of marketing management. When the implementation plan and program are finalized, an entire organization must evolve to facilitate its implementation. The implementation plan and program must specify what tasks or activities need to be carried out, what marketing expertise is needed and on what levels, and how it should be staffed. The fundamental rule in building organizational structures is that structure follows strategy in any marketing management effort. Marketing organizations are built to facilitate optimal implementation of a specific marketing action. This function encompasses the internal know-how, resourcefulness, and competitiveness of the enterprise.

Internal know-how, resourcefulness, and competitiveness require individual fortitude and professional strength, which translate into leadership. Consequently, the fourth function of marketing management requires that enterprises foster marketing leadership that is deployed when new market opportunities emerge. Typically every new product or service requires a manager who will champion the potential product or service. Sometimes a champion will emerge early on in the new development process and will continue to champion the product or service throughout its market delineation process, throughout its planning and programming process, and when a marketing organization is evolving. Most of the time, however, a champion must be found; because of this dilemma, enterprises are responsible for grooming potential leaders in marketing to manage future market opportunities. This marketing management function represents a primary internal cooperative effort between marketing and human resource management.

Overall control and monitoring of the marketing process is the last function of marketing management. Assessment of market opportunities, their planning and programming, development of marketing organizations, and their leadership represent a one-directional marketing effort that necessitates the final marketing management function: evaluation and adjustment of the entire marketing effort for a given product or service. The evaluation and adjustment effort is based on extensive feedback from consumers or users concerning their level of satisfaction with a given product or service, and on other internally and externally generated data and information.

Each enterprise may use different criteria in evaluating and adjusting its marketing effort; however, the composition of the preferred consumer or end user feedback needs to be clearly specified and monitored, depending on the product or service attributes or level of technological sophistication. This may include information about the need for technical service, recall attempts, and part or component replacement issues, among others. Internal audits include profitability, sales volume, market share, and market penetration measures. External audits, typically conducted by third-party providers, include product image, product performance, product service record, and other information specified by marketing managers. The combination of these sets of factors is used in making adjustments in the entire marketing effort for each product or service offered by a given enterprise. The evaluation and adjustment function represents an independent internal and external system of unbiased auditors who make certain that the entire marketing effort supervised by marketing managers is performing effectively and efficiently.

Although marketing management functions can be clearly defined and organizationally implemented, marketing managers do not operate in a closed environment inside an enterprise — they must also be cognizant of activities external to the enterprise. All marketing activities need to be conducted in the context of social responsibility, environmental awareness, and the prevailing technological climate. It is this external business environment that creates pressure on marketing managers and their activities.

Environmental Forces Acting on Marketing Effort

Marketing management, along with its specific functions, is designed to provide an enterprise with a system of activities that enable it to facilitate a flow of products and services through the value chain as well as efficiently and effectively serve its consumers or users. However, this rather simple process is constrained by several external forces that shape the nature of products and services and, to a certain degree, determine the potential success of each enterprise in the marketplace, along with an array of competitive challenges which each enterprise faces.

From a marketing management perspective, each enterprise operates in a uniquely structured and controlled external business environment. This external business environment consists of forces that shape the operations and strategies of each enterprise and have a direct impact on marketing management operations and strategies. The forces are generally defined as: (1) economic, (2) technological, (3) lifestyle, (4) social, and (5) ecological. Each external business environment offers a unique definition of these forces, depending on how the governing body of each external business environment legally and administratively defines these forces based on inputs from its constituencies (citizens, voters, employers, workers, customers, consumers, etc.).

For example, any state government in the United States, to a certain extent, creates its own environment for its enterprises. Each state's economic climate tends to be different depending on state taxes and how taxes are collected (state sales tax or income tax), and on the level of technology a state population tends to support as reflected in the legislative action of a state government (a high-technology state as compared to a predominantly agricultural-technology or resource-mining state). The lifestyles adopted by the population of a state also impact the character of the workforce (a rural lifestyle versus a highly industrialized urban lifestyle). The social force within a specific external business environment is a composite of ethical, political, and legal constructs that shape its social actions and reactions and grant mandates to its legislators (highly regulated business startups as compared with subsidized assisted business startups). The ecological force shaping enterprise actions is also becoming increasingly more important, and has a direct impact on a variety of marketing management operations and strategies (such as recycling, post-consumption product removal, or logistics in highly populated metropolitan areas).

Marketing managers recognize that the interpretation of external business environmental forces by consumers or users creates unique conditions for marketing operations and strategies, and must be accepted as such. In other words, the perception that consumers or users have of the environmental forces impacting enterprises may differ from the perception of the enterprises themselves. This recognition also implies that managerial action and decision making need to comply with the nature and intent of the forces in each external business environment. This is particularly significant for international marketing activities, where enterprises may function in a number of external business environments. The nature and impact of each marketing effort needs to reflect the conditions that exist within each external business environment, and needs to comply with them.

The ability of marketing managers to comply with the forces of an external business environment depends greatly on their ability to gather accurate and reliable data and information. Marketing research specialists consequently share the responsibility of assessing and processing data and information needed to provide sound foundations for managerial decision making. Marketing managers' decisions are only as reliable as the inputs on which the decisions are based. An external business environment must be constantly monitored for changes and developments, which frequently create market opportunities as much as changes and developments in the marketplace. Technological changes and advancements in an external business environment may open up enormous market opportunities for new products or services.

Governments and their agencies that shape environmental forces view their interaction as a dynamic process that is constantly evolving subject to the needs of their constituencies, especially from the perspective of consumers or users that form markets within them. In technologically advanced environments in particular, the nature and the impact of these forces changes quickly and marketing managers must be ready to respond to these changes. Most marketing managers recognize the necessity to respond to changes and frequently plan for contingencies within their marketing efforts, especially with respect to market adjustments and competitive action.

Enterprise Actions and Marketing Management

In order for marketing managers to systematically and rationally respond to dynamic forces in their external business environment, they need to understand the strategy and structure of their enterprises. It is important to understand that today the marketing effort — operations and strategies — responds to market opportunities for the entire enterprise. In reality, marketing management determines the future of the enterprise. Organizationally, marketing management begins at the top level of the enterprise and ends with the empowerment of all employees to participate in the ultimate focus on consumers and users. Conversely, top management is responsible for marketing action and empowers the entire organization, line and staff employees, to focus entirely on the satisfaction of consumers and users.

Such an orientation requires that a comprehensive mission statement is communicated directly to all employees. The mission statement is a statement of purpose; it outlines the strategic philosophy of the enterprise in a time dimension and the changing nature of its markets and products or services. In other words, a mission statement specifies the purpose for which the enterprise and its resources exist, and offers the understanding of its founders (or top managers) as to how the enterprise should proceed strategically toward ever-changing market opportunities in accordance with its available resources.

At the same time, a mission statement should offer a perspective on the enterprise's future evolution while it responds to the environment in which it functions in the present, with the full understanding that markets are not constant and change as additional scientific knowledge is generated. Consumer preferences also change to correspond to new scientific and technological capabilities embedded in new products and services.

Marketing management typically responds and operates with respect to the mission set by the enterprise, although occasionally it has an opportunity to provide input when an obsolete mission statement needs to be revised. This is particularly important in startup enterprises, where more often than not the mission statement has not been clearly set and the initial marketing and technological capabilities have not been fully realized.

In addition to a mission statement, marketing managers also need to understand the strength of an enterprise's resource base, namely its financial, physical, and human resources. Each enterprise logically owns and manages a different kind, amount, and combination of resources. The success of many enterprises depends on how they manage these resources to optimally implement market opportunities.

Financial resources need to be examined in the context of present and future opportunities. Future opportunities depend on current and past investments in the development of non-financial assets. Current investment in research and development is harvested in competitive products and services in the future. The profitability of an enterprise is closely related to the dynamics of its financial resources. Each enterprise must coordinate its marketing programs with its present financial capabilities and its future financial potential. If marketing management does not accurately gauge the responses to its marketing efforts by not generating sufficient profit, the entire financial resource base will collapse.

Physical resources are all the tangible assets that an enterprise owns and manages, and present a considerable challenge to marketing management. Traditionally, enterprises owned most of their manufacturing facilities, distribution systems (including warehouses), and transportation systems, among others. In the age of outsourcing, restructuring, and downsizing, however, many traditional physical resources have been eliminated. Enterprises have reduced their physical resources by various combinations of disinvestments, outsourcing, and leasing options.

Manufacturing facilities have been reduced dramatically and supplemented by automation and streamlined Just-in-Time inventory systems, which reduce the need for warehouses, storage facilities, and outgoing inventory-holding or staging facilities. Entire logistical systems can be outsourced, which eliminates the need for truck fleets and truck maintenance equipment. These developments have substantially changed the entire marketing management operations and strategies.

Over the past few years, human resources, as a part of the entire resource base, have also experienced a major transition. Due to several major economic trends, enterprises nowadays employ fewer employees with greater responsibilities for more sophisticated tasks than their predecessors. New technologies especially information technology, have fundamentally changed new product development, manufacturing, distribution, and communication processes. In addition to offshoring, automated manufacturing and production technologies have reduced the number of workers needed in manufacturing. Office automation has also reduced the number of workers. Even in engineering, especially in new product development, the use of computers and engineering software has dramatically reduced the number of engineers, designers, and technicians needed to design a new product or formulate a new service. Many specialized enterprises in high-technology industries have even reduced their staff of scientists and researchers and dramatically reduced their research and development efforts, which represent their future investments.

The dramatic changes in resources have also changed how marketing managers manage. Today, marketing managers need to be better trained, have a greater propensity to develop innovative and competitive marketing strategies, and possess the foresight to invest in future market opportunities. The changes in the nature and makeup of the resource base have had a direct impact on how marketing managers view internal and external marketing operations. Internally, many enterprises are showing a tendency to change the role of marketing by empowering employees to participate in the entire marketing effort and centralizing some of the basic marketing functions such as advertising, marketing research, or quality control, among others. Externally, enterprises are developing capabilities to compete more aggressively with highly structured and integrated marketing strategies. The external marketing effort requires more sophisticated monitoring systems based on shared data and information sources such as scanner data, environmental scanning, and direct consumer or user feedback. Although the fundamental marketing management functions still provide the theoretical and conceptual foundation for marketing management, enterprises and their marketing managers need to be constantly aware of how these changes impact their market and financial stability.

Marketing and financial stability today are dependent on the competitive position of each enterprise. In a highly competitive and technologically advanced marketplace, each enterprise needs to fully understand its exact competitive position. Some marketing managers suggest that it is up to them, their resources, and the entire enterprise to specify their competitive market position before they enter the market. This means that enterprises should be able to define their competitors, specify their competitive advantages, and appropriately challenge them by formulating effective marketing strategies and accurately timing the market introduction of technological advancements. Several enterprises in the information and personal communication industries are doing just that. The entire marketing effort must be gauged towards managing and challenging carefully selected present and future competitors.

Marketing Effort of an Enterprise

Today, most marketing efforts focus on the critical definition of which market segments to serve. The definition and specification of new markets and market segments require imagination, creativity, and intuition on the part of marketing managers. Based on its resource base, marketing and technological know-how, and communication ability, each enterprise needs to identify the primary market. In the framework of contemporary marketing and technological abilities, markets tend to be created rather than harvested. New technologies, products, and services require the formation of needs and expectations that can effectively utilize them. Furthermore, new technologies, products, and services require a certain level of understanding and imagination by consumers or users to integrate that technology, product, or service into their highly structured consumption functions and, subsequently, their consumption processes.

Market segments are integral parts of markets. Once a market has been defined and selected, a specific market segment needs to be accurately defined. Each potential consumer or user in that market segment must be specified based on economic, social, and psychological needs. Their perceptions, attitudes, and preferences need to be understood by marketing managers and converted into market opportunities. Potential and marginal consumers or users need to be examined on the basis of their propensity to enter the specified market segment — under what conditions and approximately at what time horizon they will join the segment in question.

The market and market segment dynamics outlined above are especially relevant for small startup enterprises that may have a new technology, that are based on an invention, or that have some otherwise protected concept or even patent that they want to bring into the marketplace. In many instances, startup enterprises face choices concerning the implementation of their intellectual property. They need to make decisions regarding which market is optimal, and under what conditions, and who will ultimately purchase the new product or service and benefit from it. Marketing managers need a great deal of information about potential consumers or users to make these decisions.

In highly competitive and rapidly changing markets, marketing managers need to understand what motivates potential consumers, or business-to-business purchase facilitators, to purchase a specific product or acquire a service. Business-to-business purchase decisions are considered to be made on economically rational bases.

Consumer purchase behavior is a major subset of overall consumer behavior. From a marketing management perspective, any successful marketing effort is ultimately triggered by consumers making a purchase decision. A purchase decision is the final step in a sequence of decisions that consumers make in order to participate in the entire value creation process. Before a purchase decision can be made, marketing managers assume that consumers first process available information about the product or service through their behavioral filters — perceptual, attitudinal, and preferential — and then determine that they may derive some level of economic, social, or psychological benefit from the purchase.

The actual purchase decision may be an instantaneous response to some ambient or situational conditions that triggered the purchase decision (an impulse decision); it may be the result of a long rational process involving systematic evaluation of relevant information subject to careful analysis of personal, economic, social, or psychological needs (a rational decision); or it may result from a combination of the factors involved in these two extremes. The actual purchase decision needs to be understood by marketing managers at several different stages. First, there are preconditions for the actual purchase decision: a systematic exploration process during which the likelihood of the decision is determined by the consumer. This estimate of the likelihood provides valuable inputs into managerial considerations about whether or not to proceed with development of the product or service. Second, when the consumer makes the decision to purchase the product or service, marketing managers determine under what conditions the decision was made and at what level of consumer commitment. Finally, the purchase decision needs to be evaluated after the purchase to determine how satisfied the consumer was with the product or service.

These three stages of a purchase decision are particularly important for products or services that are new to the marketplace and based on the latest technological developments. Consumers will make the purchase decision based not only on their economic, social, and psychological considerations, but also on their technological knowledge and perceived skills. Consequently, marketing managers have to ensure that their marketing efforts will accomplish the intended objective, but they also need to provide the necessary technological understanding for the product. This effort requires a dual communication process between marketing managers and consumers — one for marketing communication and the other for technological learning.

The final factor in marketing management is the level of consumer or user satisfaction. Consumer satisfaction provides several inputs for the entire marketing effort. An objective measure of consumer satisfaction should indicate the likelihood that consumers will repurchase a product or service. It should also indicate how willing consumers are to recommend a product or service to others. From a financial perspective, consumer satisfaction is an indicator of potential return on investment, profitability, and competitiveness. Finally, consumer satisfaction may also serve as a platform for product improvements and modifications.

Marketing management defined in the context of geographically remote industrial clusters (GRICs) serves two specific purposes: (1) it is used to formulate operational procedures and strategic options for a GRIC; and (2) it is an integral part of the operational and strategic efforts of each participating enterprise. Without well-designed and properly implemented marketing management functions on both of these levels, the entire GRIC's efficiency and effectiveness will not be realized.

Bibliography

Aaker, David A. (1995). *Strategic Market Management*, 4th ed. New York: John Wiley & Sons, Inc.

Barabba, Vincent P. (1995). *Meeting of the Minds: Creating the Market-Based Enterprise.* Boston, MA: Harvard Business School Press.

Frank, Ronald E., William F. Massy, and Yoram Wind (1972). *Market Segmentation.* Englewood Cliffs, NJ: Prentice-Hall, Inc.

Messinger, Paul R. (1995). *The Marketing Paradigm: A Guide for General Managers.* Cincinnati, OH: South-Western College Press.

Mohr, Jakki (2001). *Marketing of High-Technology Products and Innovations.* Upper Saddle River, NJ: Prentice Hall.

Schnaars, Steven (1991). *Marketing Strategy: A Customer-Driven Approach.* New York: The Free Press.

Chapter 5

Marketing Management and Cluster Dynamics

Marketing management is an integral part of all geographically remote industrial clusters (GRICs) on every level. Marketing management is a part of the operations and strategies from a GRIC's formation to the point where it is a fully functional and ongoing venture. At this point, a GRIC is expected to market itself and provide marketing expertise and skills to its member enterprises by managing an operational and strategic platform for them. Marketing managers responsible for implementing the marketing management functions and maintaining the marketing platform of a GRIC are expected, to a degree, to help chart the marketing activities of member enterprises.

This dual responsibility for marketing management needs to be clearly understood from the point of view of the entire GRIC as well as from the point of view of the individual member enterprises. One responsibility of marketing management is to create an optimal climate for marketing activities for the entire GRIC. The second responsibility is to design a marketing platform for the GRIC's members, on which the member enterprises can build an effective and efficient marketing effort for their products or services. In some GRICs, member enterprises mutually design and implement their marketing effort; while in other GRICs, member enterprises utilize the platform occasionally in developing their own marketing operations and strategies.

For individual enterprises participating in a GRIC, marketing management begins with the initial description and formulation of an initial idea for a product or service around which a new enterprise is formed. Depending on the GRIC's mission and the level of involvement, individual enterprises may benefit from the overall marketing management that a GRIC provides, or each enterprise may launch its own marketing management effort intended to deliver its products or offer services to selected business-to-business or business-to-consumer markets. Some enterprises operating within a GRIC choose to do both — participate in the GRIC's overall marketing management effort, and manage their own.

Approaches to Development and Operations of GRICs

There are two different approaches to developing and operating GRICs: (1) mutually dependent GRICs in which all member enterprises together sequentially deliver a single line of products or services to business-to-business or business-to-consumer markets; and (2) GRICs that provide a managerial platform, or loosely formed cooperative entity, from which independent members manage their own marketing initiatives.

Both of these models are acceptable and used in economic and regional development projects internationally. Some countries prefer one model over the other, depending on the degree of control various governing bodies require. Both models are frequently found side by side in countries where the emphasis is on innovation, growth of smaller manufacturing enterprises, and other economically and socially desirable alternatives for growth of new ventures.

The first approach to the formation of a GRIC incorporates marketing management into its overall structure as a component of its operational and strategic activities. Marketing managers then proceed to cooperate with each member enterprise to determine the specific role that each enterprise is asked to assume in the overall activities of the entire GRIC. Under these conditions, the marketing effort of each member enterprise is closely coordinated with the overall marketing effort of the entire GRIC and delivers only a partial value to the whole value chain serviced by the GRIC. In other words, marketing activities of the individual member enterprises are contingent upon marketing efforts of the entire GRIC. This approach is frequently referred to as being highly integrated — or, a highly integrated GRIC.

Highly integrated GRICs can be found in the mining industry, wine and agricultural producers, or suppliers to high-technology industries such as aircraft manufacturers, among others. Many highly integrated GRICs have a specific mission whereby each member enterprise performs a specific function or serves a clearly defined purpose. In GRICs that specialize in developing and fabricating agricultural equipment, member enterprises such as machine shops, tool and die makers, or software developers serve specifically assigned roles. Similar conditions can be found in marine vessel restoration services, where each member enterprise is part of a sequential process that requires unique expertise.

Several examples can also be found when a local governmental agency, university, or other public entity attempts to organize a GRIC based on a number of existing enterprises that, although seemingly unrelated, may be brought together to produce a product or service. The initiating entity may have an idea or plan of how the newly created GRIC could be managed to assist local enterprises in cooperating to implement the idea or plan. Usually, the first step in this process is for the organizing entity to establish an incubator or research park to facilitate the process. In this situation, the GRIC's management takes over the entire marketing management process.

In the second approach to the formation of GRICs, marketing management of a GRIC is completely separated from marketing management of the individual members. Each GRIC deploys its own marketing management activities; it also provides a platform from which participating members may launch their own marketing programs. Parallel to this marketing management platform, the GRIC also provides operational and strategic marketing activities designed to market its own services, membership options, and other endeavors to make certain that it will survive. If needed, member enterprises may receive assistance with marketing management under a consulting agreement. Some marketing specialists, having worked closely with GRICs and their marketing managers, recommend that a GRIC should actually maintain two different marketing organizations: its own, and the other for consulting purposes for its member enterprises.

The second approach to the formation of GRICs and the integration of marketing management into their operations and strategies is popular with smaller high-technology enterprises that are focused on scientific or technological activities and pay little attention to marketing activities. Managers of smaller startup enterprises may concentrate on developing and improving products or services still under development and may purchase, on a consulting basis, any marketing services they may need.

Such arrangements are generally found in GRICs that have been developed by universities. University administrators believe that, for example, a comprehensive university can design a marketing management platform for startup enterprises by harnessing internal expertise. Departments in business schools are asked to apply their expertise at the various stages of development faced by startup enterprises. Universities that manage incubators or business parks often have a standby marketing management platform available to startup enterprises at all times.

A number of GRICs that do not have a uniform program for participating members to market their own products or services suggest that, early in their startup stages, such members frequently do not know or realize what kind of marketing activities they will have to face and that they simply do not have the expertise to develop them. In these situations, participating members may rely on the marketing management platform provided by the GRIC; they may utilize the platform until they fully understand their own marketing needs and learn how to introduce them into their growing enterprises.

There is a common dimension in both approaches concerning the integration of marketing management. Both approaches help member enterprises identify market opportunities. In the first approach, there is a single integrated effort to identify and realize any market opportunity that might be identified by the entire GRIC. In the second approach, it is up to each member enterprise to identify its own opportunities and develop a marketing program even though, at the beginning of its operations, it may need assistance offered by the GRIC. In reality, in the first approach member enterprises also need assistance to clearly identify their unified position within the GRIC (internal marketing management) and understand the overall position of the GRIC itself (external marketing management).

In both approaches, marketing management in GRICs is used for two fundamental purposes: (1) to identify and implement market opportunities, collectively or individually; and (2) to foster a strong competitive position for the GRIC and its members.

Cooperation, Competition, and Marketing Management

One of the concerns among GRICs is the degree of relationship between cooperation and competition. The issue of cooperation is relevant for GRICs that were formed with the central idea that all member enterprises are expected to work together to form a cooperative effort in generating consumer value. The underlying assumption of this approach is that member enterprises cooperate in some sort of sequential fashion in which they do not compete with each other; instead, each member enterprise has a unique role in the value chain and its role does not compete with any other enterprise in that GRIC.

Problems may develop when an information stream throughout the GRIC is open to all participating enterprises and there is the possibility of overlapping technology. One member enterprise down the stream may significantly improve and utilize technology that is intended for use by another member enterprise even further down the stream. For example, an enterprise specializing in foundry casting may learn about a new cleaning technology, the responsibility for which was assigned to a less innovative enterprise in another part of the value chain. In this example, the foundry that cast the parts wants to clean the parts because it is more proactive and could easily incorporate the new technology into its finishing process. From the perspective of the GRIC's marketing management, such lack of cooperation creates conflicts.

It is also important to realize that in highly focused GRICs with unified sequential value chains, there is a relatively low level of competition, primarily because all participating enterprises directly benefit from arrangements of single value chains. In this type of GRICs, competition typically emerges from potential member enterprises that typically offer GRICs lower cost structures, updated technology, or some other cost-saving advantage. For example, an innovative startup enterprise focusing on automation may perceive as its market opportunity a particular process that is used in a production process within a GRIC. The process is currently provided by a member enterprise using obsolete technology that is economically inefficient. The startup enterprise approaches the GRIC and offers its services in direct competition with the member enterprise that is currently supplying the service. The GRIC's marketing management needs to decide from which service the entire GRIC derives greater benefits.

In GRICs where each member enterprise operates independently without any central cooperative agreements, there is also the potential for cooperation among the individual member enterprises, frequently on an as-needed basis. Some agreements may be facilitated by the marketing managers operating the marketing platform intended to assist the GRIC's member enterprises to speed up their product development, gather market information, design their marketing efforts, or resolve some technological deficiency. In these situations, some GRICs require that formal agreements are signed specifying the type and nature of such cooperation.

The situation is somewhat different in GRICs in which there is no clearly defined sequential value chain to which all members contribute their expertise but, from a technological perspective, the members are similar. For example, a GRIC may be formed to nurture and develop biotechnology in a region dominated by university research in biotechnology. Each participating member enterprise may function independently with its own technology and proprietary marketing operations and strategies. All member enterprises may potentially become competitors. In such situations, the GRIC's marketing managers must realize that potential conflict exists and they need to take precautions to ensure that each member's technology is secured, especially if it is in the research and development stage. The GRIC must take precautions that the facilities are secured, information technology is protected, and a proprietary climate is maintained. Outside of a GRIC, however, market competition may thrive.

Marketing Management and GRICs at the Market Level

Regardless of which approach GRICs used in their formation, they usually do not represent a major force in the market. GRICs that formed a single unified value chain and offer products or services in either business-to-business or business-to-consumer markets most likely compete with other marketers offering the same or similar products or services. Only in rare situations does market knowledge that products or services are marketed by a GRIC convey any meaningful economic, social, or psychological value or preference.

In some instances, the knowledge that a product or service originated within a GRIC may have some value to the consumer or end user, but only under special circumstances. For example, knowing that a product was developed, produced, and marketed by a GRIC may be valuable to a segment of consumers who are familiar with the specific geographic region, or to consumers who support a cooperative spirit in such areas as agriculture, furniture making, or the production of handmade items.

This phenomenon may become more important for GRICs, as some market segments focus on local or regional production and attempt to consume locally or regionally produced products. In an increasing number of agricultural segments, collective value chains play an important role in maintaining scales of production. Growers and producers frequently participate in GRICs in order to increase their production and satisfy market demand for their products.

Enterprises which operate within GRICs that maintain marketing management platforms also manage their own marketing activities. The fact that they may be operating out of a unique GRIC may have little impact on their market position. Communication with consumers or end users in today's technological climate is not an obstacle. Most logistical issues have been resolved with the restructuring of distribution centers and inventory procedures. With the expansion of offshore manufacturing and international logistical systems, consumers or end users seldom realize the actual geographic origin of the product that they consume.

Some economic and development specialists point out that enterprises which function within GRICs may be in a more advantageous market position than their non-GRIC competitors. They may have economic and social advantages such as availability of a rural labor force, combined logistical support, and utilization of local resources such as land, water, or climate. They also point out that there may be a unique knowledge-sharing environment within a GRIC, which may lead to more competitive product or service improvements.

Marketing Management at the Enterprise Level

From a managerial perspective, GRICs are complex organizations that either facilitate collective action or provide a platform for individual action in a collective setting. Individual member enterprises have choices: they may choose to cooperate with other member enterprises in a GRIC, or they may market their products or services independently. It is important to realize that all individual participating member enterprises are responsible for their own development, growth, and marketing efforts. It is not the responsibility of a GRIC's marketing managers to intervene in the marketing operations and strategies of individual member enterprises unless they are specifically asked to do so.

When a GRIC is designed to manage a single value chain with each member enterprise performing a clearly defined specific function within the value chain, individual members may, as long as they are performing this function, partially minimize their own marketing management activities. For example, they may focus only on internal innovations, product or service improvements, or any aspect of their marketing activities that contributes additional value to the entire value chain. Under these conditions, they may minimize their marketing activities outside of the GRIC.

A number of marketing specialists suggest that such an approach may not necessarily be strategically practical for their future. A member enterprise may have internal abilities and know-how to introduce more innovative products or offer more technologically advanced services. In fact, a member enterprise may have capabilities that reach far beyond the GRIC. At some point in time, the enterprise might choose to leave the GRIC in order to grow and compete more aggressively in the marketplace. Consequently, according to this view, even though a member enterprise has a specific responsibility within the GRIC, it also has a responsibility to assess its own potential and plan for its future inside or outside of the GRIC, whichever is more advantageous for its future. It is the responsibility of marketing management to constantly track each enterprise's own market potential and market opportunities.

In GRICs in which member enterprises operate independently but have the option of utilizing a marketing management platform managed by the GRIC, the individual member enterprises have ultimate control over their marketing destiny. In order to plan, operate, compete, and grow, each member enterprise needs its own unique marketing know-how in order to maintain its own market position and competitive profile.

If a GRIC member begins as a startup enterprise, it will initially require assistance with specific marketing tasks such as specification of a new product or service idea, development of a product concept, preparation of a technology brief to place the potential product on the market, in addition to other tasks that need to be performed before the product reaches a market. These marketing tasks are generally within the capabilities of the GRIC's platform managers because they are somewhat common to all startup enterprises.

The need for marketing management inputs will change as a new product evolves and a market segment is specified. Marketing management considerations internal to an enterprise will shift to include external considerations. As a product moves closer to the market and begins to take on strategic and competitive dimensions, the need for marketing management intensifies. Marketing managers need to develop competitive strategies and plans for growth, technological advancements, and other related activities.

Individual member enterprises operating in GRICs are generally viewed by economic and development specialists as independent entities responsible for their own actions. Marketing specialists perceive them in a similar way; they define them as independent marketing organizations that are able to determine their own destinies and utilize marketing management to progress towards these destinies.

Marketing Management at the GRIC Level

According to marketing specialists, marketing management at the GRIC level has two fundamental responsibilities: (1) to maintain and assure the future viability of the entire GRIC; and (2) to assist and support member enterprises with their future viability. Regardless of how a given GRIC was formed, it has the responsibility to assure its member enterprises that it will continue to function and provide a sort of safety net for them, if they need it, and that it will manage its own marketing effort to benefit the entire GRIC and the member enterprises.

It is generally understood that in GRICs with a unifying value chain, the bond between the GRIC's marketing managers and the individual member enterprises is much stronger than in GRICs where the individual member enterprises act independently and maintain their own markets. A certain level of consensus needs to be reached when the entire GRIC focuses on a market, or a number of market segments, and attempts to introduce a product or service that represents the entire membership of the GRIC.

This is a major responsibility, particularly for startup enterprises not certain about their future. However, even larger member enterprises know that by joining a GRIC they may give up a substantial portion of their previous market or the entire market, and turning over their future to a GRIC may be less than effective. This is a decision that each enterprise needs to make before joining a GRIC.

In GRICs where member enterprises act independently, marketing management serves an entirely different role — it is advisory. The assumption is that the GRIC's marketing management expertise might be more advanced than that of a typical member enterprise. Member enterprises may request specialized marketing assistance needed to improve their operations or future strategies. The relationship between marketing managers at the GRIC level and their counterparts at the member enterprise level may be of a project nature rather than an ongoing relationship.

In either approach, marketing management at the GRIC level has a wide responsibility for guiding member enterprises in their marketing activities. There is an understanding among marketing specialists that a GRIC's marketing know-how and capabilities need to be substantially better than the marketing know-how and capabilities of individual member enterprises. Marketing managers of individual member enterprises typically focus on their own marketing interests and expertise, while the GRIC's marketing managers must focus on the overall aggregate marketing efforts of the entire GRIC.

Bibliography

Bell, Geoffrey G. (2005). "Clusters, Networks, and Firm Innovativeness." *Strategic Management Journal*, 26, 287–295.

Guliani, Elisa (2005). "Cluster Absorptive Capacity: Why Do Some Clusters Forge Ahead and Others Lag Behind?" *European Urban and Regional Studies*, 12(3), July, 269–288.

Kotler, Philip (1967). *Marketing Management: Analysis, Planning, and Control*. Englewood Cliffs, NJ: Prentice-Hall, Inc.

Kukalis, Sal (2010). "Agglomeration Economies and Firm Performance: The Case of Industry Clusters." *Journal of Management*, 36(2), March, 453–481.

Mytelka, Lynn and Fulvia Farinelli (2000). "Local Clusters, Innovation Systems and Sustained Competitiveness." Discussion Paper Series #2005, United Nations University–Institute for New Technologies, Maastricht, The Netherlands, October.

Russo, Margherita and Federica Rossi (2009). "Cooperation Networks and Innovation: A Complex Systems Perspective to the Analysis and Evaluation of a Regional Innovation Policy Programme." *Evaluation,* 15(1), January, 75–99.

Smith, Madeline and Ross Brown (2009). "Exploratory Techniques for Examining Cluster Dynamics: A Systems Thinking Approach." *Local Economy,* 24(4), June, 283–298.

Chapter 6

Notes on Case Analysis

The teaching cases that follow are unique and have been written exclusively to explore marketing management and how it relates to geographically remote industrial clusters (GRICs) within the context of business-to-consumer marketing. The subject of GRICs is relatively new in marketing. From an experiential point of view, it is clear that GRICs are confronted with special operational and strategic problems and challenges characteristic of marketing management. Care has been taken to make certain that each case presented has a different set of problems, all related to marketing management.

The analysis of each case may be made from several perspectives, depending on the apparent definition of the problem. All cases represent realistic situations confronted by marketing managers as decision makers within GRICs. After reading the case, each student, in the role of a future manager, may perceive a different problem. As long as the definition of the problem is within the guiding principles of business-to-consumer marketing and reflects problems encountered by marketing managers on a regular basis, it is worthy of analysis.

The cases are not arranged in any specific theoretical or conceptual framework designed specifically to analyze these cases. The only consideration that was made in arranging these cases was managerial complexity and the boundaries of the potential decision. The managerial complexity ranges from relatively general to very specific. For example, the decision to enter and operate within a GRIC may be a relatively simple decision for a manager of a startup smaller manufacturing enterprise (SME), but a more complex decision for a well-established SME with substantial market investment. The same may apply to the boundaries of the decision. A decision that needs to be made by a marketing manager, or even an owner-manager, of an SME concerning speculative issues whether or not to participate in the formation of a GRIC at the start may be initially simple. However, as the scenario evolves and describes the conditions under which the GRIC will be formed and operate, the decision to form may present a major dilemma and may be a very difficult decision to make.

There are three major themes running through all of the cases: (1) the notion of remoteness in a highly competitive global marketplace; (2) the question of how marketing management operations and strategies may be deployed to overcome problems of delivering goods and services effectively and efficiently to consumers from remote locations; and (3) the concern of how collective and cooperative business-to-consumer marketing focus and action within GRICs can facilitate this process. The concept of remoteness is important for marketing management in the scope of the global marketplace, especially when managerial tools such as improved communication and information capabilities, offsite manufacturing, and logistical support today are readily available to enterprises operating in GRICs.

The challenges of collective and cooperative actions are also important within the framework of GRICs. SMEs in particular are not necessarily interested in collective action or cooperation unless it leads to profits. They may join a well-structured value chain that not only facilitates the sales of their products or services, but also provides an opportunity to improve their marketing or technological skills. Conversely, SMEs which are not very active in the marketplace and tend not to innovate might be more than willing to participate in a GRIC, because they have an opportunity to rely on others to market their goods or services and help them to be innovative in the future.

Most importantly, regardless of how or under what conditions individual enterprises participate in GRICs, the main emphasis is on the quality of decisions made by marketing managers. A complete marketing management framework needs to be understood in order to be able to analyze the cases in detail. Marketing managers typically make decisions using both qualitative and quantitative decision-making processes. Some of the cases provide a complete set of data that are suitable for making sound decisions. In other cases, there is very little data and in these cases it is important to generate the necessary data needed to make a sound decision.

It is also important to realize that each marketing manager may perceive a different problem and may develop a different solution to it. In actual situations, especially in large enterprises, when a decision needs to be made and the decision involves several marketing managers, an actual portfolio of decision outcomes needs to be constructed and all outcomes need to be compared. This is because individual marketing managers based on their abilities and knowledge can only arrive at optimal decisions.

A Decision-Making Approach

Although there are many approaches that marketing managers deploy in making decisions, academics suggest that there is an inherent structure that provides the framework for managerial decision making. The structure consists of several steps that provide consistency and reliability for the entire decision-making process.

The students, as future managers, need to fully understand the conventional theoretical and conceptual framework of marketing management, along with the case which is to be analyzed. It is important to realize that each individual has a unique understanding of the case. This is primarily because each individual has a different educational background, a set of practical experiences, and/or personal convictions and philosophies. Each individual will have a tendency to understand and interpret a case differently.

This diversity of ideas and approaches may lead to better decisions. The theoretical and conceptual frameworks do not necessarily change; rather, they expand. Research into the practice of marketing management brings improvements to the theoretical and conceptual knowledge. Findings from recent management publications suggest that decision makers learn by reading findings from major research studies and from ideas presented by leading management gurus.

Before an individual decision maker begins analyzing a case, he or she needs to determine his or her scope of authority. This requires that each individual select an optimal managerial position with a relevant scope of control and level of responsibilities within the boundaries of the case. Each decision maker should ask the following question: is the solution to the case being developed from the perspective of the overall enterprise, or is the decision maker examining a small aspect of an organizational issue that might only be tangentially related to the core dilemma in the case?

More specifically, the decision maker may be a marketing manager reporting to the chief operating officer, but his or her scope of control and responsibilities may be broad enough to also include financial and personnel matters. Or, as is frequently customary in larger enterprises that are not consumer-oriented, a marketing manager may be responsible only for product development, and some related issues such as advertising, and is required to coordinate closely with the sales manager on any decisions related to marketing. The main concern is to determine the decision maker's managerial position in the enterprise and his or her span of control and set of responsibilities.

The next step in the decision-making process requires a definition of the problem in the case as perceived by the decision maker. The problem statement needs to be clearly formulated using a declarative sentence, not a question, which is formulated in such a way that it can be clearly communicated to others. The problem statement should be formulated and understood in a structured enterprise setting by all individuals involved in the case for which the problem was defined. A problem statement should start with a call for action: "The problem is to ... [do something]." For example, the problem is to determine financial gains or shortfalls resulting from joining a newly formed local GRIC.

Once the problem has been clearly defined, the next step in the decision process is to examine the relevant information in the case and determine if that information is sufficient to solve the problem defined in the previous step. If the information is not sufficient, what other information does the decision maker need? Can the needed information be generated internally or should a research study be conducted outside of the enterprise? Can the information be obtained from outside secondary sources? Each decision maker may draw on primary and secondary sources of information, and may use his or her managerial skills and abilities to determine the relevancy of information for the solution to the problem in the case.

Each decision maker needs to be satisfied with the information presented in the case or gathered in addition to the case. After the decision maker has evaluated all the information available, the decision maker proceeds to list the various ways that the defined problem can be solved, since there may be several alternative options to solving the problem depending on the availability of resources and the urgency of solving the problem. Alternative options suggested to arrive at the solution of the problem must be: (1) internally consistent, (2) mutually exclusive, (3) substantial, (4) accessible, and (5) measurable. This means that each alternative option by itself is potentially capable of solving the problem. Accessibility is related to the span of control and set of responsibilities representing the managerial position of the decision maker. The concern over measurability is directly related to the outcome of each alternative option and its contribution to the quantifiable outcomes.

The outcome of each option needs to be compared to every outcome of each alternative option. Each alternative option needs to be evaluated in qualitative and quantitative terms. The first step requires that each alternative option is scrutinized from the perspective of available knowledge to determine if each alternative option meets the standards of current managerial knowledge related to it. The second assessment is quantitative, which means that each alternative option needs to be evaluated and compared using typical financial or marketing data. In cases where neither data is available, probabilities can be generated and used to compare alternative options based on the likelihood that some results will materialize that can be compared or ranked. A Bayesian probability approach is frequently used as the preferred tool for this kind of analysis.

Perhaps the most important step in the decision-making approach is to select the alternative option which the decision maker considers to be optimal. The selection is based on both qualitative and quantitative analyses combined with the decision maker's own judgment and professional experiences. The optimal decision may not necessarily reflect the highest rate of return on investment or the largest potential sales, but rather what the decision maker understands is best for the consumer and the enterprise.

A plan for implementation of the optimal alternative option needs to follow. The plan should include tentative steps outlining how the implementation will be executed, along with any requests for additional resources such as financial resources, functional personnel, and physical facilities. The implementation plan also typically includes a listing of approvals required from the various functional departments which are impacted by the decision. Depending on the organizational level that is executing the implementation process, approvals may be needed from higher organizational levels. All of these contingencies need to be included in the implementation plan.

The actual implementation begins with the draft of a project protocol that will monitor each step outlined in the implementation plan. The project protocol is designed to ensure that the problem as formulated will be resolved according to the specifications presented by the decision maker as set out in the optimal alternative option. A project protocol may not be developed for systematic execution of events or activities if the implementation plan calls for individual action by an executive, perhaps for security reasons; instead, the implementation plan may be just a mental outline of the steps that the executive needs to take to eliminate the problem.

The final step that needs to be taken in the problem-solving approach outlined above is to be sure that the implementation plan is successfully carried out and the problem dealt with. The mechanism needed to ensure that the problem is under control should be an independent process and not under the scope of control or set of responsibilities of the decision maker who was asked to solve it.

In relating the decision-making process to marketing management and to the dynamics of GRICs, it is apparent that future managers need to understand not only some of the issues concerning involvement in GRICs by individual enterprises, but also the knowledge and experience that is needed to successfully operate within their formal or informal structure. There is very little known about the dynamics of GRICs today, since GRICs are relatively new, and the array of decisions that need to be made by individual enterprises is extensive. Enterprise managers, just as much as future managers, are still learning how to make these decisions.

As suggested earlier, the following cases provide future managers of enterprises currently operating within GRICs, or those enterprises contemplating operating within GRICs in the future, an opportunity to explore some of the issues, problems, and challenges that await them. The cases are designed to offer opportunities for future managers to examine a given case from several different perspectives and to learn from these opportunities.

Bibliography

Beveridge, W.I.B. (1950). *The Art of Scientific Investigation*. New York: Vintage Books.

Christensen, C. Ronald (1987). *Teaching and the Case Method.* Boston: Harvard Business School Press.

Medawar, P.B. (1984). *The Limits of Science.* London: Harper & Row.

Penzias, Arno (1989). *Ideas and Information: Managing in a High-Tech World.* London: W.W. Norton & Company.

Tesar, George, Hamid Moini, John Kuada, and Olav Jull Sørensen (2010). *Smaller Manufacturing Enterprises in an International Context: A Longitudinal Exploration.* London: Imperial College Press.

Zinsser, William (1976). *On Writing Well: An Informal Guide to Writing Nonfiction.* London: Harper & Row.

COLLECTED CASES

Part I
Formation of Geographically Remote Industrial Clusters

There are two fundamental issues concerning the formation of industrial clusters. The first issue is whether industrial clusters can be formed through individual or collective initiatives, and whether entrepreneurs, startup ventures, and/or established small- or medium-sized enterprises can be motivated to join together and form an industrial cluster. This issue has implications for market operations, competitive position, and even individual initiatives. Most economic and regional development specialists believe that industrial clusters can be formed on the basis of someone's initiative, whereas most marketing managers do not share that belief. The second issue is what constitutes a "geographically remote" area or region. Research results from studies in sociology, anthropology, and other related behavioral disciplines, including political science, suggest that an exact definition does not exist but rather is subject to the specific context in which it is defined.

Case 1

Instinctive Formation of an Industrial Cluster*

After several years of retirement as a university professor and management consultant, Hans Novak attended a meeting with some of his former students who had invited him to talk about his experiences in helping to forge strategic alliances, mergers, and takeovers, and especially in forming industrial clusters in the mid-1990s. Hans was a professor of marketing and entrepreneurship, specializing in helping owner-managers of smaller manufacturing enterprises grow. He was a member of a small department at a state university located in a remote part of a Midwestern state in the United States.

The state is divided into two major parts: the main part represents most of the major economic activities where the state capital is located, is well populated, and is socially progressive; while the other part is rural, and is mostly surrounded by lakes, with a national forest covering much of the land mass. The university where Hans spent many of his professional years is in a major city which is accessible by only two main roads. The campus is located in the

*George Tesar, Professor Emeritus of Umeå University and University of Wisconsin-Whitewater, developed this case for educational purposes only. The case is designed to illustrate several concepts and theories in the formation and management of industrial clusters. The names of the individuals in the case are fictitious.

part of the city next to a lake. Ignoring the geographically remote location, over the years some graduates had decided to stay in the area, search for opportunities, or start their own business ventures. They produced products, managed research laboratories, or offered fabrication services to clients all over the middle part of the United States. Some of the students who had stayed and known Hans for a long time were at the meeting with him today.

In his consulting capacity, Hans traveled internationally and consulted with all types of manufacturing enterprises in several industrial sectors, ranging from processing operations like sawmills to large diversified international manufacturers of heavy equipment. His major interest was in startups, especially spinoffs in the high-technology medical equipment sector. Hans had good friends in the physics and chemistry university departments, and frequently talked with them about potentially new products and services that could be developed into commercially viable opportunities.

In private conversations with his friends and colleagues, Hans frequently emphasized that he preferred to work with the smaller high-technology manufacturing enterprises located near his university because they were more commercially flexible and willing to face new marketing challenges. What especially attracted him to the smaller high-technology manufacturing enterprises was their ability to innovate, produce a quality product, and be competitive in the market in spite of their geographically remote location. And he also liked their Internet presence. "Information technology is very important to smaller high-technology manufacturing enterprises," he frequently told his former colleagues over coffee.

Many years ago, Hans noticed an interesting phenomenon. In his travels he noticed that many smaller manufacturing enterprises gathered around universities. Some of them produced products or offered services that had nothing to do with the university itself. Owner-managers of these enterprises knew each other socially but, because of their market focus, did not professionally cooperate with each other. They would occasionally talk with each other at the local Chamber of Commerce meetings, professional association gatherings, or various local social functions, but they knew little about each others' businesses.

Hans also noticed that some enterprises had parts made at their local machine shops or components fabricated at the shop next door, but no significant or lasting cooperation was ever discussed between them. The university spinoffs, mostly high-technology and software companies that were set up in the late 1990s and early 2000s, maintained strong relationships with the university. The university's small business development center even helped them improve their relationships with various departments at the university or state governmental agencies. Because of the technological nature of their products, Hans often wondered why these enterprises did not cooperate more and create some local competitive advantages from which more of them could benefit.

Discussion about Incubators

The discussion today focused on incubators. The local business community was interested in helping the university build a high-technology incubator to facilitate more startups in the area and improve its commercial climate. The university representatives were interested, but emphasized that with cuts in state funding it would be impossible to get a project to build an incubator funded in the existing political climate.

The chief executive officer of Illuminator Incorporated, John White, suggested that the local business community could help. Others agreed. John owns one of the original highly successful spinoff companies established in the early 1990s. His company produces a line of specialized lighting products, based on a recently commercialized quartz technology, for industrial applications, and in the past few months had started exporting products to Canada and Mexico.

The type of incubator that was discussed included office and manufacturing space for potential owner-managers as well as necessary space for existing smaller manufacturing enterprises that wanted to expand or diversify into other lines of high-technology products. The incubator was to have assistance available from engineers, scientists, and other professional experts. The incubator was also to be staffed with marketing and financial specialists, including accountants, to help with day-to-day commercial activities. Hans suggested that some of his retired colleagues still living in the area would volunteer their services, but that some graduate students at the university could also provide marketing and financial support with the supervision of their professors. The university and the city would jointly own and manage the incubator.

Residency in the incubator would be for two years. Each resident would have to sign an agreement with the management of the incubator that if the new venture became profitable, it would have to share a negotiated percentage of its profit with the university and the city. There was no discussion about the potential market or technology focus for the incubator. The local business community would raise the funds to build the incubator.

Hans felt uneasy on his way home from the meeting. If the business community, many of which were his former students, felt so committed to the university and the city, they should do more than just build an incubator. "If only there was another way to cooperate and improve the business climate in the area more extensively," he wondered. After all, an incubator was just a starting point in a series of business ventures that could lead to major economic activities in this relatively geographically remote area.

When he returned home from the meeting, Hans called his friend Sue Jones, the Dean of the business school. Sue was always looking for new opportunities for her business school and, with her financial background, was especially interested in economic development in this remote part of the state. That was in fact one of the reasons that had motivated her to choose her present position.

Business School Helping to Form an Industrial Cluster

Soon after the meeting with his former students, Hans met with Sue to discuss the meeting he had attended with the local business community leaders. He wanted to visit and discuss his perceptions about the incubator. He explained that the incubator would focus on a small part of the range of possibilities that could be developed around the university. Hans also explained that some of the informal cooperation existing among the current enterprises could be structured to leverage their resources more effectively and efficiently. They could structure a supply chain consisting of local suppliers or pre-fabricate or pre-assemble products and components for large clients. Perhaps some of the smaller manufacturing enterprises in the area could restructure their operations and offer a complete line of products for both business-to-business and business-to-consumer markets. Hans and Sue agreed that they needed to meet with the Chancellor of the university to discuss these ideas. And they generally agreed that the business school would help in any future developments along these lines.

The surprise came when Sue and Hans met with Everett Highsmither, the Chancellor of the university. The Chancellor, who had just returned from a meeting with the other chancellors in the state, had learned that his campus and the surrounding business community was perceived by several well-known economists working with geographically remote industrial clusters as an industrial cluster made up of smaller manufacturing enterprises. Both Sue and Hans were amazed. They became even more amazed when Everett asked them what "geographically remote industrial clusters" were. The Chancellor clearly was not interested in an incubator.

Several leading economists in the United States and abroad have studied the formation of industrial clusters as a naturally occurring economic phenomenon. Industrial clusters can be found in almost every state in the United States, ranging from light aircraft manufacturing and farm equipment around Wichita in Kansas to the more famous high-technology cluster focusing on microelectronics and biotechnology in Silicon Valley in California. Some of these industrial clusters are huge. The recent interest among local and regional economic development communities is on smaller clusters within a definable geographic area. Given the vast area and the remoteness of the population centers in the United States, Australia, Canada, and even Northern Europe, the interest of regional economists is turning to geographically remote industrial clusters. According to them, geographically remote industrial clusters could potentially serve as economic units generating jobs, tax revenues, and stronger local economies.

In the meeting with Sue and Hans, the Chancellor posed the following question: how do incubators relate to the formation of local industrial clusters, especially in geographically remote areas? The generally accepted notion among regional and developmental economists is that geographically remote industrial clusters can be formed without incubators. In reality, incubators and industrial clusters are two different concepts; they can support each other, coexist, or be completely independent of each other. Consequently, a dilemma emerged — should the university consider accepting the funding from the local business community and help build an incubator, or should the university design a totally new model for local economic development by combining an incubator with a local industrial cluster? The decision of how to resolve this dilemma was left to Sue and her business school.

Before Sue would discuss the idea of building an incubator and forming an industrial cluster in a meeting with the entire business school faculty, she decided to talk with the members of the local business community who served on the advisory board for the business school. She explained to them that the approach she preferred would be to build an incubator first and then form an industrial cluster around the smaller manufacturing enterprises in the area. The consensus that was reached clearly supported both: the incubator and the industrial cluster. The local business community would raise the necessary funds to build an incubator, but where would the funds to form an industrial cluster come from? Would additional funds come from the local business community or would the state make a contribution to the development of the industrial cluster?

How Smaller Manufacturing Enterprises Operate and Cooperate in Industrial Clusters

During Hans' meeting with the business community leaders, it became obvious to him that not all smaller manufacturing enterprises were managed the same way; in fact, there were differences in how owner-managers managed their operations, formulated their strategies, and marketed their products or services. Some managers were only interested in producing a profitable product and making enough money to support their personal lifestyles. After all, they lived in an excellent recreational region of the country where they could enjoy water sports in the summer and ski or snowmobile in the winter. Most of the fabrication and machine shops were managed by such managers. Sometimes when the weather was good, in the summer or winter, they were known to reject attractive business opportunities just to go sailing, fishing, or snowmobiling. Hans, along with the state economic development officials and even the politicians, often wondered what really motivated these managers.

There were also managers who actively promoted their businesses among the smaller manufacturing enterprises in the region. They considered their products and services to be competitive and their capabilities were outstanding. As individual managers, many of them were good engineers, were skilled in programming the latest computer-operated machine tools, and understood the latest technology. Some of them produced their own proprietary products, but also maintained open capacity to design, engineer, and machine parts for clients. Owner-managers who actively promoted their enterprises were frequently seen driving to the nearest airport to fly to visit their clients. They liked where they lived, and they did not mind traveling to sell or explore additional opportunities. They were serious managers who were interested in their business and the place where they lived.

The high-technology firms in the area were managed by professional managers, who understood their mission and scope of operations and actively cooperated with faculty at the university by cooperating on research projects and offering internships to students. They were not necessarily concerned only with their products or services or promoting their enterprises, but paid close attention to their resources. They produced products or offered services that were well placed in the market. Most of them had international contacts and frequently responded to foreign orders. Some of them cooperated with major medical centers and specialized in fabricating medical equipment that incorporated cutting-edge technology. Sometimes they tended to look down on university research and felt that they were ahead of it.

Although the managers of all three types of enterprises interacted in professional meetings and social and civic organizations such as the Lions, Rotary International, and Kiwanis clubs, they did not think alike. Some were willing to volunteer for social activities and some were not, and their potential for social or professional cooperation varied dramatically. In their managerial roles, they tended to be relatively introverted and reluctant to discuss their operations with their equals. Some of the managers who would rather go fishing were looked at with amazement by the internationally active managers.

How these fundamentally different owner-managers of smaller manufacturing enterprises would interact in a created industrial cluster was an open question. Could university personnel assist with stimulating levels of cooperation among this varied group of owner-managers? Would they work with each other when provided with a framework or a plan to create greater local economic value? Would they be able to participate in a coherent value chain? These were intriguing questions. Sue, the Dean of the business school, believed that they potentially could cooperate; Hans, the retired consultant, was not so optimistic.

Experiences of One of the Smaller Manufacturing Enterprises in the Area

Located across town in a private industrial park is a fabricator of high-technology remote monitoring and measuring equipment. This equipment is used in various automated manufacturing processes where remote sensing devices are able to detect out-of-standard variation in the final assembly of products such as automobiles, trucks, and agricultural equipment. Alfa Limited is owned by Charles White and a few minority investors. Charles serves as its chief operating officer. He started the machine and fabrication shop shortly after he graduated from the local university, where he majored in physics. During his junior year abroad, he had an opportunity to study applied physics at a well-known German engineering school and, at the same time, spent time as an intern at a local automotive assembly plant, where he got the idea for his equipment. With his knowledge of physics, all he needed were some machine tools and fabrication equipment; the rest of the components he could outsource or purchase off the shelf from major, internationally known suppliers.

Shortly after he graduated, Charles built his first prototype, developed a business model, and looked for financing. He participated in venture capital fairs organized by the state economic development agency. There was substantial interest in his equipment by potential customers, but the venture capitalists were not interested. Charles was not experienced enough, according to one of the venture capital specialists. Subsequently, Charles approached several banks for a private equity loan, but was not successful because he had virtually no tangible collateral. Since Charles had enough funds to build his first functional unit, he decided to approach a large potential customer directly and was successful. A manufacturer of industrial earth-moving equipment was impressed and asked Charles to build a series of 10 dedicated units for specific assembly operations. This sale was substantial enough for Charles to develop a standard product line, which he then sold under the Alfa Limited brand name.

Charles believed in information technology and, shortly after he started his operations, posted a webpage on the Internet. He wanted to explore who might be potentially interested in his equipment and also to learn what potential customers look for in remote monitoring and measuring equipment. This became his only source of market information. Charles was also the only sales engineer and customer service specialist in the company. His marketing organization was minimal. He recalls that he used to travel a great deal in the beginning.

After about two years of operations, Alfa Limited started getting an increasing number of orders; a major portion of these orders came from overseas customers. It became obvious to Charles that he needed help — his shop capacity and employees simply could not manage to fabricate all the parts as well as assemble and test each unit. Charles started talking with his friends in the city who operated machine or fabrication shops. Unsuccessful in that approach, he tried one of his old classmates who fabricated heating and ventilating equipment for a local heating contractor. Charles tried to talk him into fabricating enclosures for his equipment, but his old classmate felt that the equipment was too "high-tech."

One day, with the help of the local Chamber of Commerce, Charles called a meeting of members who owned machine or fabrication shops to explain to them his needs and offered an opportunity for cooperation. Without realizing it, Charles had introduced the concept of an industrial cluster. This was at a time when specialists like Hans Novak were providing consulting services and universities were not necessarily interested in local economic development.

The outcome of the meeting was the realization that the local enterprises, mostly machine and fabrication shops, were not necessarily interested in cooperating. Several reasons were mentioned. They all had their own customers in construction, heating and ventilation, agriculture, or forestry. They were reluctant to get involved in new ventures that perhaps required new machinery and high-technology approaches. Clearly, these were their perceptions. Charles had no choice but to look for domestic suppliers elsewhere or have his equipment manufactured abroad. He decided to go abroad. As his operations grew and became more profitable, Charles expanded his production capacity and started to bring his manufacturing back home.

Hans Is Faced with a Decision to Help a Municipality in a Remote Part of the State Form a Cluster

The first meeting about the incubator generated adequate interest among the participants. Hans discussed the meeting with some of his university friends, among whom was a very active professor of rural sociology working with several wine growers in the western part of the state. Individual growers had problems — they were too small to produce ample quantities of grapes and wine individually. In addition, although the region had good potential, it was not known for wine production; it was primarily a tourist region. The situation was complicated by the fact that most of the aspiring wine growers were retired corporate executives, former advertising account managers, or retired doctors from the large metropolitan cities not too far away, who had previously owned summer homes in the area and then moved there for their retirement. The professor told Hans that the winery owners were interested in some form of cooperation and that he would discuss it with them on his next visit.

Shortly after this conversation, Hans received an e-mail from the mayor of a small city in the wine-growing region asking him for help to form a wine-growing cluster in the area. The mayor, John Staal, had attended several conferences where industrial clusters were discussed; he liked the concept and wanted to help develop wine production in his municipality. Hans had a long conversation with John. He insisted that, based on his experience in working with owner-managers of smaller enterprises, it was very difficult to motivate them to cooperate as a coherent group. John, on the other hand, pointed out that they were not typical owner-managers of smaller enterprises, but experienced professionals with highly focused objectives. Hans agreed to come for a visit to meet John and discuss the situation with the owners of the small wineries.

Hans' visit was very successful; the mayor was very enthusiastic and invited several members of the potential cluster to the meeting. They looked to Hans for guidance in designing the cluster, specifying relationships within the entire value chain, and identifying the lead players in the cluster. At this point, Hans began to wonder, "What are these people trying to do? Geographically remote industrial clusters occur as a natural phenomenon! It is virtually impossible to form a brand new cluster and make it work." Hans began to think that they wanted a wine cooperative, not an industrial cluster.

Slowly and systematically, Hans started to explain the differences between a geographically remote industrial cluster, a farm or an agricultural cooperative, and a brand new value chain. In his opinion, these three concepts were closely related. After several hours of discussion, the group concluded that they wanted to form a new cluster that would focus exclusively on growing grapes and producing wine.

The individual vineyards would pool their resources in growing grapes; they would set up wine production facilities, invite a young viticulturist looking for a challenge, and agree on the terms of cooperation. Hans became even more agitated: "This is like developing a business model for a completely new manufacturing enterprise, not a naturally evolving cluster with intentions to produce and market wine." As he was driving back from the meeting, Hans thought to himself, "Do I really want to be involved? Do I want to do this?"

Hans Believes in Naturally Occurring Industrial Clusters

The results of many studies in the past that focused on industrial clusters concluded that they evolve naturally. In one of his articles, Porter (1998) mapped over 30 U.S.-based industrial clusters which evolved naturally over a relatively long time period. Studies conducted in Northern Europe, Australia, and Canada also suggested the same phenomenon. It is only recently that some social scientists, economic development specialists, and directors of small business development centers have suggested that the concept of industrial clusters, in general, could be viewed as an innovation. Universities, municipalities, and other social entities — even in remote geographic regions — could form new clusters to help stimulate local economic growth and management activities.

Hans was aware of these events. As a faculty member, he had frequently participated in academic conferences, seminars, and discussions about them. As an academic and management consultant who always focused on managerial activities within smaller manufacturing enterprises, he was still not convinced that industrial clusters could be simply organized at the discretion of economic developers, small business development specialists, or even major commercial consultants. In his opinion, owner-managers of smaller manufacturing enterprises had their own individual agendas and were reluctant to share their know-how and experiences with others. In his opinion, they did not like to be participants in events that they could not control.

Hans reflected on his many years of experience and wondered if, perhaps, the rapidly changing economic conditions both domestically and internationally had had an impact on how smaller manufacturing enterprises compete, how they restructure their operations, and how they fit into value or supply chains. He thought about the number of his clients that had their products manufactured overseas, and how many were asked to join highly structured supply chains and had become subject to the demands of their dominant clients that controlled the entire supply chain.

Perhaps a number of smaller manufacturing enterprises located in a remote geographic area, such as the one in which he lived, would be willing to cooperate and create an innovative industrial cluster where members would help each other to add value by holding on to the resources they had. Hans wondered if the notion of industrial clusters had changed: "Instead of naturally evolving industrial clusters as they were defined earlier in the literature, are we now talking about innovative, value-creating clusters that have both public and private interests? Can these clusters be formulated in remote geographic regions as part of local economic development?"

After several hours reflecting on this dilemma, Hans concluded that he felt much more comfortable with the traditional concept of industrial clusters: naturally occurring clusters. He was still uncomfortable with the new concept that he seemed to be hearing — that industrial clusters, especially in geographically remote regions, could be considered as new social and economic development tools, that is, as social and managerial innovations.

The City Needs Jobs and Is Willing to Give Substantial Incentives to SMEs That Join the Local Industrial Cluster

Since the meeting with Hans and the Chancellor, Sue was busy talking with Bruce Flat, the city mayor, and the local economic development official representing the state, Fillip Green. The city in which the university is located is relatively isolated but closely knit. They all agreed that a new economic initiative needed to be undertaken, especially in the current economic downturn. The entire business community needed to create additional jobs. However, most of the enterprises in the municipality were smaller manufacturing enterprises and they found it difficult to look for new opportunities at the same time they were trying to fill the orders that they did have. New customers were hard to find and existing customers were not buying.

Bruce argued that the university has a great deal of knowledge in economic development; it operates a Small Business Development Center financed partly by the federal government and partly by state grants. Many of the professors also periodically receive grants to study various aspects of small business development and management; they publish articles based on their studies, and frequently consult with governmental agencies and private enterprises about new developments among smaller enterprises in general. Could this knowledge be used in the public sector to help the municipality create more jobs and a stable local economy? Sue believed that the university could help with these issues.

In her meetings with the Chancellor, Sue brought up the conversation she had recently had with Bruce. They both agreed that the university, and especially the business school, should prepare a major funding grant proposal to organize a local industrial cluster of smaller manufacturing enterprises. The proposal would provide an opportunity for both faculty and students to get involved in building a better local economic base, and at the same time give students hands-on experience in motivating owner-managers of smaller manufacturing enterprises to work within an industrial cluster. Sue delegated the writing of the funding grant proposal to Harriet Miller, the Director of the Small Business Development Center, and also promised that she, Sue, would personally see to it that the proposal received adequate attention from funding agencies.

Bruce, being a person of action, did not rest either. He decided to seek funding through different channels, and eventually received ample funding from the state economic development agency and some from the federal government. His intention was to do something innovative quickly, create jobs, and maintain or even increase the current population in the general municipal region. The key funding condition was to form an industrial cluster with the intention of developing a complete value chain for products that could be engineered and manufactured primarily within the cluster.

Initially, a meeting was held in the Chancellor's office with the Chancellor, Sue, and Bruce. After the three had agreed on the terms of their cooperation in forming an industrial cluster in the city, Harriet, the Director of the Small Business Development Center, and Hans were asked to come into the meeting to discuss their ideas about how the cluster could be organized and by whom. Hans clearly stated that before any proposals suggesting how the cluster should be organized were considered, the owner-managers of the small machine and fabrication shops in the city should be consulted. Most of all, Charles White should be made a part of the future discussions. Sue promised that she would organize a team of experienced management, marketing, and finance professors to help with the project. Sue and Bruce would oversee the project with equal authority and responsibility.

The Chancellor, a former banking executive and government regulator, asked who would direct the project. The individual directing the project would need to have a great deal of management experience, understanding of both business-to-business and business-to-consumer markets, and know-how to motivate managers. Without hesitation, Sue volunteered Hans. Hans was taken aback by this sudden turn of events. He had not expected this assignment; he did not want to take on additional responsibilities, but he did not refuse the offer. Both the Chancellor and Sue liked the idea that Hans would be directing the project.

Hans Has a Conflict — Give Up His Professional Integrity and Help Build Something in Which He Does Not Believe

From the beginning, when Hans had started to discuss the idea of an industrial cluster, he was not convinced that an industrial cluster could be easily formed by having managers of smaller manufacturing enterprises working together towards a common goal of creating a single value chain. He knew many of the owner-managers of the local machine and fabrication shops because many of them had been his students. He also knew some of the product manufacturers and engineering firms in the city, including Charles and his experiences. To view an industrial cluster — in other words, a social network — as an innovative tool in economic development was somewhat of a complex idea for Hans.

In fact, the whole idea of managing a project that would, in many ways, pressure owner-managers of smaller manufacturing enterprises into a collective effort — an effort that would take away their own strategic initiatives and operational goals — did not seem to be right. Hans believed in free enterprise and individual initiative. Yes, he sometimes argued that the world had changed and had become more global and competitive for both marketers and consumers, but he believed it to be a natural progression of things. Enterprises of all kinds had to make decisions whether or not to source abroad, import components for their products, or have their entire products manufactured abroad. Some enterprises succeeded and some did not.

117

Those were choices that managers had to make in times of economic adversity.

But now, to actually start organizing a self-sufficient industrial cluster in a geographically remote area, in a state with a relatively obsolete manufacturing base and without major high-technology input, was a difficult task for Hans. From the beginning, Hans had always believed that industrial clusters were natural phenomena which evolved over time. Hans had been asked to give up his professional integrity and help to build something in which he did not believe.

The next morning, when Hans had an opportunity to sort things out, he called Sue first to give her his decision; he simply did not believe in the project and therefore could not take responsibility for it. Sue was disappointed. She asked him to call the Chancellor and tell him about his decision. He did, but the Chancellor tried to convince Hans that he should take on the project, if for nothing else because of his past professional experience and affiliation with the university. Hans declined.

The Chancellor and Sue arranged a meeting with Bruce. When Bruce was told about Hans and his decision, he was angry. He argued that they had to make Hans take on the responsibility for the project because the city had the funds, and because they knew that the proposed grant submitted by the Small Business Development Center to the state funding agency would be funded. He also knew about the previous discussion about the incubator and the willingness of the business community to fund it. Bruce argued further that the university had let down the entire city and its business community. After all, he had held meetings with some of the managers in the city and they were willing to become part of an industrial cluster. The Chancellor asked Sue to look for another faculty member, either retired or currently employed, who could potentially manage the project. Sue believed that this would be a rather difficult task.

The City Brings in a Professional Management Consulting Firm

When Bruce returned to city hall, he called in his procurement officer, an experienced professional who had grown up in the city and attended the local university, to discuss the entire series of events and the fact that Hans refused to take on the project. After a short discussion, the procurement officer suggested that the city issue a public tender, specifically for management consulting firms, to bid on the project and both for an incubator and an industrial cluster. At first, Bruce was reluctant to even consider the idea. He asked out loud, "What do management consulting firms know about industrial clusters in geographically remote areas?"

By a series of coincidences, Bruce knew about the wine-growing region about 90 miles west of his city. He had met the mayor of that city, John Staal, at one of the mayors' meetings in the state's capital city, and had established a good working relationship with him. Bruce called John. John told him that after discussing their intentions to form a cluster in their region of the state around the production of wine, they had decided to call the chief operating executive of a management consulting firm with which one of the vineyard owners had worked in the past and asked him if his firm would take on the project of forming an innovative industrial cluster that covered the entire wine-producing value chain. The answer was that they would. And John concluded by saying, "They are working on it now."

After Bruce had completed the telephone call with John, he went over to the procurement officer, sat down, and for a while complained again about the lack of cooperation between the university and the city. After he calmed down, he told the procurement officer to go ahead and draft the tender so that he could discuss it with the city supervisors at their meeting next week.

What Was the New Industrial Cluster to Achieve?

When the procurement officer began developing the tender, he wondered what the project was going to achieve. After several hours of thinking, he developed a list of potential points that he thought should be addressed in the tender:

1. Identify machine and fabrication shops in the city interested in participating in the development and operation of an industrial cluster.
2. Organize machine and fabrication shops around product ideas or technologies with which most of them have substantial experience and which could serve as their competitive advantage.
3. Identify and organize the existing manufacturers of products and suppliers of services in the city to participate in, and perhaps lead, the industrial cluster.
4. Identify products or services that could be offered by the industrial cluster.
5. Estimate the potential market share and sales volume of the industrial cluster.
6. Identify strong leadership for the industrial cluster.
7. Develop an organizational and strategic management team for the industrial cluster.
8. Create and implement the entire value chain for the industrial cluster.

After he had drafted the tender, he passed it on to Bruce for his comments before the meeting with the city supervisors. In the margin of the draft, he noted: "How will the industrial cluster be managed, who will develop the products, and who will manage the logistical support?" "Should all these items be included in the tender?," he wondered.

The next week, on Wednesday evening, Bruce presented the tender to the city supervisors and reminded them that the city had the necessary funding but that the university did not want to cooperate on the project. A stormy discussion followed. The city supervisors wanted to hear from the Chancellor. One of the city supervisors asked, "Will there be a future for this industrial cluster located in our city in a geographically remote region of this state?"

Bibliography

Mattsson, Henrik (2009). "Innovating in Cluster/Cluster as Innovation: The Case of the Biotechvalley Cluster Initiative." *European Planning Studies*, 17(11), November, 1625–1643.

Porter, Michael (1998). "Clusters and the New Economics of Competition." *Harvard Business Review*, November–December, 77–90.

Sorenson, Olav (2003). "Social Networks and Industrial Geography." *Journal of Evolutionary Economics*, 13, 513–527.

Stuart, Toby and Olav Sorenson (2003). "The Geography of Opportunity: Spatial Heterogeneity in Founding Rates and the Performance of Biotechnology Firms." *Research Policy*, 32, 229–253.

Case 2

Athelia — How Can an Old City Survive the Death of French Shipyards?*

Athelia is named by contracting two words: "Athena," the Greek goddess of wisdom; and "Helios," god of the sun. The industrial cluster was created in 1987 in order to provide a solution for the conversion of sites affected by the closure of the Normed shipyards. By July 2011, with 283 companies and around 6,500 jobs, it seemed to have successfully replaced the shipyard. However, there are a number of issues that need to be addressed by the different partners and decisions have to be made to secure the future of the cluster.

It cooperates with a nearby major business school, providing opportunities for students to explore some of the cluster's perceived problems and possibly provide recommendations. When along with fellow students you approached Athelia Entreprendre for a project, the union was pleased to have you explore what it perceived as a crucial issue.

---

*Catherine Lions, Umeå School of Business and Economics, Umeå University (Sweden), developed this case for educational purposes only. The case is designed to illustrate several concepts and theories in the formation and management of industrial clusters.

Figure 1. La Ciotat (denoted by ★).

The Location

La Ciotat ("the city" in Latin) is a small city in the south of France (see Figure 1). It is in a nice sunny location, but it is neither Marseille nor Nice (800,000 and 350,000 inhabitants, respectively) and is far from Paris. In the 19th and 20th centuries, the site was known as a place for vacation. Since then, the city has retained its attraction for summer tourism and offers beaches, opportunities for diving, and a starting point for visits to the creeks. In the 5th century B.C., the first settlements on the route of ancient navigators were installed. During that time, the city acquired great wealth through fishing and trade. The port's activity contributed to economic development of the city. In 1429, La Ciotat became a commune by having its own rights and acted as a port. In the 16th century, the city boomed due to immigration of a part of the Genoese aristocracy expelled from Italy by local revolutions. Real shipyards were built in 1622 and were shaped as industrial organizations from 1836. The shipyards changed hands several times in the 20th century, and they were to be the economic heart of the city until the decision to close them was made in the mid-1980s. The city then experienced hard times, with a chain reaction of closures and bankruptcies as well as long strikes that affected the population both in economic and psychological terms. The city experienced a dark and painful depression during the 1990s. Prices for land and housing went down, the unemployment rate increased to more than 30%, and political turbulence did not help its recovery.

Since this dark period, La Ciotat has been trying to revive its summer tourism trade. The casino was reopened in early 2000. It is now becoming a destination for tourists traveling to Provence. The planning policy of the city has shown signs in this direction, including the development of shops and eating establishments along the beach. At the same time, the city is making use of its port facilities to set itself up as a yachting center (see Figure 2). In 2006, construction began on what would eventually be the largest ship lift in Europe. But economic and political forces are divided: opposed to the fierce defendants of the maritime tradition, more and more voices clamor for industrial diversification. The result has affected the population numbers: 32,700 inhabitants in 1975 and 31,600 in 2011. These numbers have to be compared to the average annual growth rate of the French population, 0.58%. Many are disappointed and have the feeling that after a 20-year chaotic period, the current increase of house prices should not be interpreted as a sign of vitality, but rather as a result of property speculation that could damage the fragile value of the city.

The Geographically Remote Industrial Clusters in France

An industrial cluster is defined as a site dedicated to the establishment of businesses in a given area. These areas are defined, developed,

Figure 2. La Ciotat from the sea, with the old shipyard.

and managed by the local authority that owns the territory of implantation (usually the city or the village). They gather around a common goal of growth in a spirit of partnership among the government, communities, and businesses. Placed under legal subdivision, they are usually located on the outskirts of large urban centers because of their proximity to transportation infrastructure, guaranteeing their influence at the regional, national, or international level, and a pool of labor and services. Generated by the economic transformation of the 1960s, the concept of industrial cluster, then, is viewed as a new approach to the allocation of powers to establish a better balance of wealth.

There are now 32,000 clusters in France representing a total surface area of about 500,000 hectares across the country. The key to success revolves around their ability to increase the attractiveness of their territory for economic exogenous development and to externally support the efforts of businesses nearby (local loosening). They cover a number of areas that have taken a decisive weight in the economy and belong to categories such as craft, commerce, industry, logistics, services, technology, and port. They vary in size, ranging from a few thousand square meters (craft areas) to a few thousand hectares (like the industrial areas and the 7,000-ha port of Fos-sur-Mer). But many of these industrial clusters were created too quickly in the 1970s. As a result, there are now vast surpluses of open space unsuitable for other uses. Some of these creations clearly appear inappropriate, since they fit into the decline of heavy industry like coal mining or shipyards. The sharp economic downturn and ensuing changes have left open spaces unused and economically impoverished. On the other hand, installation of large industrial parks in agricultural areas because of the low cost of land has led to criticism against the competition between industrial and agricultural land use. In France, these developments, combined with the strong growth of urbanization, have led to a policy of booking much of the land in agricultural regions in order to maintain agricultural activity, which is the only permitted activity (this is done directly by local regulation or by putting a dissuasive tax burden on other kinds of activities). Obviously one major current issue is the fierce battle between agricultural lobbies and territory developers.

Another particular feature is the structure of political power, managerial power, and financing. Managed by the municipalities, these clusters are usually controlled by a local union made up of different types of partners (municipality, county, region, state, and other communities). Finance for development comes from several layers, from municipal taxes to European Union subsidy programs.

The French Approach to a Duty-Free Zone

In 1987, to compensate for the drastic loss of industrial jobs in a number of areas, the French government decided to implement the old idea of a duty-free zone, as a bounded and bonded area where firms were granted taxation advantages. During the period of validity of the agreement, the investors gained a number of exemptions. In the case of Athelia, firms benefited from a five-year exemption from income taxes and social contributions (which are now over).

We can consider that it was actually the first French case of implementing adjustment means used by many U.S. states to reactivate sites in difficulty, using the principle of free area (deregulation, cutting of red tape, tax exemption). Following the definition of "small industrial parks, geographically defined," within which some of the constraints weighing on economic activity, prevailing in the rest of the country, were relaxed or suspended, they were supposed to be places where the state would intervene less. In the political debate in 1986, it was particularly clear that these projects aimed to be viewed not only as enclaves of geographical deregulation but also as "laboratories" for experimenting with European effects of deregulation of access to technology and public resources on the recovery of port activity. However, the debate was not always very clear: What is an economically depressed area? How to help? Since there were three sites in shipbuilding to close, they were made a priority in the program.

In theory, industrial clusters are intended to create or maintain jobs by providing new opportunities to residents in a previously distressed neighborhood by eliminating taxes and regulatory obstacles to innovation and entrepreneurship. The concept, though, periodically re-surfaces as a way to revitalize certain areas where policies of traditional development have not had the desired effect, and hence the relevance is controversial. Is it realistic to consider building effective enterprise zones in geographically remote areas, especially after a great depression? It is obvious that temporary tax exemption is not enough. Nonetheless, it creates a well-delineated zone with boundary points, impacting the property development. Littoral and port zones are of special interest for policies of localization of economic activities. Even if the classical concept is actually criticized, the neo-liberal view still supports these means of non-regulation.

In a maritime city, the territory is split into three zones with different kinds of development: the village center (including the port); the surrounding land, with major housing projects; and the hinterland, which should attract land-consuming major activities. Between ports and their hinterlands, ease of getting around is a key issue for their operations. There are also the requirements of executives and business leaders who want more environmental-quality business parks and communal living. Developing new economic activities in these areas takes two directions:

- Help create jobs for locals; and
- Provide an advantageous incentive for employers.

On the contrary, another issue that appeared to be important in the late 1980s was the support offered to individual entrepreneurs by developing a local bridge likely to welcome businesses and to create a business center to accommodate an incubator and provide small-sized offices. The aim was that large businesses should serve small ones. It may not create more jobs, but at the same time startups possessed potential knowledge and expertise that could be useful for others. It was also a method to release initiative and mobilize the skills available or accessible in four steps:

- First, gather all the potential partners and find a motivated operator — a group of entrepreneurs, a chamber of commerce or trade, or a local development agency;
- Identify the skills and then the excellence locally available, not only those of existing businesses and organizations, but also those accessible to local companies, subsidiaries, and decentralized large groups;
- Rake the ground to detect in companies, among future entrepreneurs, the full potential, and discover the project leaders — the "sleeping projects" in companies that, due to time constraints or available technology and skills, sleep in the bottom drawer; and
- Support the implementation of these projects and these local initiatives by a small field team, dynamic and effective.

How many new products, new markets, or new processes may arise from a dynamic network among companies? How many startups, finally, may emerge if the city provides better help and support to entrepreneurs?

After years in which municipalities have invested in equipment to make their land more attractive, they now find themselves in a spiral of fierce competition among companies and territories. Such competition has advantages because it requires everyone to know each other's strengths. Intense relationships among businesses and territories are driving strong local development. But if attraction of new businesses remains a common requirement, then the maintenance and development of existing businesses is also an urgent need. It is obvious that retaining firms located in a municipality is the key to successful municipal financial tranquility. The key success factor in this issue is the phenomena of outsourcing and links among business contractors, subcontractors, and suppliers that promote the economic organization of networks. For the cluster to survive, a comprehensive system is vital to the cohesion of the whole in which circulation of people, information, and goods is facilitated.

Pollution, Sustainable Development, and Industrial Ecology

In France, pollution generated in some important industrial sites is considered to be critical, since it presents significant risks to the environment and public health. An abandoned industrial site may require extensive work for reprocessing the area in the form of recovery of metallic materials, removal of surface layers of soil with a high concentration of pollutants, and re-establishment of vegetation. However, substantial resources required for conversion of the site may be too costly economically, and obviously cannot be financed by companies already in trouble or in bankruptcy. If local or state authorities do not support this cost, sites are sometimes abandoned and become "industrial graveyards."

Industrial risk management at industrial sites is an important factor of security. The danger of activity and proximity of the populations are elements entering the evaluation of risk. In Europe, the most dangerous industrial sites are classified "Seveso," in memory of the industrial disaster in Seveso. Most industrial areas are built on the outskirts of cities, for reasons of cost and land space, but the rapid growth of urbanization is catching up with the fact that an initially remote site may be found to be included in a densely populated urban area. This exposes the border populations to danger, as is often the case in the most deadly industrial disasters, such as the explosion of the AZF factory in Toulouse.

Recently, sustainable management of industrial parks has become a key issue by integrating the territorial dimension with economic, environmental, and social aspects. This management is based on new partnerships between businesses and territories. It promotes the establishment of collective management of business services and employment needs for optimizing costs.

The challenge for an industrial cluster is to ensure the commercial success of the park and economic development of establishing companies, but at the same time to prevent environmental impacts on park facilities and help companies do the same, and to promote access to employment for all and improve the working conditions of employees. The implementation of sustainable development applied to industrial clusters is based on a winning triad: management, animation, and user services. It is believed that collective approaches allow companies to pool their needs and find solutions that are more appropriate and less costly. They help find solutions to identified needs when individual solutions are not satisfactory. For different needs related to quality of life for their employees and operations, many companies — especially smaller manufacturing enterprises (SMEs) — for various reasons cannot be efficient at a viable cost due to low demand terms of quantity, frequency, or number of users. In the environmental field, SMEs face difficulties in implementing preventive actions because of three main obstacles: there is a lack of culture on this issue, that is, companies do not necessarily have enough impact on the environment to justify a position of responsible environmental approach; technical solutions are not always suitable for small amounts and do not favor the upstream process, e.g., they have difficulties in separating waste or in treating certain liquid wastes; and there are very high costs in terms of quantities generated, e.g., hiring a dump truck to move a trash can of paper or a few bottles of products. Business parks or industrial zones are typical areas where the proximity of a large number of activities should promote collective approaches. Unfortunately, this is rare due to lack of management and leadership of these spaces.

In addition, as outlined by the Centre for Young Managers, entrepreneurs in France often show lack of openness. As a result, they have little experience in networking, cooperation, and partnership, and probably fear losing their independence or that their ideas will be stolen. Fortunately, examples show us that collective approaches are relevant in many areas and help to improve operating activities and working conditions.

Industrial ecology seeks to minimize loss of material in the process of consumption and production by learning from how the biosphere works to change the industrial system so that it becomes viable. The objective is to promote emergence of synergies between companies so that they recycle their production residues (e.g., vapors, water, waste) between each other or with the communities. This approach allows optimizing the use of materials in industrial processes. As emphasized by Motoyuki Suzuki (director of the Zero Emissions Forum in Japan), after labor productivity and capital productivity, it is now time for raw materials productivity (quoted in Ecolo, 2009).

Industrial activities are heavy consumers of natural resources, and generate a number of losses as well as waste or liquid waste. Aware of these losses, companies have established systems to limit and treat them. Unfortunately, these approaches are mainly based on treatment at the end of a process, or "end of pipe." There are other losses that are rarely studied, such as heat, water, or steam, which could be recovered by other companies. These exchanges could be sources of income for a majority of companies.

To be sure, industrial ecology operations do exist in France in a number of clusters, such as the Parc Industriel de la Plaine de l'Ain in the region of Rhône-Alpes. To encourage emergence of these actions, public actors are mobilizing with the creation of a French virtual cluster of industrial ecology and an information center in the City of Materials.

Nevertheless, important work of awareness and information is still needed to encourage companies to develop an industrial ecology approach to enable them to reduce their environmental impact and save money. Similarly, the development of business parks and regulations must evolve to provide favorable conditions for implementation of this approach.

Athelia, La Ciotat

Athelia is a geographically remote industrial cluster divided into four sectors forming a geographic entity (see Figure 3). The zone consists of 80 hectares, with more than 280 companies — split into 80% of micro-enterprises and 20% of SMEs — totaling nearly 6,500 jobs. The main industries are the new technologies of information and communication, medical equipment, electronic equipment, and construction and mechanical equipment. The project was initiated by the Ministry of Industry and initially developed by La Ciotat commune, at that time governed by the communist party. Currently, the legal structure includes a number of public and private partners.

Figure 3. View of Athelia.

The level of basic facilities of the cluster has slowly improved. There are now five restaurants and one hotel (Best Western). There are still no shops or stores offering basic services. The proximity to the city of La Ciotat is an advantage, but it is very difficult to reach services without driving a car.

Athelia is divided into four sectors as follows:

- Athelia I (6 hectares — 1987): This site hosts quality industrial buildings, light production activities (high-tech), and offices (services, engineering, research and development). Being the historical part of the park, construction was inspired from Greek architecture, with columns and decorated frontons.
- Athelia II (19 hectares — 1990): This sector, which relied on the industrial area of the commune, brings together crafts and small industries on 50 lots.
- Athelia III (9 hectares — 1988): This area consists of 20 medium-sized industrial lots.
- Athelia IV (39 hectares — 1990): Offering large lots, this area has led to diversification of economic activities and implementation of a few large units.

Companies have diversified at Athelia by size. Small units are installed on lots of about 10 m^2 in "relay" buildings provided by the Marseille Provence Chamber of Commerce in Athelia II. On the other hand, there is the giant Ball Packaging Europe with 9 hectares of land and 45,000 m^2 of constructed area, and the Gemalto Research Centre which covers 12,000 m^2 of high-quality buildings, both belonging to international groups.

Given the diversity of industries, the medical and paramedical pole is well represented with the following companies: InterVascular, Euros, Roxlor, Efer, Biotechni S.A., Sopro, Novatech, Arizant France, and Hospidex France. There are also areas of activity in new technology and renewable energy companies (e.g., Uniglobe, Sea, Innova Card, STILOG I.S.T., Jacques Giordano Industries) and engineering and electronics companies (e.g., Gemalto, Principia, Bardot Group, SmarDTV, Newsteo).

Opening a New Business Site: Athelia V

Given the success of marketing activities of the Athelia sector and given the strong demand for business location, the City of La Ciotat and the Urban Community of Marseille Provence Metropolis have engaged the extension of the site by creating Athelia V, on land initially labeled "WUA Natural Area N2," non-constructible for individuals. The development of this new area of activity of 50 hectares will be carried out in accordance with insertion of a quality landscape that combines preservation of natural forest areas, limited height of buildings depending on the topography of the land, and respect for the landscaping of the surrounding area by landscaping of the building itself. But because of the economic slowdown that Southern Europe is currently facing, at the moment the project has been frozen at its early phase of construction.

Athelia I, III, and IV are quite well equipped, with appropriate public space and maintenance. Athelia I was the only one to benefit from a common architecture, and almost all buildings look like Greek temples. Other parts are rather heterogeneous in construction styles. In general, the buildings are well made and well maintained. But a few hectares are still empty and not maintained. This has created greenfield land, obviously a misused valuable asset. Another issue is proximity to the residential site, as it is being encroached upon by residential sprawl or other economic or redevelopment pressures. In this case, revitalization of the greenfield land may create conflicts of interest.

The Free Union Athelia Entreprendre

The union Athelia Entreprendre includes businesses of the area located in La Ciotat's Athelia, on a voluntary basis, with the goal to federate energies and build a common identity, followed by mutualizing actions for both expansion and consolidation. To achieve its objectives, the association has a board of 15 voluntary members (or "friendly staff") and 5 committees composed of 66 officers or employees.

It has strongly supported deployment of corporate social responsibility (CSR) within the organizations in the area. The sustainable development strategies are carried out by different thematic committees that pursue short-term goals. The five committees are: human resource, transportation, safety, waste, and renewable energy. The HR committee is currently working on a profit-sharing common system that would harmonize bonuses for employees.

According to a *La Provence* newspaper article in April 2011 (Bougan, 2011):

> Matthieu Laudet is a happy president. The union that he chairs, Athelia Entreprendre, is undertaking an increasing number of activities, and is full of projects. Members are joining their forces. As of April 2011, 149 Athelia companies have chosen to join the union — there were 141 in 2010 — out of a total of 283 organizations settled in the cluster. Something to note, and heartening to hear, from the director of Ball Packaging, which has invested tirelessly for three years in Athelia Entreprendre.
>
> At the annual meeting recently held at Hotel Ibis, Matthieu Laudet presented his vision of the role of the union: "The actions of Athelia Entreprendre should focus on sustainable development. We must make our cluster a current and future regional model in terms of sustainable development."
>
> In 2010, the union continued and extended its marketing and public relations actions to over 48 actions, including 10 open tables on Tuesdays for lunch centered around a conference guest. The main event remained the Rencontres d'Athelia, which once again encountered success. "They provide an outreach to the general public job seekers with professional HR managers," said the president. "In fact two contracts were signed in 2010; we would like there to be more, but that's something. . . . We were also present during the week of sustainable development with the action

around collection of wooden pallets, a visit to the sorting office, and discussions with Bronzo and Ciotabus, who proposed a free shuttle to lunch."

Another important issue on which the association made significant progress in 2010 was the project of an inter-company nursery. After a call for tender, the company Babilou was selected to provide a nursery with 30 cradles. "We expect the response of the social authorities," said Matthieu Laudet.

Concerning security, Thierry Chaumont (Trees Telecom) presented figures announcing that burglaries had decreased by 40% in 2010, which amounted to 17 affected companies against 25 a year earlier. In terms of road safety, ideas about how to improve traffic flow and the condition of the roads were brainstormed. The case is not simple because skills are shared with the city, the metropolis, and the county.

Regarding transportation, in 2010 a project was announced to develop the use of alternative transport modes for private cars. [Following the plan to launch a car-pooling site with "Green Wheel," the website "Covoiturage Via Athelia" has been operating since August 2012.]

In regards to the collective management of waste, the association called on businesses. A total of 23 companies participated — 50% of employees in the area! "But to get a certification, we need more," insisted the vice president Vincent Armandon (Covitra).

Finally, after being re-elected, the president Matthieu Laudet made an appointment on November 30, 2011, for members to meet new people in order to lift up Rencontres d'Athelia to another level by opening up to neighboring clusters such as Gemenos, Les Paluds, and Napollon.

Many partners of the association were present at the general meeting, including the municipality of La Ciotat represented by its first deputy, Guy Patzlaff. Regarding security issues, he said that 80 cameras would be installed in the city within three years. Currently, there are two at Athelia. "There is no reason that there may be others, but we will discuss the modalities," said the representative of the mayor.

Athelia opens every year to the public during open days. This annual event takes place in October in La Ciotat as a meeting place for Athelia firms with the citizens of La Ciotat, and serves as a tool for creating and maintaining a link between them.

The main goal at the moment for Athelia Entreprendre is to federate companies on sustainable development in La Ciotat. The waste committee has a primary mission to expand the number of companies in the area that adhere to the solution of implementing collective management of waste. Out of 180 companies in the union, about 20 are already partners. The committee plans to double the number of members and successfully attain collective waste treatment at 50% of the waste, as opposed to 35% today. Ultimately, its ambition is to remove the tax on household waste by financing the deployment of the "Collecting Waste Athelia" program by accession of all Athelia companies. The committee has also initiated computer waste recycling.

The renewable energy committee promotes renewable energy production in Athelia as a main goal of sustainable development. Guidelines are described as follows:

- Take advantage of opportunities to develop the legal and financial Athelia image in terms of environment, attractiveness, and quality of life.
- Develop Athelia Entreprendre's actions in terms of sustainable development.
- Use Athelia Entreprendre's position to support other companies in the area that are interested in participating in this program.
- Coordinate with the City of La Ciotat to expand production of renewable energy, in particular for the planned Athelia V, from solar or wind power.

A third committee working in the field of sustainable development is the transportation committee, which aims to support the implementation of a plan to improve transportation.

Every year in July, the "Athelia Night" is an exciting event, both for managers and employees. It is also a valuable public relations time, since firms invite their best customers and suppliers in a nice environment.

The Transportation Issue

La Ciotat is accessed from Marseille by local train or by the A50 motorway or Road 559 (Route de Cassis). The train is quite convenient but slow, since it stops at every village, and also the timetable is mostly tailored to commuters who live in La Ciotat and work in Marseille. So it is not easy at certain times of the day to catch the opposite connection.

The A50 motorway is the most expensive one in France in terms of cost per kilometer. Again, the flow of traffic is linked to the commuting labor to Marseille, but the good news is that it was expanded from 2 × 2 to 2 × 3 lanes in late 2011. Also, the toll station is located northwest of the town, at the entrances to the Athelia business park. Besides the motorway, La Ciotat can be reached by local and narrow roads from the north, east, and west. But these roads are dangerous, due to the slopes and curves of the surroundings (see Figure 4). The first traffic roundabout met at the exit of the toll serves Athelia I on the right; the second exit reaches the city and continues on through the county. Road 559 running through the city center serves Athelia II, III, and IV. Road 559 crosses the city of La Ciotat from west to east, linking Cassis to Saint-Cyr-sur-Mer. It becomes a city street from the roundabout at the bottom of the ramp from the highway to the district of St. John. This route connects small villages along the coast, skirting to the north from west to east along the Paris–Italy railway path.

The Environmental Issue

Athelia is currently involved in two programs: Natura 2000 and Med Zones.

Figure 4.   La Ciotat and other coastal villages (satellite map).

Natura 2000

Natura 2000 is a network of ecological sites with two objectives: conserving biodiversity and enhancing the natural heritage of territories, directly managed by the European Union. The network of sites is spread all over Europe in order to bring coherence to initiatives to preserve species and natural habitats. At La Ciotat, two major concerns are the flight of migratory birds and the quality of the seaside, showing that nature and its preservation have no borders. Two EU directives are the most important guidelines, "Birds" (1979) and "Habitats" (1992). They establish a regulatory basis for the European ecological network. Designated sites under these two guidelines form the Natura 2000 network.

The Birds Directive provides long-term conservation of wild bird species in the European Union, targeting 181 species and subspecies for special attention. Over 3,000 sites are classified as Special Protection Areas (SPAs), and La Ciotat is one of them (see Figure 5). The Habitats Directive establishes a framework for the community to measure the conservation of fauna, flora, and

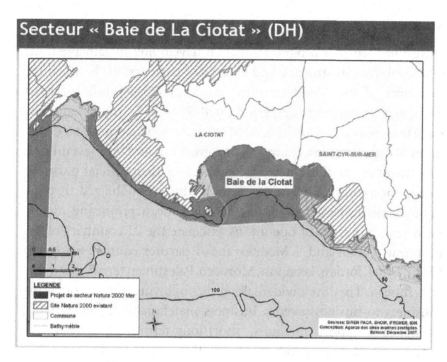

Figure 5. Map of Natura 2000 — La Ciotat.

their habitat. This directive lists more than 200 natural habitat types, and 200 animal and 500 plant species of community interest in need of protection. The Special Areas of Conservation (SACs), now numbering more than 20,000, account for 12% of the European territory and allow for protection of these habitats and endangered species.

The municipality of La Ciotat decided to enter the Natura 2000 program in 2008, after rejecting it in 2006. Even if measures are tailored to specific threats to these habitats and species, they do not lead to prohibition of human activities, since they have no significant effect on the maintenance of habitats and species. The program helps maintain biodiversity while taking account of economic, social, cultural, and regional perspectives of sustainable development. In fact, it may be seen as both an opportunity and a burden. Matthieu Laudet and Athelia Entreprendre are positioned as major actors in leveraging both the image and profitability of the cluster through Natura 2000.

Med Zones

"Invest in Med" is a program aimed at developing sustainable trade relationships, investments, and enterprise partnerships between the two rims of the Mediterranean Sea. With 75% funding by the European Union over the period 2008–2011, it is implemented by the MedAlliance consortium. MedAlliance gathers economic development organizations, chambers of commerce, and business unions. The members of these networks, as well as their special partners, gather thousands of economic actors, who are mobilized through pilot initiatives centered on key Mediterranean promising niches. Each year, hundreds of operations associate the 27 countries of the European Union and 9 Mediterranean partner countries: Algeria, Egypt, Israel, Jordan, Lebanon, Morocco, Palestinian territories, Syria, and Tunisia. They are divided along the following lines: networking (business-to-business events, business matchmaking, conferences); assistance (support missions, short/long-term staff exchanges); training (workshops); and documentation (guide books, economic intelligence reports). Other major issues addressed by the program relate to the young or female entrepreneurs, diasporas, micro-enterprises, franchising and leasing, public–private partnerships, and access to financing.

Within this framework, the Med Zones initiative is an exchange of good practices among different Mediterranean partners monitored by the Marseille Provence Chamber of Commerce and its partners, the French Chamber of Commerce in Morocco and the Foreign Investment Promotion Agency (FIPA). The Med Zones initiative aims to construct an offer for Mediterranean industrial clusters for sustainable and efficient business competitiveness and attractiveness of the territory. Based on the necessary appropriation and dissemination of the principles of sustainable development in industrial clusters, partners of Med Zones have decided, through "Invest in Med," to share their experiences and reflections to promote the general areas of sustainable activities.

The three main project objectives are:

- Identify the issues that arise in industrial clusters and sustainable development in the Mediterranean;
- Promote Mediterranean cooperation by sharing existing good practices; and
- Produce a reference work on conditions for implementation of a sustainable development policy in a cluster.

It aims at making private and public local actors understand that the label "EcoPark" gives value to a territory as a major asset in terms of image and attractiveness. Three operations have been implemented within this initiative framework: a guide of best practices was published; a workshop with companies and planners made everybody aware of companies' expectations; and a training session about sustainable planning and management was organized for the attention of technicians. This issue requires considering a new type of urbanization for future projects. If some areas are "best," indeed, many have questions about the nature and performance of services they offer to businesses.

Med Zones has chosen Athelia as a model in its guide for developers of zones. This is good for Athelia Entreprendre, which is involved in the development of Athelia V to make it a showcase in the field of sustainable development.

Due to population growth and attractiveness of large cities, the scarcity of land in the Mediterranean requires a denser economic development space and a fight against land speculation. To fight against this speculation, strategic land management is implemented with solutions like the use of long-term leases. For example, Bouskoura Industrial Park proposes leases of 17 years which are automatically renewable at the discretion of the lessee.

Home business is conducted in order to reduce "waste" of land. Different courses of action have been discussed: increased surfaces built on private plots, strategic development of buildings, and vertical division of large buildings. These strategies could reach a ratio of 250 jobs/hectare dedicated to the activity. Taking into account climatic factors, the Mediterranean is characterized by sunshine and water scarcity. These two factors have led to a rethinking of the way to develop areas as well as to integrate these elements in the design or renovation of buildings. In terms of development, this can result in management of water issues, the choice of adapted plant species, or building orientation. Similarly, important work has focused on the mastery of stormwater runoff on roadways and parking lots, water consumption, watering parks, and control systems against fire. These climatic factors may affect the services provided to companies, like establishing solar panels or water-saving technologies. As part of its action, the association Athelia Entreprendre promotes the development of photovoltaic panels on roofs of companies. It appears as a necessity for those involved in these territories to be able to create value-added business by implementing technological innovations. This desire is often found in the selection criteria of companies wishing to relocate.

Managers' and Entrepreneurs' Viewpoints

You and your project partners have now done enough research in textbooks and other literature to learn more about industrial clusters. You have also visited the cluster several times, and explored the brochures provided to you by Athelia Entreprendre on the main issues discussed by the cluster's different stakeholders. With this knowledge, you returned to Athelia to discover more about personal opinions, and you conducted four interviews.[1]

---

[1] For the convenience of the readers, only the most striking ideas are transcribed. Interviews were conducted face-to-face during the summer of 2011. The identities of the respondents have been disguised.

Interview with A.B., Plant Manager of the largest industrial firm in the cluster:

> The firm is fairly large, and Athelia implementation is a good choice for covering the Southern European market. I have experienced several shifts of majority ownership (French, American, Swedish), and the decision to grow within Athelia has been reinforced year after year.
>
> Sustainable development is the main issue. The firms like the fact that the cluster mobilizes forces in the three dimensions: financial, social, and environmental. Obviously, the dominant objective is to increase profit, but at the same time managers and entrepreneurs are quite proud of their location in a cluster known for its high-tech as well as sustainable environment. Athelia is a really good location for the firm, since the cluster does not aim to expand, but more to ensure the welfare of all stakeholders, in particular the employees. The proximity of the Calanques National Park and belonging to Natura 2000 are advantages for attracting visitors and recruiting staff. The location, at an equal distance to Barcelona and Milan, is really positive. Athelia wants to be a model in creating synergies between technology and the environment. The availability of land at a reasonable price is definitely an advantage. The surroundings are wonderful, the view is great, and the city of La Ciotat is growing as a tourist destination. The new kindergarten and search for synergies in saving energy are valuable. The facility for recycling garbage will hopefully bring the ISO 14001 label. I am currently really satisfied with the recycling process for batteries and electrical waste. The animation of the zone is highly appreciated. In order to help cooperation and synergies through business-to-business relationships, business buzzes and speed-dating sessions are organized, as well as open tables around a common interest. For an entrepreneur, there are a number of specific arguments related to Provence that are valuable and marketable.
>
> Transportation is a problem. The roads are quite okay, but trains and airports are really problematic for visitors. For staff, you really

need a car. It is almost impossible to bike. The future plan for interactive development will include a platform for car sharing, which is really good. The hotels are okay, even if there are no five-star hotels in La Ciotat. The nearest top-standard hotel is the Dolce Fregate Provence Golf Resort, 15 kilometers from Athelia, which is superb and perfect for VIP clients.

The trend is definitely toward more cooperation among the firms. And as the largest firm in the cluster, we are committed to actions. A new issue that I have brought up for discussion is a common profit-sharing system in order to increase the loyalty and motivation of employees all around Athelia.

I do think that the quality of working, living, and operating here is extremely good. Both our employees and business partners are happy with it, and it fits our strategy.

Interview with C.D., Managing Director of the Research and Training Center of a multinational group:

Our location at Athelia is mostly for tax advantages and the cheap price of land. We have recently purchased extra square meters, and the relative price/quality is more than acceptable. It is the biggest advantage of the cluster. But we don't know about the future, since the French regulation for both industrial clusters and industrial risks is not stable.

The way the cluster has grown is really not ideal. It looks like a mille-feuille gâteau, lacking coherence. The landscape is a disadvantage. Some roads have an 18% slope, which is impossible for trucks. Natural and technological risks are quite high. The roads are very bad and too busy. Transportation and safety are big problems.

Because of the specificity of activities that we have located at Athelia, we do not generate real synergies with other firms. We are not really into a network, and cohabitation with others is sometimes difficult. Our current goal at Athelia is to limit flows of goods. We will use our facilities for research, development, training, and online sales. On the other hand, it is a wonderful area to welcome customers and trainees from all over the world, even if some of them would prefer to be in the center of Paris (where we have a similar center). Our commercial staff spends most of the time traveling. They organize events where the customers are. They like to come to Athelia for meetings and project development. At Athelia, we have built a showroom, and the quality of the equipment in servers and distance connections is great.

We are happy with the Natura 2000 project. It is a factor for quality of the environment of the cluster, and actually sustainability and environmental protection appear to be the right domain for federating local firms. Since we cannot find synergies to strengthen our market position within Athelia, it is important to build a value chain for these issues. These are exactly the type of issues that are hard to go alone. Energy saving, waste recycling, and efficient transportation are value-adding services when shared. Regarding other services (cleaning, gardening, security, food, and accommodation), the offer is satisfactory. There is a shortage of intellectual services (law and audit) and no conference center.

Athelia should have a better communication plan. Interesting things are being done, but I cannot see what the governing guideline (red thread) is. It would probably reinforce the dimension of the network.

Athelia Entreprendre is a vigorous union. For sure it is the driving force for improvement of the cluster.

Interview with E.F., young entrepreneur and owner of a startup operating in the cosmetics industry:

Definitely I chose to locate my business at Athelia for the matching of the images. My company wants to base its image on the Provence asset, and sell concentrated perfumes made from local plants and vegetables. Even the view from my window is a marketing tool! I am looking for a strong address effect. I am really happy that Athelia is not in downtown La Ciotat, but in the hinterland. The sea coast cannot produce anything else other than shipyards, and this image is so specific for historical reasons. At Athelia, I can smell in the park what I am based on.

When I think about the future, I put forward the adequation between high-tech production that we develop, our market position, and our search for an image of top quality. I really want Athelia to support me in adding value for this issue.

Parallel to it, Athelia seems to have the appropriate dimension for incorporating a pattern of sustainable development — a goal in the process of environmental protection that has become essential. Our demand for quality matches the role that the cluster wants to strengthen in the economy of the area, which conveys a strong image for member firms and future investors.

Interview with G.H., Chief Officer of a medium-sized mature company operating in the robotization industry:

I did not choose the location, since I only joined the company in 2009. If I had to make the decision about the location of our headquarters and main industrial site, I would have to look for a site with a high potential of related industries and a qualified labor force. I would go where the profession is and where the competition is, as these two are key factors for decreasing costs. Regarding a qualified labor force, our business needs human capital, or more importantly, stable human capital. So the living conditions and the advantages that a specific location can offer are important. Regarding business relations, we need a network of complementary industries in order to increase the visibility of our strategic positioning. I am concerned about the location at Athelia. Our company has grown and has reached the critical size for autonomy. Its image is now rather distinctive. So we could leave the cluster, if there are no good reasons to stay. As with any network, members are free to come in and drop off. We have no specific vocation or emotion to stay at Athelia. I view this location as a temporary one for a period of time, before an international restructuring of our activities. The good reasons to stay could be cheap land to buy for extension, or an increased vertical sectoral approach integrating close partners.

A number of practical issues have to be tackled immediately. Mutualizing transportation of people is critical. This applies to all — competitors, related firms, and independent entities. All of us will gain from it. A well-monitored land must help to offer extra square meters that we need at a cheap price. For me, clearly Athelia was not a result of industrial approaches, but a political decision. Athelia has no incubator favoring innovation, and no partnership with a university for developing knowledge and research. The political authorities must work toward a densification of relationships among the firms, the population, the universities, and other research centers. It is essential to accompany innovative SMEs in their growth. Unfortunately, Athelia is not positioned on the Mediterranean Trail for High Technologies that goes from Spain to Italy, as the closest cluster (Arbois, Aix-en-Provence) is. The strategy of attracting firms by tax exemption has a limited effect. It does not work with a mature firm, when the strategy is more complex than a focus on cost optimization and when constraints appear. The question now for Athelia is to avoid drop off. Operating buildings are definitely better than empty ones.

Required

You and your fellow partners are now structuring your report to be submitted to your project supervisor at the business school. In order to discuss the situation and make some recommendations to the cluster partners, you decide to draw up a reasoned analysis, and you finally come up with the following questions:

1. When you examine the history, the location, and the topography of the area, what are the advantages and the disadvantages for a company to be located at Athelia?

2a. Obviously, firms' managers complain about transportation problems. Is this a key issue? Does it have an influence on the future of the cluster? What are your recommendations?

2b. What are the critical services that need to be offered to companies of the cluster in order to retain them?

3a. Do the activities of Athelia Entreprendre develop networking, cooperation, and partnership among companies, and do they reduce firms' fear of losing their independence or of having their ideas stolen?

3b. Does the implementation at Athelia promote the economic organization of networks connected to the phenomena of outsourcing and links among business contractors, subcontractors, and suppliers?

4a. Collective management is a new approach that aims to improve the conditions of doing business and working conditions while optimizing costs. What are the Athelia companies doing with regard to this concept?

4b. How can the establishment of a collective industrial ecology become a popular marketing tool for businesses?

4c. What do you recommend to implement for Athelia V, being a showcase in the field of sustainable development?

5a. Are companies looking to get a good image by perceiving Athelia as an "effective address," i.e., through the right balance between their market position on the one hand and the image of quality that they intend to carry on the other?

5b. How can the cluster's mindset impact the companies' marketing and outreach strategies for clients?

Bibliography

Bougan, Philippe (2011). "Athelia Entreprendre Veut Devenir Une Référence." *La Provence*, April 26.

Ecolo (2009). "Programme Economie Verte." http://wcb4.ecolo.be/?Priorite-no1-entreprendre-la/.

Case 3

Closing the Distance between Two Furniture Clusters — Möbelriket in Lammhult and Tibro Interiör in Tibro*

On a September afternoon in 2009, the cluster managers from the small town of Lammhult, located in the county of Småland in southern Sweden, Johan Sjöberg and Anders Wisth, had to leave a project presentation empty-handed. The representatives of Tillväxtverket (Swedish Agency for Economic and Regional Growth) had told them that they saw the potential for Möbelriket ("Furniture Kingdom") to become a worldwide known furniture cluster. However, Tillväxtverket would only consider granting long-term financial support if this cluster initiative reached out to other clusters, grew, and collaborated in southern Sweden. On the way home, the two entrepreneurs — the "king" and the "prime minister" of Möbelriket — discussed about possible new partners, primarily the Tibro Interiör cluster initiative in Tibro. On the one hand, there were potential opportunities, as 20 Swedish miles[1] was not a big

---

*Zsuzsanna Vincze and Håkan Boter, both at Umeå School of Business and Economics, Umeå University (Sweden), developed this case for educational purposes only. The case is designed to illustrate several concepts and theories in the formation and management of industrial clusters.
[1]20 Swedish miles = 200 km.

distance; on the other hand, Tibro and Lammhult were competitors traditionally. There were no easy answers as to how to make the clusterization work. How could the different structures and traditions be mixed? Should other clusters, such as Glasriket ("Kingdom of Crystal"), also be considered? How far could Möbelriket expand and how fast was it realistic to do that? Until they figured this out and started to implement cooperation between the clusters, approximately 1 million SEK in support was on hold.

Möbelriket

Thomas Friedman's (2005) hypothesis that the world has become flat is being challenged by the growth of cities and regions. "In terms of both sheer economic horse-power and cutting-edge innovation, surprisingly few regions truly matter in today's global economy," claimed Florida (2005). According to him, the world is "spiky," despite the global playing field having been leveled thanks to advances in technology, because innovation, economic growth, and prosperity occur in those places that attract a critical mass of top creative talent. Definitely, the European Cluster Observatory[2] puts southern Sweden (see Figure 1) along with, for example, northern Italy at the high peak on the cluster map. Many people have studied and defined Möbelriket both as an existing cluster and as a cluster initiative. Many have seen the potential for a strong cluster, which could even become a world-class cluster through collaboration with other clusters in the south of Sweden.

The furniture industry in Lammhult was established in the early 20th century. The now-prosperous retailer Svenssons actually started a small factory already in 1891, and the first carpenter workshop opened in 1919. By the 1950s, there were about 10 factories in Lammhult, each operating with more than 50 employees. Also, retailers like Svenssons strengthened their position in the town.

---

[2]See, e.g., Sölvell *et al.* (2003).

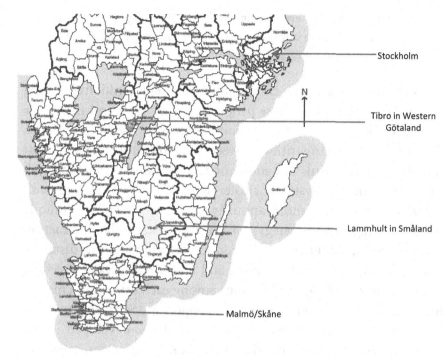

Figure 1. Map of southern Sweden (source: http://www.scb.se/Grupp/klassrummet/_Dokument/kommuner_text.pdf).

The design sector in particular boomed in the 1960s. During that time, the economy grew considerably and so did the public and residential construction sector, followed by a strong demand for interior architect services. As Anders himself said:

> Put it like this — in the 1960s when you built all those public halls, etc., and you hired interior architects that were paid to do the interior, quite a lot of the time they also designed new items, such as new products for this specific public hall, and at the same time you asked the architect to also develop some tables and lighting. Afterwards you often said to the designer, "You have made this product very well. Would it be possible to continue to produce this item?" The cost for product development had already been paid, and the designer got 3–5% in royalty on the sales of the new

product. . . . That system remains in the streets today, but there are no public halls being built, so we have a problem with the product development and designers' payments.

Möbelriket began as a collaborative marketing initiative among Lammhult's retailers by three people, Johan Sjöberg and two other managers, in 1997. However, soon after this idea took shape, they realized the similarities between their furniture industry and the already-successful "Kingdom of Crystal" in eastern Småland. The Kingdom of Crystal, a cluster with 15 glassworks and with about one million visitors annually, had implemented a unique design management strategy, which emphasized the interaction among artists, designers, and producers within cycling distance. There, famous crystal/glass artists and craftsmen worked together, transferring knowledge and feelings among each other and creating lovely masterpieces, and thus made the region and Swedish glasswork known to the world. A similar pattern could be developed in the furniture sector of Småland; the interaction between designers and producers was crucial for the companies there as well.

This new turn in the cluster initiative was put in place step-by-step through various projects. Johan Sjöberg took on the challenge, being the front face and the engine of the new cluster initiative.

Johan Sjöberg and Anders Wisth, the Driving Entrepreneurs of the Cluster Initiative

Johan has lived and worked as an entrepreneur in Småland all his life. His family, spanning back to three generations, were also entrepreneurs. As Johan said, he never thought of doing anything else other than working as an entrepreneur. When he was a schoolboy, he started the day in his family's factory before school began at 9 a.m. and went back there to work after school. During holidays he traveled with his father and uncle to places where they installed benches for churches. The family business was quite successful; for instance, his father received a gold medal for his workbench at the Sacramento State Fair in 1959.

Johan does not remember exactly how the Möbelriket project started. He just saw that one day, back in the mid-1990s, a local magazine coined Lammhult as the "Furniture Kingdom" of Sweden, parallel to the "Kingdom of Crystal" in eastern Småland. At that time, Johan was the owner/manager of the retail company Svenssons and he saw an opportunity to market Swedish design furniture retailers from Lammhult. He noted that it took 20 years for the Glasriket cluster initiative to become famous, so he calculated that it was about time to start building a famous furniture cluster. Indeed, Möbelriket was merely a marketing name at the beginning. The aim was to market the shops. They believed that together they could communicate better with the outside world and put Lammhult on the map as an interesting place in which to purchase good-quality furniture. A lot has been done since then — today, not only the retailers but also furniture manufacturers, subcontractors, designers, and educational institutions are all active in the cluster initiative (see Figure 2). With Johan's vision of creating a cluster that would be famous all around the world because of high-quality Swedish furniture designs, several successful projects have been initiated and implemented. Recently, Johan was awarded the "Entrepreneur of the Year Award" in southern Sweden, and in February 2011 he received the "Litteris et Artibus" medal from the King of Sweden for his significant contributions to Swedish business.

Johan's vision provided the ignition for the development of the cluster. He worked on project after project, guided by his "inner light" of always looking for new things and interesting possibilities. He claims that he was never the kind of person who liked to do the same things all the time. Rather, he is always looking for new happenings and new people to meet. For example, he realized the benefits of extending the Lammhult name to various industries: "A good name: Lammhult. It is famous for good things, so it will

Figure 2.   Examples of cluster members of Möbelriket.

be easier to sell. . . . So much goodwill in the word of Lammhult, but you don't need to only have it in furniture; you can have it in sausages or other things."

From the perspective of furniture companies like Lammhults Möbel AB, having the same name as the town's name was seen as an asset but it could also be a risk. The risk was connected to the social setting of Lammhult. The challenge was to provide a trustworthy setting for the company and at the same time to develop the town, the local context, so that the public and the industry would all be aware of belonging to a global context.

Johan believes in design. According to him, design is a way to get better business and a better economy. Indeed, design for him is not only about art; if it is only art, it is not a good business. One has to link design to many other things, such as the economy, ecology, quality, price worthiness, and so on. Thus, he convinced the companies around Lammhult that for furniture development they needed design and had to have contact with external designers. The new concept of "design management" created a lot of buzz. And at this moment, the other leader of the cluster, Anders Wisth, stepped in. As Anders said:

> We used to joke that Johan is the King and I am the Prime Minister of the Furniture Kingdom. So we have divided the work in that way. Johan has a stronger focus on the destination development, bringing people as tourists and working with retailers — that is his baby. Since I came on board, I have been focusing more on the strategic issues for the industry and for this sector. We have worked with the designers as one group, and we have worked with the producers as another group.

Anders came on board in 2003, around the time when Johan with two other managers started to think about extending the collaborative marketing for retailers to a more integrated cluster development program. The three saw the need for a formal structure. Johan was at that time the owner of Svenssons, which created both opportunities and limitations. One of the opportunities based on his position was that he could offer strong support for activities and programs, but at the same time his ownership in Svenssons also created limitations. Anders was known to them because at that time he was working at the TräCentre (a foundation for research and education in the wood sector) in Nässjö as a business developer. He started working on the side, with the intention to widen the work. His mission was to give the cluster idea more structure. He also saw the need for stronger cooperation within the industry and for the development of projects that had yet to be acted on by the industry. At first, Anders was involved in helping to develop the structure towards a cluster initiative. He eventually left his earlier job and started to work as a paid employee for Möbelriket.

According to Anders, "There were not that many active initiatives and projects for development in general and with a future orientation. We tried to identify areas that were not being taken care of by the existing organizations. And to say it quite simply, we are working on those things that the other organizations do not do, for example, import activities. We tried to broaden the involvement of many more actors."

Anders was intrigued by how the furniture industry really worked. After a while, he realized that the producers for the contract market were the ones that could push the industry forward. One can see how the industry works by just going to Stockholm for the furniture fair. There are at least two halls: one is called the A hall, where the contract market exhibits are; and the other is the C hall, the place of the domestic/residential market. As Anders put it:

> The DNA of our industry is such that in the contract hall that is there for the architects — the prescribers — that hall is the hall where you find all the product inventions. The architects come out with new ideas that are progressive, bold, and forward-looking. . . . So in that hall, the products are edgier, they are bolder. Going to the residential market (the C hall), you will see what you found in the A hall two years ago, because the retailers are only buying what they know they will sell. For example, old oak furniture retailers in the home market are buying old oak furniture, but that left the A hall five years ago. And this makes sense because in one whole year you can have a lot of copies because you are copying all the success factors here, but for bringing designs and creating a world-known brand you have to be in the A hall.

In contrast to the situation in the good old days of the 1960s, there are no more public halls being built, which has created problems for product development and employment of designers. Designers now "offer" to work on pure speculation. They could come up with ideas to a producer and the producer could say okay. The producer may accept an idea for production, but if the designer is to be successful in presenting such an idea to the manufacturer, he/she needs to have the product. The designer has to carry out the prototyping on his/her own as a designer. The manufacturer could then say okay and help to market the product for a commission once it is out there in the market. However, this involves a time cycle of maybe three years, from invention to commercialization in the market. Johan and Anders understand this situation, and Möbelriket tries to help the young designers. As Anders said, "This is extremely important for us to work with and we are doing that right now, so we are trying to help them and we have done that now for a number of years. And by being involved in this with Vinnova (Swedish Governmental Agency for Innovation Systems) and Tillväxtverket, we also got into the cluster standardization organization and became an accredited cluster in that way."

Projects in Möbelriket

Möbelriket has a clear focus on design-related issues. The Green Design project (2008–2009, financed originally by Tillväxtverket) intended to create a more attractive career arena for the region's eco-conscious design students and design companies. In believing that trendy and eco-conscious designers could lead the way for more young companies/students in sustainable design, Möbelriket acted as a mentor and pillar for new partnerships and business opportunities with surrounding municipalities, businesses, and universities. Altogether, the project involved 33 design companies that worked together for a year and a half. They visited New York, Poland, and Oslo, and organized many workshops on different themes. Several other sponsors joined, and in the end the final budget was between 1 and 2 million SEK. The immediate aim was to establish young design firms, give them tools and mentor them, as well as actively disseminate environmentally conscious designs. This project has since then been extended a few more years, with this group joining together in various activities. The wider objectives here are to enhance cooperation among the region's environmental stakeholders, and to increase market and new business opportunities in sustainable design.

Other important, ongoing projects include the Designers Saturday, the Furniture Parliament, and the Design Arena. Every year, on one spring Saturday, the public is invited to visit the member companies of the Furniture Kingdom as well as other house- and interior-oriented companies in the region. The purpose of Designers Saturday (which involves lectures, round trips, exhibitions, and labs) is to create interest in and develop knowledge of the importance and role of design aspects in the manufacturing of furniture, houses, lighting, etc. The aim is to get 5,000 visitors to Designers Saturday annually. Similar events are organized in other European towns, e.g., in Switzerland and Norway. For instance, in Langenthal, Switzerland, Möbelriket participates every September in a large organized trade show that attracts more than 15,000 visitors in a city that has just 20,000 inhabitants. The Furniture Parliament is also important. Every year Möbelriket organizes a seminar in Lammhult, with around 150–400 participants from the companies in Lammhult and the nearby city of Värnamo, contractors, representatives of municipalities, as well as representatives from Tillväxtverket, Vinnova, and Banverket (Swedish Rail Administration). The three broad themes of the workshops and lectures are design management, internationalization (export and import), and infrastructure for growth. Furthermore, Johan organized the Design Arena (a member of the Möbelriket cluster; see Figure 2) in cooperation with the Lammhult municipality;

this is an exhibition of furniture designs from the whole of Sweden from the 18th century until today. All of the projects are very much inter-related, with some having a stronger local focus than others. For example, *Småländska Pärlor* ("Pearls of Småland") is a collaborative project among destinations in Småland that consists of both local and region-wide projects. Local projects include the architecture and design of apartments and schools in Lammhult. Nevertheless, when a local project is organized, it has to have a wider, even international, perspective. Möbelriket tries to combine the local and global perspectives.

The Stockholm Furniture Fair is the leading arena for Nordic design, with exhibitions focusing not only on furniture but also on textiles, office furniture, and interior design. This fair is the core exhibition for Möbelriket, with nearly 50,000 visitors who are growing internationally and with participants from a broad spectrum of the public such as the furniture retail sector, design schools, and media. Every year, the Milan Furniture Fair (*Salone Internazionale del Mobile di Milano*) is held in Milan. This fair started in the 1960s. It was initially the vehicle for promoting exports among Italian furniture companies, but today it is the most highly anticipated and prestigious event in the global furniture sector. In addition, Möbelriket has participated in the Swedish–American Chamber of Commerce's "Entrepreneurial Days" event as a representative of furniture and furnishings to inspire business between Sweden and the U.S. In August 2008, a large delegation of U.S. representatives visited Sweden, and to those who had expressed interest in furniture and design Möbelriket was presented. Further direct business meetings were arranged between the Swedish and U.S. companies. For example, Möbelriket launched its young-designer scholarship scheme to support designers abroad, and Anders together with some designers were invited to North Carolina. All in all, by concentrating on the international context, the cluster tries to attract investments and interest of stakeholders in order to generate a greater society to work in. As Anders said, "The smallness can be the greatness."

Tibro Interiör

After World War II, another concentration of the Swedish furniture industry started to grow in the town of Tibro (western Götaland). It eventually became a rather impressive center of furniture producers mainly for the Swedish residential market (*folkhemmet*). During the heyday of the 1960s and 1970s, there were almost 100 furniture manufacturers in this tiny town in the middle of Sweden. However, this network of actors in one industry and the increasing power of national retail chains, including IKEA, resulted in fierce competition among the manufacturers by the 1980s. As one manager stated, "20–30 years ago the companies were fighting with each other, and hated it if the neighboring manufacturer got richer."

In 2005, the Tibro municipality produced its future vision of "Vision Tibro 2017." Since then, the work has focused on developing close cooperation between the business community and municipal activities. The starting point was the question of where Tibro would be in the longer term, and what areas would be important to invest in in order to get there. Representatives of municipal, business, and voluntary sectors and interested community residents of all ages participated in the process. Together with a research/consultancy firm, they identified future changes in the industry and new trends in the society and put them in relation to Tibro's unique assets. At the time, Tibro still had some 70 craftsmen and 40 furniture manufacturers and interior design companies (see Figure 3), and in the close vicinity there were the headquarters of the largest national furniture retail chains, such as Mio and Kinnarps. Another valuable factor was Tibro LBC, the biggest furniture distributor and logistics center in Scandinavia; previously, the companies had their own lorries, which often ran around Scandinavia half-empty. All in all, nowhere in the Nordic countries were there as many furniture

Figure 3. Examples of cluster members in Tibro.

companies gathered as there were here. The tradition of wood, furnishings, and design was profoundly rooted in the region, with the relatively long experience of handling different furnishing materials. That is why Tibro could become a natural center — a place where furniture creators meet. By early 2000, the companies started helping each other around the same time that the municipality woke up. Even close competitors could call and borrow employees from each other within a day. Each company's workforce was skilled, so people could work for any company, depending on which company had the production peak in which season of the year. Another benefit of the close network and the critical mass in one place was the access to raw material in both small and large quantities, if required by production, within 24 hours. In contrast, a single company in a remote location elsewhere often had no other choice than to order a full truckload of material, even if it could not use the whole truckload.

According to Malin Lundberg, a project manager at Tibro Interiör:

> Since 1997 we have had a development company, IUC Tibro, one out of 17 in Sweden. They work with network issues. In 2006 they got a new CEO, and he started to expand the domains of Tibro and they decided to invest in cluster development. The time was ripe for working together more. Since 2007, we have worked strategically on cluster development in Tibro and we started Tibro Interiör. We began to focus on interior aspects and produce interior products. Products are made by single companies, but also in a team of companies.

Behind the Tibro Interiör cluster initiative, launched in the spring of 2007, there are the producers of Tibro, the municipality of Tibro, and the Industrial Development Center West Sweden AB. IDC West Sweden AB is the region's development company for the industry. It is owned by more than 100 companies, and has annual sales of approximately 10 billion SEK and more than 10,000 employees. IDC is aimed at both small and large businesses, and contributes to the increase in knowledge sharing among businesses in the region and universities and colleges. IDC also contributes to the development of innovation systems and clusters in different industries. Since the "Vision Tibro 2017" program has been in place, the Tibro municipality — together with all of the companies and IDC — has organized and involved people in projects like the marketing of Tibro Interiör, competence development, "Architect Days," as well as study visits to explore new markets and visits to trade fairs. The cluster is trying to create a platform to promote Tibro as a meeting place for the industry, for example, by inviting over 100 designers and architects from Sweden, Norway, and Denmark.

According to Andreas Rapp, a project manager at Formidabel Specialinredningar in Tibro: "Thinking of a cluster is a very positive thought for me. . . . We do not want to give up more jobs, so we are handling them within a network. In the first place, it's a question of obtaining work for Tibro, of building up a network, and of working together. Make people find the portal, and I rest assured that it will help produce more jobs for all the companies involved."

Summary of the Current Situation

There are clear differences between the Möbelriket and Tibro Interiör clusters. Tibro has a very high concentration (literally within one town) of manufacturing companies focused mainly on the residential market. In fact, the fierce competition among those companies resulted in the delayed and difficult process of building trust between them. As Malin Lundberg stated: "In Tibro we did not work with strategic marketing plans; we have just started doing that now. We don't have any tradition for marketing in Tibro. Many companies are passed on from one generation to the next generation, but we have had a number of new entrepreneurs in the region, which will influence the development of the region positively."

In Möbelriket, the companies are not directly located in one city, but are scattered in various villages within a radius of 5–10 Swedish miles, with Lammhult, Värnamo, and Sävsjö being the best-known of those places. It seems easier to build trust and cooperation among these companies, as they are not producing for only one segment of the market. Rather, some companies focus on the contract market while others focus on the residential market or may be subcontractors of both. Tibro companies have a strong focus on production and have an obvious production capacity, whereas in Möbelriket there are more design-intensive companies.

Despite these differences, it is also noted that both cluster initiatives need a critical mass, especially because the biggest threats to the Swedish furniture industry are not within the country, and yet the two Swedish clusters are relatively unknown outside Scandinavia. Both Johan and Anders agree on that. As Anders stated, "In Tibro, they have more of a good structure of work than we have here, but here we have more entrepreneurship. So we need to mix those things."

During the 2009 meeting with Johan and Anders, Tillväxtverket told them that they would like the two clusters to build bridges and work more closely together. But the two clusters did not have that perspective yet. How would it be possible to find the right way to complement each other rather than to compete? Would it be possible to integrate Tibro companies in the projects successfully run by Möbelriket? Johan and Anders were excited about this new challenge, which indeed carried new potential. However, the temporary negative result from Tillväxtverket had to be communicated to other stakeholders of Möbelriket. When bringing up something less positive in discussions with partners, it is not a bad idea to think of some solutions in advance. What kind of cluster collaboration possibilities could be put on the table? Can you help Johan and Anders think through the alternatives, with potentially best first steps on a new, ambitious road?

Bibliography

Florida, Richard (2005). "The World Is Spiky." *The Atlantic Monthly*, 296(3), 48–51.

Friedman, Thomas L. (2005). *The World Is Flat: A Brief History of the Twenty-First Century*. London: Allen Lane.

Sölvell, Örjan, Göran Lindqvist, and Christian Ketels (2003). *The Cluster Initiative Greenbook*. Stockholm: Ivory Tower AB/ European Cluster Observatory.

Case 4

Social and Environmental Value-Based Cluster Development — The Dilemma of Wishing to Do Good by Selling Textile Goods*

During their business studies at Umeå School of Business and Economics (Sweden) in the mid-2000s, Jonas Forsberg and Anders Sandlund talked endlessly about starting up their own business. They perceived the freedom of being "on their own" as extremely attractive, and they continually evaluated the theories and models they had learnt in their studies in relation to actual business models. What would work and how could they build a successful business from scratch?

Before going into business studies at the university level, Jonas had already started a business as a project in high school through the organization Young Enterprise. This brought him many ideas and

---

*Johan Jansson (PhD) and Mattias Jacobsson (PhD), both at Umeå School of Business and Economics, Umeå University (Sweden), developed this case in close cooperation with redQ owners and founders Jonas Forsberg and Anders Sandlund. The case is based on actual events, and the company redQ is in full operation and development. For more information on redQ, please visit http://redq.se/ (in Swedish only).

connections with the business world in Umeå. With this experience in fresh memory, he was not content with focusing on purely theoretical learning during his years at the business school. Compensating for a lack of experience with enthusiasm and a healthy dose of naivety, he initiated a number of small business ventures, ranging from selling sponsorships to finance the construction of a sports stadium, selling advertising on a student notebook, to creating and selling a Monopoly-type board game about the city of Umeå, and conducting market surveys for local businesses. Although these ventures were fun and supplied him with many valuable experiences, he was not entirely comfortable with the prospect of sticking to this way of life for a lengthy period of time. He wanted something more substantial and enduring to put his efforts into.

Anders had always enjoyed the feeling of being independent. He moved out of his parents' house before finishing high school, and after graduation he traveled and worked his way around the globe. Motivated by two years of positive experiences in Young Enterprise during high school, he decided to go for a business degree once back in Sweden. Since Anders' parents were running a firm specializing in exclusive leather products, the idea of starting up a company was nothing new and was not the least bit scary to him. His parents' firm did some manufacturing in a cluster in Bangladesh and assembled the products in Sweden, and had operated a good business with that model for many years. Despite being successful, Anders felt that he wanted to create something of his own, and quite frankly he did not believe wholeheartedly that leather products were the future, although the idea of being closely related to a cluster setting was in itself attractive. In fact, starting a firm was a very viable option compared to the banking and auditing careers many of his peers were considering at the end of their studies. In addition, his many discussions with Jonas on different business ideas were very motivating and rewarding. They could sit for long hours and discuss business ideas when they were supposed to be writing papers or studying for exams at the business school. But although these discussions were fun and interesting, they were frustrating as well. Anders felt that the studies took up too much time and he really wanted to start something soon — almost anything — as long as it was fun and could pay the bills. However, deep in his roots he also had the conviction that what one started (a degree in business) one should finish, and so he completed his thesis after a semester at BI Norwegian Business School in Oslo, Norway. He got a final injection of entrepreneurial spirit during a six-month internship in Stockholm at Founders Alliance, an organization granting membership only to founders of successful businesses. Meeting new members every day, Anders realized that he was sitting on the wrong side of the meeting table. He was not content with listening to the already-successful entrepreneurs; instead, he wanted to be one of them. More convinced than ever, Anders returned to Umeå and reunited with Jonas. The stage was set.

The First Business Idea: Buying at Low Prices, Selling at a Profit

The spark needed to ignite the imagination of Jonas and Anders came from an unexpected source. On his way to a dinner party, Jonas rushed into a filling station in search of a proper gift for the party's hostess. Being late spring, he was surprised to find that the gift rack was still filled with Christmas angels and a lonely odd maraca. Being forced to settle for a box of chocolates, he rushed on. But the sight of the unattractive gift rack came back to him the next day whilst discussing potential business ideas with Anders. Combining previous experiences from retailing and manufacturing, they started to sketch a business model based on supplying fuel filling stations with the right products and sales materials to increase their sales of gift items. The backbone of the idea was the possibility to purchase cheap products manufactured in low-cost countries. After some research, they realized it would not even be necessary to purchase straight from the producer in Asia to have sufficient margins. Buying from Swedish wholesalers was easier and cheap enough.

Having secured a contract with a chain of 20 filling stations, emptied their savings accounts, and registered a firm, the business was now up and running. Managing the business from home took little effort and, even though the goods purchased did not always strike a chord with end customers, the two friends got started with a very limited input of time and capital. Soon they were making a healthy profit in relation to the investment. So were the four to six middlemen — agents and wholesalers between whom the goods were handed on their way from China to Jonas and Anders — and so were the filling stations. Yet, the price paid by the end customer was competitive.

The Itchy Feeling That Something Is Not Right with the Business Idea

During some business travels to China and sales talks with filling station managers, Jonas and Anders began to get the itchy feeling that something was not healthy about their business idea. At the time, in 2005/2006, the media were repeatedly reporting about the problems of "cheap" Asian labor and the quality issues of these products. Reports on child labor, union prohibitions, and workers being exposed to harmful working conditions and other dangers kept coming in at a steady stream in the Swedish business media. Since many of these stories were related to Asia and low-wage countries, Jonas and Anders could not help but notice them. Also, this was the time when environmental issues such as climate change were being hotly debated partly due to the movie *An Inconvenient Truth* with Al Gore. Jonas and Anders started discussing these issues together and also with other friends. However, having been at a business school for more than three years, they were not really used to discussing the negative aspects of the consumption-focused society. The discussion became very exasperating. On the one hand, business organizations promoting entrepreneurship and growth were seeing business opportunities in these issues; while on the other hand, environmental and labor organizations seemed to be against all types of globalization and trade of products across large distances. Was there no middle ground? Did Jonas and Anders bear any partial responsibility for this? Could they even contribute to solving some of the justice and environmental issues?

Having no previous experience in working with these issues, they realized that they needed new input in order to figure out if there was something they could do about it. Jonas studied conventional corporate social responsibility (CSR) strategies of textile clusters and multinational companies such as H&M, IKEA, and Inditex (owner of textile brands such as Zara and Massimo Dutti). He came to learn that a code of conduct is often the backbone of a large corporation's approach to CSR. It is a document that the buying organization sends to the contractors who manufacture their goods. Reading the documents, Jonas found that they stipulate how manufacturers should set up their factories in terms of working environment, fire safety, working hours, minimum wages, overtime, etc. He found that the use of a code of conduct was widely adopted and a practical tool to control production in low-cost countries, especially in the textile industry. However, he also found it hard to find out how these codes were controlled by the buyers (if at all). Instead, media reports by organizations such as Human Rights Watch and Amnesty International seemed to show that, although the codes existed, they were not followed in reality.

In parallel, Anders looked at examples of small-scale sustainable businesses that he had discovered in the Swedish media. Watabaran and DEM Collective were two compelling examples. Founded in 2001 by then-19-year-old Björn Söderberg, Watabaran utilizes an abundant resource in Kathmandu, Nepal: waste. By paying for waste paper collected on the streets and recycling it into Christmas cards, notebooks, and calendar organizers to be sold on the European market, the company helps battle the waste problem and at the same time creates well-paid working opportunities in Kathmandu (Watabaran, 2011). Building on this concept and the network created, several other small enterprises formed by the people related to Watabaran have subsequently popped up in Kathmandu.

As another example, Annika Axelsson and Karin Stenmar were looking for T-shirts produced in a fair environment and with just working conditions to sell in their Fair Trade store. Realizing that there was no such shirt or production line to be found, they decided to do something about it. Calling themselves "DEM (Don't Eat Macaroni) Collective," they started their own sewing factory in Sri Lanka in 2004 (DEM Collective, 2011). By connecting cotton farmers trying to use sustainable practices with weavers and coloring plants with high environmental aspirations, they are creating a more sustainable production chain for garments. The employees at DEM Collective work for eight hours a day and are paid a salary that can support a family. Comparing it with other textile factories, Anders found this in itself to be a remarkable feat. These examples convinced him that a practical approach, taking the local context into account, was necessary to create a sustainable business whereby both the well-being of the workers and the environment were taken into consideration.

Comparing their findings, Jonas' suggestion was to write a code of conduct, stipulating the terms under which production should be made. By sending such a document to producers, he argued, they could help improve the situation for workers in the factories. Anders, on the other hand, thought that a document would make no real difference at all. After all, it is just a piece of paper. He believed instead that there was a need for hands-on involvement by buyers in the entire production chain. "There are enough documents already. Someone needs to implement them," he said. Furthermore, Anders did not believe that the implementation could be made from Sweden; rather, they needed to form a relationship with a manufacturer or a cluster of manufacturers in order to have influence over the production methods.

To settle the argument, Jonas and Anders decided to travel to a low-cost country to study the manufacturing industry first-hand and to also see if they could come into contact with a textile manufacturing cluster. Since Anders' parents had worked as volunteers in Bangladesh in the 1970s and had many contacts there, that became their country of choice. They also knew that Bangladesh, with about 160 million inhabitants, is one of the poorest and most densely populated countries in the world (partly due to the very fertile soil), and is plagued with environmental problems such as continuous floods and cyclones with high death tolls. If Jonas and Anders really wanted to try to do something good, there seemed to be plenty to learn about and do in Bangladesh.

Arriving in Bangladesh was even more shocking than they had anticipated. The heat, the number of people, and the severe poverty coupled with obvious visible environmental problems made them acutely aware of the problems that would lie ahead in setting up some sort of business or cluster there. On their very first Bangladesh factory visit, they saw a display of codes of conduct from all of the different companies buying from the facility. Scrutinizing the contents, Jonas and Anders realized that every buyer had made their own demands on salaries, working hours, and safety measures for the factory to implement. One buyer's demands could even be contradictory to the demands from another. Still, products destined for the different buyers were produced parallel to one another. The factory visit settled the argument — writing a code of conduct was not enough if they sought real improvement. They had to completely rework their business idea if they wanted to run it with a good environmental and social conscience. Also, they began to become more critical of some of the highly publicized advertising campaigns about organic cotton and fair trade products. They had now seen the production first-hand and, although the codes of conduct seemed to have some positive effects, it was a far cry from what glossy advertising from other corporations promised. The trip home from Bangladesh to Sweden was spent in contemplation.

Digging Deeper into the Social Issues

Back in Sweden, Jonas and Anders continued their research by trying to grasp the depth of the problem related to consumption in the Western world. They discovered that issues concerning poverty in developing countries and environmental and social problems were deeply intertwined. For example, 12% of the world's population live in North America and Western Europe and account for 60% of private consumption spending, but a third of humanity who live in South Asia and Sub-Saharan Africa account for only 3.2%, according to Worldwatch Institute (2004). They also noted that the International Labour Organization (ILO) found in a study that almost 10 million people worked in slave-like conditions in Asia in 2005 (Asia News, 2005). Could something be created that would help the people in the poorer part of the world and simultaneously inform and change consumption patterns in a relatively rich country like Sweden?

With their new insights from Bangladesh fresh in mind, Jonas and Anders revisited the issue of their responsibilities as entrepreneurs and the feasibility of their business model. On the one hand, they could try to change the manufacturing industry from a buyer's perspective within their gift business. Aware that it would take a lot of time and effort to make any difference, they thought that it still might be easier to use conventional methods than to innovate. On the other hand, starting with a clean slate was a tempting alternative. What if they could design the future of manufacturing, without having to carry the weight of an existing system with all of its inherent problems?

After endless discussions and sleepless nights, the two friends decided to use the small profit they had made on the gift import business to start doing something that would be part of the solution rather than the problem. But what would the solution be? Neither Jonas nor Anders had any experience of working with sustainability. Instead of becoming experts themselves, they decided to consult organizations focusing on different aspects of the issue. For example, they asked the World Wildlife Fund (WWF) what environmental concerns needed to be addressed and Save the Children about problems related to child labor in Asia. After learning more about workers' rights from Swedish unions and the Clean Clothes Campaign (2011), they got further coaching from the ILO. Drawing from the collected knowledge of these organizations, Anders and Jonas compiled a list of four concepts on which to build sustainable production:

- Fair labor — treating workers according to the ILO Conventions and the Bangladeshi labor law, focusing on workers' right to organize and bargain collectively;
- The environment — only using raw materials that can be grown without artificial irrigation or agricultural chemicals and a production process free of chemicals;
- Worker development — helping workers attain education and knowledge that can increase their level of income; and
- Transparency — being open about the location of manufacturing facilities and the intention to be a part of developing a jute cluster, and encouraging visits from third parties.

With this new framework in hand, they started to look for a way to implement it. Visiting Bangladeshi textile factories again, this time in search of partners to work with, they soon started to question the feasibility and relevance of their way of thinking. For starters, everyone they met laughed at the thought of producing textiles without artificial irrigation or chemicals and called it impossible. Concerning workers' rights, they tried to argue that dialogue and cooperation between management and workers would be profitable for all parties in the long run. "Talking to the workers?," asked one factory owner during a meeting. "Today they work for me. If someone pays them 10 cents more tomorrow, they'll be moving on. Once or twice per year they throw a strike, causing delays in the production and costing me huge sums in delay fees. And when it's time for national renegotiations of minimum wages, their demands are outrageous. If I raise their salaries, there will be nothing left for me. They are driving me out of business! Why should I even consider talking to them?" The tone used by union representatives (if there were any) was equally harsh: "Today I have a job; tomorrow the factory is out of orders and I don't have a job anymore," said a young woman representing one of innumerable union organizations. "We work 16 hours per day and hardly make enough money to feed ourselves, let alone our families. Time and time again we try to talk to the factory boss, but he won't even listen to our demands. The police beat us up when we try to protest, but what other choice do we have than to fight?"

The tension between workers and employers was thick enough to touch, and Jonas noted that this was not the right environment for a sustainable production mindset to grow. Anders agreed, but also felt that they had not seen the whole truth yet. "The root of the problem does not lie here," he said. "We're missing an important piece of this puzzle. What's really creating this untenable situation?" "The inability to understand the other party's perspective?," Jonas suggested. "No, the lack of resources," Anders replied. He argued that the pay the factory received from Western buyers was insufficient to pay the workers, let alone adapt to environmental practices. Jonas countered that just more money would be no good without an ongoing dialogue between parties on how to divide the resources fairly. They finally agreed that the situation would not change unless more resources were added by buyers and the dialogue between workers and factory owners improved. They also reached the conclusion that getting involved in and changing an existing production chain would mean more hassle than starting a new factory or a cluster of factories from scratch. By selling straight from their own factory to buyers in Sweden, they could influence the wages paid as well as ensure a functioning communication with workers. They would also be able to handle some of the dire environmental issues that kept showing up during their research.

Environmental Problems with Textiles and the Decision to Focus on Jute

Warming to the idea of starting their own factory, the obvious question was what to make. Jonas and Anders wanted to produce something useful that people actually needed, and not just more trinkets that people bought for fun in a throw-away fashion. What about clothes? However, in their research they saw that the textile industry was extremely problematic from both social and environmental aspects. For example, in regard to water, about 7,000 to 29,000 liters of water are required to produce a single kilogram of cotton depending on the irrigation method and degree of efficiency, and about 60% of the water used to irrigate cotton is lost to evaporation and poor irrigation practices (Klohn and Appelgren, 1998). Somewhere in the region of 76 million acres of land is currently utilized for the production of cotton globally (Kooistra *et al.*, 2006). According to some estimates, cotton covers 2.5% of the world's cultivated land and yet uses 16% of the world's insecticides, more than any other single major crop (Environmental Justice Foundation, 2007). Anders and Jonas concluded that cotton was not the textile fiber to grow in Bangladesh to solve environmental issues. The water was needed to grow food, and the price and environmental impact of insecticides to grow cotton were problematic in such a densely populated country. They looked for another textile fiber that would be more environmentally sustainable and less dependent on chemicals from large multinational corporations.

During their travels in Bangladesh, they had heard about what locals called "the golden fiber." When researching raw materials, they started asking questions about it and soon got introduced to jute. They learned that Bangladesh was formerly known as the "country of jute" due to being the world's leading exporter of this product. Bangladesh used to be one of Great Britain's most profitable colonies, delivering raw jute to mills in southern England. There, the fiber was made into large jute sacks used for storing grain and other commodities, as well as trusses for the shipping industry. In the 1950s and 1960s, almost 80% of the world's jute was produced in Bangladesh. But due to several setbacks and the introduction of cheaper substitutes such as plastic and synthetic fibers, the world trade of jute halved from the 1970s until the early 2000s (Food and Agriculture Organization of the United Nations, 2002). Although balanced to some extent by increased consumption in Bangladesh, in 2010 jute products made up only 3% of total exports from the country (Economist Intelligence Unit, 2010). However, something was going on in several areas of Bangladesh in order to rectify this trend.

Jonas and Anders came into contact with the Jute Diversification Promotion Center (JDPC) and the Bangladesh Jute Research Institute (BJRI), two governmental organizations in Bangladesh focused on bringing jute back to the market. With their help, it was possible to assess the potential of this golden fiber and what clusters of organizations and companies existed. First and foremost, Jonas and Anders looked at jute's potential in manufacturing versatile textiles, but quickly realized that the material was too rough to produce wearable garments. Searching further, they saw a strong potential in making reusable and biologically degradable shopping bags from jute canvas. In fact, they noted that several eco-initiatives carried out by supermarkets in Europe often used what looked like jute bags. Another option that looked promising was the widespread knowledge of Bangladeshi jute workers of how to make home interior items from jute by hand. It seemed as if there was potential to participate in or be part of developing a cluster of jute growers and manufacturers.

Researching the potential for each option, Jonas looked more closely at making shopping bags. He found that the demand for alternatives to plastic bags was soaring as the environmental trend swept over the Western and Northern consumption markets. He asked potential customers such as supermarket chains and clothing chains, and received positive feedback on the concept of responsibly produced and environmentally friendlier bags. Anders took a closer look at jute handicrafts. He found a vast array of applications, ranging from rugs and baskets to spa and bath products and accessories. When they met to discuss their options, both of them were enthusiastic about their own niches. Jonas argued that the potential market for shopping bags was larger than that of jute handicrafts. Anders agreed, but countered that a handicraft production would be cheap to set up, whilst the size of the initial investment to make bags would be substantial. The smallest setup of machinery to handle the latter task would cost in the region of 10 million SEK.[1] This was far more than the capital they had accumulated in their previous business endeavors. Anders also had an ace up his sleeve: Granit,[2] a Swedish chain of home decoration stores, had decided to buy handcrafted jute goods from them if they could produce the products responsibly in Bangladesh. That settled the issue. Granit had 16 shops in Sweden and one in Oslo, Norway, which made it a heavy argument. They would focus on jute handicrafts to begin with.

Setting Up the Manufacturing Cluster in Bangladesh

Looking at where to establish themselves, Anders' and Jonas' attention was initially focused on the Bangladeshi capital of Dhaka and its surroundings. Because of the relatively steady supply of electricity and the proximity to administrative functions, this area seemed like a natural choice. However, the size and layout of most available industrial facilities were adapted for garment factories, and the jute mills in the area — even though for sale — were far too large for the two entrepreneurs to consider. Looking for other alternatives, they went to the district of Natore, 200 kilometers northwest of Dhaka, to visit the village where Anders' parents had done volunteer work 30 years ago. Whilst relatively well connected to Dhaka, four-and-a-half

---

[1] About 1 million Euros or 1.4 million US dollars.
[2] *Granit* translates to "granite" in English. See http://www.granit.se/ (in Swedish only).

hours away by bus, to Jonas and Anders it felt like this region was light years away from the mega-city buzz of the capital city. The roads were narrow and winding, electricity was available four hours a day (to those fortunate few connected to the grid), and the standard living quarters for one family consisted of a single room with walls and a roof of corrugated tin. The main source of income in the region was agriculture; hence, the men worked in the fields while, due to lack of employment opportunities, the women were left to take care of the home and family. Jonas and Anders had heard that some women had organized into small groups, producing jute handicrafts together to generate some extra income, and that the groups in turn had formed a manufacturing cluster. First and foremost, the cluster enabled the women to deliver on orders too large for a single group to meet. The formation also shared knowledge on production methods, cooperated on sales efforts, and coordinated their purchases of raw materials from nearby farmers. Being focused around the village of Bagatipara, the cluster was also loosely associated to similar structures all over the Bangladeshi countryside.

The two Swedish entrepreneurs met with cluster representatives to explore the possibility of marrying Bangladeshi handicraft traditions with social and environmental values, aiming products for Western consumer markets. The initial response from the cluster was mildly positive, but Jonas and Anders soon realized that their key success factor — the practical implementation of responsible production methods — would prove to be quite a challenge to achieve in an already-formed cluster.

The cluster was headed by Gita, a strong leader who was used to getting her way. She did not agree with the notion that all workers should be given the chance to influence their own situation organized in a union. Since the right to organize and bargain collectively ranked high on Anders' and Jonas' list of priorities related to workers' rights, they debated how to approach the resistance from Gita to this idea. They interviewed some of the workers in the cluster to understand the relationship between them and Gita in depth. The conclusion was that the cluster often benefited from having a strong leader in their external relations. Gita was the one who secured orders, bargained for better prices on raw materials, and made sure the goods were delivered. On the other hand, she did not involve others in her decision making and she did not treat the workers equally. Jonas and Anders were unsure of how to handle the situation. Their business model was built on an inclusive management philosophy, and involving all workers in the change process would be important to succeed; yet, they were dependent on the cluster leader Gita to hold the group together and to manage the production. As a gentle first step, Jonas and Anders invited local union representatives, who informed the workers of their rights according to Bangladeshi law and how to form and operate a local labor union. Jonas and Anders then left it up to the workers to either start up their own union or not.

When paying salaries to the participating producer groups, the cluster operated on a payment per piece basis. The standard originated from the payment method of the buyers, paying a fixed price per piece. This meant that the level of income often fluctuated heavily from month to month for the workers, and that there was no salary at all if there was no order. Jonas and Anders wanted to change this procedure to make sure that all workers would have a steady income, so that they could more easily plan their lives. Getting the workers to agree on a new model based on monthly salaries was not a problem. The challenge came when it was time to decide the amount payable each month. The entrepreneurs had heard of a model called "Living Wage," where salaries are calculated based on the cost of living in a particular area. On the one hand, this model would ensure that workers were able to survive and support their families on the salary they received. On the other hand, the amount would be calculated by the employer, thus not making it possible for the workers to have their say in the matter. Another way would be to negotiate the salary with worker representatives. The question was who to negotiate with and whether the worker representatives would be a reasonable counterparty. Another question that arose in regard to the manufacturing cluster concerned the number of employees that could be included. Due to the informal way the cluster was set up, Jonas and Anders did not want to start their endeavor by unintentionally creating enemies within the cluster. Could this also be solved using worker representatives?

The producer groups in the cluster were used to working at home, producing in between chores and with the help of other family members. It was a flexible solution that enabled the women to take care of the household and still make some money. However, Jonas and Anders found that this model presented a problem in terms of who was actually making the product. There was no way of knowing whether it was the woman herself or her children who were producing the product. How could working conditions be controlled and child labor be avoided in these types of conditions? On the other hand, it would make the lives of the working women more complicated if they had to go to a certain location (like a regular factory) every day to work. Jonas and Anders tried to find arguments for how to encourage the women to work together in one place with controllable conditions. Could there be some positive outcome for the women to manufacture the products in a common place that would get them to agree to the change? In the end, it had to boil down to a managerial decision. Even though Anders and Jonas worked hard to adapt to local customs, Bangladeshi practices fell short when they were up against principles necessary to achieve sustainable production. Therefore, after much debate and checking of available options, a village house with five rooms was rented and turned into a production facility. The location of the house was chosen with care in order for it to become a hub in the jute cluster later on. If everything turned out well, the house could work as a model factory on which other local collaborators could model their production and manufacturing operations — a way of leading by example in the cluster. Another possibility would be to turn it into an exhibition house, so that both ends of the chain (jute growers and potential retail customers) could get an insight into the cluster operations. Other organizations such as JDPC and BJRI would also be invited to have a presence in order to develop the cluster even more. The decision to rent the house in the center was thus a strategic one that would have to be evaluated later on, when manufacturing was in full operation and the cluster formation had developed. The two entrepreneurs also made a mental note to evaluate this decision when manufacturing was in full operation later on.

When evaluating the production methods from an environmental standpoint, Jonas and Anders came to notice that many of the production methods suggested by JDPC and used by the production cluster in Bagatipara included environmentally hazardous glue. Many products were also colored either by spray painting or by submerging the product or raw material in large vats filled with dyeing chemicals that were sometimes hazardous. The glue did not impact the aesthetics or the durability of the final products, but shortened production time. Although skeptical about the harmful glue and colors, Jonas and Anders surveyed the target markets and found that the use of colors would greatly increase their ability to sell their products. They even got an order from a large chain of stores, requesting colored products. The use of glue and chemically dyed colors was common practice all over Bangladesh and was a deeply rooted method within the cluster around Bagatipara. It made the goods cheaper to produce and more attractive to customers. What bothered Jonas and Anders was the environmental impact of this method. They could potentially keep the method for starters to lower startup costs and increase initial sales, and then phase it out as soon as they found more environmentally sound alternatives. But how would it affect their long-term ability to build a consumer brand around socially and environmentally sustainable production? Would this be one of the trade-offs they would have to make in order to actually get the business up and running? Another problem with not using this dangerous method would be to actually explain this decision to the manufacturers and workers in the cluster. They already had some experience of trying to discuss values regarding socially and environmentally sound production. Would they be able to explain that the profitability of the cluster and business endeavor would likely increase in the short term by using the glue and colors, but suffer in the long run? Jonas and Anders argued back and forth while working on the first order that they could produce without the chemicals. But a decision had to be reached within the next few weeks.

Thinking about these issues, Jonas and Anders went back to Sweden to find customers and a location for their Swedish office. Anders would have a decision to bring back to the cluster and the workers when he came back to Bagatipara to check on the quality of the first order.

Setting Up the Office in Sweden and Finding More Entrepreneurs Interested in Sustainability

When looking for a suitable office for the Swedish part of their operations, it felt important to the former business students to be able to continue their learning through interaction with experienced business owners and managers in startups like themselves. Having been introduced to BIC (Business Innovation Center) Factory, a business incubator of newly established companies in Umeå, they filed an application to become a part of this startup cluster and soon got accepted. They were quick to settle in and started looking for ways to improve the exchange of knowledge among companies. Even though they found the dialogue with their peers at BIC Factory very rewarding, the level of commitment to sustainability varied among companies, and Anders and Jonas felt the need for another forum for these thoughts. Therefore, they invited other sustainable companies in the area to an initial meeting with the purpose of creating a cluster focused on sustainability. The group, numbering 10 companies in total, discussed different ways of starting a cluster. One business owner suggested that they should start by erecting a sustainably designed office building where they all could move in. Hence, they would create a natural meeting point for sustainable companies. Another entrepreneur argued that the first step should be to find a financing partner. Whether it be the local municipality, the Swedish government, or the EU, an external financier would enable them to employ a project manager who could facilitate the interaction among companies, thus making it efficient and viable in the long term. A third opinion was that they could keep the cluster informal, while finding hands-on activities that they could build the cluster around. The activities could include holding workshops, starting information campaigns, or selling a commonly developed product within the sustainability scope.

Neither Anders nor Jonas had been involved in starting a cluster from scratch, and they were uncertain about which suggestion to support. They also thought that participating in a cluster like this could have both advantages and disadvantages. For example, they might develop valuable business partnerships. But contributing to the cluster activities would also take time, and perhaps even money. Another issue would be to find entrepreneurs that shared some type of similar values that social and environmental sustainability should be prioritized before monetary profits. Maybe a "sustainability cluster" would attract organizations that just used the word "sustainability" as a marketing claim in order to sell more and take advantage of a growing trend.

Getting the First Contract and Establishing the Ingredient Brand

Returning to Sweden after setting up production in Bangladesh, redQ's first market priority was to secure a first order from Granit. As mentioned earlier, Anders had an initial contact with the Swedish store chain prior to starting actual production in Bangladesh.

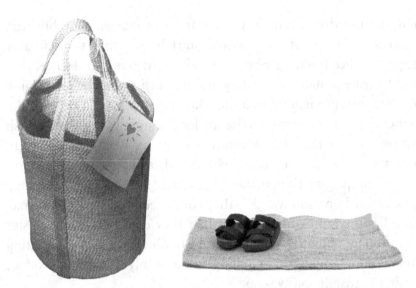

Figure 1. Doormat and cylindrical storage bag delivered to Granit. The pictures are not true to scale.

The Granit chain owned 17 stores in Sweden and Norway selling home decorations and small furniture items, with a focus on storage solutions, to environmentally conscious customers. After showing samples, having negotiations, and waiting nervously for a few weeks, the order for doormats and cylinder-shaped storing bags made of jute arrived (see Figure 1 for a display of these products). It was a large order for a startup, but far from enough to build a successful business in the long term. Also, future orders from the chain were conditioned on the customers' reception of the products when they reached the stores. Thus, Jonas and Anders had to develop the market further.

The initial responses when they started calling potential customers were quite cold, with the standard answer being that sustainability was a hot trend but nothing a customer would pay more to get. Anders and Jonas realized that they would be able to sell more products if they reduced prices to the level of competitors with less ambitions regarding sustainability. But even though they felt that their cost of production was competitive, their expenses were higher than those of their competitors due to paying higher wages and paying more for raw materials. Lowering prices would erase the profit margin from their calculations. And although profits were not the main aim of their business, they still needed to survive on profits — otherwise the business would not be very sustainable, especially for the manufacturing cluster that they had started to tie up. They had to find another way, or at least a good balance between price and acceptable margins.

Another approach would be to infuse more value into the redQ brand as such. If it was perceived as more valuable and really contributing to sustainability, it might be easier to convince retailers to actually give the products a try. They really needed a brand strategy that would match their sustainability criteria. During their process, they had come to think of their brand not primarily as a consumer brand, but as a business-to-business brand that retailers could trust for sustainability, like Gore-Tex in the beginning. This would make other textile brands and designers able to use the redQ materials in their products if they wanted to be sustainable. But how would these values be communicated, and which retailers had end customers that would find this interesting and valuable? To Jonas and Anders, this seemed to be a key issue to solve in order to get the first retailers and orders on board.

Finding Retailers and Designers with Similar Values

Jonas and Anders scanned the market for companies with a sustainable profile, the theory being that these companies would be able to see the added value redQ created for them as well as for the end customer. Run by the Swedish clothing designer who has lent her name to the company, Gudrun Sjödén Design (Gudrun Sjödén, 2011) was identified as such a company. During an initial meeting, the parties concluded that they shared the same values and that Gudrun Sjödén could motivate a slightly higher purchase price by the added value that redQ's responsible production represented to the end customer. Jonas and Anders received designs for a round striped carpet made from jute that would fit with the company's general design profile. The telltale signs of a Gudrun Sjödén product are the vibrant colors that have survived many fashion trends, even when black and gray were at the center. So once again the coloring issue appeared on the agenda, and this time it seemed really important to solve. For the striped carpet, Jonas and Anders were able to identify a coloring pigment extracted from the catechu tree, which is common in Bangladesh. Verifying that the colorant and the coloring process were not harmful, they agreed to make the product for the trial order. Luckily, the products and colors were well received by Gudrun Sjödén and their customers (see Figure 2 for a display of the carpet).

After delivery, more design suggestions arrived from the designers at Gudrun Sjödén, this time with even more coloring on the products.

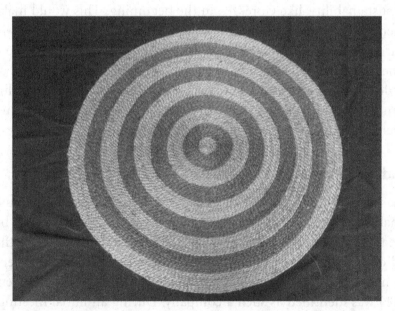

Figure 2.   Colored carpet delivered to Gudrun Sjödén. Note that the picture is not true to scale.

The size of the order they had placed for the carpets clearly showed that Gudrun Sjödén could rapidly become redQ's largest customer. But how would redQ be able to deliver on the wish for all of these different and vibrant colors? There would be no problem to solve the issue technically; numerous coloring plants all around Bangladesh were up for the task. However, none of them colored without chemicals. Also, some colors proved to be much more difficult and hazardous than others, which made the color range quite limited if sustainability was going to be part of the process. Arguing back and forth, the two entrepreneurs were torn between on the one hand securing growth and the possibility to do more good in the future, and on the other hand producing with methods not consistent with their core values.

When discussing the issue with the manufacturing cluster members, Jonas and Anders were positively surprised to note that they now understood the conundrum better than the last time. It seemed as if the value discussions of fair trade, environmental sustainability, and prioritizing these types of values before financial profit were starting to have an effect in the cluster. Some of the cluster members and workers were actually becoming quite good ambassadors for these values. Thus, it seemed as if the discussions over the many months since the initial contact were actually starting to pay off. This led a manufacturer in the cluster to arrange a contact with a coloring plant focusing on traditional and non-toxic plant-based coloring. Discussions were held in parallel to discussions with the designers at Gudrun Sjödén. Finally, it seemed as if the values that Jonas and Anders were building their redQ brand on were working more as a contribution to the discussions and negotiations between stakeholders than as a barrier. Could this type of process be used even when discussing with retailers that were not so focused on the environmentally and socially aware consumers?

The Importance of Designers and the Commercial Value of the Manufacturing Cluster

During the discussions with both Granit and Gudrun Sjödén, the redQ team learnt several things that proved important in their coming endeavors. For example, they came to realize the importance of good designers that knew both the market and how jute could be used in different products. Jonas and Anders had primarily focused on the function of the products, i.e., that they should be sturdy, durable, as smooth as possible, and of course appealing. Now they realized that designers were a bit like famous chefs at restaurants. If a particular experienced designer came up with a design, it was sometimes possible to intuitively relate that design to the actual product. Their designs worked as trademarks. Being the connection between the designers at Gudrun Sjödén and the manufacturing cluster, Jonas and Anders also learnt a lot about the process and what they could actually do with jute. The material kept surprising them in its versatility and, for every new product successfully produced, they realized the enormous potential of the material for all sorts of applications. That Jonas and Anders had good connections with several manufacturers in the cluster in Bagatipara also added to the complexity of what could be achieved. By combining different competencies, methods, and raw material treatments, more members of the cluster could be involved. This also meant that the cluster was on the whole becoming more knowledgeable about which designs were attractive to the Western consumers, and several times during their visits Jonas and Anders would get very good suggestions and prototypes for new products that they could bring back home to potential customers in Sweden.

These two realizations — the importance of designers and the value of the manufacturing cluster — turned out to be very important when they met a young designer at the largest furniture fair in Sweden in 2009. Her name was Linda Zetterman, and she immediately warmed to the social and environmental core values of the redQ brand. She had long nurtured a dream to do something more sustainable in her previous work, but a real opportunity had never presented itself. In discussions with Jonas and Anders, she promised to make a few sketches on designs for jute and another material abundant in Bangladesh, namely rattan. After a few meetings and a visit by Anders to Bagatipara with the sketches, some test products like slippers, stools, and carpets (see Figure 3) were manufactured by several of the workers in different parts of the cluster. The three entrepreneurs decided to publish pictures of the products on their website under the name "Linda Z by redQ," and at the same time offer the products to Granit and another large retail chain in Sweden.

A Breakthrough Contract and New Challenges

Whether it was the cooperation with Linda or successful networking at trade fairs and other meetings, one previously cold contact suddenly became super-hot. Anders and Jonas had contacted this retailer early on, but the discussions had never really amounted to anything interesting (other than a nice pat on the back saying that they were doing something unusual and interesting in the business). The retailer had close to 80 major outlets in Sweden and had recently purchased another chain in home decoration with about 30 stores. Now all of a sudden, they were interested in placing a major order for redQ products that would be sold in all stores across Sweden. It seemed to be a combination of an environmental wake-up call and a wish to renew some of the traditional products and designs associated with the two retail chains.

Jonas and Anders were of course very happy about this interest, but also noticed that the terms and conditions of the order were very hard to negotiate. Everything seemed to be standardized in terms of amounts, dates, payment, and quality criteria. Would they be able to pull this off? Upon signing the order (for more products than they had sold in total previously!), they would be bound to several clauses

Figure 3.   Above: Products developed together with Linda Z. Below: Jonas (right), Anders (left), and Linda (middle) at a furniture fair. Note that the pictures are not true to scale. Above photos by Anders Kylberg; photo below by Kristina Grahn.

connected to substantial fees. For example, if they could not deliver all of the products on the agreed-upon date, the retail chain would subtract a percentage of the payment as each week passed.

Another restriction concerned the products. The retail chain wanted an exclusive right to sell some of the more exclusive designs (which they would help design with their own design team) for a very long period. If redQ decided to make something similar to these products, they would likely face severe legal battles in the future. The problem was that the designs seemed to be quite general; how could they not produce products in the future that were not similar? This raised several issues on how designs are actually protected that they really needed some expert help on.

A third problem was related to the redQ values. Filling this type of order size, where some products could be thought of as "wear and tear" stuff — was that in line with the values Jonas and Anders (and now the entire cluster in Bangladesh) wanted to promote? Could they meet this order while adhering to the rigid sustainability values they had set up? That the cluster needed to be expanded was not a problem; the issue was whether they could get enough workers and manufacturers together without compromising on the quality of the products and the values they wanted to support. A new trade-off was emerging that they felt they needed to address before signing the order.

What seemed to be the big breakthrough for redQ turned out to be the biggest challenge as well so far. And it seemed to Jonas and Anders that several of these issues were intimately connected. It was not at all like the textbook cases they had studied at the business school, where there had always seemed to be a clear separation between branding, manufacturing, design, marketing strategy, and core business values. These all seemed like new problems and issues that were hard to solve in the long run due to the constantly changing circumstances and demands by retailers. What would be the way forward? What did they really want to achieve with redQ?

Bibliography

Asia News (2005). "Almost 10 Million People Work in Slave-like Conditions in Asia." May 5. http://www.asianews.it/news-en/Almost-10-million-people-work-in-slave-like-conditions-in-Asia-3324.html/ [accessed October 10, 2011].

Clean Clothes Campaign (2011). "Improving Working Conditions in the Global Garment Industry." http://www.cleanclothes.org/ [accessed October 10, 2011].

DEM Collective (2011). "Välkommen till Dem Collective." http://www.demcollective.com/ [accessed October 10, 2011].

Economist Intelligence Unit (2010). "Country Report — Bangladesh." http://www.eiu.com/ [accessed October 10, 2011].

Environmental Justice Foundation (2007). "The Deadly Chemicals in Cotton." Report prepared in collaboration with Pesticide Action Network UK, London, UK.

Food and Agriculture Organization of the United Nations (2002). "Agricultural Commodities: Profiles and Relevant WTO Negotiating Issues." http://www.fao.org/righttofood/KC/downloads/vl/docs/Agricultural%20commodities%20-%20Profiles%20and%20relevant%20WTO%20negotiating%20issues.pdf / [accessed October 10, 2011].

Gudrun Sjödén (2011). "Gudrun Sjödén." http://www.gudrunsjoden.com/ [accessed October 10, 2011].

Klohn, W.E. and B.G. Appelgren (1998). "Challenges in the Field of Water Resource Management in Agriculture." In *Sustainable Management of Water in Agriculture: Issues and Policies,* Paris: OECD, pp. 31–39.

Kooistra, K.J., R. Pyburn, and A.J. Termorshuizen (2006). *The Sustainability of Cotton: Consequences for Man and Environment.* Report 223, Science Shop, Wageningen University & Research Centre, The Netherlands.

Watabaran (2011). "Om Watabaran." http://www.watabaran.se/watabaran/about.aspx/ [accessed October 10, 2011].

Worldwatch Institute (2004). *State of the World 2004: Special Focus — The Consumer Society.* New York: Norton.

The Textile Firm ZEEL S.A. or the Never-Ending Story of Marketing as Levitt's "Cinderella"*

Introduction

As occurs in other traditional manufacturing sectors (TMS) such as footwear, toys, or furniture, the European textile industry tends to be focused in geographical clusters. For example, in Italy the cluster in Prato with 1,643 firms stands out, in Portugal the cluster around Porto has 1,087 firms, and in Spain the cluster in Alcoi-Ontinyent has 811 firms (see Figure 1). In fact, some estimates suggest that in Southern European countries more than 25% of TMS activity is carried out in a regional organizational model in the form of a network (Boix, 2009).

Some of the reasons that help to explain the tendency to concentrate geographically are found in the advantages that firms in an industry obtain from a regional network model. A. Marshall (1890), whose work centered on the study of the textile industry in Manchester (UK), pointed out the important external economies that resulted from the division of labor between specialized units

*Francisco Puig and Marcelo Royo-Vela, both at University of Valencia (Spain), developed this case for educational purposes only. This work is part of a broader investigation, "Location and Competitiveness in European TMS," which is financed by the Research Project GV/2011/025 of the Generalitat Valenciana (Spain). Although some names are fictitious, the case is based on a real situation.

Figure 1. Examples of geographical agglomerations of textile firms in the EU (source: Bureau van Dijk, 2008).

(machinery and workers) and a location that provided certain socioeconomic elements (industrial environment). The characteristics of these smaller manufacturing enterprises (SMEs, with less than 250 employees) and the empirical evidence that related greater competitiveness to location meant that politicians, businessmen, and academicians saw a model in that type of network organization that permitted smaller firms to compete with large, vertically integrated firms. This influence was named the *cluster* or *industrial district effect*.

After the oil crisis of the 1970s ended, in many business environments expressions such as "Now the problem of the small business is not its size, but the being out of touch" started circulating, with paradigms such as Silicon Valley–technology (USA) or Sassuolo–ceramics (Italy). So much so that in the 1980s, articles on clusters and industrial districts (see, e.g., Becattini, 2004; Porter, 1990; Saxenian, 1994) as well as the socioeconomic and business reality that existed in those regions became consolidated at all geographic levels into concentrations such as the one in Alcoi-Ontinyent.

Alcoi-Ontinyent's Industrial Cluster

Like any industrial cluster, the one named Alcoi-Ontinyent (hereafter, "CAO") has diffuse geographic limits, given that for administrative aspects the firms and their locational decisions have defined its frontiers. Therefore, in order to identify the cluster we had to turn to one of the most widely accepted techniques in the literature, which is based on the specialization coefficient (Puig and Marques, 2011).[1]

The application of this technique identified a geographical area formed by eight towns with almost 200,000 inhabitants (some 30,000 being directly employed in textiles), measuring around 4,000 km², and located approximately 150 km from Valencia and Alicante and 400 km from Madrid. In this area the majority of textile firms are SMEs (99%), which are very specialized (vertically disintegrated). Their location, the large number of jobs, the structure of the firms, and the strong compatibility between the productive activity and the

---

[1]The specialization coefficient (SC) is a statistic used to assess the presence of an activity (in our case, home-textile production) in a specific territory related to the presence of this activity in the overall reference population. Its mathematical expression is as follows:

$$CE_{ij} = \frac{E_{ij}/E_j}{E_i/E_n},$$

where E_{ij} refers to the volume of employment in the activity i in the territorial entity j, E_j indicates the total employment in the territorial entity j, E_i shows the total employment in the activity i at the national level, and E_n represents the total volume of employment at the national level.

Table 1. Towns in the CAO.

Cluster Alcoi-Ontinyent	Occupied Textile Clothing	Specialization Coefficient
Banyeres de Mariola	1,304	28.25
Agullent	444	27.52
Albaida	1,012	24.45
Bocairent	627	19.96
Ontinyent	4,407	19.30
Muro de Alcoi	960	18.08
Cocentaina	1,313	17.99
Alcoi	5,071	12.75
TOTAL	15,138	17.10

Source: Instituto Nacional de Estadística (2004).

socioeconomic aspects of the zone mean that we can affirm that it is a true geographically remote industrial cluster (GRIC). For example, there are 444 people in Agullent dedicated to textiles — 27.52 times more than the national population that works in the same sector (see Table 1).

The CAO's evolution, in a way, has been similar to that of a product's life cycle: birth, growth, and maturity (and perhaps decline). The reasons for its present-day situation can be summarized in one word: globalization. For the European textile industry — and other countries such as Canada or the USA — the free trade agreements (World Trade Organization, 2008) led to an invasion of Asian products, which have been seriously threatening its survival. This is because to face up to greater and fiercer competition, the firms opted to increase imports, subcontract the more labor-intensive activities, or relocate. In such a way, it could be said that for the European case the most visible result of this greater globalization and of the firms' strategies has been the transfer of productive activity to areas with lower salary costs (Morocco, Turkey, or China) and a greater intensity in commercialization and marketing activities.

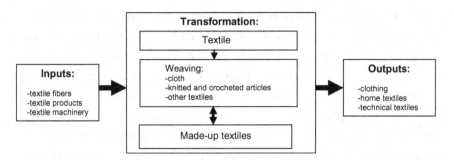

Figure 2.   The textile-clothing production process.

Recent studies point out that regionally the result of the globalization process (especially from 2005 to 2010) has been unequal and heterogeneous, as the final textile products offered by each region are very different, ranging from those more intensive in labor ("low-tech") to those more intensive in capital ("high-tech"). For example, according to the productive process in the textile-clothing industry (see Figure 2), we can observe textile activities or subsectors centered on the initial and preparatory operations of spinning (Inputs); others are more linked to spinning, weaving, and textile ennoblement or finishes (Transformation); and yet others are linked to the production of final products (Outputs). Those more linked to the final product (home and technical textiles) are the ones that have a greater added value and are less affected by globalization.

In addition, at a company level, the decisions relative to the level of vertical integration (make-or-buy) and the relocation of productive activities and subsectors have had a significant influence on performance and survival. An example of this is ZEEL S.A., a company whose revenue and return on assets (ROA) grew about 6% a year on average during the period 2005–2010.

The Company ZEEL S.A.

ZEEL S.A. is an SME founded in 1976. It is located in Agullent (Valencia) in the heart of the CAO. It has 64 employees, and invoiced almost €15 million (US$20 million) in 2010. Its principal subsector is home and technical textiles. For home products, its principal clients are in Central Europe (Germany, France, Italy, Portugal, Morocco, etc.) (60%), while its market for technical products is mainly national.

Its competitors are Asian countries whose labor is cheaper. With respect to its suppliers, though some raw materials are bought around the world, many parts of the productive process are subcontracted to firms in the CAO. It is also noteworthy that ZEEL S.A. maintains a strong regional association with different university institutions, business organizations, and technological institutes.

The key to its success could be that, since the late 1990s, ZEEL S.A. has opted for diversification related to textile products with a strong innovative component (thermal insulation, acoustic absorption, ecological materials, etc.). In the beginning, this required a large expenditure in facilities and machinery. Over the course of time, this strategic commitment to innovation permitted a robust repositioning in the competitively hostile surroundings of the textile industry. However, this commitment seems to have obscured the company's marketing subsystem, thereby limiting its growth.

The Function of Marketing in ZEEL S.A.

The marketing manager of ZEEL S.A., Anabella Ruiz, is worried about the negative effect that globalization is having on the CAO. Many of its suppliers are becoming marketers of imported final products, and consequently the cluster's model is beginning to break up. Others are following this trend, which has plunged her into greater uncertainty. Not only is there a shortage of marketing synergies within the cluster, but there is also the belief that ZEEL S.A.'s market orientation (as a marketing philosophy) is no longer appropriate. She summarized the situation in the following way: "We are losing sources of external economies, and at present, the commercialization of our products is neither technical nor efficacious." All in all, a worrying panorama.

Although Anabella's academic formation is adequate and she has many ideas, it is not easy to put marketing into practice or for her to be listened to. Fortunately, the company allowed her to be part of its design team together with the innovation, production, and sales departments.

The meeting with García, the sales manager, was not altogether satisfactory. The sales team was only worried about pricing and selling, but there was neither a correct discount policy nor an analysis of the product portfolio. The sales team had very little negotiating range with the clients. They only had two possible tariffs and they ignored the product margin they were selling. Worse was the lack of flow of marketing information between the company's different departments, and the lack of continuity in the decisions taken. At least Anabella could act as an intermediary between the designer of the products and the yearly collection, and between the designer of the catalogue and the image to be transmitted. Thanks to Anabella's mediation, the projected image now has value and is coherent with the target market segment and position sought. However, the day-to-day routine is making the process of analysis, planning, organization, and control of marketing difficult. There is no time to think.

The information about the competition is different. Here, several departments — principally technicians — are participating with the objective of testing competitors' products. Nevertheless, the information is not being used to improve marketing, but only to see the deficiencies of the competitors' products against ZEEL S.A.'s products. The products are always subjected to all of the technical tests and possible certifications with the clients in mind.

Marketing System

There are problems with ZEEL S.A.'s strategic marketing, in part created by an organizational structure problem. Unlike the majority of the firms in the CAO, there is a marketing department (although consisting of Anabella alone) and there is operational marketing; however, the marketing department is subordinate to the sales and production departments, which are orientated to sales and the product, respectively.

The company's webpage clearly shows a philosophy of corporate social responsibility. It is very concerned about the environment, the workers, and the suppliers. But aside from the product and brand portfolio, press cuttings, sponsorships and contests (that is to say, public relations), as well as the actual webpage, the company's marketing is not clearly shown. Thus, the flow of information and production seems to head in the same direction, that is, from the company to the marketplace.

The company, lamented Anabella, does not count on specialized personnel, or a research and development department coordinated with the marketing department that deals with detecting needs or improvements by the technological progress of existing products. There is not really a flow of information from the market to the company by means of a marketing department or function; instead, the process of innovation depends on the chain of supply, i.e., the suppliers of raw materials. "It is funny," Anabella said ironically, "Not only am I subordinate to production and sales, but moreover, innovative ideas have their origin in the chain of supply." These suppliers can supply a determined input, such as natural soybean, bamboo fiber, or artificial polyester fiber. The question that is asked in the company is: "Given our technology, what type of product can we manufacture with this textile fiber that may be accepted in the market?"

At present the price variable is of utmost importance, as it has become fundamental in relation to the acceptance of the product in times of crisis. So much so that once an innovation based on an input is defined, the production function explores ways to minimize costs, and then later looks for the external support from technological institutes or universities that certify the corresponding quality. In this way, the trinomial innovation–efficiency–guarantee facilitates access to a new segment or client, as in the case of the product SonoZEEL® and the construction sector.[2]

On other occasions — and this now seems more like a subsystem of marketing intelligence — the idea or opportunity for a product originates in the information supplied by the sales team, that is to say, the people who the clients talk to. As such, the company initiates manufacturing capability once the minimum production quantity restrictions have been overcome. Another route to innovation is based on manufacturing products that already exist in the market using the company's own technological capability, for example a product based on polyester such as a blanket, making good use of the *made-in effect* which in this case is positive for a country like Spain. Thanks to this effect, ZEEL S.A. has a competitive advantage over blankets manufactured in China.

ZEEL S.A.'s internationalization process is nothing special in relation to the other firms in the CAO. There was no obvious strategic planning for entry into exterior markets. It happened with a very gradual domino effect via exportation, which in turn resulted in the creation of the export department within the company. A common denominator among the firms in this region is that exportation existed practically from the beginning, but without prior planning, let alone a search for synergies. As with the majority of textile firms in the CAO, ZEEL S.A.'s internationalization was a reactive strategic action: there was an excess of productive capacity for the national market, so an outlet for the excess was sought at an international level.

---

[2]SonoZEEL® is an innovation based on polyester matting that offers better results, and can act as a substitute to the habitual fiberglass or rockwool as a thermal and acoustic insulating component in construction, especially in partition walls. It is not really an innovative product as it already existed, but it was given a new application in the construction sector as a thermal and acoustic insulator in contrast to the habitual use of polyester wool as a filling for eiderdowns or blankets.

The marketing system in response to international competition, especially from China, should be highlighted. ZEEL S.A. counts on an added value transformed into a competitive advantage: service. As Anabella stated, "People need something more than what is supplied in the containers full of products from the Asian manufacturers, and we as producers have presence, proximity, technical and productive flexibility, and design capability. All of this implies something that notably sets us apart: the power to render the service that clients require."

Besides this strategy of service orientated to the client, ZEEL S.A. is present in a variety of segments and uses a differentiated group of marketing strategies to achieve the commercial objectives, which are fixed annually. This is shown in Table 2.

Restrictions to Proactive Marketing

Anabella thinks that her company gives a lot of importance to the establishment and development of relationships of commitment and confidence with the clients. Likewise, she considers that ZEEL S.A. is a serious and responsible company: "We do what we say we will, laboratory tests are always the basis of our work, and I always back up the characteristics of the products that we deliver to our clients with technical reports," Anabella said. She added, "They see us as serious, responsible, and reliable producers. We are present in several technological institutes that carry out the tests on the products that we deliver to the clients." Hence, she enthusiastically underlines the level of satisfaction measured during the last year for the brand Milenio®, which scored about 8 on a scale of 10 points; ZEELsa® and SonoZEEL® also scored similarly.

The mechanisms for communication with clients depend on the customer. There are occasions when the wholesaler calls the factory directly and makes an order. The international area is different, and ZEEL S.A. tries to adapt to the preferences of the clients by sending agents. For example, a client in Saudi Arabia may need a high-context

Table 2. Segments and marketing strategies.

Segment/Client	Positioning	Brands (registered)	Product	Distribution	Communication	Price (profitability and margin)
National market: • Manufacturers of upholstered furniture and their networks of decoration shops • Wholesalers • Advisors, architects and designers, interior decorators International market: • Wholesalers-distributors • Manufacturers of upholstered furniture	Price–quality: medium-high	Milenio®	Upholstery	Direct and/or through agents	Catalogues and samples; Proposte Fair (Italy)	High (good profitability and margin)

(Continued)

Table 2. (*Continued*)

Segment/Client	Positioning	Brands (registered)	Product	Distribution	Communication	Price (profitability and margin)
Spain and Portugal: • Wholesalers • Retailers • Baby/childcare retailers (age 0–4 years) International market: • Wholesalers with their own network of retailers	Price–quality: high (the only better fibers are natural fibers like camel fiber, wool, etc.)	ZEELsa®	Blankets	Direct and/or through agents for zone and distribution channel	Catalogues and samples; Gentextil Fair (Germany)	High (low profitability and margin)
National market only (due to transportation costs): • Home use (textile upholsterers and mattress makers) • Technical use (construction material suppliers and soundproofing system installers)	Manufacturer of ecological brand, healthy and innovative	SonoZEEL®	Unwoven textiles (polyester wool)	Direct and/or through agents specialized in the segment	Partners' catalogues (construction material suppliers); sponsors of acoustic congresses	High (good profitability and margin)

commercial visit with all that it signifies. Anabella centralizes all of the information and the contacts with the clients. She acknowledges that there is no immediacy, but there is a desire to listen to the client. Nevertheless, she admits that she lacks time and personnel to be able to have more direct contact and primary information about the clients. Given the size and position of the marketing department in the company's organizational structure, Anabella thinks that the level of interdepartmental collaboration, especially with the production and sales departments, is not as efficient and efficacious as it could be. Therefore, the company is slow in relation to developments and requests. Production holds back lines and launches. Anabella misses being able to think with more tranquility, and having the time and energy to finish things: "We are very efficient at beginning and pushing potential projects, but we rarely finish them."

Anabella is proud that the company, with the brands Milenio® and ZEELsa®, is present at the two most important trade fairs in the sector at the European level. They present their yearly collection in Italy at the Proposte upholstery and decoration fair — a very restrictive and selective fair, where there are only 120 expositors. Clients are usually very loyal to products, factories, and brands. Even the invited guests are filtered to decide who can visit the fair. In addition, the company is present at the Gentextil Fair in Germany with the brand ZEELsa® and its collection of blankets.

Marketing Communication

In addition to the communication used in the different segments, Anabella pays a lot of attention to public relations and sponsoring to transmit an image of ZEEL S.A. as an innovative company, in addition to trying to maintain good relationships and the reputation of the company with the local communities, universities, business trusts, suppliers, and workers. Thus, they generate publicity and press communications in a systematic form in national and local newspapers. The same can be said about the radio, along with appearances and news items on national TV channels. The company is also featured in interviews and news reports on the regional TV channels, in specialized sectoral magazines, and in the publications of technological institutes and associations. They sponsor football and darts teams, acoustic congresses, and design contests directed at local university students. This latter action aims to develop the renown and image of an innovative company, considering future clients and workers at ZEEL S.A. In Anabella's words, "The design contest is fantastic in relation to the image of ZEEL S.A. in the CAO, as it has influence in the university population, allowing us to create a source of recruitment and the development of a real social network."

Anabella has not forgotten information technology, and she is beginning to develop the bases for a presence on the Internet. She is aware that if the company does not do it, others — be they clients, consumers, or competitors — will occupy that space. There are principally two planned instruments: a ZEEL S.A. blog, where they can upload different articles about the cluster, the company, the brands, innovation, etc.; and the management of social networks through a community manager with a profile more related to marketing than information technology.

Having reached this point, Anabella recognizes her limitations and the need to consult with firms specialized in virtual media planning such as Media Planning and Zenith Media. Between her and other specialists, they will establish a strategy to follow and decide which networks they should be in; one possibility is "LinkedIn," considering the technical and professional segment. Anabella thinks that this is a way to reach many people at a low cost and to analyze the feedback in terms of interactions and bi-directionality.

Final Reflections

For decades, the cluster effect permitted small textile manufacturing firms to be very competitive. However, globalization has provoked the closure of many firms, and has also forced others towards the relocation of their productive centers to regions with lower salary costs. In some cases, such as that of ZEEL S.A., globalization has led to a reorientation of firms' activities toward those with greater added value: innovation and marketing.

Faced with this globalization, ZEEL S.A. has managed to react efficaciously, but only partially. Nowadays it is considered by the stakeholders to be a solid and innovative company; and in spite of its reduced size, the fact that it is a manufacturer means that it can offer. integrated solutions to its clients based on service. This aspect is in part inherited from the cluster in which it is located. But also, this intensity in the development of abilities and know-how to produce better has limited the company in developing other skills more linked to marketing activities. All of this leads us to say that they do not know how to carry out better marketing.

Anabella is one of the few marketing managers in the CAO. She is far from the model of those firms where a well-developed marketing department exists. In addition, her manager focuses mainly on sales and catalogues. Anabella wants the marketing department in her firm to undergo more development and have more resources and personnel, as occurs with some other leading firms in the sector.

Bibliography

Becattini, G. (2004). *Industrial Districts: A New Approach to Industrial Change*. Cheltenham: Edward Elgar.

Boix, R. (2009). "The Empirical Evidence of Industrial Districts in Spain." In Becattini, G., M. Bellandi, and L. De Propis (eds.), *A Handbook of Industrial Districts*, Cheltenham: Edward Elgar, pp. 343–359.

Bureau van Dijk (2008). "Amadeus — A Database of Comparable Financial Information for Public and Private Companies across Europe." https://amadeus.bvdinfo.com/.

Ghauri, P. and P.R. Cateora (2006). *International Marketing*, 2nd ed. Berkshire: McGraw-Hill.

Instituto Nacional de Estadística (2004). *Censos de Población y Vivienda 2001.* http://www.ine.es/censo/es/inicio.jsp/ [accessed August 19, 2009].

Kohli, K.A. and B.J. Jaworski (1993). "Market Orientation: Antecedents and Consequences." *Journal of Marketing,* 57(3), 53–70.

Lambin, J.J., R. Chumpitaz, and I. Schuiling (2007). *Market-Driven Management: Strategic and Operational Marketing,* 2nd ed. Hampshire: Palgrave Macmillan.

Marshall, A. (1890). *Principles of Economics.* London: Macmillan.

Morgan, R.M. and S. Hunt (1994). "The Commitment-Trust Theory of Relationship Marketing." *Journal of Marketing,* 58(3), 20–38.

Porter, M. (1990). *The Competitive Advantage of Nations.* New York: The Free Press.

Puig, F. and H. Marques (2011). *Territory, Specialization and Globalization in European Manufacturing.* Abingdon: Routledge.

Ravald, A. and C. Grönroos (1996). "The Value Concept and Relationship Marketing." *European Journal of Marketing,* 30(2), 19–30.

Saxenian, A. (1994). *Regional Advantage: Culture and Competition in Silicon Valley and Route 128.* Cambridge, MA: Harvard University Press.

World Trade Organization (2008). "Textiles Monitoring Body (TMB) Agreement on Textiles and Clothing." http://www.wto.org/english/tratop_e/texti_e/texintro_e.htm/ [accessed January 14, 2008].

Case 6

Interactive Recycling — Service Innovation in a Green Cluster*

Be Green Umeå

"What is going on with this region?," the man thought as he was biking down Östra Kyrkogatan on one of the many crowded bike paths in the city. The wind whispered in the birch trees as he continued towards the old city hall. "If they want to change this town into a city where everyone bikes, why not design more bike paths? This is getting ridiculous!" He was on his way to return a rental bike that he had been using for free during the last week. He parked the bike outside the old city hall and stepped into the office, which was being used by one of the projects aiming to create a sustainable region.

Carina was in the office talking to some of her colleagues around the coffee machine. Carina saw the man coming into their office with the bike key in his hand.

"Hi, are you here to return the bike? Did everything go well?," Carina asked.

"Yes, it was great! I would also like to congratulate you and your team on the new program. I saw it in the newspapers this morning," the man said.

"Thanks! It is so exciting that it is a five-year project. I am actually on my way to the town hall for a meeting about how we are going to

---

*Tomas Blomquist, Sofia Isberg, and Helena Renström, all from the Umeå School of Business and Economics, Umeå University (Sweden), developed this case for educational purposes only.

work," Carina responded. The man left and Carina took her cup of coffee and walked over to her desk.

"I need to make some notes on what's going on and what I need to do," Carina thought as she sat down and found the keyboard under a pile of papers and started to type:

Green Citizens of Europe[1]

The Umeå region has about 150,000 inhabitants, and it consists of six small municipalities working together to create a sustainable region. During the last decade, the region has become one of the fastest-growing regions in Sweden and the development of the university is an important part of this growth. The region has been able to attract a young population with ambitions to change society and the way resources are used.

Local politicians, the business community, the university, and the political parties in Umeå have all been strongly involved in the development of the region. Examples of developments are several different programs ranging from railroad projects and biofuel development from forestry products to the development of windmill parks. In these cases, the region has been a partner and sponsor in different activities with the help of several other sponsors. Some of the sponsors and partners have been the County Administrative Board in Västerbotten, Region Västerbotten, the Swedish Agency for Economic and Regional Growth (Tillväxtverket), and the European Union.

Within the cluster, there are a number of both ongoing and past projects. Past projects were the creation of the first sustainable car block including a car dealer, a filling station, and a restaurant. Another project is the initiative to become a world leader in sustainable building and construction in cold climates. A third project is the use of fast rechargeable buses. A fourth project has the aim of making Umeå a sustainable city with no CO_2. A fifth is the

---

[1] The project "Green Citizens of Europe" was awarded the prize for the Best Urban Planning Project in Sweden in 2011.

reconstruction of several flats installing information technology (IT) solutions for monitoring energy use and waste. A sixth would be the construction of Sweden's largest solar power plant. The list of initiatives could be longer. The common denominator is the aim to change the region into a green region. Many of the projects aim to change tangible experiences of the region, but more and more they emphasize the importance of influencing the citizens' behaviors, attitudes, and values.

The new project "Green Citizens of Europe" will fit into this stream of projects to create a sustainable region, a project where Umeå will take on a leading role in the development of a new and sustainable Europe. There will be a need to coordinate with other large projects such as "Umeå — European Capital of Culture 2014" and ongoing infrastructure projects, together with initiatives taken on national and EU levels. Projects within Umeå unite public organizations, policy makers, local and national firms, and universities. They have made the region into a dynamic web of activities. This will create challenges when coordinating activities and finding ways to put together project groups to be able to utilize benefits from the different projects.

Carina turned around to Emma, one of her colleagues at the office. "Do you have an idea of how many sustainable projects we have in the region and in the city?," Carina asked.

"I guess there are several, and many of them are perhaps overlapping regarding means and aims. I would call Albert at the municipality planning administration. He will know about all projects," Emma responded. "He will probably give you a list on what is going on in the Ålidhem district, where they are going to rebuild large parts of the blocks of apartments. I also heard that they are planning to work with both the local housing company Bostaden and the waste management company UMEVA on different projects in order to find new ways to improve the level of recycling. Have you heard about it?," Emma asked.

"I heard about it in a meeting some weeks ago, but I definitely need to know more if I am to work on these types of issues. I will call Albert right away," said Carina.

FältCom — The M2M Company

Three blocks from the old town hall, Kalle, a reporter for a technology magazine specializing in business development, was on his way to FältCom to interview Mikael, the CEO of the company. FältCom is a fast-growing company in the city. FältCom received the 2009 award prize for the best export company in Umeå.

Kalle took the elevator up to FältCom's office where Mikael was waiting. They picked up coffee from the coffee machine on their way to the conference room. On the table, Kalle saw an approximately 12 cm × 12 cm large box made of aluminum. He recognized it from FältCom's webpage and the picture he had seen. It was easy to see that it was a technology gadget full of different connectors for connecting Internet Protocol (IP) cables and inputs for digital and analog sensors.

"Is this a Mobile Internet IP Server (MIIPS)? And is that the outer part of your system used to gather input from different devices?," Kalle asked.

"That's right. It is present in a wide range of products such as safety cameras, alarm systems and eco-driving devices for trucks, equipment for process monitoring, and much more," Mikael said.

"How did the company start and why Umeå? And what is this type of business?," Kalle asked while picking up his notebook and pens out of his backpack.

"The large distances here in the north of Sweden meant that we developed solutions to handle different problems and control processes remotely at an early stage. The problems these distances have caused resemble the challenges multinational companies meet when they need to safely monitor equipment and processes in different parts of the world. Our product and the system around it help companies to safely manage and monitor equipment remotely with the highest standard of encryption and data transfer," said Mikael, pointing to the robust aluminum box on the table.

"Would you say that you are in the telecom or the IT industry?," Kalle continued.

"You could say it's telecom. We use the term 'M2M,' machine-to-machine. Our niche is to ensure communication between different machines, M2M," Mikael said with a smile.

Kalle continued, "But how did you come to this point of development? What is the history of the product and the company, and what does the business model look like?"

Mikael turned around and picked up another box. "This one is smaller than the first, but with the same robust look. This is where it all started," said Mikael and put it on the table.

"This company started as a pure product company and it was really set up for product sales. The founder, Bosse, is retired now. He built up a company called TeleAlarm Care, at the time a sales unit within the phone company Telia. TeleAlarm Care was then acquired by Securitas. As a severance pay he received a spin-off product, an elevator phone. It was with this lift phone that he started this company, using the spin-off product the new owner did not have any interest in," Mikael said as he pointed to the elevator phone on the table.

Mikael continued: "We have more or less abandoned elevator phones as a product today, together with the pure product business model. Elevator phones are a 'one-time offer' that you sell and then it's done. It is expected that the lift phone should be installed and be able to operate during the period of the elevator's whole life span. If it is used in an office or in residential buildings, it could last for many years or decades. Lift phones and alarm systems are partly using the same standards, and that was a starting point for the development of the M2M system MIIPS, which is another part of the company. It is a systems business built around an M2M system for mobile communication between several systems. Through our

MIIPS system, we can both monitor and maintain other systems. It is a systems business. Here we have turned the business model from being product-oriented to a model that is more focused on selling services around the product." Mikael brought out some brochures that showed sketches of how systems operate with different equipment to be able to remotely communicate with different MIIPS units and server solutions that collect and control the operation.

"This must have been an exciting journey. It sounds like the MIIPS has a completely different business model," Kalle said as he looked at the brochures.

"Yes, that's right," Mikael continued. "We have made a business transition. I am an engineer, and we were all engineers in the beginning with a clear focus on the product. Now we have moved towards a focus on the customers and their needs. This is a transformation and we are still in it. We continually spend time talking about who we are and how we are working to reshape and change our business model. This is important and we must work on it to be able to be competitive."

"How do you work with new customers and their request for solutions?," Kalle asked.

"Looking at the development of new offers which use the MIIPS system, we have to be very product-focused to produce the first products, systems, and services. But then you have to twist this to become more market-oriented. We are not fully market-oriented, but we have come a long way," said Mikael.

Kalle thought: "Surely they have come a long way. They are growing continuously and are taking orders from prestigious clients such as TeliaSonera, the Swedish Transport Administration, Schenker, and Multicom. Security companies all have tough requirements on the solutions and their functions." Kalle looked up from his notes and asked, "But what will the future business model look like?"

Mikael continued, "Personally I believe that there is no future in selling hardware. If you are to have a future, you must have a business model that uses our unique offer and combines it with different services and features. If we can make services and features that meet our customers' needs, it will become a very strong and unique offer. We manufacture our hardware in China and the cost is reduced year by year. There is a risk that the profit margins will be lower on the hardware and at the same time we will need to allocate more and more money to storage as the sales increase. Following these developments, we have perhaps 10 years left before many of our competitors could do the same thing. Being able to incorporate services and service innovations into our product will be crucial for the growth of this company."

Mikael and Kalle were interrupted by a knock on the door. "Excuse me, I am sorry for interrupting," Maria said as she opened the door. "I need to talk to you about a client and I cannot wait!"

Mikael said, "OK! Sorry Kalle, back in a few minutes."

"That is fine! I'll wait," Kalle responded. He took out his laptop and searched for the County of Västerbotten. "Mikael said that many of the problems linked to large distances in the north of Sweden also constitute problems for many international firms. Could that be true?"

Kalle's Internet search on Västerbotten revealed the following information:

> Västerbotten is a county in Sweden, about 650 km north of Stockholm, with around 260,000 inhabitants. Traditional industry based on ore, forests, and water has been important for the area, but new types of industries are growing and becoming more and more influential for the growth of the region.
>
> Skellefteå and Umeå are the two largest cities in the region, with the city of Umeå as the largest with 114,000 inhabitants. About 85% of the region's workforce is found here, and almost 90% of the region's gross regional product comes out of these two cities. Umeå is a young university town with about 35,000 students and a large university hospital, and constitutes one of the most

expansive regions in Sweden. The city has recently been appointed the "European Capital of Culture 2014." Apart from these two cities, the county of Västerbotten is one of the most sparsely populated areas in Sweden with 2.8% of the Swedish population living here. The size of the region is the second largest in Sweden (about the same size as Denmark), which means that there are large distances between small villages and municipalities with, on average, 4.7 inhabitants per square kilometer. Europe's largest nature reserve, Vindelfjällen, is in the northwest part of the county, and the distance between the coastal areas and the mountains on the border to Norway is about 400 km.

"400 km! If you have these types of distances, you don't want to drive and check out if the equipment is working or not. I can see the point of being able to remotely control and overlook equipment at a distance. With the combination of mobile technology, it would be easy to install an MIIPS in almost all places on the globe. This company must have the potential to grow globally if they will be able to scale up their operations," Kalle thought.

Mikael returned before Kalle had sorted out all of his thoughts. "We need to continue another day; this seems to be taking longer than I expected. Could we see each other again on Wednesday next week at 9 a.m.?," Mikael asked.

"Yes, that would work for me," Kalle responded.

Kalle thought about the meeting and what the CEO of FältCom had said while he was walking down to one of the cafés: "What FältCom is experiencing is quite a relevant problem for many of the smaller technology-based manufacturing companies that are found in the area. FältCom is not alone in its struggle to compete with low-cost production in Asia, where it is only a matter of time before the technology is copied and used by competitors. The problem for these types of companies is that they may not be big or financially strong enough to explore and develop the technology much more. They need to focus on what their engineers are able to innovate, and at the same time understand the possibilities the technology offers when it comes to developing content and services that are valuable for the end users. But are they really up to the challenge? Do they have the ability to go through the process of transforming the business model as well as the organizational culture from an engineer/product-focused company to a company focusing on maximizing customer value through highly skilled employees developing innovative services together with the customer?"

Everyday IT

In another part of the town, a group of researchers at the Umeå School of Business and Economics and the Umeå Institute of Design came across a call for applications focusing on new and innovative projects that combined research, design, and IT development. The call "Everyday IT" was meant to lead to innovations focusing on how technology could help the everyday activities of people. The call was brought up during a meeting. As a result of this, a series of meetings started. After several meetings with FältCom, Umeå Institute of Design, Umeå School of Business and Economics, the municipality of Umeå, and several other stakeholders, a proposal was sent in and FältCom took on the role as project owner. The project proposal could be summarized in the following way:

This project seeks to change households' behavior and attitudes to waste management, and thereby improve the contribution that individuals' daily behavior provides for the creation of a better environment and a more sustainable society. The overall aim of the project is to develop an interactive information service that helps individuals and households to make environmentally sound decisions regarding waste management. We start from households and individuals — those who, in their everyday lives, choose to sort or not to sort their household waste. How can an everyday activity be made more enjoyable and interesting so that the individual understands the benefit for society that their individual actions contribute to?

In the project, design methodology will be used to formulate the problem from three perspectives: users, society, and business. The focus is on service and on finding new concepts for further development of a technology already used to provide decision support and collect information at a distance in various situations.

The project will develop a prototype for interactive and structural services. FältCom can further develop this prototype in order to sell it to other residential and recycling companies in Sweden and in Scandinavia. At the societal level, the project will increase the level of awareness among citizens and policy makers about new innovative methods of waste separation and recycling, leading to a more sustainable society.

In the proposal, a figure was drawn showing all partners that would be involved in the project (see Figure 1). Six months later, the proposal was approved and the project started.

Many Ideas Coming Together

The first meeting among partners involved in the project took place in the conference room at FältCom. Representatives of the Municipality of Umeå, the housing company Bostaden, the waste management company UMEVA, the design school, and the business school were present. After the first round of greetings, Tomas, the project manager at FältCom, presented the different products and services that FältCom had developed. After his presentation had been made, Tomas asked Carina to describe the project "Be Green Umeå."

Carina started: "I see this project as an important part of the development of 'Be Green Umeå.' 'Be Green Umeå' is Umeå Municipality's project office working on sustainability in the region, and we emphasize that it is important that people become motivated and engaged in recycling. We use a variety of small activities where people can test ways to act more sustainably, and hopefully afterwards

Figure 1. Groups and stakeholders involved in the interactive recycling project.

maintain a new behavior. Our experience from sustainable travel patterns is that you need to motivate and engage people to be able to change behaviors."

The representative from UMEVA continued the meeting, describing the work that the waste management company was already doing, explaining the methods for measuring the weight of the waste in terms of different properties, and talking about ongoing projects, technical devices, and facts and figures. "We are currently involved in projects that rebuild recycling rooms. UMEVA and Umeå are actually quite unique, since we started to collect data so early on. We both weigh garbage and recycled material, and we are able to collect data on each garbage room. Each and every trash and recycling bin has a unique number, and we collect data from the bins every time we collect garbage and recycled material. Everything is organized in a database according to each bin, fraction of waste, weight, date, and address of garbage room. The data are not on an individual level though, but rather more aggregated. This information is used to invoice the landlords. We have a lot of information about waste disposal in Umeå, and if you need figures on how much we collect I am the person to talk to!"

Tomas asked if it would be possible to use radio-frequency identification (RFID) tags so that people could log into the recycling room, throw away their waste, and then log out again. "Could we measure the weight in the garbage rooms directly?"

The representative of UMEVA responded, "It would be possible, but it would mean that we need to install weighing machines under each bin and that will be expensive. Compared to the solution we have today where each truck measures the weights, it would be very costly but surely it would be possible to do."

"But is it really the weight we are interested in?," Carina asked. "We are more concerned about teaching people to sort their waste; the recycling room must be built in a pedagogical manner to ensure that the residents understand where to throw glass, paper, and plastic. Or even better, to ensure that they buy less and reuse more so that we could decrease the amount of waste."

At this point, the representative of the housing company Bostaden AB entered the discussion: "Together with UMEVA we have a couple of projects to upgrade some recycling rooms, but also to make new recycling rooms where we use new technologies. But as always, we need to work in close collaboration with the residents living in our houses and with the local proprietor managers. Our clients and their interest always come first, and we need to think about the costs. If the system — or what you call it — costs too much, no one will be able to buy it."

"You are right, we need to find a solution that is commercially attractive to the housing companies," Tomas commented.

"We will get more knowledge about many of these things during the first phase of the project," said the representative of Umeå

Institute of Design, who continued: "During that phase, we are going to consider the service design by looking at household recycling processes, and follow a normal customer journey from the store to the waste bin and look at critical touch points where they make different decisions."

"Yes, we need to look at the users to be able to develop services and we need to understand what they value," said one of the researchers from the Umeå School of Business and Economics.

The meeting and the discussion continued, and ideas on how to proceed were discussed along with issues touching upon how to create an interactive recycling room. Tomas showed examples of other innovations made by FältCom, and also the 12 cm × 12 cm box that constituted the device that enabled communication between different machines. Jan-Olof from UMEVA followed the presentations with interest and asked questions about technical aspects and specifications. The meeting ended in a good atmosphere with a working plan for the coming months.

Different Perspectives Meet

Yet again, the next meeting took place at FältCom. Some weeks had passed since the results from the pre-study of recycling behavior had been presented by the design students. Tomas, the project manager at FältCom, opened the meeting by showing the device again. "This is what we will use."

The participants looked at the box and one of the service designers asked, "But don't we need to know what type of service we should develop before we decide upon the technical aspects?"

"No," Tomas said. "This machine can do more or less everything that we want it to do. But we have skipped the interactive part; it is too hard to incorporate."

"But wasn't that the main idea of the project?," Carina asked, unable to hide how surprised she was.

"Well, yes, but then we started looking at how to gather information about households' recycling habits and realized that this could cause integrity problems," Tomas added. "It is better to develop a service based on information from all households in the area. So it would be interactive in a way, but not on the individual level."

The group discussed the prototype and various types of needs that different stakeholders might have. UMEVA, the waste management company, highlighted the needs that Bostaden, the housing company, might have. "Recycling rooms are rather expensive to build and one of the more common problems is the risk of fire. A fire warning system would probably be a good idea to put into the box," UMEVA's representative said.

"Well, we can look into that. It is probably not such a hard thing to do," Tomas said. He added, "The property owners are our most interesting stakeholders, so we need to make sure that they are interested in the service. Otherwise, there is no need to develop anything."

"Well, I don't know if I agree with you there. Our main stakeholders here are the citizens of Umeå. If this service raises the costs for recycling and is not developed on the basis of their needs, we are not really interested in the project," Carina said. "From our point of view, it is better to develop something that really contributes on a long-term basis to the recycling behavior of citizens and we do not want to rush things. We need to really think this new type of service through."

"I understand," Tomas said, "but we need this prototype to be developed into a commercialized product as fast as possible. A few changes and problems along the way is how technology has always been developed. We put it on the market as fast as possible to see how it works."

"But wait a minute," one of the service designers said. "Isn't it better if we think this through from the start? For example, many of the citizens that live in the areas where we would like to implement the service are not Swedish-speaking. If we need to communicate with them in different languages, we might also need sound as a complement to written information."

"OK, I haven't thought about that. I need to check with the engineers about this," Tomas said.

"Yes, I think that we need to sit down and really analyze what types of needs the end users might have before the technology is developed any further," one of the service designers said. "That's what we always do when starting a project."

"Well, you could say that we have already done that quite thoroughly when the design students were working on their project," Tomas added. "We can't spend too much time on this now. We have to get this project running smoothly. I hear that we have many different viewpoints on this, but I think that we need to end this meeting here and I will contact all of you for meetings where we will discuss those issues further. Thank you for coming today and thank you for interesting discussions!"

One of the representatives of the business school in the project had mostly observed the participants at the meeting, and thought to herself when leaving the conference room that it had been an interesting and important meeting. The different interests represented by the members of the project group would be a true challenge. And not only did they have differing interests, but there were also differences in culture and how projects were developed. "I can understand that FältCom wants this project to be developed as fast as possible, while the other members of the project group don't have the same urgent time constraints," she thought to herself. "It will be really interesting to see how this journey will end."

Acknowledgments: The authors of this case would like to thank the participants in the project "Interactive Recycling Rooms," financed by Vinnova.

Part II
Internal and External Information Needs of Geographically Remote Industrial Clusters

In order for geographically remote industrial clusters (GRICs) to function, they need an extensive amount of internal and external information. They need information concerning their mission, resources, and internal arrangements, but at the same time they need information about markets, competitors, and the external business environment. Marketing managers responsible for an entire GRIC need information to manage the GRIC, but they also need information concerning their member enterprises and their operations and strategies if the GRIC is an integrated value chain. If it is not, the GRIC's marketing managers need information to understand how to facilitate successful development of their independent enterprise members. The need for external information is particularly important in cases where the technology on which member enterprises were founded is quickly becoming obsolete.

Internal and External Information Needs of Geographically Remote Industrial Clusters

Case 7

Downturn for a Manufacturing Company in a Geographically Remote Industrial Cluster*

After several years as a teacher in marketing, Rolf Svensson had decided to do more consulting. One day he met with an old student of his, Marianne Svansten, who was now working in a large international company. Rolf had the idea that he had been invited to this meeting to talk about the role and significance of marketing. He had primarily done consulting in businesses related to the consumer sector, and therefore he was a bit surprised when this invitation to meet with Marianne Svansten came, as she was working in a manufacturing company. The invitation had been very formally addressed, which made Rolf even more confused about what situation he was going to encounter.

Marianne Svansten knew about Rolf Svensson's background as a university teacher with a special interest in service marketing. Rolf had done several research projects within service marketing, but he did not think that this was the reason he had been invited to the Viking Company. He thought the invitation might be due to his teaching in marketing in general. Rolf had been lecturing in marketing for more

*Gert-Olof Boström and Britta Näsman, both at Umeå School of Business and Economics, Umeå University (Sweden), developed this case for educational purposes only.

than 20 years, and his knowledge and experience in this area were extensive. In all of his classes, Rolf was always stressing the significance of marketing in a firm. None of his students could have missed this message from Rolf Svensson. He was the crusader of the importance of marketing. This label had given him several consulting jobs over the years, helping firms to understand the potential of marketing when used right. Lately Rolf had done quite a few jobs regarding social marketing.

The Situation

Before the meeting began, Rolf was offered the traditional cup of coffee. He and Marianne Svansten sat down in a meeting room. As soon as they sat down, Marianne started to explain the present situation to Rolf. There has been a drop in demand for all the companies in the industry. This drop is natural, as the economy is in a downturn cycle. The problem is that the Viking Company has experienced a significantly larger drop in the demand for their products compared to the competitors and the other parties in the cluster. In the past four months, the company has lost about half of its sales volume, which is significantly more than the competitors have lost.

Rolf Svensson knew about this problem for the Viking Company, as he had read about it in the local paper. There was a big article on the front page of the local newspaper that day, and the news had also been on the local radio. About 50 people at the assembly line will have to leave the Viking Company. This page of the paper was totally covered by a photo of a group of sad people who will have to leave the Viking Company in six months, if the market situation for the company does not change dramatically compared to the present situation.

The cutdown of personnel in the Viking Company also concerns other groups of workers. Engineers, software programmers, etc. will also have to leave the company. The drop in sales affects all different categories of personnel in the company. Rolf got the impression in the meeting that Marianne Svansten is also a bit afraid of losing her job.

The problems for the Viking Company do not only concern this company. A cutdown in the demand for products from the Viking Company naturally affects all firms in the supply chain (read also "cluster"). But the Viking Company seems to be the one that has been hit hardest by the decreasing demand.

Marianne is deeply concerned about the drop in demand for the products that the Viking Company manufactures. She is not at all convinced that the drop in sales for the Viking Company is due to an "ordinary" recession in the market. According to Marianne, there are probably more factors affecting the situation for the Viking Company. Therefore, she let Rolf know that she had taken some steps of action in the situation. From her face, Rolf could see that Marianne was not going to tell him more about these steps, at least not for now.

In order to inform Rolf Svensson about the background of the Viking Company, Marianne and Rolf agreed that he should meet with Martin Lundgren, who has the overall responsibility for the marketing and information department. But before this meeting, Marianne wanted to give Rolf her view of the situation in the company. According to her, the history of the company is an important factor for understanding the present.

Marianne Svansten had worked as a market analyst in several different companies in many countries before she got the position as manager of the marketing department in the Viking Company two years ago. This experience has given Marianne a unique position in the Viking Company. She is the one with the most recent experience from other industries and other companies in the whole managerial body of the Viking Company. Very few of these people have had any experience of external work. Most of the men "came up the hard way" in the company — they started at a low position in the Viking Company and worked their way up.

The market that the Viking Company operates in is very small. The total number of units sold worldwide is about 2,500 pieces a year. The actual number is difficult to find out, as some manufacturers do not want to reveal their sales. In some countries, one type of the machines that Viking sells does not need to be registered, which further complicates the chances to get an exact number of the total volume for the world market. Therefore, the volume of the world market is a bit unreliable. To some extent, the number is based on advertisements about purchases of machines in the newspaper. But the number of 2,500 units is a sound estimate, according to Marianne.

Marianne Svansten continued to talk about the industry characteristics, as she is so fascinated by it. None of the industries that she had worked in before was like this one. There is a very close monitoring of each other in the industry. "You cannot do anything in this industry that the competitors do not know about," said Marianne with a sigh.

By and large there are three large manufacturers in the industry that are acting on the world market. In addition, there is a large number of smaller actors that are present in the Nordic countries. "So I hope you get the picture," said Marianne to Rolf. "Every step you take is carefully monitored and evaluated by your competitors."

The three largest manufacturers are all from traditional areas in this industry: Sweden, Canada, and Finland. The Canadian company Robert Moose is a manufacturer of mainly Lynx machines. The Robert Moose Company is a member or subsidiary of a large corporate group, and thus has access to large financial resources. This company is seen as a very important company in the group. Therefore, the Robert Moose Company will continue to operate in the market regardless of whatever financial situation arises in the market.

The Robert Moose Company has been manufacturing machines in this segment for more than 100 years. However, within the industry in which the Viking Company operates, the Robert Moose Company has only been active for 25 years. There is very limited knowledge in this company about how to handle situations of decreasing demand from the market, as the company has never experienced anything like the present situation.

The Finnish company Sisu Yxi is a very strong family-owned company run by its founder, Jari Tuomikoska. This company was founded more than 50 years ago. From the start, the Sisu Yxi Company has specialized in making these types of machines. Their knowledge in this area is large. One indication of their knowledge (and business skills) is the fact that this company has developed a very strong financial basis.

The smallest competitors are both small and local. First, there is the national company Oskarsdunge, which originated from a small town with the same name. It is a typical family company that operates primarily within close range of the company. Then there is the Lynx Machine Company; this company is a challenger with poor financial results. And finally there is Log Life, a Finnish company close to bankruptcy. No one in the industry thinks that this company will survive the present downturn. "These actors, the small ones," said Marianne, "are of most interest from a national perspective. Internationally these firms are not such a big threat even if they sometimes manage to export a machine."

The German company SHM, which also operates in this industry, is in a situation similar to that of the Finnish company Lynx Machine. There is, however, one significant difference between these two companies: SHM has access to capital due to the investment group that owns this company. Therefore, it is hard to know what SHM will do; whether it is a competitor to consider or not, Marianne is not sure.

There are of course variations among the different manufacturers' machines, as Marianne pointed out. But the customers do not consider these differences to be of any significance when comparing the quality of the different machines in the market, especially between the large manufacturing companies' machines, according to surveys conducted by the Viking Company. Therefore, there is an endless struggle to win over customers. Due to the perceived similarities in quality, the fight is very much about price — a price war.

"However," said Marianne, "the situation cannot be reduced to the machines themselves only. The best way to explain the complexity is by putting the service the machine performs into the value chain. We are now looking at the contribution of the firm that offers the service that the machine performs. The firms operating these machines sell a service for which the machine is the key. This service is offered within a restricted time, e.g., in three weeks we will have done this job. The crucial factor for fulfilling this promised deadline is the function of the machine. Thus, the accessibility to a garage that has knowledge of performing the service of the machine and repairing it is also an important factor when customers decide which machine to buy."

The large manufacturers charge a higher price but also have larger service networks. This means that there are short traveling distances to any machine. Oskarsdunge has chosen a somewhat different strategy to compete; they have few but very loyal customers. The machines of Oskarsdunge are priced in the same range as those of the three large manufacturers' machines, but this firm cannot offer as much service. Oskarsdunge's strategy is to be strong in certain geographical areas and the company has no aim to cover all geographical areas, even nationally. In those areas where the company is present, they take extremely good care of the customers they have.

The smaller manufacturers cannot of course have dedicated garages in any large geographical area. Thus, these firms cannot compete with service in the same way as the larger firms do. These smaller firms just focus on price, which has been a successful strategy. As Marianne stated, "Their comment to a customer who says that he will not buy their machine due to the lack of garages is, 'With our low price, you can buy a new machine more frequently and in that way eliminate the need for a garage.'"

Rolf waited for Marianne to continue with her description of the manufacturers in the market, but there was no continuation. Thus, Rolf came to the conclusion that these are the significant actors in the market. Rolf was surprised by the small number of actors on the market, and he realized that this structure of the industry would have some specific characteristics. He did not have to wait for long; Marianne continued and told Rolf that this manufacturing structure really gives a specific framework for competition.

"Let me give you an example," said Marianne. "We changed the light in the photos of our machines published in the material that we give to potential customers. Within four weeks, another manufacturer changed their photos so they were similar to ours. Let me put it another way: All firms in this industry, both we and our competitors, are quite careful not to offend any customers. To try something new is therefore a challenge, and if someone tries something new that seems to work out then we all adopt it very quickly."

The business is very conservative, since most of the customers are men in their 60s who have been in this business their whole lives. The top management in the Viking Company also shares the same characteristic. Therefore, much is done as it has always been done. The motto in the industry is to "play it safe," i.e., to be in line with the values of men in their 60s.

Viking's customers are located all over the world where the activity that Viking's machines perform is mechanized. In those parts of the world where this process is not mechanized, there are no present customers; however, there might be potential ones. Viking's customers are found in most European countries, Russia, Oceania, North America, and South America. "Here we have another challenge," said Marianne. "Our customers are at very different technical levels. There is a discrepancy of more than 20 years in the various geographical areas."

The Meeting with Martin Lundgren

Martin is a man who has come up the hard way in the company. He joined the company more than 40 years ago in the factory at the assembly line. Martin is very proud of his long experience in the Viking Company, which gives him an overview of what has happened in the company. He can relate every new activity to what took place in the past.

It is obvious that Martin Lundgren has a background in manufacturing. His technical expertise is constantly evident when he talks, which of course is natural due to his background. It is also understandable due to the soul of both the Viking Company and the industry. A critical means for competing is technical news. There is a constant need for technical news, according to Martin, in order to keep current and new customers interested in the company's products.

Martin became very enthusiastic when describing the products. "It is really very technically advanced equipment," Martin explained. "We use the analogy of flying a jet plane in order to grasp the technical level of the situation. The Viking Company has one machine called the 'producer,' which is the first one in the process. This machine prepares the raw material for transportation. This machine is constantly in contact with the next stage in the value chain in order to process the raw material in the most financially rewarding way."

Martin continued: "The other machine we have collects the raw material that the 'producer' has prepared and transports it to collection points. Inside each machine is a computer that calculates today's performance and sends a report to the next actor in the value chain, the one who will process the raw material in the next phase. There is also a computer in each of the machines that monitors the machine. If anything is getting worn out or is approaching breakdown, the computer automatically orders new parts from Viking's spare parts center."

"Our customers are extremely demanding because they are buying high-technology complex products, which they have limited possibilities to repair themselves. A breakdown most often means that a technician has to come and repair the machine. We therefore," said Martin, "have mobile technicians that come to the spot for service."

"An additional factor that strongly affects our customers' financial sensitivity is the low margins. They have very low margins in all the jobs that they are doing. A figure in this context is 5%. The users of our machines usually get a revenue between 3% and 5% for a job. It is therefore extremely important that the machine does not stand still due to breakdowns or any other malfunctions. The machine cannot stand still because then the customer will lose a lot of money. So in our company there are about 80 engineers taking care of the customers' problems before the machine reaches the customer. By offering the customer a high-quality technological product, we provide our customers with an efficient tool for performing their jobs. As long as we have high technical quality, we will sell," said Martin. Rolf could see from Marianne's face that she did not totally agree.

"So you're from the university," Martin continued. "Well, we have good cooperation with both the engineering department and the agricultural department at the university. These institutions really contribute to our competing power. Let me tell you about one development project that we have with the engineering department," said Martin sounding very enthusiastic. Then he seemed to realize that it might not be so good to talk about this secret project with an external consultant. Instead, he ended the discussion by saying that the university is a key partner in the cluster, helping the Viking Company to manufacture their technologically high-quality machines.

The Viking Company is currently owned by a very large international corporation, Steel Corp. They manufacture and sell military equipment, construction and mining equipment, and industrial machinery all over the globe. In 1999, Steel Corp. realized that it did not have any businesses within the industry that the Viking Company operates in. In order to make their assortment complete, Steel Corp. bought the Viking Company. The Viking Company is a very small part of Steel Corp.'s turnover, about 3%; nevertheless, it is a significant player in order to make Steel Corp. "complete."

Steel Corp. is very successful and it is the largest company in their business. They have very high standards, and are known for their impeccable quality and Just-in-Time method of manufacturing and delivering their machines. Steel Corp. has proved to be a very good and stable owner of the Viking Company.

The Viking Company has a history going back more than 100 years. Around the end of the 19th century, Johan Persson, a blacksmith from a small village, made the first products in the firm. The name of the company at the time was Persson's Smide. Johan Persson was a man of great vision and invented a lot of products that helped farmers in their daily work. The demand for these products increased, as mechanization was a way to be more efficient.

Persson's Smide stayed in the family and Persson's sons took over. In the 1950s, they started to explore new segments and a dispute occurred in the family. The part that today is the Viking Company was sold to Göran Persson, the grandson of Johan. Göran Persson got into contact with Lennart Olsson, and together they started to manufacture the Viking Company's products. Their different areas of knowledge — Göran's knowledge of steel and farming combined with Lennart's knowledge of hydraulic pumps — ensured an immediate success.

For many years, new inventions came out of the company mostly pre-ordered by other local companies that had some technical problem that needed to be solved. In the 1960s, more and more of the requests started to come from one segment of customers. This large demand for equipment soon made Viking specialists in this specific area. The company built up a good reputation and reports of their high-quality machines spread by word of mouth. Before long, word about the Viking Company was out nationally and more and more requests came in. The first country outside Europe that the Viking Company exported to was Brazil. The first customers in this country were three entrepreneurs who had heard about the Viking Company. These entrepreneurs had plans in which the Viking's machines seemed to be very useful.

Unfortunately, Göran Persson died of a heart attack on one of his trips to Brazil. This situation put the company into a state of shock; Göran Persson was a very strong leader and he had been the person with the business strategies. Lennart Olsson was more of a skillful inventor but not a businessman.

Hans Nilsson, an engineer in the company who had an interest in doing business, took over the position that Göran Persson had occupied. The Viking Company expanded in more countries, but did not make any money. Thus, the financial situation of the Viking Company forced the owners to sell the company and a large tractor manufacturer finally bought it. This course of events resulted in profitable cooperation for several years.

The Viking Company became an even more high-tech company, testing all kinds of materials both for their own industry and for the tractor industry. For engineers, working in the Viking Company was seen as a very good career move. Many new inventions were made in the company, and it was considered to be one of the technical leaders in the industry. The competitors copied more or less everything that the Viking Company made. Thus, the company was always at least one step ahead.

A couple of years later, the tractor manufacturer decided to redefine their business and concentrate only on building tractors. The Viking Company had become too specialized and hence too far apart to fit into their business group anymore. The selling price tag was high, and at this time an investment company came into the picture and bought the Viking Company. The international investment company Introwest bought the Viking Company. The board of Introwest had decided that the company should widen their business, and the Viking Company seemed to be a sweet deal.

During the years with this owner, Introwest, Viking's only strategy was to survive, since no investments were made. There was a strict demand that the Viking Company should perform according to a budget that did not contain any means for development. Introwest just wanted to earn as much money as possible, and they did not care about the future of the Viking Company. The competitors soon started to catch up in technology and the Viking Company was no longer the natural leader. The engineers were worried and wondered what was going to happen to their company, the company that they had been loyal to for so many years.

Finally, the situation became unbearable and the customers deserted the Viking Company. Introwest managed to sell the Viking Company to Steel Corp., since this company would fill a gap in its product mix. Steel Corp. comes from a setting where its business tradition is different from that of the Viking Company. Steel Corp. was very anxious to find out everything about the company they had acquired, and therefore immediately sent a delegation consisting of engineers and economic personnel. These people liked what they saw and were very happy with the 210 employees.

"Over the years, there have been many downturns," said Martin. "I can remember the one we had in the beginning of the 1980s. I had just worked in the Viking Company for six months and then the recession came. The demand for our products literally died. But we managed to survive," said Martin with pride in his voice. "We cut down and survived."

With these words the meeting was over, Rolf Svensson realized. Martin seemed to have a strategy ready for the situation; there was no doubt about that. The firmness with which he was handling the situation was somewhat shocking to Rolf. With his background from the university, he had expected to find another approach to the present situation in the Viking Company.

The Industrial Cluster of the Viking Company

The country that the Viking Company operates in is known for being successful in this sector. There are many companies located in proximity to the Viking Company that do business in this sector. Thus, several of the suppliers to the Viking Company are located relatively close by. With regard to this constellation of firms and their geographical position, the cluster could clearly be defined as an industrial cluster in a geographically remote area.

The country that the Viking Company is located in is also a peripheral country regarding geographical distances. On the other hand, this country boasts the world-leading industry within which the Viking Company operates. The mechanization of this sector started in this country to a great extent, and it is therefore an extremely interesting market. Nowhere else can one find such knowledgeable and demanding customers. If you want to be a company that develops this type of products, this is the market for you. It is so important to be present in this country that the world leader in the industry has set up a large facility in this country.

The Viking Company may be defined as a smaller manufacturing enterprise (SME) based in a geographically remote industrial cluster. Three of the hardware (read "steel construction") suppliers to the Viking Company are located at a distance of 60 km. All of these suppliers are world-leading firms in their respective segments.

Looking at the software suppliers that the Viking Company uses, they are mostly located at an even smaller geographical distance, and most frequently these firms are very small — micro firms. These firms are highly specialized in a specific sort of programming. They are often startups from the university, that is, some students started a firm after finishing their studies. These firms contribute essentially to the development of the Viking Company. Today, the lion's share of the developments in the machines are based on information technology (IT).

The Meeting with Fredrik Andersson

After a week, Marianne Svansten called Rolf Svensson and said that it was essential that he meet Fredrik Andersson. Fredrik was a newly employed market analyst at the Viking Company; Marianne had hired him. He had been at the company for six months. This job was his first one; he had been studying marketing at the university before he was employed by the Viking Company. His first task was to conduct a survey of the people who had bought a new machine in the last six months.

Fredrik Andersson was now going to present the results from this survey. Martin Lundgren, Marianne Svansten, and Rolf Svensson had all got their coffee, so the meeting could start. Fredrik began by telling the group that he would just give the highlights from the survey, as they only had an hour for the presentation.

Fredrik started his presentation by saying that the buyers of these machines are small firms; 87% of the firms have between one and three employees. Most of them (42%) are run by father and son. The father is typically in his 60s and is the one who runs the business, while the son is the operator of the machine and he is between 20 and 30 years old. Every third year, 63% of the firms in the survey buy a new machine. The process of buying a new machine is a continuous one. The owner of the firm decides this process, and his decision is very much affected by the operator of the machines.

The buyers do not identify any large differences between the machines in the market. They are by and large comparable in quality, according to the buyers. The most significant difference that the buyers identify between the machines is the color.

A critical dimension for the buyers is operating hours. They want to secure themselves with as many operating hours as possible. A breakdown would be devastating for them and for the present job. The service organization therefore plays a significant role in achieving the highest ratio of operating hours possible.

Of the interviewed persons, about 65% of them use the Internet during their leisure time. Many of them (80%) visit YouTube in order to find video clips showing the machines in action that they operate in their working hours. About 98% of them look for news about the machines or for supporting articles.

Rolf's Solution

It is now two weeks since Rolf Svensson was in the meeting with Fredrik Andersson. Rolf is sitting in his car on the way to the Viking Company. Now it is time for his meeting. There is no doubt about the expectations placed on him. To underline the expectations, the Viking Company has flown in two people from the headquarters of Steel Corp., in addition to the CEO of the Viking Company, to participate in the meeting. Now they all want to get the solution for the Viking Company. What should Rolf tell them?

Case 8

Saab — A Case of Emergency*

"It is merely a coincidence," Nick Lindh thought as he hung up the phone and turned on his old Acer laptop. While waiting for the computer to start up, he wondered if any of his former colleagues at the statistics department perhaps could calculate the probability that he, out of all, would be asked to do this job. "Whatever the probability is, it is slim," he thought. His former colleague Morgan Johnson had asked him to join him in a project and to come down to Saab and share some of his views on marketing in general and marketing management in particular.

Morgan was not a Saab employee but a senior partner at one of Europe's top management firms, and had worked with Nick on several occasions. Morgan had been a mentor to Nick since the 1980s, and the two had become close friends over the years. They had recently worked together in a brand development project that had turned out well, so Morgan felt confident about assigning Nick to the Saab task. However, Morgan did not know that Nick had studied Saab in depth for over two decades and was quite a specialist on the organization, nor did Nick mention it either since he did not consider that an important piece of information.

The reason Nick had studied Saab for such an extended period of time was due to some advice one of his old professors had given

---

*Carl Patrik Nilsson, of the Stockholm Institute of Communication Science (STICS), developed this case for educational purposes only.

him back at his old business school. His professor had told him to do the following: (a) pick a company that you find interesting, that you think could be managed better, and that you also think will stay around for some time; (b) make that company your hobby object of study and try to learn everything about that company; and (c) try also to understand all marketing and management theories you have ever learned by applying them to whatever is going on in this hobby project of yours. Saab was Nick's hobby project, chosen more than 25 years ago among thousands of other companies that he potentially could have picked. Over the years, Nick had come to consider Saab an "invaluable source of insights into marketing," as he used to phrase it.

Nick had been a marketing consultant at a small firm for the last ten years, and he had been a full partner for the last two years. Before his current job, Nick had worked as a senior brand manager for many years, and prior to that he had started off his career as an assistant at the statistics department at his old university. It was a great job, where he learned a lot about how stats could be used to get on top of things. In connection to his work, he had continuously updated his theoretical skills by adding one or two marketing or management courses per year to his CV. He had done so ever since he graduated from his home university. He considered practical experience to be valuable and theoretical insights imperative, especially when working in complex industries. Nick could understand that some practitioners did not particularly value theories that had intuitive characteristics. However, there were not only "intuitive theories," but also a growing number of counterintuitive theories that you either knew or did not know. If you did not know them, your intuition would tell you to manage your company in an intuitive way, which thereby meant a less favorable way than what the best managers did.

The next day, Nick met with his former colleague over breakfast in a spacious conference room at Morgan's favorite hotel. It was not so much a breakfast as a business meeting. Morgan had barely said hello before he started updating Nick about the client. The art of updating people was Morgan's specialty, and he always believed that the more background information the better. So the first thing he did was to give Nick a compressed historical snapshot of Saab:

Nick, I do not know if you know this or not, but most people are unaware of the fact that Saab started out as an airplane manufacturer in 1937. Not only was Saab an airplane manufacturer, but the company was actually formed partly from the remnants of a failed and reconstructed train set and locomotive manufacturer, *Aktiebolaget Svenska Järnvägsverkstäderna* (ASJ). ASJ had formed an airplane division, *Aktiebolaget Svenska Järnvägsverkstäders Aeroplanavdelning* (ASJA), which was then merged with Saab. Initially, Saab manufactured German Junkers Ju 86K and American Grumman fighter planes, both manufactured under license. In 1940, the company started the development of an entirely Swedish bomb plane, the B17, which was followed by the B18. The B18 was, as a matter of fact, the fastest bomb plane when it was introduced in 1944. So you can imagine that Saab already had great engineers from the very start.

Nonetheless, following the end of WWII Saab had, like many other fighter plane manufacturers, an overproduction of airplanes and needed to transform its military production into some kind of civilian production. Consequently, a team of engineers, designers, and technicians put together what was to become Saab's first product, the Saab 92. The car was first presented in 1947 and launched in 1949, and full-scale production was initiated that same year.

That Saab started production of cars was actually the result of an analysis of the company's options as well as its capabilities. This environmental scanning and analysis took place in late 1944 and early 1945. The top management had realized that sales of military airplanes would decline when the war ended. Thus, the managing director at the time, Ragnar Wahrgren, discussed options with his management team, such as prefabricated houses, kitchen furniture, motorcycles, and cars of course. Eventually the choice fell on cars. One problem, though, was that no one within the company had any experience in the car industry. Hence, in charge of the development of Saab's first car was an aircraft engineer who specialized in wing design for fighter airplanes. Consequently, aerodynamics was deemed important, which is evident from the design of Saab's first car — viewed in profile, it has the same shape as the wing of an airplane.

Together with aerodynamics, the first Saab had to fulfill two more absolute requirements: to be unpretentious and to use front-wheel drive. It had to be unpretentious since Europe was rather poor after WWII, and it had to use front-wheel drive since this layout has many and obvious advantages compared to rear-wheel drive, for instance on snowy and icy roads.[1] Furthermore, you can save a lot of precious space when opting for front-wheel drive since you can make the engine and drivetrain in one compact piece — something that many rear-wheel drive manufacturers discovered some 40 to 50 years after Saab did.

So if you are still with me, Nick, we have here a company whose first product was developed based on simplicity, aerodynamics, and front-wheel drive. The company was very proud of their creation, and from that point onwards the company chose a path that deviated quite a lot from those paths chosen by other manufacturers. Saab came to be the slightly odd outsider cousin among the car brands, an image that the company proudly clung to in heart and spirit.

During the following years up until 1989, when the company was still independent and Swedish-owned, Saab achieved quite a number of technological breakthroughs even though the company was small. These breakthroughs boosted the Saab staff's confidence that they were on the right track and doing the right things.

---

[1]Vehicles with front-wheel drive have a better grip on sandy, muddy, snowy, and icy roads. Since the engine on most cars is placed in the front, this means that cars with front-wheel drive will have more weight and thereby more downforce (than cars with rear-wheel drive) on the front wheels, which is transformed into better grip.

However, in 1989 Saab's relative independence came to a halt. The American car manufacturer General Motors acquired half of the company and assumed leadership over Saab. The first thing they thought about was to put in place appropriate goals and adequate strategies.

After the historical snapshot, Morgan filled up his mug of coffee and went on talking about Saab's goals and core strategy.

Goals and Strategy

Morgan said:

> Nick, as I guess you remember from your days at the business school, goals provide organizations with an outline that can guide actions. A goal can be defined as a future state that an organization or individual strives to achieve. Clearly defined goals help organizations coordinate activities and predict and plan for future events. Organizational goals usually have four basic purposes: (a) they provide guidance and direction; (b) they simplify and aid planning; (c) they motivate and inspire employees; and (d) they are crucial in the evaluation and control of organizational performance.
>
> Part of planning and setting goals is environmental scanning, which is the practice of monitoring and analyzing a company's market environment. The input from the scanning is used to adapt to the ever-changing world outside of the company. In the process of adapting to the environment, plans have to be revised, strategies fine-tuned, and goals and objectives recalibrated. Some organizations are stiff and inflexible, while others have the ability to adapt to changes and better achieve a strategic fit between strategy, environment, and organization.
>
> To perform well in the marketplace, the top management ought to choose the right strategy and course of action in order to achieve company goals and to generate sustainable profits. When it comes to the selection of a general strategy to create competitive advantage, there are basically three strategies to choose among. A company can choose cost leadership, differentiation, or focus as

a general strategy. The focus strategy can in turn be divided into two substrategies, cost focus or differentiation focus.

Cost leadership is a straightforward strategy. It simply means that the company aims at being the company with the lowest costs in its industry. Differentiation means that the company strives to be unique in some sense along some dimensions widely valued by buyers. The third strategy, focus strategy, rests upon a narrower competitive scope where the company tailors its strategy to serve a specific segment in the industry while excluding others. The focus strategy can be executed using either cost focus or differentiation focus.

In Saab's case, the main goal for the organization and the marketing department, set in 1989, was to reach a production level of 150,000 units per year, which was a very ambitious but in no way impossible goal to achieve considering that the global sales totaled 103,591 in 1989. However, GM could have had a better start with its newly acquired brand, since sales dropped the following year to 87,356. Despite the drop in sales, Saab and its marketing department were steadfast and committed to their goal for the next 20 years even though they never reached it. The closest the company came to reaching this goal during the 20-year period was in 2006, when 132,957 cars were sold. Thus, Saab fell short by 13% and made a loss equivalent to 1/6th of the total revenue that year. Hence, it is unlikely that the company would have reached breakeven, even if it had reached the goal of 150,000 produced units. In the years after 2006, sales fell sharply, reaching 93,388 in 2008, 38,756 in 2009, and 31,696 in 2010, a year when many car manufacturers saw sales recover sharply after the financial crisis.[2]

The strategy that GM used for Saab was based on a mix of efforts designed to achieve competitive advantage. Saab was the world's smallest standard car manufacturer but now with the strength of the biggest manufacturer in the world — GM. Thus, GM's strategy

---

[2]The prelude to the financial crisis started in the spring of 2008, with the fall of the investment bank Bear Stearns. The crisis escalated in the autumn of that same year with the fall of the investment bank Lehman Brothers.

for Saab was to build further on Saab's high-quality cars through economies of scale in production and thereby reinforce the cost leadership strategy.

In addition, there were synergy effects to be gained by coordinating distribution so that Saab, Opel, and other brands in the GM portfolio could use each other's dealership networks. Coordination was also to be achieved in the area of product development so that platforms, engines, and components used for the various car brands in the GM portfolio (Opel, for instance) could be shared and used in upcoming Saab models. GM and Saab also came up with a bold idea to really speed up product development[3] and save costs at the same time. The idea was as simple as it was brilliant: to develop two new Saab models based on two already-existing cars. Thus, the Subaru Impreza and the Chevrolet TrailBlazer were transformed into the Saab 9-2[4] and the Saab 9-7, respectively. This last move was part of an effort to broaden Saab's product portfolio and appeal to additional segments in the market and thereby increase total sales.

Morgan took a deep breath and a big gulp of piping hot coffee from his mug, and went on:

In addition to the mix of efforts that I just told you about, Nick, GM and Saab crowned their marketing strategy by setting a very attractive price on their valuable offer. In a study by an independent consultant, it was found that Saab managed to keep prices only slightly higher than the Japanese car manufacturer Toyota. Taken together, this was the essence of Saab's strategy, and it was appreciated and applauded by Swedish as well as international media. There was also this Swedish "car professor," later stationed in Copenhagen, who praised the GM–Saab strategy. So things could not have been better.

---

[3]The Saab 9-2 was launched in 2004, and the Saab 9-7 in 2005.
[4]The model number on the first Saab from 1947 was "92."

"Nick, what I have told you so far sounds pretty good, doesn't it?," Morgan asked Nick. Nick nodded. Morgan then continued:

Well, before going any further I would like to read to you an excerpt from two business journals that sheds some light on how Saab's business was doing during this time period and actually all the way up until today, which I have now been updating you about. It goes like this: "Despite over 60 years in the car industry, Saab has very seldom managed to run its business at a profit. From day one, Saab has been a project producing cars and losses and most recently only losses. When looking at the company's financial statements, it becomes obvious that Saab has not produced a profit in the last 14 years; instead, the company has lost 2,000 Euros per car on the 1,372,873 cars the company has produced during the same time period. Former CEO of Volvo Cars, Pehr Gyllenhammar, claims that Saab in fact has generated a profit only on two occasions during its 60-year-long history [Cervenka, 2008; Heimersson, 2009]."

"So now the media have finally realized that the company is really sick?," Nick inserted. Morgan nodded and added, "Yes, but they have no clue what kind of disease Saab has contracted and, moreover, why this disease has remained untreated for such an extended period of time. Well, now it is your job to know, Nick, and before I start asking you questions I will add some more history for you."

Morgan went on with his lecture:

Nick, while you were struggling to finish your degree at the business school, you know, in the last years of the 1980s, the two companies Scania and Investor, who owned Saab at that time, scanned and analyzed Saab's business environment. As a result of that analysis, they came to the conclusion to sell Saab to General Motors. As I mentioned previously, half of the company was sold in 1989 but the other half was not sold until the year 2000.

When GM acquired half of Saab in 1989, Saab got a new CEO, David Herman. Herman held the post for two years while Saab was integrated into the GM organization. Herman was then superseded as CEO by strongman Keith Butler-Wheelhouse. Under his management, things would change somewhat, in addition to the changes we have already talked about, that is.

Butler-Wheelhouse's plan was to increase the speed of the product development using the means already mentioned previously. Things had just been taking too much time in the past. For example, Saab's first car, the Saab 92, had developed into the Saab 93, which in turn was developed into the Saab 96. The Saab 96 was in production for 20 years before the production of it was discontinued in 1980. Even though the 96 had a new model name, it was still based on a car constructed in 1947.[5] Another Saab model, the 99, was an additional example of slow development, where basically the same car was produced from 1967 until 1987, when that model was discontinued.

Not only did the new CEO Butler-Wheelhouse see opportunities to speed things up and to add new models to Saab's product portfolio, but he also thought that Saab should start using rear-wheel drive for its most luxurious models. When GM bought Saab, they did so with a certain purpose. GM wanted to add a premium brand to their portfolio of existing brands. The premium brands that Saab was to complement in GM's portfolio were Corvette and Cadillac, both using rear-wheel drive. Thus, for Saab to fit into the picture, the car ought to have rear-wheel drive. Furthermore, a look at other premium brands supported GM's idea about the concept of rear-wheel drive. Brands like BMW, Mercedes, Lexus, and of course also Porsche and Jaguar were all using rear-wheel drive. Moreover, Toyota's premium model Celica, which was highly successful in the 1970s using rear-wheel drive, lost almost all of its attractiveness when Toyota decided to turn it into a front-wheel drive vehicle.

However, GM's will to change to rear-wheel drive on Saab was not welcomed by the engineers or anyone else at Saab. This started a

---

[5]The 93 as well as the 96 were based on Saab's first car, the 92, which was constructed in 1946–1948.

lengthy debate and power struggle within the company that went on during the first half of the 1990s. According to interviewed staff at Saab, Saab Tech, and GM, a lot of time and energy was spent on the wrong things during this period of time. One of the interviewees said, "We were not even going in circles; we were trapped in a maelstrom bringing us to places we didn't want to go. GM wanted us to start using rear-wheel drive, and we were stalling and delaying or at least trying to — not really the best combination to speed up product development." In the end, GM gave up and Saab released their largest model, the Saab 9-5, with front-wheel drive in 1996.

Sorry for going on and on, Nick, but the story of Saab is quite interesting and that is why I am forgetting about the time here. Anyway, to see whether you are still with me, I would like to hear what you have to say about the following questions.

Morgan took a pause to fill up his coffee mug and wrote four questions on the whiteboard.

Morgan's First Set of Questions

Morgan wrote the following questions on the whiteboard:

1. When Saab developed its first car, three factors were deemed important. Why were these three factors important, and do you agree with Saab's notion that these three were the most important?
2. Discuss and elaborate on the following issues related to Saab:

   a. Which management philosophy is Saab using and is it appropriate for the company? Furthermore, what would you as head of the marketing department do and say about the longstanding goal that the company was aiming at?
   b. In what way could Saab create synergy effects and were there any potential downsides related to those synergy effects?
   c. Which strategies did Saab use and were they appropriate for the company?

3. Did Scania and Investor arrive at the right conclusion in their environmental analysis when they decided to sell Saab? Why or why not? Was it the right decision by GM to acquire Saab?
4. What would you have done regarding the decision to use rear-wheel drive or front-wheel drive? Which marketing arguments or other arguments would you bring forward to support your decision?

Since Nick had already given the subject quite some thought over the last two decades, he thought he would enlighten his mentor a little bit and give him an appetizer of his exceptional knowledge of Saab. So he fired away answers to all four questions that took everything that Morgan had thought of into consideration, along with a number of other issues that Morgan had not considered or even thought of.

Morgan was flat-out mesmerized and very impressed, and thought he had made a surprisingly excellent choice when choosing Nick for the project. With a smile on his face and with his coffee mug filled up, he continued to update Nick and resumed his lecture:

So here GM had bought the smallest car manufacturer of standard cars in the world, and they wanted to integrate this odd bird into the GM family. The Saab organization, located in an arctic country, Sweden, and in a remote area in that arctic country, Trollhättan, was not the easiest to manage. They were right out stubborn, you see, and had fixed ideas about how things were supposed to be done. Not only was Saab stubborn, but the entire cluster of suppliers, in which Saab was an integrated part, was stubborn. It could not have been easy for the GM managers to start doing business with this small-minded company and the fragmented network of smaller manufacturing enterprises [SMEs] that came along with it. From GM's point of view, Saab was just not able to see the big picture.

Morgan then took a gulp of coffee and browsed through some of his papers while mumbling something about the arctic car cluster.

While Morgan was mumbling, Nick's thoughts began to wander. He thought of his own family and their relation to the Saab brand. He figured that they had been pretty much in Saab's core segment. When Nick was seven years old, his father, an academic and lecturer in marketing management, had come to the conclusion that Saab was a suitable brand for the family. Ever since then, Saab had been an important brand in Nick's life. After all, he met the brand every morning and afternoon when he got a ride to and from school, and during summer vacations he spent a lot of time in the backseat together with his brother and sister going back and forth to their summer house in the Scandinavian mountains.

Nick's dad had a total of four Saabs before he quit driving, and he had had five Fords before that. He was pretty unlucky with his Saabs or perhaps lucky, depending upon the perspective. Nick's father only bought one Saab and got the other three for free. The first one was a used Saab 99L, which he bought when it was only three years old. He had that car for almost 10 years, and Nick's dad used to say that that car was the best he had ever had. The second was a brand new Saab 900GL and was paid for mostly by subsidies from the state, the municipality, and a mix of insurance companies. They were nice enough to pay for it because of a hip injury he had developed. A few years after Nick's dad bought the car, he underwent surgery to remove the damaged hip and thereby overcame his handicap.

Unluckily, when Nick's dad was finally free from his handicap, the car was stolen and set on fire by those who stole it. But he was not sad for long, since the insurance company stepped in and gave him the chance to buy a brand new Saab 900 Turbo. That was a great car both Nick and his dad agreed upon. However, one sunny morning Nick was on his way to the business school with his dad's car when a lady, also driving a Saab, made a left turn right in front of

Nick. Nick slammed into the side of that Saab 99 at 70 km/h.[6] Nick stepped out of the wreck shocked and dizzy, but most importantly alive and without a scratch on him. The lady suffered a slight head wound mostly because she had not worn a seatbelt, according to the police officers when they arrived on the scene. The policemen and firemen cleaning up the scene also informed Nick that he would have suffered serious, if not fatal, injuries had he been driving another car brand.

So that sunny morning could have been Nick's last one had it not been for the safety features of the brand he was driving. As for the lady, she was lucky that Saab was the first car manufacturer in the world to include collision protection elements in the doors already back in 1972 — about 20 years before the other safety giant in the industry, Volvo, introduced side collision protection. Nick thought to himself that perhaps his story and others' alike with more meaning and content would have appealed to a greater extent to an academic target market with an above-average education. Nick had never been a fan of the shallow unfocused marketing communication that Saab had been using over the last 20 years. "Well, maybe my story would have suited Volvo better than Saab," Nick concluded. After the accident, Nick's father got another Saab 900 from the insurance company, which is still being used to this day by one of his grandchildren.

At this point, Nick stopped daydreaming and returned to Morgan's presentation.

"Allow me to repeat myself," Morgan said. Nick smiled when he realized that his mentor had caught him daydreaming. With a fresh mug of coffee in his hand, Morgan went on.

---

[6]70 km/h is equivalent to 45 miles per hour. The European New Car Assessment Programme (Euro NCAP) usually tests cars at a speed of 55 km/h or 35 miles per hour.

Innovation and Product Development

Morgan continued:

> Nick, we both know that companies use innovation and product development to battle each other, but all companies are unfortunately not successful in this respect. A number of interviews that I have personally conducted with Saab managers, engineers, designers, and all kinds of staff show that they really have taken this issue to heart. It seems as if they really have understood that this is important. One manager who I interviewed captured it in three nice sentences: "To be innovative and to develop new products is a cornerstone in the renewal that companies undergo constantly. Companies that want to remain on the market and survive in the fierce competition had better innovate or perish. At Saab, we are dedicated to innovation and product development and, as a bonus from our efforts in building the car with the best quality, we will have a product that sells itself."

As if Morgan had heard what Nick had been daydreaming about, he then started to talk about safety.

Safety

Morgan stated:

> Well, you know, Nick, Saab has been brilliant when it comes to new and odd ideas. Throughout the 1970s and 1980s, Saab was astonishing in their innovation abilities. For instance, in 1972 Saab inserted shock-absorbing bars in the doors to protect the driver and passengers in the event of a side collision. This side collision protection was developed and put in place 20 years before Volvo, positioned as "the world's safest family car," developed the Side Impact Protection System (SIPS).
>
> In fact, in various tests and measurements of safety Saab has been found to be safer than Volvo in a majority of cases during

the last two decades, both in real accidents and simulations.[7] However, while Volvo has marketed itself as a safe family car and positioned itself as safe, Saab has kept silent about its safety. Saab was the first car manufacturer in the world to introduce many other safety components as well, so let me mention a few: in 1964, twin diagonal brake systems, so that in case one system fails there is always a back-up; in 1967, energy-absorbing zones in the front and the rear; in 1972, side collision protection; in 1983, brake pads without asbestos; in 1993, Black Panel, which is a system to reduce unnecessary or redundant information and thereby enhance the driver's night vision when driving at night time; and in 1997, Saab Active Head Restraint (SAHR), which is an active protection against whiplash injuries.

In a comparison among brands over the last three decades, Saab comes out as the safest car (in reality) during a majority of years — a fact that almost no one has any knowledge about. There you can talk about satisfying the customer beyond his or her expectations. The only problem is that the customer will only find out about this if he or she ends up in one of the most violent car accidents possible. If it is a less violent accident, it does not matter which car you are in, but when a collision is really violent you would wish that you had bought a Saab.

Turbo

"The coffee is really good here at my favorite hotel, isn't it?," Morgan said. He filled up his mug once again, smiled at Nick, and went on:

The engineers at Saab were not only good in innovating new safety components; they were really good in all kinds of innovation. Their biggest innovation was perhaps not in safety, but in how to get as

[7] See Folksam's (2003, 2005, 2007, 2009) research reports on car safety and comments on the research reports (Auto Motor & Sport, 2009; Sterner, 2010).

much horsepower as possible out of an engine without increasing the number of cylinders or increasing the cylinder volume. Other manufacturers who wanted more horsepower from their engines would increase the number of cylinders to 6, 8, or even 12, and also the cylinder volume from, say, 2 liters to 4 liters or more. The problem, though, is that big engines weigh considerably more than small engines and they consume more gasoline as well. Even though Saab at that time only used 4-cylinder engines with 2 liters of cylinder volume, their engineers chose to stick to that engine size. They figured that a little bit of engineering magic could get just as much horsepower out of the engines without having to increase the engine size, and Saab's new magic was the Turbo.

Nick, as you know, Saab did not invent the turbo. However, Saab was the first car manufacturer that could harness its power. The Saab engineers, under the direction of head engineer Per Gillbrand, came up with a beautiful solution so that the turbo could be used in standard cars. The key to the success story was the invention of the wastegate valve. The wastegate allowed Saab to domesticate the turbo and increase the engine power by 50% and reduce the fuel consumption at the same time. It was the kind of product attribute that is a dream for both engineers and marketers.

Saab included the new attribute in the 99 model in 1977, and full-scale production started in 1978. That same year, in 1978, Saab launched the Saab 900 and the top-of-the-line model was the Saab 900 Turbo. It became an instant success on the market and the delivery time to get a new Saab 900 grew rapidly. By the end of that year, customers had to wait more than 10 weeks for their new cars and delivery times just continued to grow longer. The marketing department was very excited about this success. In retrospect, the Saab 900 Turbo might have been Saab's most successful model on the market and the company was indeed booming.

A few years later, in 1984, Saab developed a new big and luxurious family car, the 9000 series. This was to be the stepping stone to the premium segment. When the 9000 arrived in the U.S., it was categorized as a "large car" by the Environmental Protection Agency (EPA)[8] — that is, a car in the largest category. For Saab, this recognition by the EPA was very valuable, since the Audi 100, BMW 5 Series, and Mercedes 280 were in one size category below the Saab 9000. Consequently, Saab had finally reached the top of the pyramid. The sales success from 1978 was repeated in 1984–1985. Shortly after the launch of the 9000 series, delivery times started to grow, which the marketing department knew was a foolproof sign of imminent success.

Biopower

Morgan continued:

Nick, let me finish this innovation part by saying just a few words about Saab's BioPower model. In 2006, Saab introduced biopower as a new concept. The concept rests upon a slightly modified engine and fuel system so that the engine can run on up to 85% ethanol and 15% gasoline. The engine can also use ordinary gasoline, but then there is no biopower effect of course.

Running a car on ethanol is positive for the environment in that it produces less carbon dioxide and other harmful emissions. Ethanol is also a recyclable fuel type, since it is the end result from, for instance, corn or wheat that has been mixed with yeast and water in a fermentation process.

A final advantage of ethanol compared to gasoline is that the engine power increases by about 20%. The engineers that were working on the fine-tuning of the engines were euphoric when they discovered this. As one of the engineers put it, "We did nothing and got 20–30 more horsepower for free." Everybody was happy.

---

[8] According to the U.S. EPA, the Swedish-built Saab 9000 is the most fuel-efficient automobile in the agency's "large car" size class. In addition, the Saab 9000 is the only import to achieve "large car" status, which the EPA determines as a function of interior volume (Saab, 1992, 2012; Environmental Protection Agency, 1986).

Market Segmentation and Positioning

All of a sudden, Morgan went quiet! He was gazing into nothingness and chewing on his tongue in a peculiar way, as if something was missing. A quick look down in front of him revealed the problem immediately. He had allowed himself to run out of coffee. There were only fumes left in his mug, and that was almost as embarrassing as running out of fuel on the Autobahn. A few seconds later, Morgan's mug was full of pitch-black coffee again and he went on as if nothing had happened: "Nick, you remember that market segmentation is at the core of marketing?" Nick nodded but said nothing, so Morgan continued:

A crucial aspect of segmentation is to evaluate the segment in terms of:

(1) attractiveness (such as size, growth, profitability, and scale economics); and

(2) whether the segment matches the company's objectives and resources. This is simply a question of whether there is a match between the segment and the company. If there is a match, the company will be able to serve the segment by satisfying customer needs better than competitors and will thus do so at a profit.

To Saab's delight, one can assume, the famous marketing professor Philip Kotler has been kind enough to point out in textbooks that Saab should belong to the same "well-to-do" segment as brands such as BMW and Mercedes [see Kotler *et al.*, 2005, p. 412]. However, BMW and Mercedes are about 10 to 20 times bigger than Saab in terms of production, which means that in order for Saab to compete with these two giants Saab should be more differentiated, unique in their product design and promotion, and ... and ...

Morgan went quiet again. "There was one more thing I wanted to say here," Morgan added. "Something about that all these mentioned aspects should also be reflected in something or somewhere. Umm . . . ," he mumbled and then his eyes went blank.

"It must be all that coffee," Nick thought. "Perhaps decaf would do the trick," Nick speculated in silence.

Morgan caught himself drifting away, and then he refocused and started again. "It is gone; I have forgotten it. Let us go on instead," Morgan said. And on he went:

> One Swedish professor in marketing said: "In view of Saab's relatively limited production output, one could almost say that Saab's cars are 'built by hand.'[9] Saab sells fewer cars than BMW and Mercedes, so in order to find car brands with equally limited production output as Saab, we have to look at Porsche (75,238 cars in 2009) and Jaguar (52,500 cars in 2009). Both those premium brands sold more cars than what Saab did in 2009, which is rather surprising."
>
> Saab's top management has had a wish for Saab to belong to the premium car segment, but at the same time the car has had the image of being a *folkbil* [people's car], which has complicated the task. Saab's management has actually, from time to time, expressed the view that Saab is a *folkbil*, which in Swedish means "a car for everyone." Saab has successfully conveyed this notion in their PR campaigns, and all Swedish car industry journalists except one have given strong support to this idea. Most of the journalists believe that the *folkbil* idea is the very reason behind Saab's successes over the years.

"Okay, Nick," Morgan said, "we are about to come to an end here, so listen up and fill up your cup!" Morgan continued:

> The final step in the segmentation process is to position the company's offer in the marketplace. Positioning is a matter of how your offer is perceived by your prospects on important attributes.

---

[9]Saab's cars are not actually built by hand; it is just a metaphor for limited production. Saab uses relatively efficient means of production in their factories.

Consequently, positioning is about what you do to the mind of the customer through all kinds of market communication.[10] Among the important aspects of positioning, two are especially relevant here — namely, to find a distinctive and unoccupied position for your brand; and secondly, to be first with the new attribute.

Saab has in the past, as we have seen, developed many new product attributes that were new to the industry, which in turn constituted excellent opportunities to position Saab's offer on the market. The development of the turbo back in the late 1970s serves as a good example. Possessing an attribute like turbo, which no one else has, is a dream scenario for any marketer working with positioning. Both before and after the turbo, Saab focused on safety; and during the 1990s and early 2000s, they focused on the "Born from Jets" tagline and also the very successful and awarded "Release Me" campaign. In connection with the ethanol strategy in 2006, Saab positioned itself as the "biopower" car, which resulted in the best sales ever that year.

"Oh, aah," Morgan said, "now I remember what I wanted to say when I interrupted myself and went blank just a few minutes ago. Perhaps you remember that I said that 'all these mentioned aspects should also be reflected in something or somewhere'; I should have added '... reflected in Saab's ....' Yes, now I remember," Morgan stated triumphantly before he went on: "But it should not be necessary for me to say this to you, since it is quite obvious what I wanted to say and you seem to be on top of everything today, so you tell me instead, Nick," Morgan said with a smile.

Nick flashed away the right answer instantly and added with a grin, "Well, I could have helped you right away when you started drifting away, but I thought I would check how your memory is doing nowadays and it seems to still be intact." Morgan laughed dryly as he was tired of talking and was suffering from a serious coffee deficit. Then he replied with five more questions.

---

[10]Note that product, price, and place are also means of communication.

Morgan's Second Set of Questions

Morgan wrote another set of questions on the whiteboard:

5. When and how are innovation and product development good tools to make a product "sell itself"?
6. In connection to the launch of Saab's 900 and 9000 models, the delivery times grew rapidly and the marketing department was excited and jubilant on both occasions. In your capacity as a prominent marketing specialist, how would you interpret the sales successes of the 900 and 9000 models in 1978 and 1984, respectively? And what factor or factors were mostly behind the success?
7. Did Saab's 9000 series become a premium car through the EPA classification? What is your opinion, and what arguments do you have that support your opinion?
8. What were the advantages and disadvantages when Saab introduced ethanol as a new fuel, and did the micro/macro environment play a role in any way?
9. In your opinion, should Saab be a *folkbil* ("people's car") as it has been in the past and should Saab try to go after the "folks segment"? Furthermore, which positioning concept should Saab try to establish over the next few years?

In addition to Morgan's five questions, there was actually one more question related to what Nick had been daydreaming about:

10. Why do you think that Nick concluded that the story about his own car accident (as a potential means for marketing communication) perhaps "would have suited Volvo better than Saab"? Was Nick's conclusion correct or incorrect, according to you?

Morgan listened carefully to Nick's answers to his questions, and then he said: "Before we finish off today's lecture, there is one more thing that our client Saab would like to have your opinion about. Let me present the situation to you," Morgan said with a friendly smile and went on:

> As you know, in 2009 and 2010 Saab was on the very edge of bankruptcy when the Dutch car manufacturer Spyker assumed leadership over the company. When the worst crisis was over, Saab's top management realized that GM had not managed Saab's product portfolio particularly well. The product development, which GM had promised and planned to speed up, had come to a complete halt. New product launches had thereby been either stopped or postponed.

The Meeting

Morgan continued with his presentation:

> In early 2010, shortly after Spyker had acquired Saab, the new chairman together with the CEO and the rest of Saab's top management held a meeting where they looked at Saab's product portfolio using Boston Consulting Group's well-known matrix. They did not really like what they saw. There were no question marks, stars, or cash cows, and the car production in the factory had been standing still for way too long. However, the top management had not come to the meeting empty-handed. The projects that GM had halted could be resumed relatively easily, and at that meeting the top management had brought along four dossiers filled with documents describing four potential products. The halted product development projects were perhaps the answer to all the product development problems that had hung over Saab like a dark shadow for years.
>
> At the meeting, the CEO put the dossiers and documents on the table in front of them. Inserted in the first dossier were technical drawings, specifications, and pictures related to the new Saab 9-5 Sedan, which was only a few months away from being launched. In the second dossier were documents and pictures of the new

9-5 Station Wagon, which could be launched as soon as six months after the 9-5 Sedan. The third dossier was thicker than the others. It consisted of, among other things, a set of beautiful sunset pictures from a photo session in Acapulco with the brand new Saab 9-4X Crossover SUV, which was to be produced in Mexico. The 9-4X could be launched at about the same time as the 9-5 Station Wagon, about half a year after the 9-5 Sedan.

The fourth and last dossier was filled with documents that showed the much-wanted and upcoming Saab 9-3 Sedan, which could be launched about two years after the Saab 9-5 Sedan. In that fourth dossier, the CEO and the chairman also found an odd-looking pinkish document marked with a red sticker and the text "Urgent." The pinkish two-page document was written by a technical consultant who concluded that the product development process could be speeded up even further. If certain measures were undertaken, the Saab 9-3 Sedan could be launched one and a half years after the Saab 9-5 Sedan.

The assembled managers looked up after they had gone through all of the documents. They were all smiling at each other, out of relief. The future did not look that bad after all, and they knew exactly what to do next.

Morgan's Last Question

Morgan ended his lecture by saying, "Nick, since you have provided me with great answers to all of my questions, I would very much like to hear what you would have decided in this last situation." He then proceeded to write the following question on the whiteboard:

11. What would you have done when launching Saab's new products on the market?

Morgan filled up his coffee mug one last time, smiled at Nick (you), and waited for his (your) answer.

Bibliography

Atuahene-Gima, Kwaku (1996). "Market Orientation and Innovation." *Journal of Business Research*, 35, February, 93–103.

Auto Motor & Sport (2009). "Folksam: Sveriges Säkraste Bilar!" May 5.

Barney, Jay B. and Ricky W. Griffin (1992). *The Management of Organizations*. Boston: Houghton Mifflin Company.

Bearden, William O., Ahmet H. Kirca, and Satish Jayachandran (2005). "Market Orientation: A Meta-Analytic Review and Assessment of Its Antecedents and Impact on Performance." *Journal of Marketing*, 69, April, 24–41.

Cervenka, Andreas (2008). "Saab har Förlorat 45 Miljoner i Veckan — I Elva år." *Svenska Dagbladet Näringsliv*, December 3.

Day, George S. (1994). "The Capabilities of Market-Driven Organizations." *Journal of Marketing*, 58, October, 37–52.

Dibb, Sally (1998). "Market Segmentation: Strategies for Success." *Journal of Marketing Intelligence & Planning*, 16, 394–406.

Dibb, Sally, L. Simkin, W. Pride, and O.C. Ferrell (1997). *Marketing: Concepts and Strategies*. Boston, MA: Houghton Mifflin.

Environmental Protection Agency (1986). *1986 Fuel Economy Guide.* Washington, D.C.: U.S. EPA.

Folksam (2003). *Folksams Nya Ranking: Hur Säker är Bilen?* Stockholm, April 2.

Folksam (2005). *Folksams Nya Ranking: Hur Säker är Bilen?* Stockholm, April 21.

Folksam (2007). *Folksams Nya Ranking: Hur Säker är Bilen?* Stockholm, November 8.

Folksam (2009). *Folksams Nya Ranking: Hur Säker är Bilen?* Stockholm, May 5.

Franke, N., P. Keinz, and C. Steger (2009). "Testing the Value of Customization: When Do Customers Really Prefer Products Tailored to Their Preferences?" *Journal of Marketing*, 73(5), 103–121.

Green, P.E. (1977). "A New Approach to Market Segmentation." *Business Horizons*, 20, 61–73.

Heimersson, Staffan (2009). "Inte Bitter men Förbannad." *Fokus*, August 21.

Hunt, Shelby D. (2002). *Foundations of Marketing Theory: Toward a General Theory of Marketing.* Armonk, NY: M.E. Sharpe.

Kalwani, M.U. and D.G. Morrison (1977). "Some Factors in Industrial Market Segmentation." *Industrial Marketing Management*, 9, 201–205.

Kotler, Philip (1991). *Marketing Management*, 7th ed. London: Prentice-Hall International (UK) Limited.

Kotler, Philip (2000). *Marketing Management: The Millennium Edition*, 10th ed. London: Prentice-Hall International (UK) Limited.

Kotler, Philip (2002). *Marketing Management*, 11th ed. Englewood Cliffs, NJ: Prentice Hall.

Kotler, Philip, Veronica Wong, John Saunders, and Gary Armstrong (2005). *Principles of Marketing: Fourth European Edition.* Essex: Pearson Education.

Levitt, Theodore (1960). "Marketing Myopia." *Harvard Business Review*, 38(4), July/August, 45–56.

Lönegård, Claes (2008). "Saabs Utdragna Dödskamp." *Fokus*, December 5. http://www.fokus.se/2008/12/saabs-utdragna-dodskamp/.

Mahajan, V. and A.K. Jain (1978). "An Approach to Normative Segmentation." *Journal of Marketing Research*, 15, 338–345.

Moorman, Christine and Roland T. Rust (1999). "The Role of Marketing." *Journal of Marketing*, 63, 180–197.

Nilsson, C. Patrik (1997). "Saab — Ett Skolexempel på Misslyckad Marknadsföring." *Resumé*, No. 24.

Nilsson, C. Patrik (2009). "Tveksamt om Saab Klarar att ta Tillvara en Sista Chans." *Dagens Industri*, March 21.

Nilsson, C. Patrik (2010). "Saab and the Perpetual Marketing Failure: More than 50 Years of Marketing Myopia." Paper presented at the 25th SVU World Congress in Tábor at the special session on "Coexistence of Management, Marketing and Technology in a Global Context," Tábor, Czech Republic, June 27–July 3.

Porter, Michael E. (1985). *Competitive Advantage: Creating and Sustaining Superior Performance.* New York: The Free Press.

Pröckl, Eddie (2009). "Nästa Saab Byggs i Trollhättan." *Ny Teknik,* January 15. http://www.nyteknik.se/nyheter/fordon_motor/bilar/article492615.ece/.

Reeves, Rosser (1960). *Reality in Advertising.* New York: Alfred A. Knopf.

Ries, Al and Jack Trout (1982). *Positioning: The Battle for Your Mind.* New York: Warner Books.

Saab (1992). "1992 Saab 9000 Rated Most Fuel Efficient 'Large Car' by EPA." Press release by Saab. http://www.saabhistory.com/.

Saab (2012). "Saab History 1984 — Saab 9000 Turbo." http://www.saab.com/.

Sharma, Subhash, Richard G. Netemeyer, and Vijay Mahajan (1990). "In Search of Excellence Revisited: An Empirical Evaluation of Peters and Waterman's Attributes of Excellence." In Bearden, William O. and A. Parasuraman (eds.), *Enhancing Knowledge Development in Marketing,* Vol. 1, Chicago: American Marketing Association, pp. 322–328.

Sterner, Marianne (2010). "Vi Har Gjort Världens Säkraste Bil." *Vi Bilägare,* July 12.

Svedberg, Tomas (2009). "Förre Volvobasen: Rädda inte Saab." *Göteborgs-Tidningen,* August 22. http://gt.expressen.se/nyheter/1.1679640/forre-volvobasen-radda-inte-saab/.

Welch, David and Dan Beucke (2005). "Why GM's Plan Won't Work." *Bloomberg Businessweek,* May 9. http://www.businessweek.com/magazine/content/05_19/b3932001_mz001.htm/.

Wills, Gordon (1985). "Dividing and Conquering: Strategies for Segmentation." *International Journal of Bank Marketing,* 3(4), 36–46.

Wind, Y. (1978). "Issues and Advances in Segmentation Research." *Journal of Marketing Research,* 15, 317–37.

Other Sources

Interviews conducted with:

- Saab Information Department, March 2009 and April 2010
- Saab marketing managers and representatives, February 1997, March 2009, April 2010, and May 2011
- Jaguar representative, April 2010
- Porsche representative, April 2010
- Toyota managers and representatives, March 2009 and April 2010.

Case 9

Connecting Strategy with Functional Practice in the Automobile Industry*

This case concerns the creation of a shared vehicle platform between two organizations (brands) in the automobile industry cluster in the northern part of Europe. Many famous automobile brands are situated in the cluster. This cluster has expanded over time, and within the cluster it is possible to find all types of organizations that relate to the automobile industry. The two organizations that are in focus for this study will be referred to as Chrome and Explorer.

The innovation process took place at two development sites. The Chrome organization was situated at site Alpha, while the Explorer organization was situated at site Beta. These development sites were situated in two different European countries. The basic idea behind the collaborative endeavor was to create a vehicle platform by sharing parts and still protect brand identities. However, this was easier said than done. The managers of the organizations found it challenging to connect strategic intentions with functional practice,

---

*Thommie Burström, of the Umeå School of Business and Economics, Umeå University (Sweden), developed this case for educational purposes only. The case design illustrates the need to include several concepts and theories when managing inter-organizational collaboration in industrial clusters. The names of the individuals and companies are fictitious.

and they realized that they had to coordinate and organize a complex web of interrelated business, structural, process, and technological interfaces.

Dealing with Business Interfaces

Tomas, who was head of the Engineering Department (Chrome, site Alpha), reflected on the situation. The two organizations were on the whole acting on the global market but aiming at different customer segments. The Chrome brand was aiming for the premium segments and had a very successful past; revenues were very high and the organization was seen as powerful. The Explorer brand was aiming for more low-level segments and was less successful. The Explorer brand showed positive revenues, but these revenues were significantly lower compared to the Chrome brand. Therefore, seen in relation to power, the Chrome brand possessed much more financial power than the Explorer brand.

In order to balance the relationship between the two organizations, they came to an agreement whereby the more powerful organization (Chrome) should finance the larger part of shared technology in the platform. Each organization should therefore finance their branded costs. Consequently, each organization was responsible for creating its own successful business case.

The managers of Chrome and Explorer organized a special group targeting areas suitable for branded or non-branded solutions. The group targeted and presented solutions for 90% of all areas in the vehicle platform. These solutions were on the whole accepted by the managers of both Chrome and Explorer. Nevertheless, the remaining 10% to be decided upon were very critical areas. It was decided that a decision should be made on the remaining 10% as the innovation process continued.

As the innovation process continued, it soon became obvious that it was difficult to maintain the market distance between Chrome and Explorer. In particular, the managers of Chrome saw a risk in sharing too much technology with Explorer. If customers started to view Explorer as an alternative to Chrome, Chrome's market share could be lost. Its image could also be lost. In turn, the managers of Explorer noticed that there was a cost increase in the innovation process. In order to balance that cost increase, the managers of Explorer would have to make a price adjustment. But by doing that they risked losing their customer segment, which expected fairly low-priced products. Tomas therefore formulated a question that he intended to bring to the next steering committee meeting:

- How are we going to keep the strategic market distance between the organizations so that we avoid cannibalization and yet achieve large-scale advantages?

Tomas thereafter continued to reflect on issues related to the business interface. There was also a decision to integrate an external engine supplier in the innovation process. This external engine supplier was trusted by the organizations and they had experience of previous collaboration. Since the automobile industry was striving to become "greener," a strategic decision was made to create hybrid cars — that is, it was supposed to be possible to drive the car through the use of electricity or gasoline as a power source. However, electrical engines had already been created through earlier innovative activities performed by the external supplier. There was therefore a mismatch in the strategic fit between the two organizations and the engine supplier. As a consequence, the two organizations wanted the supplier to adjust the engine to fit the body of the car, while the engine supplier wanted the organizations to adjust the body of the car to fit the engine. Furthermore, the external engine supplier already had other customers that were dependent on the present shape and status of the electrical engine. These customers were not interested in making any changes to the engine.

On the one hand, the external engine supplier argued that it was impossible to perform changes to the engine. Engines were also licensed according to certain standards, and changing these standards would bring substantial costs in the form of penalties. On the other hand, the managers of Chrome and Explorer claimed that in order to meet customer demands their cars had to be styled according to novel architecture.

The strategic mismatch between the organizations meant that the innovation process came to a standstill. Changing the external engine supplier was not an option. Tomas therefore formulated another question to bring to the next steering committee meeting:

- How are we going to create novel car bodies and still use engines provided by the supplier?

Dealing with Structural Interfaces

Mattias, who was acting as Chief Project Manager of the Commonality project, reflected on the problem of creating structural interfaces. Just as in any other innovation process, there was a need to create governance structures in order to control and guide the innovation work. It had therefore been decided that the innovation process would be governed by three steering committees. Two steering committees were branded, and the third committee was seen as a Commonality committee.

It was further decided that the actual product development was to be performed by the project members of three projects. Two of these projects were aiming for the creation of branded parts of the platform, and one of the projects was a Commonality project where project members were working on creating shared technology. It had also been decided that each project should be governed by its own unique steering committee (see Figure 1).

Mattias thought, "Well, it looks good on paper." As it turned out, governance of the multi-project setting became more complex when managers at Chrome and Explorer decided to use the vehicle platform in different ways in order to meet customer needs.

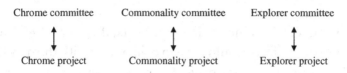

Figure 1. Governance.

In the automobile industry, organizations create series of vehicles (sets of models and variants) in order to meet different customer needs. For example, the BMW 3 Series and BMW 5 Series are examples of two series. In this case, the managers of Chrome had decided to use the vehicle platform as a dynamic base and principally create series as customer needs changed. Simultaneously, managers at Explorer decided to use a fixed number of series. They argued that this way of working would make it possible to communicate a clear offer to customers. It would also be more cost-efficient.

As a consequence of the series decision in Explorer, the workload increased for the Chief Project Manager of the Explorer project (each project was managed by a Chief Project Manager). Thus, strategic managers at Explorer created yet another project. The new project would be run by a new Chief Project Manager responsible for organizing series. It was very unclear how governance would be performed in relation to this project. The project could be seen as a fourth ordinary project, in which case it would have the same status as the other Explorer project. However, the new project could also be seen as a subproject of the ordinary Explorer project. Mattias was worried about this structural interface and decided to formulate a question that he would bring to the next steering committee meeting:

• How should the new fourth project be governed, and what status should it have?

Mattias then continued his reflection on structural interfaces. The creation of the new project could have consequences for the Chief

Project Managers of the other two projects. If the new project were to have the same status as the ordinary projects, then the Chief Project Managers of all projects would have to collaborate with the new Chief Project Manager. If the new project were to be seen as a subproject, collaboration could be delegated to the Chief Project Manager of the Explorer project.

Another complex issue to deal with in the structural interface was the role and place of the external engine supplier. The commitment of the external engine supplier was low. The engine supplier only had one representative in the Commonality project, and all questions regarding engines and hybrid engine development should pass through the Commonality project. However, due to the low degree of commitment, the Chief Project Manager of the Explorer project had contacted the engine supplier at site Beta instead. This way of working was not in line with what had previously been agreed, and it came to the knowledge of the Commonality committee. The managers of the Commonality committee were not sure how to deal with this issue. There was a risk of miscommunication. Mattias, who was supposed to organize the collaboration with the engine supplier, therefore decided to formulate yet another question to bring to the next steering committee meeting:

- Should we try to make the Explorer project terminate this interaction, or should we take another approach?

Finally, there was a lack of strategic synchronization. The managers of the Chrome organization/project had started their work three months before the managers of the Explorer organization/project. Consequently, since the project managers of the Chrome project had already started their activities, so did the project managers of the Commonality project. This unsynchronized start created problems for Mattias. He found that he was supposed to collaborate with the Chief Project Managers of the other projects, but since they were not in sync, it was almost impossible to come to any major agreements.

Mattias therefore decided to formulate a final question to bring to the steering committee meeting:

- Should we force the branded projects to synchronize their development process?

Mattias was well aware that this issue was a very sensitive issue to approach. For example, the Chief Project Manager of the Chrome project actually wanted to increase the speed of the development work. If allowed to do so, the gap between the two projects would widen, making it almost impossible for Mattias to coordinate the creation of commonalities. Nevertheless, managers at the Chrome brand intended to industrialize their product six months before the Explorer brand. Mattias therefore respected the need for an increased speed of development; still, he felt under a lot of pressure due to the responsibility for multi-project coordination.

Dealing with Process Interfaces

While Tomas was reflecting on problems with business interfaces, and Mattias was reflecting on difficulties with structural interfaces, Niklas, who was a strategic process manager, reflected upon challenges in creating practice-based process interfaces. The organizations had come to an agreement that they should use one and the same new product development process. It was argued that, even though the process was more familiar to one of the organizations, it would be easier to "come to terms" if they used the same type of innovation process. This way of organizing was very successful. Through the use of a shared innovation process, project members could find a shared language and they could use the same instructions as a guide when being uncertain of what actions to take. Still, it remained to put strategic intentions into action. The action was very much influenced by core values, decision-making practices, and cost follow-up practices.

Core Values

It was expected that the project members would coordinate and integrate as they saw fit. That is, the project members were expected to self-organize, and only when they were unable to solve issues would organizing be performed through negotiations between the managers of the steering committees. It was also expected that the innovation process would be guided by the core values relating to each organization. However, Niklas found that while it was obvious to the project managers of the Chrome and Explorer projects what core values to be guided by, it was not obvious to the project managers of the Commonality project (see Figure 2).

Niklas found that the steering committees spoke with different voices when trying to guide the projects. Both Chrome and Explorer occupied co-shared positions in the Commonality steering committee. However, the managers of the Commonality steering committee came from lower ranks in the organizations. They did not have

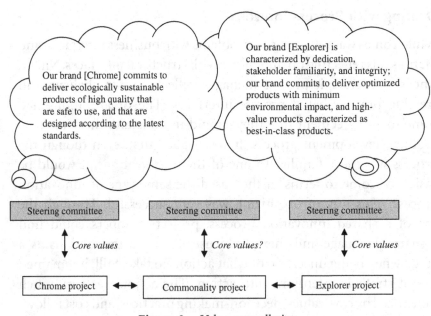

Figure 2. Value constellation.

the same power as actors in branded steering committees. As a consequence, they did not manage to create ongoing communication with the managers of the branded committees. Thus, most of the shared organizing efforts were performed in positions that were hierarchically lower or higher than at the level of steering committees. For the project members, this situation meant that value-related novelty, differences, and interdependencies were challenging to understand. For example, the project managers were guided by the information in a brand distinction document that clearly stated the level of differentiation/commonality for the majority of components; however, key components still needed to be decided upon. The project members therefore had to consult different steering committees in order to reach a final decision on interdependencies relating to commonality.

Brand core values and approaches to creating customer value were deeply rooted in the traditional way of working at each site/brand. The two brands had by tradition implemented their unique ways of balancing features and costs. These different approaches did not mean that one brand did not care about costs, or that the other brand did not care about features; it simply meant that the managers of the organizations had very different priorities in the initial phase of product development. The managers of Chrome were willing to take higher risks in costs in order to protect its premium image, while the managers of Explorer advocated cost efficiency and were therefore more unwilling to take risks related to costs. Nevertheless, the remaining key commonality issues were supposed to be negotiated in the project setting.

Negotiating key commonalities was challenging, since managers of the parent organizations, and their related projects, were naturally guided by traditional brand core values when deciding on the value approach related to commonalities. However, the project managers of the Commonality project and its committee were guided by diverse core values. For branded projects, traditional brand values were explicitly communicated from brand to project in branded product and project prerequisites. For the Commonality project and its steering committee, the work pattern looked a bit different. In the Commonality project, the Product Planner had to interpret branded product prerequisites and requirements in order to create product prerequisites directed for commonality. Hence, during this activity the Product Planner, and later the Commonality project members, tried to interpret customers' shared values. For example, when items were removed or changed by one brand, the project managers of the Commonality project had to make a complex interpretation in order to understand the meaning and impact of the change.

Furthermore, the project managers translated the meaning of features into value-related terms: "leading," "among the best," and "competitive." Thus, the value profile of each brand was expected to be illustrated by different combinations of such value-related terms. That is, when brands used the term "leading," such a statement had to be understood in relation to some certain specified value aspects (targets and requirements). For example, the level of fuel consumption is a certain value aspect. If a brand wanted to be "leading," a target level of fuel consumption had to be identified. However, fuel consumption is affected by sources such as engines, air resistance, and tires. Some of these sources were seen as areas for branding, while other sources were seen as areas for commonality. It was difficult to understand how such interdependencies would be differentiated or shared in the new products. Tensions therefore arose when actors early in the process found that product prerequisites, through the use of value terms, communicated very similar vehicle profiles. For sure, in relation to commonality aspects, values should be very much alike, but overall profiles should be differentiated.

It was earlier in this case illustrated that in order to communicate the product offer to customers, the brands also worked on creating product series. Niklas found that the creation of such series was part of the boundary challenges that faced the project members. Each series was supposed to be novel and yet linked to traditional product traditions. Product series were also seen as an important way of differentiating brands, despite sharing technology. Therefore, the project managers elaborated on using combinations of several narrow series or a single broad series. Nevertheless, the brands performed an unsynchronized startup phase: while one brand decided on a concept and continued by investigating other development issues, the other brand tried to understand intra-brand product interdependencies.

Development of the vehicle platform was also affected by estimations of future sales volumes. Predictions of higher sales volumes brought possibilities to invest in more features, and also signified lower costs per item produced. Of course, future sales predictions differed between brands; this was not a problem in relation to branded issues, but it was a problem in relation to commonality issues. For example, in the Commonality project, branded expectations of future price and market demands were transformed and integrated into commonality aspects. But since commonality aspects were structured to integrate the view from the two brands, with different views on estimated changes, price and market mechanisms became less understandable for actors in the Commonality project compared to members in branded projects. The Commonality project and its committee therefore had to balance different views on estimated changes, and on the effects that price and market changes would have on the platform.

Related to the development of the platform was the idea of using parts that were already in production by implementing a carry-over strategy. It was argued that the use of these components and parts would be beneficial for the platform, and it would increase the speed of product development. The intention of using a carry-over strategy was good, but Niklas found it difficult to implement this strategy in practice, since the brands had different experiences of these parts and components that originally had been developed to fit a single brand strategy. Hence, while one brand saw the carry-over strategy as more or less unproblematic, the other brand had to evaluate and understand all consequences of using that strategy.

Niklas also found that connected to all development issues was the issue of how the brands should be positioned in the market. It was not so easy for the projects to obtain a clear-cut answer, since they communicated with different steering committees. This issue was treated through ongoing dialogues throughout the project setting; the dialogues found a more substantial content as product development continued. Niklas still found it necessary to create an answer to the question:

- How should organizations and steering committees guide the project managers through the use of core values?

Inter-project core value issues

Niklas also identified some other core value issues. The project managers were not equally attached to organizational values. For example, engineers were generally more influenced by traditional brand values than purchasers were. The purchasing function had been organized in an aligned fashion. Thus, despite acting at different sites, purchasers found it easier to balance traditional brand values than their fellow engineers did. There were simply fewer product development issues on which to disagree.

Each function had worked out strategic approaches in relation to its own area. For example, the manufacturing function explained key issues related to the manufacturing process. These approaches were communicated in project prerequisites, and had been weighed against each other in earlier projects. Nevertheless, although the actors had experience of previous common product developments, they still worked on understanding and accepting each other's approach to value creation.

Moreover, although the project managers were performing activities in different projects, they still shared knowledge and understanding of diverse brand values. Thus, this knowledge was shared, but knowledge of how to integrate and coordinate diverse values was lacking. Therefore, actors representing various functions were collaborating, but this collaboration concerned integration of work routines, not brand values. There were regular cross-project meetings, but these meetings were not specifically concerned with values but only with issues like costs or features.

In order to understand how competitive a certain feature would be, actors used value expressions such as "leading," "among the best," or "competitive." By combining such feature definitions, they could describe brand profiles; these expressions were related to competitors with respect to brands in isolation, not with respect to each other. Thus, during meetings the project members viewed value expressions as integrated, while the practical application of value expressions was separated. Simply put, on a strategic level, brands identified competitors in a certain segment and created profiles in relation to these actors. However, since the brands targeted different segments, they adjusted the use of value terms to their own situation. Consequently, since both brands wanted to be on top of their respective segments, it was almost impossible to see a difference between the created brand profiles in prerequisites and requirement specifications.

Niklas also found that the project members had some difficulty understanding ongoing organizational changes in relation to values. Some branded functions were becoming integrated; thus, the relationship between brands and people in projects was also changing. One department had reorganized and integrated across sites and brands, and therefore "spoke with one voice." Another department tried to find a similar way of working, and networks were created in other functions. In these networks, discussions were held in order to balance commonalities and branding. Hence, brand value integration could be discerned, but it was difficult to state how far such integration had penetrated. The question still remained:

- How should the project managers deal with the situation of being guided by diverse core values?

Decision Making

Niklas also reflected on the fact that in any new product development project managers need to make a lot of decisions. However, Niklas found that making decisions in an inter-organizational multi-project setting where organizations compete and collaborate at the same time was very challenging.

Organizational intentions were communicated to projects through product prerequisites, which in turn were translated into project prerequisites by the project managers. The Commonality committee/project was responsible for integrating branded prerequisites, but the mandate to achieve such integration was less clear. These actors could only act on decisions made by all projects in consensus. When commonalities were not decided in consensus, decisions could be blocked by other committees/projects.

Niklas could see that most mandates in relation to product decisions for branded committees/projects seemed quite clear, while mandates for the Commonality project and its steering committee were less so. Branded steering committees were entitled to make product decisions, while projects should make project decisions. The Commonality steering committee and project were supposed to play similar roles as branded committees and projects, but many commonality-related decisions caused ambiguity, since the technology decided upon often had interdependencies with branded parts. When details at the front of the vehicle were being decided, these decisions clashed with decisions that had been made about the details pertaining to the rear of the vehicle. This made it hard to understand and create clear areas of decision.

Since there was an ambiguity over decision areas, actors in projects could not know how stable and definite a product development decision actually was. Brand-related committees/projects had control over branded development. Therefore, decisions taken on branded issues were more stable than decisions relating to commonality. Decision stability was also affected by changes made through the carry-over strategy. Changes could affect technological interdependencies, in which case previous decisions would have to be reviewed. Due to the multitude of these decisions and their ambiguity, actors in projects prepared for eventualities.

Niklas identified one clear distinction in relation to mandates between steering committees and projects. This distinction concerned the right to open gates. The Commonality steering committee did not have the same power as the other two steering committees. Thus, gate opening concerning the Commonality project became ambiguous, since all three committees had to have a say. The Commonality steering committee was able to put pressure on brands if they had not reached their commonality targets. Nonetheless, the managers of Chrome and Explorer had the last word, since they held the monetary resources; and because the brands were gate openers, the project members could be expected to act in accordance with brand directives rather than with directives from the Commonality steering committee.

Niklas could also see that related to the challenge of creating decision stability was the issue of decision cultures. Since this was a phase of early product development with a high degree of ambiguity, many decisions were unstable and many decision iterations were being performed throughout the project setting. That is, decisions were either rejected, modified, or negotiated. It is important here to point out that there is nothing wrong with decision iterations; it is the way many actors make decisions in early phases of product development, although this is not acknowledged. Nevertheless, Niklas found that decision iterations varied by committee/project.

First, at the boundary between the Chrome project and its committee, the decision-making culture called for consensus. Second, between the Explorer project and its committee, managers were performing decision making according to another principle. These managers saw decision making as important, as a way to communicate progress. Thus, although managers made decisions, these decisions were often taken as recommendations. Third, since the Commonality committee/project depended on decision making in branded committees/projects, decision integration was more reactive than the way in which branded projects made decisions. The project members of the Commonality project could proactively make decision proposals, but usually had to wait for decision iterations to take place in branded projects. Therefore, the variety of decision cultures became an inter-organizational managerial challenge.

Since the branded committees had the right to decide on product prerequisites, they also had the right to decide on costs and features. However, the managers of the two brands had also agreed to share some costs and features. Therefore, in relation to commonality cost, mandates were ambiguous, since some of these costs/features had already been decided upon while other costs/features were still to be negotiated.

Niklas also found that decision making related to time management was complex. Organizing product development in relation to time constraints is difficult, especially when managers are trying to control inter-organizational time constraints. In this case, some managers wanted to make changes to the time schedule. The managers of the Commonality project used a master time plan. In this plan, the brands had different deadlines. It was possible to deviate from this plan, within limits. The Commonality steering committee/project had to balance branded time plans against the master plan, but had no mandate to order changes. Therefore, the Commonality committee/project had to point out time-related consequences, sometimes claiming that the issue in focus was an agreed commonality area and that therefore other committees/projects had to comply, or negotiating in order to convince other projects to make changes, so that the master plan could be followed. On the other hand, branded projects were also caught up in mutual agreements concerning commonality. Thus, branded projects could exercise decision rights as a way to make timely changes and create separation, but only if they were willing to pay the price of torn-up agreements.

There were also occasions when committees made separate decisions on the same type of matter. That was not a problem as long as the decision subjects concerned isolated branded issues. But due to technological interdependencies, many parts and components were connected. When these interdependencies could not be balanced at the committee level, issues were brought to decision-making bodies higher up in the organization. However, this transfer of decisions made it difficult for project actors to understand decision-making processes.

Strongly connected to mandate-related tensions was the role of the Chief Project Manager (CPM). The CPM's role and boundaries in each project and in relation to steering committees was unclear. The CPMs of branded projects did not have the role and mandate of a business project manager to balance customer product prerequisites and decide on the best business case. However, each CPM had to ensure that his project created project prerequisites and requirement specifications in order to achieve balanced targets. Hence, in branded projects the CPM had responsibility for business proposals but not for proposal authority and decision rights.

For the CPM of the Commonality project, mandates took on yet another character. Due to the strong interdependence with branded committees/projects, role performance was even more ambiguous. There was a responsibility to create project prerequisites and requirement specifications relating to commonality. However, since business cases were owned by brands and communicated through branded projects, the Commonality project's CPM was responsible for creating commonality business case proposals without being able to communicate directly with business case owners. Hence, integration and coordination of business proposals and business cases became separated in relation to customers, both in terms of planning and action. Mandates therefore had to be further understood, negotiated, and elaborated.

As work with the platform continued, it became a challenge to understand which actor owned integration and coordination rights in relation to the complete vehicle offer. As product development continued, the product became more detailed and there was a need to decide on issues relating to the complete vehicle. Branded committees/projects saw themselves as owners, since they were responsible for business results. At the same time, the members of the Commonality committee/project saw themselves as owners, since they had the platform responsibility. Niklas therefore saw it as necessary to find the answers to two questions:

- How should we have organized in order to create a more transparent and efficient decision structure from the very beginning?
- What should we do in order to create more transparent and efficient decision structures in the following work to come?

Cost Follow-Up

Niklas further identified that it was challenging to perform inter-organizational cost follow-ups. The two organizations had to provide resources so that cost follow-ups could be organized and performed in a similar and consistent manner. In this respect, the two organizations co-owned the problem of cost follow-ups. All projects had a responsibility to perform cost follow-ups, but not the authority to tell their respective line organizations how this was to be done.

The managers of Chrome and Explorer had organized differently in order to perform cost follow-ups. The managers of the Explorer project could quite easily organize the cost follow-up process, while the managers of the Chrome and Commonality projects at the other site had to turn to various engineers in the line organization. The managers of the Explorer project were working in a more standardized (as in "hard," core formal routines) way with cost interdependencies. Those standards had to be adjusted to the complex project setting. As for the managers of the Chrome and Commonality projects, they were used to working with less formal cost follow-up routines. However, the managers found it difficult to balance the resources needed in order to anchor the process at two sites, and were therefore trying to integrate shared routines on how to organize cost issues.

Furthermore, since the projects were still in an early phase of product development and were working with a new cost follow-up tool, it was not easy for the managers to understand how different types of cost issues should be organized. Since cost follow-up was of mutual interest, managers were searching for a solution that was related to cost follow-up practices. However, many ongoing parallel changes had to be understood and taken into consideration as well. For example, there were complex cost interdependencies with multiple projects outside of the project setting, and there were also changes in managers working with cost follow-ups (the Explorer project) and uncertainty over who would work with cost follow-ups (the Chrome and Commonality projects).

Another challenge was to keep track of how costs changed when brands wanted to add unique features and drive branding instead of commonality, which resulted in higher project and product costs. And since the project managers were still developing their cost follow-up tool, a definite answer was hard to reach. Hence, projects could not always balance changes and costs. The answer from the brands, when there was a cost increase, could be that projects should "assimilate" costs into the rest of the project. However, when using more glass, steel, and man-hours, assimilation was very difficult, especially since the projects could not know what other changes might come later.

Cost decisions were also difficult for the project managers, since the brands were not equally cost-sensitive. The project managers thus had to understand how to balance the brands' cost sensitivity, desired features, and future market position. Written documents in the form of prerequisites and requirement specifications were supposed to support the decision process, but it was not always easy to find a balance between what was specified and the costs. For example, the features expressed by the Explorer brand were not balanced in relation to the intended costs. The managers of the project setting therefore tried to find an answer to the following question:

- How should we create more efficient cost follow-up routines in our inter-organizational collaboration?

Dealing with Technological Interfaces

Malin, who had the role of strategic geometry manager, found difficulties in creating technological interfaces. New product development was supported by the use of computer-aided design (CAD). The use of CAD early in the innovation process was strategically important, since it could reduce the use of physical prototypes. Thus, the innovation process would be both faster and cheaper, since the creation of physical prototypes takes time and is expensive.

Through the use of CAD, engineers could create very detailed digital models of all parts in the car as well as a model of the final car. The CAD modules give a hint of how data, information, and knowledge complexity can be communicated when dealing with specific product development issues. However, if the project is large, many more or less interdependent CAD modules are used to communicate and organize complexity. For example, a complete car with all of its complexity may be visualized by configuring CAD modules representing the different parts of the vehicle.

Malin knew from experience that new product development related to a car is performed concurrently by engineers in different departments using their own computers and digital tools. Each engineer creates parts related to his or her area of expertise. So from time to time, there is a need to stop the development work and evaluate the work done by different engineers. However, a CAD module, with all of its details, carries a lot of digital information, which makes it difficult for the system, for example, to rotate the module on the screen. The amount of digital information therefore needs to be reduced when making evaluations. Hence, the project members used an *automatic configuration tool.*

This meant that in order to provide other project members with geometry-based product information, the car models were translated into lightweight CAD formats to be more manageable. The lightweight CAD format made it possible to review, for example, how the gearbox fits with the engine or how suspenders fit with the body of the car. Simply put, engineers and all other project members could get the bigger picture of their performed new product development achievements. The downside of the lightweight format is that it is not possible to make any changes in the digital geometry that is visualized.

Malin knew that the dream scenario was to perform product development until a milestone was reached, and then there would be a freeze in product development whereby the development work would be evaluated. After evaluating the quality of the performed development project, the members would make necessary improvements and new product development would continue. Nevertheless, the use of CAD systems in the early phase of new product development also resulted in some problems in practice.

Malin, who was responsible for coordinating and integrating the work with CAD systems, was worried. The ideal situation would be to use only one CAD system. There had actually been a strategic decision and agreement to use only one type of CAD system. However, in practice three different CAD systems were in use. Consequently, the project members needed to act within a multi-CAD environment, which was somewhat problematic.

One of the CAD systems in use was very old. It was only used by engineers at site Beta. This system had not been updated for years. The information in the system was not in English, which meant that there was always a need for translation when using data from this system, since the business language was English. The system was still in use because it contained data relating to older products. However, some parts from older products were being used in more novel products. It was also impossible to use the old system in combination with the configuration tool. Malin therefore asked herself what to do with this system:

- Should we update and only keep this CAD system alive until we don't need it any more, or make an effort to translate all information inside the system and then put the system to rest? Translating all information might be unnecessary and would cost at least 1 million Euros.

At site Alpha, two other CAD systems were in use. Different engineering departments preferred the use of the respective systems. The choice of using which of the two CAD systems was affected by traditions and emotions. Any specialist who had learned how to work with one system would have to re-learn if changing the system. However, it was more complex than that. New product development was performed in close relationship with suppliers and customers, and so the work of engineers was connected to systems in other distant parts of the innovation cluster. Thus, changing CAD systems would lead to consequences that were difficult to identify and understand. Malin therefore asked herself how to deal with the situation:

- Should we keep to the initial decision and use only one CAD system, or should we actually learn how to manage a multi-CAD environment?

There were also other problems. Engineers at site Beta had, in line with the strategic agreement, initially used only one CAD system.

However, since some project members at site Beta had to collaborate with project members at site Alpha, which used a more modern system, they found it necessary to start using two CAD systems in parallel. Malin therefore asked herself:

- Should I intervene and prohibit the use of two CAD systems at site Beta? It involves costs and there is also a risk of path dependency, since once you start using a system it gets stuck in the organization. On the other hand, I can see that the work runs more smoothly now that we use both types of CAD systems.

Finally, the most immediate problem to deal with was that when trying to integrate data from both modern CAD systems in the automatic vehicle configuration tool, the whole system collapsed. Parts in the form of digital modules were not connected as they should be; the picture on the computer screen therefore showed modules randomly placed all over the screen, making evaluation impossible. In order to deal with the problem, a momentary solution was to create engineering task forces that manually translated data to fit into the automatic configuration tool. But that work took three weeks, which delayed the project and made customers feel uneasy about the development situation. This issue added to the uncertainty of how to work with CAD systems.

Malin understood that there was a mismatch between planning and actual performance, and she recapitulated:

- We have made a strategic decision to work with one type of CAD system, but that does not work.
- We do not know what to do with the old CAD system at site Beta.
- We do not know how to deal with the situation of using two modern CAD systems in parallel, since we cannot integrate the use of these systems in the automatic configuration-packaging tool.
- Engineers at site Beta have started using two CAD systems in parallel in order to make product development work in practice,

but this action is not in line with the decision to use only one CAD system.

Overall, the managers were dealing with complex practice-related development issues stretching from inter-organizational strategic levels to inter-organizational functional levels. Tomas, who had heard of all the problems in the organization, felt that as Chief of Engineering he had a responsibility to call for a meeting with Mattias, Niklas, and Malin. At the meeting, they all presented their knowledge of the present situation. After the last presentation, they all fell silent. After a while, Tomas spoke up and formulated the obvious remaining question:

- What should we do now?

Bibliography

Bengtsson, M. and S. Kock (2000). "'Coopetition' in Business Networks — To Cooperate and Compete Simultaneously." *Industrial Marketing Management*, 29, 411–426.

Müller, R. (2009). *Project Governance.* Aldershot: Gower Publishing Company.

Müller, R., K. Spang, and S. Ozcan (2009). "Cultural Differences in Decision Making in Project Teams." *International Journal of Managing Projects in Business*, 12(1), 70–93.

Nohria, N. and R.G. Eccles (1992). "Face-to-Face: Making Networked Organizations Work." In Nohria, N. and R.G. Eccles (eds.), *Networks and Organizations: Structure, Form and Action*, Boston, MA: Harvard Business School Press.

Olson, E.L. (2008). "The Implications of Platform Sharing on Brand Value." *Journal of Product & Brand Management*, 17(4), 244–253.

Olson, E.L. (2009). "The Impact of Intra-Brand Platform Sharing on Brand Attractiveness." *Journal of Product & Brand Management*, 18(3), 212–217.

Orlikowski, W.J. (1992). "The Duality of Technology: Rethinking the Concept of Technology in Organizations." *Organization Science*, 3(3), 398–427.

Ottosson, S. (2002). "Virtual Reality in the Product Development Process." *Journal of Engineering Design*, 13(2), 159–172.

Case 10

Cluster Development and Marketing Challenges for a Regional Biorefinery Cluster*

In Sweden, economic welfare has often relied on wood resources. Almost 80% of the Scandinavian nation's land mass is heavily forested. These areas are part of the taiga biome (or boreal forest), which covers large parts of the Northern hemisphere. Taiga wood is known for its high quality and long fibers that develop during a lengthy growth process.

Industrial development in the northern part of Sweden has relied heavily on logging and processing of forest resources into traditional wood products (i.e., paper, timber, and furniture). Due to the presence of sawmills and paper factories, several wood-based industry clusters have developed in this part of Sweden. Historically these clusters have focused on producing traditional wood products. In recent decades, however, one particular setting in northern Sweden

*Andrew Arbuthnott and Johan Jansson, both at Umeå School of Business and Economics, Umeå University (Sweden), developed this case for educational purposes only. It was compiled from published sources, and is intended to be used as a basis for class discussions rather than to illustrate either productive or unproductive industry cluster developments and marketing practices.

has differentiated from the status quo and developed a new regional biorefinery industry cluster, creating highly refined and innovative products from wood.

Biorefinery industry concepts are multi-faceted industrial facilities or systems that integrate biomass conversion processes and equipment to produce fuels, power, and chemicals from biomass and are analogous with petroleum refineries, which produce multiple products and fuels from petroleum (Kamm *et al.*, 2006). In this case from northern Sweden, biomass, mainly raw forest material, is refined into products that have a higher market value. The International Energy Agency (2008) defines biorefining as the sustainable processing of biomass into a spectrum of bio-based products (food, feed, chemicals, and materials) and bioenergy (biofuels, power, and/or heat).

Based on adding value to renewable forestry resources, industry clusters centered on refining raw forestry (biomass) face a myriad of challenges. There are often heated debates — held at local, national, and international levels — on the amount of wood that can be removed sustainably from forests. In Sweden, and within the taiga biome, it may take 80 to 100 years for a pine tree to reach full maturity. Traditionally abundant forestry resources are becoming scarcer, as private and public sector actors discover that more and more commercial products, such as fuel, can be derived from wood. In addition, remote wooded areas have high value for international and domestic tourism as well as recreational activities such as hiking, skiing, fishing, etc. Thus, sustainability challenges are evident.

This case concerns a regional biorefinery industry cluster, which operates within one of Sweden's geographically remote regions — Örnsköldsvik.[1] Figure 1 illustrates the industry cluster's geographic location in Sweden, Scandinavia, and Northern Europe. Although the industrial activities within the Örnsköldsvik biorefinery cluster

---

[1] Translated from Swedish into English, *Örnsköldsvik* means "Eagle Shield Bay."

Figure 1. Location of Örnsköldsvik.

initiatives are diverse, this particular case focuses on the cluster's formal development organizations and marketing of ethanol as a biofuel for transport, and some specific challenges faced during this process.

The Örnsköldsvik Region's Industrial and Societal Setting

The Örnsköldsvik region is located along the Gulf of Bothnia, and positioned approximately 530 kilometers north of Stockholm, the capital of Sweden. The geographically remote and predominantly rural Örnsköldsvik region is an administrative part of Västernorrland County, which in recent years has been one of Sweden's *least* enterprising counties. With circa 55,000 inhabitants and a population density of 8.5 inhabitants per square kilometer, the Örnsköldsvik region is sparsely populated.

The largest and most dominant businesses in Örnsköldsvik operate within the forestry, pulp-and-paper, and engineering sectors. A military vehicle production sector, small local tourism, and professional service divisions also operate in the region, alongside a now-budding biorefinery sector. Of the region's working population, 27% are employed within manufacturing — which is almost twice as high as the national Swedish average (18%). The region's deep-water port provides local businesses with opportunities to export and import numerous raw materials and manufactured goods.

Industrial facilities, processing systems, and socioeconomic developments in Örnsköldsvik trace back to the early 20th century, when many sawmills were built and pulp-and-paper production became most dominant. However, in the 1990s, whilst Sweden's wood-based industries faced severe economic difficulties, the Örnsköldsvik industrial and societal setting also suffered (Peterson, 2009). Many businesses closed, downsized, or relocated to more centrally located regions in Sweden. Around 5,000 jobs were lost. During that period of socioeconomic decline, it was common for local people to describe their regional community as *Dövik*, meaning "Dead Bay."

Local Industry Cluster Development

Within industrial and post-industrial nations, regional industry cluster development tends to be initiated by either governments (i.e., top-down) or local business communities (i.e., bottom-up). Despite a large number of "top-down" clustering initiatives that exist, cluster researchers and practitioners (e.g., Sölvell *et al.*, 2003; Ffowcs-Williams, 2004) suggest that regional industry clusters driven from the bottom-up are more dynamic.

During the late 1990s, various Örnsköldsvik regional business leaders, entrepreneurs, and politicians realized that new business and industry concepts were needed in order to prevent further socio-economic decline. International competition in the traditional pulp-and-paper industry and varying price levels of such products were negatively affecting the region. Local industry and government actors discussed how more value-added products could be produced and marketed in ways that would create more profit and more jobs, and thus renew the regional industry setting (Croon, 2005). Among many alternatives, a new regional biorefinery industry and cluster located around an old industrial site became an important renewal initiative.

As noted in Arbuthnott *et al.* (2010), the new regional industry initiatives were conceived during the latter half of the 1990s when a small group of managers, entrepreneurs, and local industry developers met informally to discuss ways to rethink, renew, and revitalize the region's local industry setting. Over time the group met more regularly. Accordingly, they developed a list of over 50 potential industry renewal ideas that could be expanded into new business and industrial processes within their struggling region. The ideas were diverse. Nonetheless, they all concerned exploiting the region's raw forestry material, wood and chemical processing expertise, and strong industrial infrastructure in order to create new products, services, and firms. As such, the core idea was to create pioneering industry facilities and processing systems, which could integrate biomass conversion equipment and processes to refine raw biomass — mainly forest material — into new value-added products.

The informally organized group founded a formal not-for-profit organization, and initiated a local cluster concept, under the name "Processum Biorefinery Initiative" (hereinafter "Processum"). A central motivation for initiating the new "regional industry" cluster was stimulation of new, collectively orientated business within the region.

Meanwhile, the Örnsköldsvik municipality created a long-term development scheme and renewal project encompassing five strategic "regional excellence" areas. Each area aimed for the region to be world-class by the year 2015. The emerging biorefinery industry initiatives fell within the local government's "Beyond Oil — Industry Development in a Sustainable Society" area.[2] Professor Charlie Karlsson (2008) indicates that when private and public organizations cluster within a specific region, potential collective benefits may be realized.

The potential production and distribution output of Processum's regional cluster initiative was broad. New textiles, fuels, food additives, pharmaceutical aids, energy and heat, soil enhancers, and paints and solvents were possible to create and refine from forest resources. One particular production in this distribution and innovative business concept was bioethanol fuel, for individual consumer and public transportation usages. Such ethanol initiatives had high economic value, societal significance, and market potential. Consequently, ethanol fuels made from forestry-related biomass became a high-profile business concept, stemming from the emergent regional industry cluster.

As an organization, Processum was what Professor Michael Porter (2008) would consider an "institution for collaboration" (IFC). Porter emphasizes the importance of IFCs that create specialized arenas for interaction between cluster participants. It is known that

---

[2]Other strategic excellence areas that the local government championed were: "Worth Seeing," aiming to develop local tourism; "Finally at Home," aiming to develop the quality of life and attractive accommodation; "Skills for the New World," aiming to develop skill provision and higher education; and "More City," aiming to develop local attractions, establishments, and venues.

the performance of a cluster depends very much on the strength of interaction among its private, public, and non-profit sector participants. The presence of IFCs allows for, and encourages, fruitful socioeconomic interactions and enables a collective group of organizations to manage their activities, which also influences the way in which a cluster's resources and the like are organized (Saxenian, 1996).

Moreover, if one considers the contextual setting of the geographically remote and predominantly rural Örnsköldsvik region, the Processum organization also resembled parts of what we commonly know as community development corporations (CDCs). A CDC can take the form of an umbrella-like organization that addresses a variety of economic, social, cultural, and environmental issues (Bessant, 2005, p. 54). Key features of the CDC model include:

- community-based, community-oriented, and community-controlled development;
- integrated economic, social, and cultural goals (e.g., business and economic development, employment, and training);
- reliance on volunteer time and resources (e.g., board members, committee work, administrative support, and local leadership and expertise);
- multiple sources of funding;
- reinvestment in the community;
- networks, partnerships, and collaboration with private and public institutions; and
- short- and long-term community capacity-building strategies such as capital projects and asset development.

The formal organization's vision was to stimulate the Örnsköldsvik region towards becoming a creative and leading region in the development of biorefineries, with wood and energy crops as a basis. As the emergent biorefinery industry cluster's lead organization, Processum established an independent board of directors.

The board consisted of entrepreneurs and managers from local research, manufacturing, consultancy, chemical processing, and forestry businesses, as well as government officials who showed an interest in developing new process industry activities for the Örnsköldsvik region. The board invited numerous organizations and businesses to be A-, B-, or C-level members of the local industry clustering initiative. It was also made possible for organizations to apply to become a member. The type of membership within the cluster development organization determined the amount of funds contributed to the formal clustering initiatives. A-level members would contribute the most funds, and C-level members the least.

After about two years of operation, Processum had developed seven new businesses and gathered 14 local organizations into various biorefinery industry initiatives. Motivated towards regional industry development, yet at the same time maintaining a not-for-profit focus, an important impetus within Processum was that funding and earnings generated would not be distributed directly to members or shareholders. Instead, the organization's earnings would be continually reinvested to promote and support new biorefinery businesses and industrial processing activities in the region. A financial overview of the cluster development organization is presented in Table 1.

A further criterion for the success of the cluster's collaborative organization, and thus critical for developing the new biorefinery industry cluster, was the initial recruitment of a leader and "spider in the web" of the clustered organizations. The entrepreneurs and managers responsible for the new industry cluster initiative worked together, and recruited a chair of the board. The ensuing chairperson had no professional or personal experience within the Örnsköldsvik region, and limited experience in processing and biorefinery industry operations. Nonetheless, the emerging cluster's chairman had what local entrepreneurs considered the necessary networking, facilitation, and business collaboration skills for gathering people and companies

Table 1. Financial overview of the cluster's development organization.

	Jan 2010–Dec 2010	Jan 2009–Dec 2009	Jan 2008–Dec 2008	Jan 2007–Dec 2007	Jan 2006–Dec 2006	Jan 2005–Dec 2005	Jan 2004–Dec 2004	Jan 2003–Dec 2003
Employees	13	13	11	8	4	2.2	2	0.4
Turnover (in thousand SEK)	14,507	12,443	9,107	8,047	4,426	3,744	3,662	744
Net Result (in thousand SEK)	42	47	64	24	19	6.7	6	0.9

Source: AffärsData.

together, sourcing public and private resources, and encouraging new development projects between local firms.[3]

The Processum organization began to develop the regional biorefinery cluster from the ground up, mainly through assuming responsibility for facilitating new business and research development projects among its members, and offering and promoting the projects' results and benefits to members. The allocation of the organization's, and its subsequent projects', resources was not evenly distributed. Instead of awarding each organization involved in the industry cluster the same share, Processum allocated resources to those businesses, entrepreneurs, and organizations that showed the most interest, and to those whom the board considered would advance the cluster's business and research activities.

Over time, Processum worked towards building new collaborative business and research projects for the emergent cluster. An important requirement in the collaborative organization's selection of new business and research projects within the cluster, as well as decisions concerning what to use financial, physical, and human resources on, was that at least two or more local companies needed to be involved. It was not sufficient for only one company to be involved in a project.

Subsequently, the cluster's development organization began operating towards two main areas of development. One operative area concerned expanding and retaining membership, support, and resources for their "Biorefinery of the Future." The other area concerned identifying and exploiting complementarities among various business units, people, and firms within the area. In addition, Processum began developing new business and R&D projects, and at the same time started handling new business and R&D projects on the other local firms' behalf. Whenever a new business idea, research project, or development initiative was not part of a member's core

---

[3]As part of his new position, the cluster's inaugural chairperson moved from Stockholm and became a permanent resident in Örnsköldsvik.

competence (or core interest), they were encouraged to hand it over to Processum for further development.

Moreover, in order to develop campaigns that would benefit the emerging regional cluster and integrate the new industrial ideas into the local community, Processum interacted with local government authorities. The cluster's businesses began collaborating with local primary, secondary, and tertiary education providers — often with Processum providing the initial push — so that local upper secondary pupils could go on field trips (four per year) to see and learn about the newly developing biorefinery industry and clustered firms. New chemistry-based and industrial processing science programs were developed (e.g., a "Green Chemicals without Oil" course). Additionally, a 12-month traineeship was established to integrate recent university graduates into the newly combined regional biorefinery activities. Funded and facilitated by the not-for-profit-based Processum, over a 12-month period six local university graduates, and future employees of the cluster, were recruited and introduced into the biorefinery initiative. The trainees worked on development projects that aimed to create new biorefinery industry products, processes, and systems within and between the cluster's core firms (Arbuthnott *et al.*, 2010).

The emergent regional cluster also championed agreements with local universities. Processum was responsible for recruiting senior scientists and professors into the cluster. These persons were encouraged to work directly alongside the local businesses and actualize R&D for the biorefinery industry. The integration of university actors into the local industry initiatives allowed for direct interactions between the cluster's core firms and a nearby university. This became important for driving the cluster's research and development projects that were based on wood and chemical processing, process engineering, and process controls. Meanwhile, it gave the clustered businesses an opportunity to meet with university researchers face-to-face, and discuss current and future problems and projects. In some instances,

311

new ideas turned into tangible action; and proposals for new business were created and potential patents developed.

By 2010, more than 25 locally operating businesses and organizations had become active in the Örnsköldsvik regional biorefinery cluster.[4] The cluster's activities had also spread into the neighboring Umeå region. For the remote regional business setting, the period in which the biorefinery cluster was initiated and materialized was one of the strongest in decades. In order to further their regional biorefinery developments, the innovative cluster was awarded 17.4 million Euros in European Union structural funds in late 2009. In addition, after evaluation by national and international expert cluster review panels, 10 years of future funding and support — approximately 11 million Swedish kronor (SEK) per year — was offered to the cluster initiative via the Swedish government's VINNVÄXT regional industry development program.

Marketing Challenges

Although there were numerous marketing challenges to overcome during the cluster's initial development, some issues proved more challenging than others. One particular challenge for some companies within the emerging biorefinery industry cluster pertained to marketing the development, production, distribution, and sale of bioethanol fuel to domestic and international consumers.

The development and sale of bioethanol fuel were handled by a private research conglomerate operating in Örnsköldsvik and engaged within the emergent biorefinery cluster, Swedish Ethanol Chemistry. A need arose, however, for another organization that could take care of local communication and education issues related specifically to bioethanol fuel, and spread information about using ethanol as an alternative fuel for private and public transport.

---

[4]Various private, public, and not-for-profit organizations engaged in the biorefinery industry cluster are listed in the Appendix at the end of this case study.

To meet this purpose, it became necessary to enter into a broad collaborative effort in which many local organizations could have a stake in ensuring the success of the cluster and of the bioethanol initiatives. Within the region, those organizations responsible for encouraging a transition from the fossil-fuel-dependent transportation systems to fossil-fuel-free ones were gathered into a not-for-profit-based organization. In late 2003, the organization was created by 15 municipalities in the Västernorrland and Västerbotten counties, two county administrative boards (in Swedish: *Länsstyrelsen*), a county council, several state authorities, three Swedish universities, and ten of the industry cluster's companies. These actors branded, and named, the new organization BioFuel Region (hereinafter "BFR").

In addition, both the EU and the Swedish Energy Agency contributed funding for an ethanol pilot plant in Örnsköldsvik, which was inaugurated in the first quarter of 2004. Whilst the industry cluster's private research conglomerate would concentrate on R&D and hands-on industrial development processes, the public BFR organization would promote the regional cluster's respective ethanol ventures and lobby municipalities to contribute funds for biofuel-related business and social initiatives.

According to a report by Lars Christensen (2005), there were primarily four interrelated contextual factors driving the development of BFR. The first factor concerned the long-term and genuine interest in regional energy issues. Local utility companies (i.e., Övik Energi, Skellefteå Kraft, and Umeå Energi) had begun to diversify their core business, resulting in an array of new wood-based products (e.g., home heating pellets).

The second important factor concerned environmental awareness and the move towards a sustainable business logic. Seven persons in the BFR leadership were actively engaged in other environmental organizations, which supplied the organization with a valuable network and competence in how to finance and support environmentally focused initiatives. As one of the BFR founders stated: "Firstly it is about 'saving the world,' then it is about 'having fun,' and finally about 'making money' — and in that order."

The third contextual factor concerned the knowledge among the process leaders in driving a change process, and finding institutional support for ideas and actions. The members of the group could be considered lobbyists at different local, national, and international levels, which influenced policy-making over time. BFR thus possessed good knowledge on the broader institutional prerequisites for handling regional and national policy development in accordance with their own goals.

The final factor, according to Christensen (2005), that served as a catalyst for the BFR initiative concerned the EU Directive 2003/30/EC, often referred to as the "Biofuels Directive." The passing of this directive gave legitimacy to the local initiatives, and functioned as a driving force and a vision of the future with concrete goals of biofuel production in Europe.

Accordingly, in order to adapt to changing regulations and changes in the political climate, BFR's purpose and vision experienced several strategic changes. Söderberg (2010) notes that two periods could be discerned to have dominated the agenda during different phases of the BFR initiative. The first phase, from 2003 to 2006, was characterized by the underlying problem of the fossil-oil-dependent transport sector and unemployment. In response, BFR sought to achieve a combination of attaining self-sufficiency regarding transport fuels and promoting supranational policies and national investments in specific biofuels; bioenergy was mainly viewed as a potential regional growth sector. Söderberg (2010) labels this period as the "bioenergy for self-sufficiency" phase. In the second phase, from 2007 to 2010, the perception of the underlying problem changed towards emphasizing the problem of the oil-dependent transport sector in the region and climate change issues on the world's environmental agenda. Consequently, BFR's marketing aims changed to achieve a societal transition toward renewable energy within the region. During this second period, bioenergy was considered a more potential green regional growth sector, and Söderberg (2010) names it the "bioenergy for green transition and growth" period.

Based on the contextual factors, and during the different periods, BFR initiated several marketing-related activities in order to meet challenges that arose.

Marketing Ethanol as a Fuel for Transport

With the vision of being a world-leading actor in the transition to biofuels and products from renewable resources, BFR's three focus areas were defined as follows:

- to be the knowledge leader in social adjustment;
- to be the driver of industrial and regional development; and
- to work for increased supply of renewable raw materials.

According to BFR, their most recent strategy as of 2011 was to "mobilize, engage, and activate as many potential development forces in the region as possible by being a catalyst, venue, and coordinating body for public bodies, companies, and universities" (www.biofuelregion.se).

Marketing Ethanol Factories

In order for municipalities to participate in BFR initiatives (and thus for inhabitants to support the development), an early marketed idea was the rollout of localized ethanol factories in different towns and cities. This idea was based on the notion that the pilot development factory in Örnsköldsvik would, in the near future, be successful in producing bioethanol from woodchips. When the plant was constructed in 2003–2004, BFR more or less promised many municipalities and local energy companies that they too would "get their own factory" that would contribute to growth, employment, and transition to a fossil-fuel-free society. In addition, for the first few years, progress in the ethanol pilot plant in Örnsköldsvik was reported widely in local and national media, at congresses, and in periodicals. Various regional actors seemed to interpret this to mean that "their own factory" would be just around the corner. However, this did not occur, and as such proved to be a serious communication challenge for BFR and the emergent industry cluster.

The technological developments and the pilot ethanol plant in Örnsköldsvik were more problematic than expected. Accordingly, BFR's stakeholders and network partners became impatient. Some accused BFR of over-promising and under-delivering on this issue. In response, BFR communicated externally that they had never "promised factories" and that the development of ethanol factories was dependent on the pilot technology being successfully implemented. Some actors in the BFR umbrella organization also communicated that the external actors' initial investments in and enthusiasm for the pilot ethanol facility had contributed to a belief in the success of the process, yet in reality very little had come out of the BFR initiative.

To conclude, initial enthusiasm was needed to attract interest and finances, yet some actors were often too caught up in external communications, so they did not have time to consider how BFR could promise factories. BFR did not have the financial ability or purpose to develop ethanol factories. This had to be mobilized by other actors in the regional network and cluster. To this day, the challenge of communicating bioethanol development with enthusiasm, and at the same time stimulating realistic expectations, remains a key marketing challenge for BFR.

Mobilizing Knowledge Development

One of the most active working groups in BFR's organizational structure since the beginning has been the knowledge and involvement group. Within this group, several volunteer working groups were developed. In turn, these groups created small-scale public education schemes and public awareness ventures regarding bioethanol as transport fuel. This was done by engaging upper secondary schoolteachers on specific workshop days, where they would be able to meet the challenges that a transition from a fossil-fuel-dependent society entails. Some schools and teachers were more active than others were, but overall this educational and societal engagement project was successful in bringing about a discussion of problems and issues concerning the transition. In addition, it was well in line with the core values of BFR, i.e., building a sustainable future for our children and grandchildren with minimal dependency on foreign oil. In the next step, the teachers used material developed by BFR about renewable resources, climate change, and problems with fossil oil extraction in discussing these issues with their pupils. Moreover, other public educational organizations were involved and helped in arranging workshops based on the material for people outside the traditional education system.

Framed as education and knowledge development, much of the material developed carried BFR's core values. BFR used scientific sources in a positive manner to mobilize a regional awareness of transition in the region. This can be thought of as marketing through the use of mobilizing social movements at different levels of society. Within the mobilized knowledge, traditional values and norms were open for discussion. In the regional forum that BFR created, solutions to challenging environmental problems were handled at a local level. Some of the cluster's ethanol-focused projects also joined forces with similar initiatives on a national scale for lobbying and on a European scale for applying for EU funding. Nonetheless, not all inhabitants or firms in the region were convinced.

Promoting Infrastructure and Procurement Activities

An early challenge identified by BFR concerned different public procurement rules. These rules, usually constructed for the efficient use of public funds, had few criteria pertaining to local self-sufficiency and environmental responsibility. Thus, efforts both locally and nationally were made on trying to influence policy-makers to change these rules. Some of these efforts were successful in combination with EU regulations concerning biofuels. As a result, BFR was able to influence participating municipalities to start replacing their petrol vehicle fleets with vehicles fueled by bioethanol (E85). This created a localized demand for ethanol vehicles. Sweden's Ford dealers noticed this demand and were successful in marketing the Ford Focus Flexifuel (E85 and gasoline) car, which in 2004–2005 was the most sold alternative fuel vehicle in Sweden.[5] The Ford dealer in Örnsköldsvik was the most successful dealer in Sweden when it came to selling flexifuel/bioethanol cars. A local taxi company also got involved and developed a green-car-only fleet.

The increasing national and local demand for bioethanol kept offering business opportunities to one of the clustered companies (SEKAB), yet it also created challenges. The main challenge was to convince fueling stations to invest in pump systems for E85 fuel. This was to some extent solved by the Swedish government implementing a fuel directive demanding that fueling stations above a certain size should have to offer E85. Nonetheless, another challenge concerned the procurement of enough bioethanol in order to meet the demand. Since the ethanol pilot plant in Örnsköldsvik did not produce enough to meet the market demand, the company had to import ethanol from Brazil, and then distribute it throughout Örnsköldsvik and the rest of Sweden.

Moreover, in relation to the price of petrol and diesel fuels, the demand for E85 became rather volatile. It appeared that when petrol/diesel was less expensive than bioethanol, consumers would fill their vehicles with those fuels, and vice versa. This was detrimental

---

[5]According to "green motorists" in Sweden, the Ford Focus Flexifuel was the car that encouraged the transition to alternative fuel cars. It was named the greenest car in Sweden in 2006, 2007, and 2008 (see Jansson, 2009).

to SEKAB's business and negatively affected BFR's initiatives. The challenge regarding how to market the fuel on factors other than "just" price continues to haunt the region's bioethanol initiatives.

Communicating the Local Example to an International Audience: The BEST Project

A strategic goal for the BFR collaboration is to scale up local funding with national and international grants. Another goal is to continuously learn from BFR's activities, share knowledge, and show it to interested parties. For example, the bioethanol pilot plant regularly entertains national and international groups to show how they have met technological challenges. Another example is the use of "lighthouse tours," where students, companies, authorities, politicians, etc. are guided through different parts of the BFR cluster and partake in their initiatives.

Merging these two strategic goals together (i.e., securing funding and promoting the region), BFR partners have been involved in several EU projects. In May 2003, the EU enacted a ruling referred to as the Biofuels Directive (2003/30/EC). Under this directive, Europe established the goal of reaching a 5.75% share of renewable energy in the transport sector by 2010. The Biofuels Directive was amended in 2009 to a minimum goal of 10% in every member state by the year 2020 (2009/28/EC). In order to reach these goals, a number of research and demonstration projects were initiated concerning renewable energy in general and biofuels in particular within the Sixth Framework Program (FP6), called "Sustainable Energy Systems." FP6 was a program for research and technological development from 2002 until 2006, set up by the EU in order to fund and promote European research and technological development. Within this program and based on this funding, a demonstration project — BioEthanol for Sustainable Transport (BEST) — was created and coordinated by the Environment and Health Administration of the City of Stockholm from January 1, 2006 to the end of December

2009. The project consisted of ten regions around the world and four universities, and the work was carried out in nine work-packages.

Within the BEST program, several international actors (e.g., from China, Brazil, Holland, and Spain) were invited to BFR to take part in the development and learn from mistakes and successes. In relation to the BEST program, research programs studying consumer behavior were also carried out showing that consumers in the BFR were more positive and knew more about bioethanol than citizens in other cities of Sweden (see Jansson, 2009). However, several challenges also developed in the BEST project that made an international rollout of the BFR concept problematic. For example, the different policies concerning ethanol as a vehicle fuel and the different levels of consumer awareness around the world of dwindling fossil oil resources became hard to handle.

Remaining and Future Marketing Challenges

Initiating the regional industry cluster and not-for-profit collaborative organizations appears to have been a useful way to meet certain regional, environmental, and local industry challenges in the Örnsköldsvik region. Concerning bioethanol development, the initial enthusiasm and motivation among a few tight-knit individuals led to local, national, and international attention, which few imagined was possible in the beginning. Based on the uniqueness of the regional setting, the local biorefinery industry's clustering activities, and certain high-profile product development initiatives, numerous marketing challenges were encountered and future marketing challenges are expected to arise.

Bibliography

Arbuthnott, A., J. Eriksson, and J. Wincent (2010). "When a New Industry Meets Traditional and Declining Ones: An Integrative Approach towards Dialectics and Social Movement Theory in a

Model of Regional Industry Emergence Processes." *Scandinavian Journal of Management*, 26(3), 290–308.

Bessant, K.C. (2005). "Community Development Corporations as Vehicles of Community Economic Development: The Case of Rural Manitoba." *Community Development*, 36(2), 52–72.

Christensen, L. (2005). "Formering för Samhandling: Framväxten av BioFuel Region [Formation for Cooperative Efforts: The Development of the BioFuel Region]." ISA/NUTEK/VINNOVA, Stockholm.

Croon, I. (2005). "Utveckling, Förnyelse, Omvälvning: Grodor Blir Prinsar och Tvärtom: En Vandring i en Industri och ett Land i Förvandling." Spearhead, Stockholm.

Ffowcs-Williams, I. (2004). "Cluster Development: Red Lights and Green Lights." *Sustaining Regions*, 4(2), 26–32.

Fromhold-Eisebith, M. and G. Eisebith (2005). "How to Institutionalize Innovative Clusters? Comparing Explicit Top-Down and Implicit Bottom-Up Approaches." *Research Policy*, 34(8), 1250–1268.

International Energy Agency (2008). "IEA Bioenergy Task 42 on Biorefineries." Minutes of the Third Task Meeting, Copenhagen, Denmark, March 25–26.

Jansson, J. (2009). "Car(ing) for Our Environment? Consumer Eco-Innovation Adoption and Curtailment Behaviors: The Case of the Alternative Fuel Vehicle." PhD thesis, Umeå School of Business and Economics, Umeå University.

Kamm, B., P.R. Gruber, and M. Kamm (2006). *Biorefineries — Industrial Processes and Products*. Weinheim: Wiley-VCH.

Karlsson, C. (2008). *Handbook of Research on Cluster Theory*. Cheltenham, UK: Edward Elgar Publishing.

Peterson, C. (2009). "The Demise of the Swedish Model and the Coming of Innovative Localities?" In Kristensen, P.H. and K. Lilja (eds.), *New Modes of Globalizing: Experimentalist Forms of Economic Organization and Enabling Welfare Institutions*, Helsinki: Helsinki School of Economics, pp. 202–238.

Porter, M.E. (2008). "Clusters and Competition: New Agendas for Companies, Governments, and Institutions." In Porter, M. (ed.), *On Competition*, Boston: Harvard Business School Press, pp. 213–304.

Saxenian, A. (1996). *Regional Advantage: Culture and Competition in Silicon Valley and Route 128*. Cambridge, MA: Harvard University Press.

Söderberg, C. (2010). "Environmental Policy Integration in Bio-energy: Policy Learning Across Sectors and Levels?" PhD thesis, Department of Political Science, Umeå University.

Sölvell, Ö., G. Lindqvist, and C. Ketels (2003). *The Cluster Initiative Greenbook*. Stockholm: Ivory Tower AB.

Appendix: Private, Public, and Non-Profit Organizations Engaged in the Regional Biorefinery Industry Cluster

- Akzo Nobel Surface Chemistry — chemical production and development (www.akzonobel.com)
- ÅF — industrial processes and infrastructure projects consulting group (www.afconsult.com)
- BioFuel Region — regional promotion and collaboration for renewable fuels (www.biofuelregion.se)
- BRUKS — provision of wood-processing, bulk materials handling, and bioenergy solutions (www.bruks.com)
- Brux — conference center, restaurant, and local real estate management (www.brux.se)
- Domsjö Fabriker — cellulose/ethanol/lignosulfonate development, innovations, production, and sales (www.domsjoe.com)
- EcoDevelopment — sustainable development consultancy and project management (www.ecodev.se)
- Energitekniskt Centrum i Piteå — R&D center for renewable fuels (www.etcpitea.se)

- Etek Etanolteknik — pilot plant for ethanol production and processes (www.etek.se)
- Eurocon — independent consultancy (www.eurocon.se)
- Holmen Skog — forestry, timber procurement, and timber trading (www.holmenskog.com)
- Innovationsbron — commercialization of research-related business ideas (innovationsbron.se)
- Kvaerner Power — design and manufacturing of chemical recycling and energy production systems (www.akerkvaerner.com)
- Länsstyrelsen Västernorrland — county administrative board (www.y.lst.se)
- M-real Technology Center — R&D and process/product development (www.m-real.com)
- Metso Power AB — biomass processing technology development (www.metso.com)
- MoRe Research — independent R&D, chemical analysis, and physical and paper analysis (www.more.se)
- Örnsköldsvik Kommun — regional municipality (www.ornskoldsvik.se)
- Övik Energi — energy production and distribution (www.ovikenergi.se)
- Processum — regional biorefinery cluster development (www.processum.se, www.bioraffinaderi.se)
- SCA — development and manufacturing of wood-based products (www.sca.com)
- Sveaskog — forestry, timber procurement, and timber trading (www.sveaskog.se)
- Svensk Etanolkemi — ethanol development and production (www.sekab.com)
- Umeå University — tertiary research and education (www.umu.se)

Part III

Marketing Management Operations and Strategies of Geographically Remote Industrial Clusters

Marketing management operations and strategies are central to the entire notion of forming geographically remote industrial clusters (GRICs). It is important to examine some of the fundamental notions of how GRICs are organized and managed. The main question to ask is: How do GRICs benefit from marketing management? Why is marketing management such an important tool in GRICs' operations and strategies? Are economic and regional development managers correct in their assumption that GRICs can be managed in the same way as conventional enterprises?

Case 11

Sweet and Sound with Xylitol*

In 2004 at the Finnish Embassy in Seoul, Korea, the CEO of Lotte Confectionery Co. Ltd. and Chairman of Lotte Group, Kyuk-ho Shin, received a badge of honor from the President of Finland for his and Danisco Korea's General Manager Won-jang Cho's tireless work in promoting Finland Xylitol chewing gum in Korea. Their marketing was so successful that the general awareness of Finland became very high among Koreans — and much higher than that of other Nordic countries. The favorable attitude towards Finland that the Finland Xylitol chewing gum marketing helped in creating is worth millions of U.S. dollars for Finland. This case will describe the success of marketing Xylitol chewing gum in the geographically remote Korean cluster.

Danisco

De Danske Sukkerfabrikker ("The Danish Sugar Factories") was founded in 1872 as a merger of several local Danish sugar factories. Sugar was extracted from sugar beets, and it has been a profitable business for Danish farmers through decades. One source of competition is the sugar extracted from sugar cane in warmer climates, which has a competitive advantage as the yield

---

*Jens Graff, of the SolBridge International School of Business, Woosong University (South Korea), developed this case for educational purposes only.

is higher. But the global market for sugar has been regulated by tariffs, quotas, and subsidies, so a real competitive global market for sugar does not exist. However, the Doha Round of the World Trade Organization has the freeing of agricultural product trade high on its agenda, which posed a threat for Danisco's long-term sugar production.

De Danske Sukkerfabrikker realized early on that this situation was not sustainable in the long run, so in 1989 they lessened their dependence on sugar and diversified into food ingredients and changed the company's name to Danisco. Before that, however, they had expanded their dominance in the European sugar market by acquiring competing sugar factories in Sweden, Finland, Poland, and Germany.

De Danske Sukkerfabrikker/Danisco is known for being a serious producer with good relations with its suppliers (including participating farmers), customers, and governments, and they keep their assets (for example, buildings) in very good shape. The Dow Jones Sustainability World Indexes (DJSI World) track the performance of the leading companies in the sustainability field, and assess companies' financial, social, and environmental policies and performance. Approximately 10% of the largest 2,500 companies in the Dow Jones Global Indexes are selected, of which only six companies are in the food industry category. In 2004, for the third time Danisco was ranked second in the index for food companies as a result of its dedicated effort in all areas related to sustainability.

In 1999, Danisco acquired the Finnish food and sweetener group Cultor and integrated it into Danisco with its headquarters located in Copenhagen, Denmark. The objective was to establish a Nordic-based, world-class supplier to the global food industry. Cultor was a major producer of xylitol. At the end of the 1990s, the competition in the xylitol market heated up due to increased Chinese production.

This caused pressure on prices of xylitol on the world market and problems for Danisco. Danisco initiated efficient production measures to cope with the new challenges. The demand for xylitol, however, remained good.

In 1999, Danisco acquired a 50% stake in the American company Genencor. Genencor was established in 1982 and has been a frontrunner in industrial biotechnology. It is mainly a research and development company that covers biotechnology and enzymes for food, laundry detergents, and ethanol processing. It focuses on biodegradable products for different purposes. Genencor is a valuable asset for Danisco, and it became a division under Danisco in 2005 when Danisco acquired the remaining 50% of shares.

In 2008, Danisco sold its sugar division to the German-based Nordzucker AG, and became a truly ingredient- and enzyme-producing company. In 2009, the total revenue for Danisco was EUR 1.8 billion and its international presence could be found in about 40 countries worldwide.

In May 2011, the American chemical giant DuPont acquired Danisco. DuPont wanted to strengthen its food ingredient and enzyme business to become a world leader in these fields. DuPont had a revenue of USD 31.5 billion in 2010, with 60,000 employees in approximately 90 countries around the world. It was ranked 86th in the Fortune 500 list of U.S. industrial/service corporations. On their website, Danisco/DuPont wrote:

Danisco's and Genencor's attractive industrial enzymes and specialty food ingredients businesses have clear synergies with the
DuPont Applied BioSciences and Nutrition & Health businesses.
This combination advances both companies' global efforts to
provide sustainable solutions to a growing global population,
particularly in the areas of food, bioenergy, biochemicals and
biomaterials. Together, we will be a world leader in industrial
biosciences and nutrition and health. [Danisco, 2011]

Lotte Confectionery Co. Ltd., Korea

Lotte was established in Japan by a Japanese-educated Korean businessman in 1948. After the normalization of Japan–Korea relations in 1965, Lotte established Lotte Confectionery Co. Ltd. in Seoul in 1967. Today, Lotte Group consists of over 60 business units with 60,000 employees. Lotte Group is involved in such diverse businesses as candy manufacturing, hotels, retailing, heavy chemicals, construction, and entertainment.

Lotte is now one of Asia's leading producers of confectionery and related products, with more than 200 products being sold in more than 70 countries. It is currently the third largest chewing gum manufacturer in the world. The company's core products are chewing gum (Juicy & Fresh, Spearmint, and Fresh Mint), biscuits, candies, and chocolates. Lotte's chewing gum and Ghana chocolate brands have remained long favorites for more than 40 years. Xylitol chewing gum is currently enjoying popularity as a functional food item.

Lotte has a vision of becoming the world's leading confectionery company by producing quality products that are traditionally flavored and have a global touch. As of 2011, its international expansion has been concentrated in Asia and Russia.

The Product

After the Korean War ended in 1953, Korean companies started producing chewing gum. Chewing gum originates from the chicle tree, which has its natural habitat in Mexico.

Xylitol is a sweetener naturally found in fibers of different fruits, vegetables, and birch trees. It can substitute sugar, and it can be taken by people with diabetes without contributing to high blood sugar level. Finnish researchers found in the 1970s that xylitol was less harmful for teeth than other sugar types, and it is recommended as a product for caries prevention. Its discovery is especially linked to the Finnish dentist, Dr. Kauko K. Makinen.

Xylitol-based products are allowed by the U.S. Food and Drug Administration to make the medical claim that they do not promote dental cavities. The biggest producer of xylitol is the Danish ingredient company Danisco.

Xylitol is reported to have medical benefits such as building immunity, protecting against chronic diseases, and providing anti-aging benefits, besides clearing the nasal passages, preventing ear infections, and reducing intraocular pressure. It is also reported to help in preventing diabetes and obesity, as xylitol has about 40% fewer calories and 75% fewer carbohydrates. Xylitol is slowly absorbed and metabolized, so the blood sugar level is only slightly increased; therefore, xylitol is a good choice for diabetics. The sweetening effect of xylitol is the same as for sugar, and a 1:1 amount is used in recipes.

It is recommended to use xylitol products after eating. It can be taken as gum, mint, or candy. Before going to bed, it is also recommended to use xylitol toothpaste, mouthwash, or nasal spray. Its use as a food additive is approved by the World Health Organization. Xylitol looks like snow-white sugar.

For teeth, xylitol is a better sweetener than normal sugar (sucrose). Sucrose gives nutrition to bacteria, which consume the sugar and leave acids that can eat away the enamel on the teeth, which causes tooth decay and cavities. Xylitol does not break down like sugar and helps to keep a neutral pH level in the mouth. Bacteria in the mouth are unable to digest xylitol, so their growth is reduced. In addition, bacteria do not stick well on the surface of the teeth, so plaque decreases.

Today, people say yes to xylitol and no to sugar. It is the first "happy" drug in Korea. Like Viagra for men, it makes people happy without any side effects. People all over the world have become more concerned about their health. They are now thinking more about prevention of diseases, whereas previously the focus was on treatment of diseases. People are starting to recognize the importance of healthy food and the link between well-being and food, and companies are increasingly thinking about consumers' health.

The Korean Market for Chewing Gum[1]

The Korean chewing gum market in 2011 was worth USD 280 million. Nearly 80% of the chewing gum sold here is xylitol-based. The overall market has experienced a downward trend over the last few years; this includes both sugarized and xylitol chewing gum, although sugarized gum has suffered a larger decline.

It is expected that the chewing gum market will decline further. It is believed that consumers are becoming more relaxed about the health benefits of xylitol and focusing more on its refreshment benefits, which are often offered more vividly by sugarized chewing gum.

The five-year forecast for the chewing gum market predicts further decline in all categories. About a 20% decline over the next five years in value terms, and about 7.5% in volume terms, is expected. In particular, the functional chewing gum market is expected to decline by over 10%, corresponding to a 2.2% decline per year over the next five years. The slowdown in the chewing gum market is believed to be caused by the general recession and rising food prices, which reduce individuals' real incomes. This could be especially true for the relatively high-priced Xylitol chewing gum.

In 2009, Lotte enjoyed 63% of the overall chewing gum market in Korea, followed by Haitai (17%), Orion (14%), and other companies (6%). Specifically, in the functional chewing gum segment (xylitol), Lotte had an overwhelmingly high market share of 86% over Haitai's 14%.

About 95% of chewing gum is distributed by grocery retailers. Internet retailing, vending machines, and other non-grocery retailers make up the remaining 5%. It is a product that is very intensively

---

[1]Market data in this section are delivered by Danisco Korea.

distributed, as sales success is very much related to easy access to the product for consumers.

Marketing

The first chewing gum produced in Korea was a regular sugar-based type. In the 1990s, the Korean company Haitai marketed their first sugar-free chewing gum. It was sweetened with sorbitol and branded "Denti-Q." In 1997, Lotte began its marketing of Xylitol chewing gum. It was labeled with an "F" (for "fortified") after the Xylitol name.

When xylitol chewing gum was marketed in Finland and Sweden, PR efforts were successfully directed towards dentists. As opinion leaders, they could recommend xylitol products to their patients, who trusted them. The same strategy was followed in Korea by Danisco Korea. Messages showing the caries prevention benefits of chewing gum with xylitol were distributed through dentist clinics on postcards free to grab for their patients. Lotte chewing gum was marketed as something you chew after you have brushed your teeth and before you go to bed; it was not marketed as a substitute for brushing teeth.

Danisco Korea and Lotte conducted market research on consumers' preferences about price, design, and taste. Since expert groups generally have a great influence on consumers in the market, Lotte tried to get support and trust from the experts by holding seminars for them. These seminars were primarily targeted at dentists, but other non-governmental organizations (NGOs) were targeted too. People normally trust NGOs. In these seminars, postcards with cartoon figures promoting the message about caries prevention were given to dentists for them to hand out to patients.

Danisco Korea and Lotte also used the Internet. Newspaper ads and TV commercials were able to show Xylitol's effectiveness in terms of quantity and quality, but the use of Internet websites enabled people to get more information about xylitol and Finland, and also grabbed a lot of attention from customers. A Second Life virtual world was even launched in 1999 for dentists.

Lotte changed the culture in their company and became a health-conscious company. Today, Lotte's main target group is families. Mothers buy Xylitol chewing gum for their children. Lotte projected an image of an eco-friendly company by making use of Finland's green image in its advertisements. People now think of Lotte as a company that takes care of consumers' health.

The PR strategy for Xylitol was to change the recognized brand name from "Xylitol" to "Finland Xylitol." This was easier for consumers to pronounce and gave the product more validity.

The story of Xylitol and Finland was of great interest to the mass media. They wrote many editorial articles about it. Because people normally believe information supplied by the mass media, today there is a high level of awareness and understanding about Xylitol. Now, people understand the value and benefits of Xylitol.

Marketing the Xylitol chewing gum in Korea was not an easy task. Xylitol as a sweetener was about ten times more expensive than sugar. Should Xylitol be marketed as chewing gum or medicine? The first campaign failed. It was impossible to deliver the value (caries prevention), it was impossible to deliver the credibility, and it was impossible to deliver the brand.

After this initial failure, the established concept was overhauled. The logical appeal with caries prevention was changed to an emotional appeal, "no sugar" was changed to "one of the sugars," and the brand "Xylitol" was extended to "Finland Xylitol." "Xylitol" was a difficult brand name for Korean people to perceive and pronounce, so it was decided to extend the brand name to "Finland Xylitol." This turned out to be a very good idea, as will be described later. As you might remember, the xylitol ingredient is sourced from Finland where it is extracted from birch trees.

Danisco Korea chose a dental positioning. The high price of xylitol demanded a high price for the chewing gum in shops. There was a need to justify the higher costs through added value in terms of consumer benefits. The value was dental benefits and health. Since dentists were already using xylitol products and had explained its advantages, consumers would believe Xylitol's effectiveness.

Danisco Korea formed a partnership with Lotte in 2000. At the time, Lotte was already the biggest supplier of chewing gum to the Korean market, ahead of producers like Haitai and Orion. It was decided that Lotte would handle the consumer-directed marketing communication, while Danisco Korea would manage the PR activities targeted at the value network of Danisco Korea. This network consisted of industrial customers, trading partners, distributors, regulatory agencies, dentists, dental universities, PR/advertising agencies, and the media. Danisco Korea's dental PR activities in 2000 comprised the following:

- TV (10 programs, 95 minutes);
- Radio (8 programs, 13 minutes);
- Newspapers (96 articles);
- Magazines (45 articles); and
- Industry publications (15 articles).

Lotte's positioning strategy was to appeal to consumers' concerns about their health. This involved telling consumers that taking regular sugar was bad for their teeth. In general, Lotte positioned itself as a green, environmentally friendly firm. Lotte's marketing communication used Internet and print advertising as vehicles. They promoted the Finland image heavily. The marketing communication was so successful that a consumer survey in 2001 placed Xylitol as No. 3 among the most remembered brands in Korea; No. 1 was a popular TV series ("Friends"), and No. 2 was a sales mileage card ("OK Cashbag").

The coupling of Finland and Xylitol was so strong that it benefited Finland's image as a country. A public opinion survey report on Finland's image, published by Korea Gallup and sponsored by the

Embassy of Finland, showed that 78% of Koreans were aware of Finland, of which 31% liked the country. Finland's main image factors were "natural image" (40%), "North Europe" (28%), "cold" (17%), and "has a good natural environment" (15%).

The survey result showed that Korean people linked Finland's image with a natural image (40%), a social/cultural image (39%), and a commodity/product image (31%). These three image components contributed to the total country image in similar proportions. Xylitol gum accounted for the biggest proportion of unaided awareness with 29%. In the reported commodity/product image category, Xylitol accounted for 96%, far exceeding that of Nokia which showed only 4%. Respondents who linked Finland with natural and social/cultural images were generally highly educated (some at the college level) people in their 30s and 40s, while respondents who linked Finland with a commodity/product image tended to be junior high/high school students aged from 13 to 19 years old. In the same survey, Xylitol's image was characterized by concepts like "cool," "clean," "fresh," "credible," "green color," and "environmentally friendly."

The success of Xylitol was due to a range of activities. Danisco ensured close coordination of its marketing efforts with dental NGOs. The PR activities directed towards dentists, hygienists, professors, teachers, etc. meant that Xylitol attained strong credibility among dental experts, which carried over to consumers.

The coupling between Xylitol and Finland turned out to be an inspired move. Many similarities between Finland and Korea were highlighted, such as the success of companies on the world market in both countries (Nokia in Finland and Samsung in Korea). Furthermore, both countries had saturated Internet and mobile users, making Internet communication relevant and successful.

In 2000, Mr. Kyuk-ho Shin, CEO of Lotte Confectionery, made a wise decision to focus on Xylitol again. He had a dream of making Lotte the top gum-producing company in the world. He developed new supply channels, using for example discount stores, home shopping networks, vending machines, and door-to-door sales.

The packaging of Xylitol chewing gum is in stick packs, tablet packs (blister packs), and bottle packs. About half of the sales are in bottle packs. Tablet packs and bottle packs signal "medicine" and are labeled accordingly as "Dental Health Gum," and the xylitol content is high (86%); while the stick pack is the traditional chewing gum packaging with lower xylitol content (37%). On the packages is written "100% xylitol from Finland" and "Prevents cavities," so the Finland image is still strong on their packages, although the brand name is now "Xylitol" and not "Finland Xylitol" anymore. As of August 2011, the price for consumers for a stick pack of Xylitol was KRW 500 (USD 0.50), and KRW 5,000 (USD 5) for a bottle pack.

The Korean Culture

South Korea is a highly information technology (IT)-experienced country. It is a national policy that every household should have broadband connection, and this aim is close to being fulfilled — even in rural areas. Maybe because Korea is so densely populated and so urbanized, Koreans have a special love for electronics. In every mom-and-pop store, retailers watch TV when they are short of customers, and taxi drivers also have small TV screens in their cabs so that they can stream TV when they are not driving. For young people, it is very popular to meet at PC game sites in town.

Koreans are also interested in health and well-being. Kimchi is categorized as a world food, and it is regarded as very healthy. Kimchi is a Korean dish made of fermented vegetables, which traditionally is made in the autumn when it is time to harvest different kinds of vegetables. A traditional Korean meal consists of a range of different kimchi types served in small bowls on the table for the diners to pick. There is very little meat in the traditional Korean menu, as meat is expensive and there is not a big tradition for eating much meat. Koreans often use the phrase, "It is good for your health." Hence, nearly every dish in the menu is praised for some health feature. This might explain why Xylitol became so popular in Korea — because "it is good for your health."

The rising incomes in Korea and effective marketing from Danisco Korea and Lotte were success factors for Xylitol. They made some good commercials that became widely loved by the Korean audience. The main story in the commercials was centered on a father who had brushed his teeth and was getting ready for bed. But his wife shouted at him, "Haven't you forgotten something?" The father then remembered that he had forgotten to chew Xylitol gum. At that point in the commercial, a central figure — an old Finnish man with a large beard — appeared and shouted, "*Hyvaa Hyvaa*," meaning "good job." His outfit was green, signaling the green and clean Finland. There were several versions of this commercial, but the old Finn became a beloved figure appearing in them all.

The author of this case moved to Daejeon, Korea, in September 2009. At that time, it was not everyday that you saw a foreigner in the streets. In some city quarters, some people looked at foreigners as aliens. Daejeon is a city of 1.5 million people located in the middle of South Korea. In the capital, Seoul, the situation is, of course, a little different, but still the number of foreigners is quite small.

The English-language proficiency is very modest in Korea, both among older people and youngsters. The Korean government is very actively promoting English learning among people, but the very modest English proficiency in general in Korea is an obstacle in business-related matters and in the social context as well. This also means that the influence from outside through media is limited. Additionally, the fact that geographically South Korea is a peninsula with a hostile border to North Korea has kept out frequent neighbor contact and solidified the Korean culture.

As mentioned before, Koreans are very health-conscious people. Everywhere in condominium sites, parks, and nature tracks, you will find workout equipment for public use. And Koreans use it! Typically, an installation has 4–6 pieces of equipment for strengthening one's legs, torso, and arms. The Korean menu is very rich in vegetables, and Koreans eat a lot of different fruits, roots, beets, and vegetables that are supposed to be very healthy. Ginseng extract, ginkgo extract, and different roots are common drinks in Korea, and one can find small, family-owned shops with extract facilities in numerous places.

The very health-conscious Korean culture has definitely been a plus for the marketing of Xylitol in Korea. Consumers are knowledgeable about food ingredients and desire them for their health reasons. So, xylitol is just another ingredient that is desired for its health reasons.

Korea's business environment is very much concentrated around the big conglomerates (*chaebol*). They are big family-owned companies like, for example, Samsung, Hyundai, and Lotte. They typically carry out business in many different fields; for instance, Samsung's activities include shipbuilding, household appliances, computers, and electronics. Samsung alone accounts for about 10% of the Korean GDP, so such *chaebol* have the immediate attention of the government. Recently, the government has urged the *chaebol* to help small- and medium-sized companies and other smaller manufacturing enterprises (SMEs) to grow and internationalize. All in all, Korean business life has been very nationalistic and inward-looking: "We do it the Korean way!" This has meant, for example, that Koreans stick to a common software system; and if a feature is not present, they develop a system themselves even though they could easily buy the system abroad. So when Lotte marketed a chewing gum with a special sweetener, the Koreans accepted it and stuck to it. It has become a national, beloved brand.

Remote Geographical Regions

This case tells the story of how a geographically remote country, South Korea, used the image of another geographically remote country,

Finland, in the marketing of a consumer product with ingredients from the geographically remote Finland. In a way, you could argue that South Korea is a geographically remote cluster in itself. Only in the last few decades has it aggressively participated in international trade, and its status as a peninsula with a hostile country at its only land border has been a factor explaining the special Korean culture.

Olav Sorenson (2003, p. 515) writes: "Social networks influence the geographic distribution of industries because networks do not randomly link individuals. Rather, people interact most frequently with those who live in close geographic proximity and with whom they share backgrounds, interests and affiliations (often referred to as social proximity)." It can be claimed that because of the special Korean conglomerate (*chaebol*) structure, interaction and cooperation take place within these *chaebol* as all companies within a *chaebol* are "part of the family." Besides, the very collectivistic, hierarchical, and masculine Korean culture also ties business people together, for example, at after-work dinners and drinking sessions where subordinates socialize with their bosses. Danisco Korea's successful cooperation with the Lotte *chaebol* automatically gave it access to Lotte's chewing gum manufacturing and the retailing arm of Lotte, which is the biggest supermarket retailer in Korea.

Michael Porter (1990) concluded in his extensive research of country-specific advantages that companies could gain from cooperating with each other and that these advantages were most likely to materialize if the companies were located in geographical clusters, where spatial distances are small between cooperating partners. Danisco Korea and Lotte provide an example of a fruitful cooperation between an ingredient supplier and a chewing-gum-producing company which is also one of Korea's biggest *chaebol*, which includes retailing among its activities. Lotte is Korea's biggest food retailer. In addition, the special Korean culture, as just described, is a third player in this successful "cluster" case.

South Korea has 50 million inhabitants covering an area of about $100,000 \, km^2$. As South Korea is a mountainous country, its population is concentrated in low areas. This makes South Korea one of the most densely populated countries in the world. Its capital, Seoul, has about 10 million inhabitants, but during the day this number can swell up to 13 million. In fact, about half of Korea's population live in Seoul and nearby municipalities.

The American-based DuPont acquired Danisco in May 2011 and merged it into its DuPont organization. Geographically, remoteness can be seen as a sequence:

- DuPont, USA
- Danisco, Denmark
- Danisco subsidiary in Korea (Seoul)
- Xylitol ingredient from Cultor, Finland (subsidiary of Danisco)
- Factory for xylitol production, located in a relatively remote area in Finland.

That Lotte's Xylitol chewing gum became such a profound success was not in the cards from the beginning. As described earlier, the first marketing activities were not successful. It was not until the brand name was transformed to "Finland Xylitol" and the appeal to dental care was made that the marketing became successful. This probably hit upon a trend in Korea at the time, when Koreans were beginning to be more outward-looking and more concerned about their health. Nevertheless, Korea has a very special culture colored by the Korean War of 1950–1953 and its aftermath, during which the country's infrastructure was built up and an industrial base for growth was established. After the war, Korea focused on three industrial areas: shipbuilding, car production, and electronics. Today, it boasts of a worldwide presence in all three sectors. Korea is now the world's leading shipbuilding nation, and its car industry is booming. It is also the world's biggest producer of semiconductors and flat-screen TVs. The rapid economic growth has meant that Korea is now regarded as a developed country and a member of the G20, which held their 2010 summit meeting in Seoul.

Unlike other manufacturing companies, Danisco tries to focus on R&D and marketing, as can be seen from the example of the success of Danisco Korea. Danisco Korea and Lotte formed a good partnership. They analyzed changes to their product's image and planned important PR strategies together. This was the first example of "living together" in the history of both companies, and led to great success.

As a multinational company, Danisco has a typical value network to nurture. The production of xylitol takes place in a remote region in Finland; its headquarters is in Denmark; and its marketing success story is in Korea and is staged by its Korean subsidiary. Since May 2011, Danisco has been managed by DuPont, USA, and has been integrated into DuPont's overall value network.

The supply chain between Danisco (Denmark), Cultor (Finland), Danisco (Korea), and Lotte (Korea) has functioned very smoothly over the years. One explanation for this is the success of Xylitol chewing gum in Korea, which meant that Danisco had a big, stable, and even growing market for its xylitol ingredient, from which all partners in the link profited. Most of the time, it was "business as usual." The players in the value chain could rely on each other.

Other members of the value network also worked together in an enthusiastic manner. Regulatory agencies were keen on xylitol because of its health benefits and as an obvious substitute for traditional sugar; dentists were happy because they could recommend a substitute for traditional sugar; dental universities acknowledged the virtues of xylitol through scientific research; PR/advertising agencies were able to convey a good message to the Korean audience; the media liked the product and could write about its health qualities; industrial customers had an ingredient by which they could differentiate themselves; and traders/distributors had a successful product to sell.

In a way, you could claim that Korea is a big cluster in itself. Although Korean *chaebol* do compete internally (e.g., Samsung Electronics versus LG Electronics in 3D flat-screen television production), they also cooperate with and supplement each other. And until recently, Korea was considered a remote cluster by most businesses around the world. But there is a drive and enthusiasm in Korean business culture. Korea's politicians and business community are extremely proud to be a member of the G20 group of countries and to have held the first Asian G20 summit in 2010. The current President of South Korea, Lee Myung-bak, has traveled to African and Central Asian countries on promotion tours for Korean products, and he has been very successful in signing giant construction contracts for petrochemical plants, energy-producing plants, other industrial products, and condominiums. Moreover, he has been eager to source for oil and minerals. This government–private cooperation is very typical for the Korean cluster as well.

Although government–private cooperation is not unique to Korea, the magnitude of cooperation and the vital role played by the Korean President is striking. For example, in 2011, he was instrumental in getting contracts for building a nuclear plant in the United Arab Emirates, newly developed jet fighters for Indonesia, and a giant petrochemical plant in Kazakhstan.

Conclusion

Given that xylitol is an important ingredient (sugar component) for chewing gum production, Danisco Korea has played a major role in designing the marketing communication plan, which communicated "Finland Xylitol" to the consumer market. The consumer-directed marketing communication is carried out by the Korean *chaebol* Lotte, which is one of the biggest marketers of confectionery in the world.

Danisco Korea can be regarded as part of a remote geographical cluster. How is it that Danisco Korea became such a success, an envy of global competitors? What factors worked together in Korea to create this success? Can this be repeated in other countries?

Case Questions

1. How can Danisco/DuPont utilize the Korean Xylitol success in its global growth?
2. How do you perceive the production of xylitol in Finland by Cultor, Danisco, and now DuPont in light of the Chinese aggressive expansion of xylitol production?
3. Overall, how could Danisco strengthen its cluster benefits?
4. The sale of chewing gum in Korea — including Lotte's Xylitol gum — is now facing a declining trend. What would you propose to turn this trend to an upward trend again?

Bibliography

[Anonymous] (1999). "Danisco to Acquire Cultor." *Eurofood*, March 11. http://findarticles.com/p/articles/mi_m0DQA/is_1999_March_11/ai_54207965/ [accessed July 12, 2011].

Danisco (2000). *Danisco Annual Report 1999*, p. 9.

Danisco (2011). "About DuPont." http://www.danisco.com/about_us/dupont/about_dupont/ [accessed July 11, 2011].

DuPont (2011). "Company at a Glance." http://www2.dupont.com/Our_Company/en_US/glance/index.html/ [accessed July 7, 2011].

Lotte Confectionery (2007). *2007 Business Report*. http://eng.lotteconf.co.kr/IRFiles/01.pdf/ [accessed August 27, 2011].

Porter, Michael (1990). *The Competitive Advantage of Nations*. New York: The Free Press.

Porter, Michael (1998). "Clusters and the New Economics of Competition." *Harvard Business Review*, November–December, 77–90.

Sorenson, Olav (2003). "Social Networks and Industrial Geography." *Journal of Evolutionary Economics*, 13, 513–527.

Xylitol (2011). "The Sweet Solution for Better Health, Naturally!" http://www.xylitol.org/ [accessed July 25, 2011].

Acknowledgments: The author of this case would like to thank Won-jang Cho, General Manager of Danisco Korea, who was a primary source of information about Danisco Korea and its cooperation with Lotte Confectionery, Korea. The author would also like to thank Hee-Seung Lee, a Korean teaching assistant, for his help in translating Korean text and providing input about the Korean culture.

Case 12

Revitalizing Agro-Machinery Manufacturing in Tanzania — The Case of IEL*

Historical Development

Intermech Engineering Limited (IEL) is a small-sized agricultural engineering company located at 81/E Kihonda Industrial Estate in Morogoro town, approximately 200 km west of Dar es Salaam. It started in 1994 as a subsidiary of Intermech Ltd. (IL), which was a trading company that represented British firms in Tanzania in the energy, sugar, and precision measurement fields. Peter Chisawilo, an engineer and founding Managing Director of IEL, was once an employee of IL. Peter worked at IL for several years before he came up with the idea of establishing IEL as a fully registered and operational company. IEL operated as a subsidiary unit of IL until 1999, when IL was restructured. One outcome of IL's restructuring was the formal incorporation of IEL as a limited liability company under the Companies Ordinance (Cap. 212) with Registration No. 36372 on May 27, 1999.

During its subsidiary status, IEL operated from an engineering workshop that was owned by the Small Industries Development Organization (SIDO). SIDO is a public organization established

*Daniel W. Ndyetabula, of Aalborg University (Denmark), developed this case for educational purposes only. The author would like to thank Peter Chisawilo, Managing Director of IEL, for his time.

by the Government of Tanzania in 1973 to, among others, advise potential entrepreneurs on technology design and plant layout. According to Peter, the workshop was outsourced to IEL from SIDO after he showed the desire to operate a manufacturing enterprise on a commercial scale in 1993. This outsourcing from SIDO was also in line with the government's policy of privatization that was implemented during the 1990s.

Since 1999, IEL has operated as a company that provides a range of agro-engineering services such as machinery designing, production, and installation, and plant commissioning. IEL's current focus is on the manufacturing of agro-food machinery and equipment, which are mainly sold domestically to small and medium agro-food processors in Tanzania. Although plant commissioning is one of IEL's services, there has never been a substantial market need for such service, and IEL is thinking of concentrating only on the designing and manufacturing of agro-processing machinery.

Motivation behind Enterprise Establishment

Between 1967 and 1991, Tanzania followed a socialist economic philosophy, whereby a large parastatal sector was built to carry out activities in such sectors as agriculture, transport and communications, mining, education, health, and fisheries. There was, therefore, a substantial increase in state intervention into the economy, especially in the agricultural sector where the manufacturing of agro-equipment and machinery was highly regulated. There were two main state-owned manufacturing factories, one in Mbeya (ZZK) and another in Dar es Salaam (UFI), both of which are no longer operational.

After the failure of socialism in the late 1980s, Tanzania embarked upon economic transformation through the privatization of all sectors of the economy, and so the country now needed an alternative for agricultural equipment manufacturing. The population of the farming families was growing very rapidly and there was a demand for primary agricultural production equipment as well as processing machinery, both of which were being imported after the failure of socialism but were too expensive for smallholder farmers to afford. To justify his belief about the market for agricultural processing machinery in Tanzania, Peter and other colleagues from IL conducted a country-wide study that concretized his perception that farmers in Tanzania needed affordable and locally made processing machinery. He then in 1993 pursued the establishment of IEL, which was subsequently fully registered as a limited liability company in 1999. The establishment of IEL was thus carved out of an increasing demand for agricultural processing machinery in Tanzania and other African countries, where agriculture is dominated by numerous smallholders and is the main activity of the economy.

With ambitions to support smallholders in Tanzania, Peter's objective was to use his engineering knowledge and the knowledge of others to create an agro-machinery manufacturing enterprise. In this endeavor, Peter sees himself as fitting into a small enterprise rather than a larger one. The reason is that small enterprises allow room for multiple tasks, interaction, and greater involvement in technological and business development processes as a whole. After 17 years of operation in Tanzania, IEL is now an important agro-machinery manufacturing company, not only in Tanzania but in the Central and East African region, with an investment turnover of US$300,000 per year.

Location, Activities, and Organization

The 81/E Kihonda Industrial Estate, where IEL is located, accommodates several small- and medium-sized manufacturing industries. The industries in this area manufacture a range of products, most of them being ceramic materials, garments, beverages, soaps and detergents, and packaging sacks. The emergence of this industrial cluster is not by instinct. Being uniquely located, the municipal authority of this small town had planned for the 81/E Kihonda to be an industrial investment area. The town is uniquely located because all major transport routes to the mainland pass through Morogoro. For example, the Tanzania–Zambia Railway (TAZARA) and the central railway line (Tanzania Railway) pass through the region; the Dar-es-Salaam–Dodoma–Tabora–Singida highway goes through Morogoro; and the Tanzania–Zambia (TANZAM) highway connects the region to the Iringa, Songea, and Mbeya regions, and to the neighboring Zambia and Malawi in the south as well as Rwanda and Burundi in the west. The developed infrastructure facilitates access to most of the neighboring regions and countries throughout the year. Focusing on the location of IEL, Peter is very satisfied that his enterprise is located at this famous industrial area as he can easily and cheaply transport both raw materials and final products. The location advantage also enables his company to easily network and keep in touch with important business partners.

Most of the enterprises in this area are producers of garments and ceramic materials. According to Peter, these enterprises see each other less as competitors and more as partners because the market for garments and ceramic materials is still growing. Being in such close proximity to each other, the garment and ceramic enterprises are therefore able to network and share a lot of technological information. Unfortunately for Peter, there are not as many agricultural manufacturing enterprises in the area.

IEL's activities are operationalized in a small enterprise model, in which Peter as the Managing Director oversees all operational activities both as a manager and as an employer (owner-manager). IEL began with five employees, with Peter as a qualified engineer and four other engineering technicians. Today IEL has 14 employees, out of whom 2 are engineers, 10 are engineering technicians, 1 is an accounts assistant, and 1 is a marketing officer. There are three operational departments (see Figure 1) under which production activities are coordinated. Peter defines himself as a key player and orchestrator of company activities both by his ability to share and

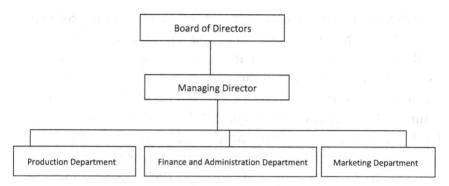

Figure 1.   Organizational structure of IEL.

use his engineering knowledge to design and produce appropriate machinery for those customers he has knowledge about, and by his experiential managerial skills to run the company profitably.

Investment and Enterprise Financing

Peter likes the fact that small enterprises are more diffuse and ambiguous compared to large enterprises. Initially he did not know how to finance the company's startup. The demand and market signals had made him ambitiously think of using his knowledge to fill the market gap and earn a living, but without regard for the capital investment requirement. In 1993, he started negotiations with SIDO to hire and privately run the workshop, but early talks failed as SIDO wanted to get rid of the workshop and so they were looking for someone to completely buy the workshop. After much thought, Peter agreed to sign a buyout contract with SIDO that required him to pay a total of TShs 55 million in installments. Upon signing the contract, Peter paid TShs 25 million out of his own savings for the first installment. This important step left Peter broke. He had no operational capital to start machinery production work. He approached IL for support and received a grant from IL of TShs 10 million, and this was the starting revolving capital which was backed up by the anonymous business "angels" who supported Peter's investment endeavor.

Peter recognized the importance of producing a prototype, but with the financial constraints and his adamancy on market availability for agro-processing machinery he had to make efficient use of what little operational capital he had. So his focus was on the production of a product ready for sale. Having made some efforts to promote the production activity of IEL, they managed to get an order for the cassava processing machine (chipper) from cassava-producing groups in rural Morogoro. This is where the first production attempt started with the mobilization of four semi-skilled technicians. They purchased the raw materials, mainly iron steel, from a variety of raw material suppliers in Dar es Salaam and produced the machinery for the group customers. Peter considers this first company product as a business prototype, as IEL was able to make money out of it.

The machines, although convenient, were mechanically operated by handles to produce cassava chips. Peter admits that the machines were not the best or the most efficient, but nevertheless they did contribute to reducing the drudgery of human beings and enhancing overall productivity and production.

IEL's investment was mostly on the technology (the workshop acquired from SIDO) and on the revolving capital (purchase of raw materials), and during the first few years of operation IEL was production-oriented. However, the company has grown substantially and has extended its market to the neighboring countries of Kenya, Rwanda, and Burundi. In 2005, IEL paid the last TShs 25 million to SIDO, and since then they have been operating from their own workshop.

Company Products, Innovation, and Market Entry

A few years passed before IEL started to produce modernized and automated products. In fact, the manually operated products that IEL produced during the early years after its inception were to meet the market need in terms of affordability. The company was also prototyping with these manually operated products, which were mainly for cassava processing. They were sold to individuals and groups of farmers.

As time passed, Peter had to carry out a campaign to innovatively trigger and enter a new market. First, he linked IEL with the University of Dar es Salaam's College of Engineering and Technology and the Sokoine University of Agriculture's Department of Agricultural Engineering for all product design and innovation activities. IEL therefore enjoys technical support from the two universities in terms of all product innovation and development strategies. In this arrangement, IEL takes in engineering and agro-engineering students for industrial attachments. Students participate in design and development projects under the supervision of professors from the two universities and a local supervisor from the company, who is usually Peter. With this arrangement, new products are designed based on the needs of the market in Tanzania and in neighboring countries.

Second, Peter linked IEL to the Private Agricultural Sector Support (PASS) in order to enter a new market for its products. PASS is a trust working to commercialize agriculture in Tanzania through the provision of credit guarantees and other financial services to smallholders. In this understanding, PASS-guaranteed clients who require agro-processing machinery are advised to get an invoice from IEL. Since 2003, therefore, IEL has become a supplier of agro-processing machinery to several PASS agro-processor clients in Tanzania.

Another market that IEL penetrated in 2004 was the market for different processors, which has been mainly dominated by two government agricultural development programs: the Participatory Agricultural Development and Empowerment Project (PADEP), and the Agricultural Sector Development Program (ASDP). Processing machines such as oil expellers, oilseed millers, and sorghum dehullers are usually bought under the two programs.

IEL also sells its products to different non-governmental development organizations that have agricultural projects in Tanzania.

Table 1. The products of IEL.

S/N	Product	Price (US$)
1	Cassava chipper	950
2	Cassava grater	1,250
3	Manual cassava chipper	300
4	Cassava press	495
5	Forage chopper	750
6	Starch extractor	2,750
7	Manual starch extractor	800
8	Groundnut decorticator	150
9	Sorghum dehuller	2,145
10	Thresher	2,250
11	Oil expeller	4,400
12	Maize desheller	2,500
13	Maize sheller	950
14	Horizontal feed mixer	1,750
15	Vertical feed mixer	3,500
16	Grain cleaner	1,250
17	Grain huller	650
18	Palm oil digester	2,250

Some of these organizations include Plan International, Participatory Agricultural Management, FOODNET, the International Institute of Tropical Agriculture, and others. Recently, individuals and groups of farmers from Kenya, Rwanda, and Burundi have placed orders for cassava processing machinery. Peter feels the market pressure that IEL is now facing, and he is afraid that the growing demand for their products may soon surpass the company's capacity.

Most of what IEL currently produces (see Table 1) are automated machines, some run by gasoline/petrol and some electrical. The prices of IEL's products range from USD 150 for the cheapest product (manual) to USD 4,400 for the most expensive one (automated).

Raw materials are mostly supplied to IEL by different suppliers in Dar es Salaam. The company purchases steel and motors from the domestic supply companies. The materials are transported to

Morogoro by roads using hired trucks. The suppliers are actually not manufacturers of the raw materials, but they import them from India, Malaysia, and China. Some materials are bought in parts for assembly into a finished good, and some are bought to manufacture originally designed machines.

Sales and Marketing

From its inception in 1994, IEL had a specific focus to fill the smallholders' domestic demand gap for agro-processing machinery. Peter was surprised when IEL received an order from smallholders in neighboring countries. The company had not advertised itself extensively to the extent of receiving orders from abroad. Peter believes that the customers from outside Tanzania may have obtained information from smallholders in Tanzania or other sources, but not from IEL as it had not advertised itself outside Tanzania. To penetrate the domestic market, Peter implemented a special marketing strategy in which he paid physical visits to PASS, PADEP, and ASDP. This was during the early days of IEL's operation. The marketing activity is now performed by the marketing department. IEL's first product order from the farmers' groups was obtained through a similar approach, when Peter had to physically pay a visit to Morogoro district council offices and promote IEL.

Having managed to penetrate most of the smallholder markets in Tanzania, the marketing department of IEL has developed an online selling and product ordering system available on the company's website (www.intermech.biz). The company communicates with clients through this system about new orders. There is a special order form that clients have to fill and submit to IEL. The marketing department then processes the filled order form by preparing a contract which will have to be signed by both parties, before the product is manufactured and made available for either pickup or delivery to the customer's premises. Customers have a choice of two options for getting their final products: they can either pick up the products themselves from the IEL workshop, or they can have the products delivered by IEL to anywhere within Tanzania. The transport costs of the products for the latter option are factored in the product price.

IEL's current sales figures reach US$300,000 per annum with products which, according to Peter, do not possess all attributes needed by the customers. Peter's ambition is to see IEL expanding in terms of technological capacity. He is happy to manage a company of small size like IEL, but with modern and sophisticated technology suitable for the production of high-quality machinery whose value is well appreciated by customers. IEL has since 2008 been implementing a retained earnings strategy in order to finance its mission to purchase state-of-the-art technology for the high-quality products.

Growth Strategy and Future Plan

In its attempt to serve small agro-processors in Tanzania, IEL experienced an increase in demand for agro-processing machinery mainly from PASS-guaranteed customers. This put a lot of pressure on the production capacity of IEL. To deal with this, IEL developed an ongoing five-year plan to expand the production workshop. According to this plan, IEL would purchase state-of-the-art workshop machinery by the end of 2011 that would be operational by early 2012. Along with workshop expansion, IEL planned to increase qualified manpower by employing two more engineers and six engineering technicians by the beginning of 2012. Peter sees the marketing efforts that IEL has made so far as the most important strategy to deal with market developments. The company's five-year strategic plan is a response to the increased market demand for agro-food machinery.

Another important strategy in IEL's five-year plan is to improve the company's website and use it as a major medium for product and company marketing. The marketing department has recently published a catalogue of all IEL products, which provides detailed product information and specifications. The company does not have plans to hire a permanent information and communications technology (ICT) specialist in its ongoing five-year plan on the grounds that specialists are still very expensive to employ permanently. So IEL will continue to hire specialists on short-term arrangements to manage the company's website.

Given that IEL has been badly affected by the regular power cuts in Tanzania, the company has also made plans to purchase a standby generator by 2013. This will reduce the likelihood of power rationing, which the Tanzanian industrial sector has been accustomed to over the last decade. To implement this generator purchase plan, IEL has applied for a specific loan amounting to TShs 50 million from one of the local banks through PASS guarantee. The company has received a 50% guarantee from PASS to purchase a generator that will serve as an alternative power provider in case of blackouts.[1]

Collaborations and Alliances

From IEL's perspective, collaboration and alliances can be discussed in terms of two dimensions, namely marketing and industrial development. In the marketing dimension, IEL has been strategically linked to organizations that are potential sources of customers for IEL. PASS, PADEP, and ASDP are the key sector collaborators forming IEL's customer base. The company has been able to market its products to a wide range of customers through different organizations with which IEL maintains a mutual collaboration.

In the second dimension, IEL is linked to different stakeholders such as the United Nations Industrial Development Organization (UNIDO), SIDO, Tanzania Industrial Research and Development Organization (TIRDO), and Tanzania Engineering and Manufacturing Design Organization (TEMDO) for industrial development

---

[1] Recent follow-ups on the implementation of the five-year plan revealed that five personnel (one engineer and four engineering technicians) have been employed and the website has been improved as planned.

purposes. With these organizations, IEL receives industrial research information about both the agro-processing products and market demands. IEL is currently attempting to link itself to the workshops of the Vocational Education and Training Authority (VETA), which are located a few kilometers away from the IEL workshop. This alliance will benefit IEL through the involvement of VETA engineering students in their industrial attachments and through the use of VETA workshops to develop some products cheaply, particularly during blackouts because VETA workshops have standby generators. The VETA workshops will also provide an opportunity for IEL to test the assembled and manufactured products. Peter is happy that the management of VETA is willing to collaborate with IEL, and efforts are already underway to sign an agreement with VETA.

IEL has also developed an informal relationship with small food vending entrepreneurs who bring food (breakfast, lunch, and fruit) to the workshop for the workers. This is common to all industries around Kihonda. There are numerous food vendors, and they earn their living from the small businesses of supplying food to employees of the companies in the industrial area.

Challenges

Despite the increased market demand for agro-food processing machinery in Tanzania, the agricultural manufacturing sector still faces a number of challenges. Peter has identified a few challenges in relation to his experience with IEL. First, almost all of the required raw materials are still imported. The supply companies purchase these materials from other countries — a situation that makes the materials expensive, perhaps due to taxation and high shipment costs. The ultimate effect of high taxation and shipment costs is the high price of the final goods produced by IEL. Peter sees this as a problem because most of IEL's customers are integrated small processors who cannot afford such expensive machinery.

Second, IEL is threatened by counterfeit raw materials. There is a rising influx of counterfeits in Tanzania in almost all imported products, be they for domestic or industrial use. Between 2006 and 2007, IEL had to change the suppliers of raw materials three times due to the supply of low-quality raw materials which were found to have been imported from China.

Another key challenge to IEL in the small manufacturing industry is, according to Peter, the regular power cuts. Workshop activities are entirely dependent on the electricity that is supplied by the monopoly company, Tanzania Electric Supply Company Limited (TANESCO). Tanzania's power is hydro-generated and hence dependent on the water availability in the rain-fed man-made dams. Because of climate change effects, the country has been experiencing extreme water shortages in the dams since 1992, thus causing power rationing almost every year. Blackouts are therefore a common occurrence in Tanzania, and the industrial sector is the most affected. IEL does not have any alternative source of power in case of power cuts, and so blackouts affect a lot of IEL's production plans. Even when power is available, it is very expensive in Tanzania compared to neighboring countries like Kenya and Uganda. Some orders are not fulfilled in time due to the power uncertainties. To counteract the impacts of what Peter calls the "fatal power effect," IEL has included the purchase of a standby generator on its five-year plan agenda.

Company managerial issues are also a challenge for IEL, since Peter has had to stretch himself too thinly by moving back and forth between the company's activities both as an engineer who is involved in the design and manufacturing of the machinery and as a manager who oversees the company's operational, financial, and marketing activities. This has been slowing down some of the important operational activities, particularly during the early days after the company's inception when Peter had to go out to promote and advertise the company and its products himself. Currently Peter is still handling several activities of the company. He intervenes in most activities of the marketing, finance, and production departments.

Bibliography

Kimambo, C.Z.M. (2005). "Stimulating Small and Medium Enterprises Development for Poverty Reduction through Business and Technology Incubation." In *Proceedings of the Engineers Registration Board's (ERB) 3rd Annual Engineers' Day — Vision 2025: Engineering Contribution in Poverty Reduction*, Dar es Salaam, March 18–19, pp. 109–125.

Madsen, E.S., V. Smith, and M.D. Hansen (2003). "Industrial Clusters, Firm Location and Productivity: Some Empirical Evidence for Danish Firms." Working Paper 03-26, Aarhus School of Business, Denmark.

Mwamila, B.L.M. and A.K. Temu (eds.) (2005). *Innovation Systems and Clusters Programme in Tanzania*. Proceedings of a National Stakeholders Workshop, Bagamoyo, Tanzania, January 24–25.

Mwamila, B.L.M., L. Trojer, B. Diyamett, and A.K. Temu (eds.) (2004). *Innovation Systems and Innovative Clusters in Africa*. Proceedings of a Regional Conference, Bagamoyo, Tanzania, February 18–20.

Nadvi, K. and S. Barrientos (2004). *Industrial Clusters and Poverty Reduction: Towards a Methodology for Poverty and Social Impact Assessment of Cluster Development Initiatives*. Vienna: United Nations Industrial Development Organization (UNIDO).

Oyelaran-Oyeyinka, B. and D. McCormick (eds.) (2007). *Industrial Clusters and Innovation Systems in Africa: Institutions, Markets and Policy*. New York: United Nations University Press.

Porter, M.E. and G.C. Bond (1999). "California Wine Cluster." Harvard Business School Case No. 9-799-124, Harvard Business School, Boston, June 22.

Solvell, O., G. Lindqvist, and C. Ketels (2003). *The Cluster Initiative Greenbook*. Stockholm: Ivory Tower AB.

Skagenfood A/S in the Northern Jutland Seafood Cluster — Decisions to Develop the Business*

The Seafood Industry — Structure and Developments

Fish and products related to fish are important contributors to economic well-being in many coastal communities both in the developed and developing world. On a global scale, the demand for fish is increasing. In developed countries, over the last few decades seafood has changed from being an inferior source of nutrition for poorer populations to an increasingly valued product that can cost more than alternatives such as pork, beef, or chicken. About 75% of global fish production is destined for direct human consumption. Since the 1990s, the amount of fish produced for human consumption has increased twofold. Approximately 40% of all fish output is traded internationally, which makes seafood one of the most intensively traded commodities in the world. Trade in fish and seafood is a global business. In terms of value, the volume of fish and fish-related products exported from developing countries is significant; it is more than that of nuts, spices, beverages, cotton, sugar, and confectionery combined.

---

*Arnim Decker, of Aalborg University (Denmark), developed this case based on information provided by Skagenfood A/S in Northern Jutland in Denmark for instructional purposes only.

Half of all fish traded are fresh fish, while less than the other half of the market is made up of products like frozen, canned, and cured fish. The rest is mainly used as feed for land animals like pigs and chickens in the form of fishmeal and oil (33 million tons per year), and increasingly for raising aquatic species such as salmon, shrimp, sea bass, etc.

In many countries, especially those from the developing world, fish serves as an important source of protein. However, quality and safety are becoming issues of major concern. Natural fish resources are rapidly depleting; overfishing has become a huge problem, together with the loss of habitat as a result of environmental pollution. The UN Food and Agriculture Organization now assumes that 75% of all available fishing grounds have been fully exploited or overexploited, or are in the process of being depleted. Since 1974, the quality of fisheries has been declining with little potential for further expansion or exploitation.

Misguided policies like poor fishery management and misleading subsidy policies have contributed to substantial overcapacity of fishing fleets in developed, but particularly in developing, countries. Large fishing fleets with industrial processing capacities on board contribute to the degradation of the biosphere by overexploitation of marine resources. Marine ecosystems are hurt because, in the process, unwanted species are caught and discarded without productive use. Fishing practices damage the natural habitat; for instance, fishing nets drag over the seabed, thereby destroying it. Inadequate fishing gear can damage the natural environment; undesired bycatch, which could have been avoided, can lead to unnecessary loss of biomass. As fish is becoming an increasingly valuable and finite resource, it is important to maintain and manage the livestock carefully. This poses a number of significant challenges to all participants in the value chain — from producers, traders, processors, retailers, through distributors and marketers to the final end consumer.

Fish Harvesting and Processing — The Product Life Cycle in the Seafood Industry

Fish is a perishable and delicate product; thus, processing and transportation are important to ensure that the quality and safety of the product are not affected. If treated properly, fish can be a healthy source of nutrition, but these properties will get lost if it is not treated properly. Inadequate handling can reduce the nutritional value of fish. Fish processing includes all processes tied to fish and fish products, from the time fish is harvested (caught) to the time fish is delivered to the consumer.

The global seafood industry is estimated to have a value of US$400 billion. It is characterized by a high degree of complexity, for there are a number of steps which take place before a freshly caught fish appears on the dinner plate.

The largest companies engaged in catching, processing, and distributing fish and fish-related products usually run their own fishing fleets. In 2002, there were approximately 1.3 million ships in operation that were larger than 10 meters long. In addition, there are about three million smaller fishing ships in operation, many of which are not decked (have a non-covered hull) and are run by wind or man power. Asia accounts for about 80% of them.

Typically, larger-sized decked vessels have a length of 10–15 meters. Only a small minority of vessels are longer than 24 meters; overall, there are about 50,000 of this kind of ships in existence, with China operating about half of them. Larger ships are often called "factory ships" because they have automated facilities on board that allow them to start processing the product right after fish has been caught. Freezing systems allow the fish to be stored for a longer period after it has been processed.

Even before a fish has been caught, there are sustainability issues that need to be taken into consideration to fully understand the supply chain. What fishing gear is being used? How much fuel does a vessel consume? While catching is going on, is the sea floor being damaged in the process? What about bycatch, if there is any — what happens to it? For example, an undesired effect of unwanted bycatch is the destruction of younger fish which cannot be processed because they are too small, yet they did not have sufficient time to grow and reproduce. Throwing back young cod which did not survive the catching process into the sea is a waste of natural resources. Destruction of the environment as well as destruction of biodiversity point towards the need to optimize the supply chain.

In Europe, as in other parts of the world, there is a plentiful number of seafood producers. All of them are, in one way or another, linked to a value chain composed of fisheries, processors, distributors, and consumers. Depending on the particular region, climate, species, retailer, and end-user demand, there are substantial differences in how the value chain functions. Once fish has been caught, it is transported to and landed in a port. In some cases, fish can be processed and deep-frozen right after the catch. On other occasions, fish which has been landed in one port may be auctioned and resent to another location in a different country for additional processing. Fish from different ships, locations, and dates of catch may even be mixed and resold in one batch. More processing steps can be added in a different location until it is finally packaged, branded, and passed on to a distributor who supplies a local retailer.

Fish can be processed to varying degrees: it may be sold as one whole fresh piece at the counter of a street market, it may be sold in the form of fillets, and sometimes it becomes part of a pre-prepared meal. Fish can be sold in fresh form, or it can be deep-frozen. Supply chain complexity has an impact on efforts to achieve sustainability, as it can be difficult to verify the claims of vendors that fisheries have been exploited in a sustainable manner due to the complexity of the supply chain. Thus, complexity results in a situation whereby it is difficult to prove whether the fish provided by seafood suppliers is from a sustainably managed stock. The need to trace fish products as they make their way through the supply chain towards the consumer is increasingly becoming an issue of concern at the level of high-ranking policymakers.

Threats and Challenges to the Seafood Industry: Depletion, Global Warming, Population Growth

Marine fisheries are under threat on a global scale. This is widely expected to lead to a significant slowdown in production, which could impact employment, fishing fleets, and prices and varieties of available fish. Aquaculture-based production is currently the fastest-growing sector, which enables the general fishing industry to maintain its growth, albeit at a slower rate.

Demand will grow in the future, both in developing and developed countries. This increase in demand will come primarily from developing countries, where there is a rising need for animal protein. Japan is currently the largest importer, with China catching up fast. Due to supply and demand mechanisms, the price of fish is increasing and this will continue into the future. As the resources of prime species are steadily dwindling, demand is gradually shifting towards lower-value species. Prices will balance demand and supply. As many Chinese citizens are now becoming wealthy, they are generating a significant aggregate demand for prime salmon products (like wild salmon), while less valuable species originating from Asia (for example, pangasius) are being exported to European markets. Price shifts result from increased demand in the marketplace and erratic supply conditions. At the same time, the seafood industry is fully exposed to globalization trends. Among other factors, this is a result of increasing demand from Asian markets, especially China. At the other end, there is an increasing demand for exotic fish species coming from American and European markets.

At the level of developing countries, there are a number of significant issues that need to be solved. For instance, giant tiger shrimp farms, which are run in countries with a tropical climate, can cause significant damage to the environment. To create space for these fish farms, natural mangrove forests are cut down and destroyed. After a short time, the seabed on which the mangroves used to grow is wasted by the shrimp-farming activities, leaving behind a desert. Shrimp farmers then move on, cut down a new area of mangrove habitat, and continue with their destructive activities.

Although fish processing activities are important, a large portion of the value is captured by trading, distributing, and selling high-quality fresh and live fish. For many companies in the sector, activities lower downstream in the value chain hold interesting potential for further business development.

Marine Stewardship Council Certification

The MSC Ecolabel

In response to the growing problem of non-sustainable fisheries, both the United States and the European Union have started to focus their attention on the introduction of certification schemes to prevent unwanted seafood from entering and being supplied to their national markets.

Currently, one of the most important ecolabels that can be found on the market is the Marine Stewardship Council (MSC) label. The MSC was established by the World Wide Fund for Nature (WWF) and Unilever as an independent non-profit organization, and was founded with the aim to promote sustainable fishing practices. It runs both an ecolabel and a sustainable fishery certification program. The label has become widespread in use, and there are now more than 1,300 companies and fisheries that have been granted MSC certification on their products. In practice, this means that seafood products which carry the blue MSC ecolabel are guaranteed to originate from a fishery that operates in an environmentally responsible way. It does not contribute to overfishing or destruction of the natural habitat.

The Quest for Sustainability along the Supply Chain from Fisheries to Consumers

For preservation and sustainability reasons, it is important to be able to understand and track the fisheries' supply chain. This can be a challenging task because of its complicated and fragmented structure. The ability to track the product along the supply chain is essential for successful certification. If implemented in the right manner, tracking systems can have a multitude of positive effects such as the achievement of a higher grade of sustainability, and maintenance of health and quality standards. End consumers will have more confidence in the end product.

For more than 15 years, consumer campaigns have tried to boost sustainable seafood practices by targeting the retailer–consumer end of the value chain in the seafood industry. For instance, in the 1990s there were campaigns called "Give Swordfish a Break" and "Take a Pass on Chilean Sea Bass." However, these campaigns only achieved limited success because they did not distinguish between those companies that fished sustainably and those that did not. For companies using non-sustainable fishing methods, there were no sufficient incentives to change because the demand for their product was stable anyway. Consumer-oriented campaigns like these do not help consumers to distinguish between "good" and "bad" producers.

One way of dealing with this problem is to establish product certification. Certification of products provides consumers with information about the producer and the origin of the seafood.

Another approach to aim for sustainability is the production chain view — that is, by looking at how products are processed during the life cycle, how they are affected by the production process, and what impact on the environment these activities have. This view takes the perspective that members of the value chain have an influence over each other and their environment as the product moves through the production chain. It would be interesting to see how sustainability is achieved at the point where linkages between members of the supply chain exist. Are they wasting resources, or are they producing and interacting in an efficient way which does not harm the environment? This view takes a holistic perspective, but unfortunately it is difficult to put it into practice because supply chains are so fragmented and difficult to overview. Nevertheless, this may provide an interesting alternative for companies which are highly vertically integrated. These companies are able to document from where they sourced their fish, and that they are able to act in an environmentally responsible way. Combined with the right marketing strategy, this may open up new market opportunities as the general public becomes more aware of sustainability issues.

The Northern Jutland Seafood Cluster

The semi-peninsula of Jutland is located in Northern Europe. It is connected to Germany in the south, and towards the north across the Skagerrak sea lies Norway. Towards the east side is Sweden, which can be reached by a two-hour ferry ride from the Northern Jutland port of Frederikshavn. Most of the way from the German border to the northernmost tip of Jutland is covered by a highway; the distance is less than 400 km, which equals to about a five-hour drive.

Northern Jutland is divided from the rest of the peninsula by the Limfjord, a natural stretch of water which cuts through the peninsula from west to east. This waterway can be used for smaller- and medium-sized vessels and was traditionally used as a transport route, but it declined in importance during the post-war period. The northern and southern parts of Jutland are connected by several bridges, and by a highway tunnel in the city of Aalborg, the most important location in Northern Jutland with around 100,000 inhabitants.

Northern Jutland is surrounded by two seas. To the east is the Baltic Sea, which stretches as far northeast of Europe as Finland and Russia. On the Baltic side of the peninsula, there are a few little harbors which are sometimes still used by small fisheries, but in general they have now been overtaken by vessels like motor and sailing yachts for free-time use. Compared to the North Sea which is to the west of Northern Jutland, the Baltic Sea area is characterized by somewhat milder sea and weather conditions.

In contrast, the west side of the peninsula has long sandy beaches and lacks natural harbors. On this side, the weather conditions are often very rough and windy, with high swells and strong currents. Nevertheless, fishing in this area has had a long tradition as well. For centuries, fishermen pulled their boats out of the water up onto the beach because there were no natural harbors. This tradition was maintained by a number of fishing communities along the west coast of Jutland, and is still alive in some places.

Over the last century, two new artificial harbors were constructed to compensate for the lack of natural harbors. To the extreme west of Jutland lies the port of Hanstholm, with its modern facilities making it the most important fishing harbor in Denmark. It also has ferry connections to locations like the Faroe Islands in the North Atlantic.

At the northern end of the confluence of the Baltic Sea and the North Sea is the city of Skagen, which is also the northernmost city of Denmark. Once a remote fishing location, it has since been developed into a modern maritime port after it became connected to the rest of the country by a railway line and a country road. Today it is an important harbor both for commercial and free-time use, with modern facilities for the landing and processing of fish and seafood. There are maintenance and installation facilities for ships with dockyards and related services, making it one of the locally most important harbors for fishing and other maritime activities.

Hirtshals, a Central Location in the Northern Jutland Cluster

Located between Skagen and Hanstholm lies the city of Hirtshals, which is the third important harbor in the Northern Jutland area.

The town and its harbor lie on an exposed location in the west coast of Northern Jutland. Hirtshals is located at a picturesque spot with a superb view of the North Sea. It is surrounded by an attractive landscape with long stretches of beaches and dunes. Weather conditions are rough and often stormy. During the summer, temperatures average between 15 and 20 degrees Celsius; during the winter, temperatures range between below 0 and 5 degrees Celsius. Because of the Gulf Stream which passes through the North Sea, temperatures seldom get extremely cold in the winter, despite the fact that Hirtshals is located on a rather high northern altitude. Its northern location means that there are long summer days with up to 18 hours of daylight in June, while during the winter months days are short with down to just 7 hours of daylight.

The town profits from its favorable location as a traffic node and connection point between several Scandinavian locations and the Atlantic Ocean. This factor also makes it a popular destination for tourism in the summer. There are a number of hotels in the area, in addition to many summer houses and camping sites. The population doubles during the summer months, with tourists mainly from Denmark, Germany, and Sweden. Throughout the year, many day tourists from Norway take advantage of the frequent ferry connections between Hirtshals and nearby Norway to do shopping and profit from comparatively low prices. Many of them visit the Hirtshals Oceanarium at the North Sea Centre, which has a giant aquarium with a large amount of different North Sea fish species and other attractions. This establishment also functions as a research and development (R&D) center for maritime research, and allows for the organization of conferences and consulting activities.

Local Population

Over the last decade, the population of Hirtshals has fallen slightly. The age distribution of the population is increasingly becoming a problem, as the 60+ generation is growing while the younger age groups of up to 40 years are slowly decreasing. This distortion of the age structure can be partly explained by limited employment opportunities in the local economy. The same applies for training and education. Therefore, many young people move to the city of Aalborg, which lies 70 km to the south, to study at the local university. Others may choose to go to the capital city of Copenhagen to study or search for job opportunities there. Once young people have left and settled elsewhere, they will usually not return to Hirtshals. The town of Hirtshals is mainly populated by citizens of Danish ethnicity, although there are some foreign citizens from Europe and Asia.

Economic Activities

The main economic sectors in the town are transport, logistics, fisheries, fishery-related industries, and tourism. The fishing activities are partly based on demersal fish (species that live on or near the sea floor), like prawn, plaice, saithe, cod, haddock, and lobster. The pelagic fisheries (fish that appear in large schools) aim primarily for herring and mackerel. The importance of fish landings to the local economy has decreased over time, which has had negative impacts on fish processing and other related industries. In fact, the Hirtshals fishing fleet decreased by 20% between 2003 and 2009. This can be partly attributed to the fact that some activities related to the fishing industry have moved to the neighboring port of Skagen, located right at the top of the Northern Jutland peninsula. Another reason is that fishing quotas have been sold away to other places and are no longer available for the fishing fleet in Hirtshals, which needed to be reduced in number as a consequence. However, the decline in fishery-related activities is compensated by a growth in the transport and logistics sector, due to the good connection by sea and to the highway network within Denmark and the rest of Europe.

The harbor is the center of economic activities, including international fishing-related activities. Because of its favorable location, Hirtshals also serves as a regional transport center for people and goods between areas in Scandinavia and the European continent. The harbor serves as a link between destinations across the North Atlantic, to Western and Southern Europe, to the Baltic states, and has direct connections to Kristiansand, Stavanger, Larvik, and Bergen in Norway. One of the two ferry companies which operate from this port, Color Line, has around 2.4 million passengers per year. About 60% of the Hirtshals port turnover originates from passenger and goods transportation.

On land, the town is well connected through the E39 highway and a railway connection. Thus, Hirtshals enjoys good links to the regional, national, and international traffic system. There is also a small airport about 30 km from Hirtshals that can be used for national and international flights. The municipal administration plans to further develop the infrastructure in order for Hirtshals to experience continuous improvement.

However, there are also some problems in the area. A number of large food processing factories in the area have closed down (including a slaughterhouse, a biscuit factory, a brewery, and a large dairy processing facility), mainly because the factories have moved to less costly locations. The Danish economy is characterized by a high level of taxation. Wage levels are also high in comparison to other places, especially Eastern Europe. As a result, many operations with high manual labor input (industries which are "wage-heavy") have closed down. Consequently, a number of industrial activities have moved out of Denmark into neighboring countries, or even further away into Asian locations.

Employment in the Fishing Industry

In 2007, Denmark adopted a system for new fishing quota regulations to reduce overcapacity and to improve the economic performance of the national fishing fleet. In Hirtshals, however, this resulted in a 30% reduction of the active fishing vessels, with a corresponding reduction in the number of jobs on the ships. Over the last few years, older vessels have been taken out of the fleet and have been replaced by larger and more modern ships, resulting in fewer but larger and more efficient units. Therefore, there is a decrease in needed manpower on board as less manual labor is required. The demand for maintenance and repair services is also declining as a result. Many of the Hirtshals-based skippers and seamen have taken advantage of these adjustments as an opportunity to retire. Yet unemployment among sea personnel has risen nevertheless. Currently, although the fishing industry is still important for employment in Hirtshals, its relative importance is in decline as many jobs are shifting into the transport and logistics industry.

Further Plans for Development of the Northern Jutland Seafood Cluster

There are plans to further develop the area; different stages of implementation have been reached at the national, regional, municipal, and local levels. Like in other European countries, in Denmark there is a national policy to ensure an equal balance of living standards in all regions of the country. In the capital, the Danish Ministry of Food, Agriculture, and Fisheries has drafted a strategic plan for further development of Danish fisheries and aquaculture. The aim is to ensure that "fisheries and aquaculture once again become a dynamo for development in fisheries dependent areas and also that Denmark can sustain or improve its regional balance" (European Commission, 2006).

In addition, the plan highlights the need for a healthy and active local economy that offers sufficient attractive job opportunities for young people in the area. At the local level, the municipality has further plans to develop and strengthen the food production, transport, and logistics sectors, together with tourism. These goals are to be achieved by combining private and public investment funds, and also by using financial development funds from the European

Union. For instance, one concrete goal is to attract Norwegian fish landing in the port of Hirtshals over the next few years.

Currently, the Hirtshals Transport Center provides forwarding/shipping agent services, various truck services, and a drivers' lounge. Its vision is to become the major regional fishing port and develop into an important center for fishing-related support activities like provision of logistics and maintenance services. Once fully developed, the transport center will also provide a complete infrastructure to facilitate transport of goods and passengers.

Example of a Large, Vertically Integrated Company: Royal Greenland

There are a substantial number of smaller players in the market, but some companies are of significant size. One example is Royal Greenland, a company that traces its roots back to 1774 when all trade with Greenland was a monopoly controlled by the Kingdom of Denmark. In the 20th century, the company was taken over by the Greenland Home Rule Government in the form of an independent limited company, and is today considered as the economic flagship of Greenland. The headquarters are operated from Nuuk in Greenland. Due to the close historical ties which still connect Denmark and the Arctic island of Greenland, Royal Greenland manages an important part of its operations from the Northern Jutland capital of Aalborg, which allows the company to profit from close proximity to the Northern Jutland seafood cluster.

The company is to a large degree vertically integrated, running its own fishing fleet, modern production facilities, and a widespread sales organization. The fisheries where its vessels operate are mainly located in the Arctic seas around Greenland. Fish is also sourced from small local Greenlandic fishermen who operate as individuals. This constitutes an essential source of income for those remote and isolated fishing communities which are scattered along the coasts of Greenland.

The company owns several production facilities in several European countries. In addition, it operates facilities to process cooked and peeled prawns in Canada, where the raw material is frozen, cooked, and peeled, and then the prawns are delivered to distributors. Back in Denmark, the company owns two factories where prawns originating from Greenland are processed, along with mussels and crayfish. It also produces surimi, a kind of mince composed of several white fish that is popular in the U.S. Moreover, at the Aalborg operations center, the company maintains an innovation center where new products are continuously developed and tested.

In the Baltic town of Koszalin on the Polish coast, the company manages a relatively new operation which was established in 2008. The site is equipped with modern equipment that enables it to handle small-batch processes. This allows for flexible handling of small-quantity orders and labor-intensive products at very competitive costs. For instance, the facility specializes in refining breaded flatfish, fish in puff pastry, stuffed fish, and high-quality salmon from Norway or halibut from Greenland. The company is also proud of its salmon tournedos which can be grilled on a barbecue — a product that has won international praise.

The company's largest production facility is located in the North German town of Bremerhaven, around 100 km to the west of Hamburg. This factory, which is the largest of its kind in Europe, is geared towards high-volume production. This highly automated facility produces more than 2.5 million meals per day, mainly using Alaska pollack, cod, hake, and other white fish. The end products include breaded and buttered fillets and portions, natural fillets, and other ready-made meals like soups and fish in sauce. The machinery enables the company to ensure high quality and cost-effectiveness by aiming for high-level economies of scale.

The company sources fish from both Greenland and other worldwide locations. It employs a dedicated sourcing team whose members possess broad knowledge about the seafood industry and markets. They maintain contacts in diverse locations like Alaska, Russia, China, and Iceland. Fish can come from wild fisheries or fish farms. Suppliers are also chosen according to their ability to comply with Royal Greenland's quality demands.

In terms of distribution and branding, the company provides for many players in the seafood market, from canteens to supermarkets and discount stores. Although it sells its products under different brands, on the package there is usually a reference to Royal Greenland. The company claims that it takes its responsibility as a large seafood producer seriously, and uses its strong market position to help develop a basis for sustainable use of fish food-related resources.

Other Players in the Supply Chain

Apart from Royal Greenland, there are a large number of other players in the seafood market whose products can be found as fresh fish in food markets or deep-frozen products in local supermarkets. In addition to large, vertically integrated companies like Royal Greenland, who operate their own fishing fleets and control all the links of their supply chain right until the end product, there is a multitude of small- and medium-sized players.

Some companies specialize in buying and processing seafood that will be processed as animal feed. There are also companies who engage in auctioning, storage, transportation, and other distribution tasks. Another important sector to take into consideration is builders of vessels for fishing, for example, fish trawlers. There is a large industry which supports the seafood industry, from ship construction to repair and maintenance services.

An important part of the global industry is the producers from developing countries that can come from a wide range of countries, such as Chile or Vietnam. For many of these often poorer and less developed countries, exports of seafood are an important part of their income and are important both for their national economy and for smaller local communities. Although there are many responsible actors, a number of environmental problems originate out of these countries. Fishing activities conducted in these countries are sometimes harmful to the environment. Lack of capital and inefficient fishing methods, as well as insufficient training and knowledge, can lead to undesired consequences for the natural habitat. In most cases, products from these countries enter the European and U.S. markets in the form of unbranded products. Local traders may repackage them and provide them with their own brand, which makes it difficult for consumers to trace where the products originally come from.

Aquaculture, also known as aquafarming, is the farming of seafood such as fish, shrimps, or mussels. There is a worldwide trend towards aquaculture, which can be conducted in freshwater or saltwater and allows for controlled conditions. It can be contrasted to the commercial fishing of wild fish which live freely in nature. Aquaculture is used to cultivate a wide range of seafood.

For many participants, aquaculture is an attractive alternative to fish caught in open waters. The reason is a chronic misbalance between supply and demand in the seafood market. While consumer demand is rather stable, supply of wild fish can be highly erratic as it depends on a multitude of circumstances which are difficult to foresee and control. These circumstances include temperature changes, diseases, and other factors. In comparison, fish farming allows for a much better control of the breeding environment. As the industry in general is dependent on a stable supply, fish farming in aquaculture is becoming increasingly attractive and as a consequence is showing significant growth.

Recognizing this trend, the local community in Hirtshals has started to plan for the development of a local aquaculture industry which will be run in an environmentally sound manner.

Skagenfood A/S, a Smaller Company within the Northern Jutland Seafood Cluster

Skagenfood A/S is a small company run and founded by a married couple, Betina Kühn and Peter Bagge-Nielsen, who founded the company in 2002. The vision of the company is to produce extraordinary food experiences with the use of high-quality raw ingredients. Skagenfood A/S delivers fresh seasonal seafood directly from door to door, both to end customers and canteens. Betina and Peter founded the company based on the realization that, even though the sea around Northern Jutland provides the region with a large variety of seafood, the average Danish family knows this only to a limited degree. Consequently, the variety and quantity of seafood on their table leave considerable margin for improvement.

Before starting the company, the married couple conducted some market research where they found out that many Danish consumers expressed a latent wish to increase their consumption of seafood. Seafood is seen as healthy and adds additional culinary experiences to the normal diet. Moreover, respondents felt that the offerings in supermarkets were too limited in terms of quality, quantity, and the variety available. Based on these observations, Betina and Peter recognized an interesting opportunity.

To exploit this market opportunity, they founded the privately held company Skagenfood A/S with the aim of providing a larger variety of seafood to Danish families. The company operates via a subscription sales model. This concept also exists with other food consumer items, for example, wine. A company offers subscription contracts to end consumers, who pay a fixed monthly fee and in return receive a couple of wine bottles every week; different products are on offer every week, so the consumer can enjoy a varied collection of different products. Skagenfood A/S follows the same concept in its delivery of pre-prepared seafood dishes and provision of raw seafood. Its products are delivered directly to the door of the end consumer. The pre-prepared meals allow for a great deal of convenience, and enable consumers of Skagenfood A/S to enjoy a wider variety of different dishes than they would otherwise enjoy. By paying a monthly fee, customers will receive meals, for instance, once a week. The company has about 11,000 regular customers throughout the country, which they serve with 18 employees.

The delivered items are usually pre-prepared meals, but it is also possible to deliver raw materials only. Delivery intervals are either on a weekly basis or once every fortnight. The company makes it a point to use raw material from small fish trawlers based along the coast of Northern Jutland. These smaller ships normally stay out at sea for one or two nights only, and then return home with their fresh catch. According to Skagenfood A/S, little time is lost at sea so that the ships return when their catch is still very fresh. To avoid unnecessary loss of time, Skagenfood A/S avoids trading through middlemen. Because they usually buy fresh from the producers, Skagenfood A/S is mostly able to document the catch, recording from which boat the raw material originated and on what day and time. This allows for transparency along the complete delivery chain towards the end consumer.

The company tries to source fish caught in Danish waters and landed through Danish ports as much as possible. However, sometimes this is not possible, for instance, when bad weather conditions prevent the small fishing ships from venturing out so they have to stay in port. In such cases, Skagenfood A/S may also deliver Norwegian salmon or other exotic overseas species. Because Skagenfood A/S purchases seafood directly at fish auctions, they can bypass middlemen. As this part of the supply chain is cut out, valuable time is saved and the fish can arrive at the customer's doorstep much fresher.

Guaranteeing a continuous cold chain throughout the distribution channel is very important, so the company has to make sure the necessary infrastructure for cooling is in place. Once Skagenfood A/S has received a catch, the fish will be hand-filled, packaged, and directly sent to the customer. Transportation is carried out under optimal conditions by contracted suppliers. The company uses isolated boxes that keep the temperature down between 0 and 2 degrees Celsius until the food reaches the customer. Specially developed packaging material ensures a continuous cooling down until the customer has received the product. According to the company, it is best if the meal is cooked and consumed right after delivery; nevertheless, the food will still be safe to eat for a few more days and provides a good culinary experience if stored properly in a fridge without losing taste or freshness. The company also makes special meals for children.

To extend its offering, Skagenfood A/S also sells packets with vegetables or fruits in addition to the packets of seafood. On its website, the company provides recipes for consumers to cook the seafood they have received. The vegetable and fruit packets serve as complements so that customers can easily follow the recipes provided by Skagenfood A/S without needing to go out and search for those necessary ingredients at the local store.

Skagenfood A/S's Business Model

Skagenfood A/S's vision is to deliver dinner experiences made of high-quality ingredients to the customer's doorstep. Customers will pre-order the fish, and it will be delivered on a specified day and time. The products vary each time a new delivery arrives; the fish comes ready-prepared with a varying assortment of vegetables and fruits out of ecological production. The company employs traditionally skilled craftsmen to prepare the meals; industrial production methods are avoided. Fillets are cut by hand and the meal packages are manually packed. The meals are delivered to the customer's doorstep by contracted suppliers who work closely with Skagenfood A/S.

As of now, the company delivers within Danish territory. As it is located in the northern tip of the Jutland peninsula, this means that it is more than 400 km away from the important population center and capital of Copenhagen, which is on the island of Zealand on the eastern side of the country. The company calculates that it is logistically able to deliver to end customers three times a week. It is only through the scope of operating on the basis of a nationwide distribution system that enables the company to achieve sufficiently critical mass; otherwise, it would not be able to cover its overhead costs.

As we pointed out, the company distinguishes itself from its competitors by shortening the supply chain. Other companies deliver fish products which have gone through multiple steps in the supply chain. In the usual supply chain model, once a fish has been caught and landed in the port, it will be brought to a cooled storage facility until it can go into auction. In the auction, a buyer will bid for the fish, which will subsequently go to a wholesaler. Then other buyers — e.g., traders on local street markets, supermarkets, canteens, and restaurants — will purchase the material and sell it to the end consumer, either fresh or prepared as a meal.

Skagenfood A/S shortens this supply chain, meaning that it takes significantly less time for the fish to arrive on the table of the end consumer. Basically, they achieve this by circumventing the wholesaler and retailer; instead, they directly purchase fish at the auctions themselves. As steps are cut out, fish will be much fresher when it reaches the consumer.

Skagenfood A/S has developed its distribution chain such that it allows for a high degree of transparency. Traceability is a competitive factor that is becoming increasingly important. To make sure that fish comes from sustainable fisheries, consumers want to know where the fish has been caught and where it has been landed. In the traditional supply chain — where the fish passes through multiple steps from auctions, storage, distributors, wholesalers, and retailers towards the end consumer — it is practically impossible to trace the origin of the original fish product. Fish from different locations, ships, and catch days are mixed and mingled. Thus, it is impossible for consumers to verify a seller's claim of sustainability. In contrast to this, Skagenfood A/S knows where their products come from and they can prove it to their customers. For consumers, this feature is becoming increasingly significant; for Skagenfood A/S, this feature can be helpful to carve out a unique selling proposition.

Making Consumers' Lives Easier

Fish is a delicate product and is comparatively difficult to prepare for many private households. Fish bones are often difficult to extract; a cook needs to have the right tools and special knowledge on how to cut the product. Another issue is choosing the right conditions for cooking; for frying, for example, the pan needs to have the right temperature and the fish should not be left in the pan for too long or too short. This can be too complicated for many private cooks. Skagenfood A/S allows these households to consume fresh fish despite not having much knowledge about cooking.

Many private households do not know a lot about buying fish. It is difficult to tell whether the fish is still fresh when it is lying on the counter of a supermarket; sometimes, it could have been there for several days. In many places, street markets are only held once a week.

Skagenfood A/S's business model enables it to exactly forecast the quantities it needs to buy at the auction hall, as it has already received orders from its customers beforehand. Therefore, the company can buy a few types of fish in comparatively high quantities, resulting in price advantages at the auction and thus compensating for the small size of the company at the purchasing level.

To summarize, by designing its value chain in this way, Skagenfood A/S has taken advantage of its geographical proximity to fisheries and its embeddedness into the local seafood-related cluster to design a supply chain that provides a competitive superiority over other players in the market. As Skagenfood A/S is not a large company, it is not well positioned to exploit economies of scale and achieve cost advantages. But a redesign and streamlining of its supply chain has enabled it to carve out a special market niche in this competitive market.

Reasons Why Consumers Choose Skagenfood A/S

Skagenfood A/S recently conducted a survey among its existing customers. The company found out that:

- 90% appreciate the freshness of Skagenfood A/S's product line;
- More than 70% think that purchasing at Skagenfood A/S is easy and comfortable;
- 47% say that by buying from Skagenfood A/S, they can get products they would not be able to find in the local supermarket;
- 45% say that their diet is becoming more varied;
- 35% cite the possibility of accessing healthier food; and
- 25% appreciate that they do not have to worry about going out and shopping for dinner.

Furthermore, the majority of customers appreciate that the lunch boxes are accompanied by a recipe, which enables end users to easily prepare tasty and healthy meals, and that the food comes from ecological production. Two thirds of all consumers positively recognize that mostly raw material sources from Denmark are used (traceability). One third think that the prices are competitive; however, this last point indicates that two thirds of existing customers regard the product as relatively expensive.

The Challenge: Take Advantage of the Booming Consumer Market in Northern Germany?

Denmark is a small country, and the much larger German neighbor (in terms of population, geographical size, and GDP) is not far and easy to reach across the southern border. Seen from the north, the next major metropolis is Hamburg with a population of 1.7 million inhabitants. Compared to this city, the whole population of Denmark is just 5.5 million inhabitants. For a small company based in Denmark, this city alone presents enormous market opportunities. Even though it would mean crossing borders, Hamburg is just a six-hour drive away from Skagenfood A/S's headquarters, and is even easier to reach than Copenhagen itself.

Being a port city of major international importance, Hamburg has always had a maritime tradition. For instance, the *Fischmarkt* ("Fish Market") is a Hamburg institution that draws in a large number of both locals and foreigners. A typical Hamburg citizen has a propensity for the consumption of seafood; there are a number of typical local dishes which are based on fish or other maritime species.

By the summer of 2011, the German economy had clearly emerged from the financial crisis and had already entered into a new boom phase, taking advantage of its favorable domestic cost basis together with market opportunities in the booming East Asian economies. The Northern German market, including Hamburg and the surrounding region, could present interesting opportunities for a smaller company like Skagenfood A/S. Hamburg, with its port and its central location as a trading hub, was traditionally well positioned to profit from opportunities stemming from international trade. The result is a wealthy and large group of upper- and middle-class citizens who are willing to spend money if it fits their needs and lifestyle. Like in other large German cities, single households are becoming more prevalent while there are relatively few children. A typical Hamburg household for which Skagenfood A/S would aim could consist of one or two members with a high level of income but with little time to buy food in the market and to cook it at home. For example, instead of going out to a restaurant and inviting friends, many people would prefer to stay at home and invite friends over. Many individuals lack time to shop and do not have sufficient cooking skills. This is where a company like Skagenfood A/S could come in.

Consumer Demand for Sustainable Seafood

Market research shows that European citizens are generating an increasing demand for fish products that have been sourced in a sustainable way. Non-governmental organizations are putting more and more pressure on retailers to stop merchandising fish species which they consider as being under threat. As a result, retailers are starting to withdraw unsustainable products from their shelves. This has led to a market where it is becoming increasingly normal practice to offer sustainable fish.

To gauge the market opportunities in Hamburg, Skagenfood A/S consulted a marketing specialist who conducted some research into that area. According to her, there is sufficient evidence that consumers prefer ecolabeled food if given the choice. However, the question is whether consumers are willing to pay a premium for ecolabeled food. According to the consultant, the answer is not always clear and depends on various factors, for instance, the fishery. Seafood markets are complicated and are influenced by many factors. It is hard to insulate the influence of the ecolabel from other factors, like general marketing activities, availability of supply, competition from alternative species, changes in the consumer markets and their dynamics, and of course seasonality. The consultant found that when consumers are confronted with fish products that are ecolabeled together with some that are not, they would prefer the ecolabeled product as long as the price difference is not too high. But it is not clear if this applies to pre-cooked fish meals of high quality, as this concept is still new in the market.

The consultant found out that consumers generally find over-fishing important enough to start thinking about buying other fish species which are less threatened. However, they would not choose to replace a preferred type of fish with an inferior one just because the less preferred one comes with an ecolabel. The consultant advised Skagenfood A/S that it would definitely be a good idea to apply for MSC certification. Yet, as there are numerous other competitors who are already using this label, the company should do more to differentiate itself in the marketplace.

Bibliography

European Commission (2006). "Assessment of the Status, Development and Diversification of Fisheries Dependent Communities: Hirtshals Case Study Report." MRAG Consortium: Socioeconomic Dependency Case Study Reports, p. 10. http://ec.europa.eu/fisheries/documentation/studies/regional_social_economic_impacts/hirtshals_en.pdf/.

Case 14

Growth Challenges in Small Manufacturing Ventures from Emerging Economies — The Evidence from Moldova*

To Grow or Not to Grow?

This is not a rhetorical question for Tamara Popa,[1] the co-owner and Executive Director of VM-Plumcom Ltd. Clearly it is the former part of the question that is on Tamara's agenda. The challenge thus is *how* to grow — a challenge that has been amplified over the last couple of years by the global economic crisis and recession, especially in the international markets VM-Plumcom Ltd. has been serving.

After the onset of the crisis in 2008, the revenue of the company dropped by 12% in 2009, with export sales dropping by 14% as compared to 2007. As the number of orders decreased during this period, VM-Plumcom Ltd. even stopped the production process in 2010 since the stock had piled up during the previous year. On top of the global economic crisis, Moldova also experienced severe drought that heavily affected the yield of fruit and vegetables, which are the company's raw materials.

*Romeo V. Turcan, of Aalborg University (Denmark), developed this case for instructional purposes only with permission from the management of VM-Plumcom Ltd.
[1] The author would like to thank Tamara Popa for her time, her tremendous support, and not least her patience in the preparation of the case.

Despite all of this, Tamara strongly believes in a positive outlook for her business. Sales picked up in 2010 and reached the 2007 level. In a way, this was due to the fact that two years ago VM-Plumcom Ltd. received organic certification that brought new, bigger business opportunities. Tamara has plans for the medium term to invest in and launch new products such as nut kernels; puree, juice, and nectar from peach, apricot, and apples; dried vegetables; and frozen fruit and vegetables. To achieve these objectives, Tamara expects to invest over US$3 million in new equipment and production capacity, and increase the number of permanent staff to between 100 and 150 employees over the next three years.

The Emergence of the Venture

VM-Plumcom Ltd. is a family-owned business. It was founded in the spring of 2000 by Tamara and her husband, with their two daughters being the other two founding members. The company provides the basis for the establishment of an industrial cluster in a geographic area where smaller enterprises are just beginning to be established and are learning how to cooperate. VM-Plumcom Ltd. is in the business of processing fruit and vegetables. Currently, its main product range consists of dried fruit (e.g., prune and cherry with or without stones, skinned apple rondelle, whole or sliced pear, dog rose (*Rosa canina*)) and prune and apple jam without sugar. The contribution of jam products to the total revenue is approximately 65%–70%, with dried fruit accounting for the remainder.

Prior to starting her venture, Tamara worked as the Executive Director of one of the largest fruit and vegetable processing enterprises in Moldova. Being frustrated mainly by the red tape and lack of support to induce dramatic changes in the organization, Tamara left her employer and decided to start her own venture. Apart from her drive and motivation for success, Tamara brought to the new venture her knowledge, experience, and understanding of the market and the business.

Initially, Tamara and her husband formed a sole proprietorship to collect fruit and vegetables, process them at various producers of canned fruit and vegetables throughout the country, and sell the finished goods. This business model turned out, however, to be quite expensive and ineffective. Tamara and her husband then decided to create a limited company that would incorporate all of those functions in aiming at a better performance. Three former colleagues joined Tamara in the newly established company, covering the areas of marketing and sales, engineering, and accounting.

In 2000, Tamara bought 9,800 m^2 of industrial land on the outskirts of Ungheni on which there was a decommissioned enterprise. With an initial investment of €10,000, Tamara managed to start up the company, and began to produce and sell their first products in 2001, generating just over 31% of their revenue from international sales (see Table 1). The company's current yearly production capacity is 300 tons of dried fruit (prunes, apples, and pears), 60 tons of stoneless dried cherries, 400 tons of prune jam, and 200 tons of apple jam. From the date of its inception, VM-Plumcom Ltd. grew rapidly both in size and scope. Before the crisis in 2008, the average growth rate of employees per year was about 30%, while the annual total revenue grew on average by 45%.

Internationalization: East or West?

Right from the company's inception in 2000, Tamara was aware of the fact that she had to target international markets, as the local market was too small and was exhibiting the emergence of intense competition. The question, though, was where to go: east or west? Given Moldova's historical ties with Russia, the Russian market — and, for that matter, the markets of other Commonwealth of Independent States (CIS) countries (the former Soviet Republics, with the exception of the Baltic states) — would have been a natural choice for an international market entry, as it has been for a large number of entrepreneurs from Moldova.

Table 1. Aggregate growth data of VM-Plumcom, 2001–2010.

	2001	2002	2003	2004	2005	2006	2007	2008	2009	2010
Number of Employees	15	22	35	40	45	45	65	72	70	56
Product Range	Dried prunes, dried apples	Dried prunes, dried apples	Dried prunes, dried apples, prune jam	Dried prunes, dried apples, prune jam, apple jam	Dried prunes, dried apples, prune jam, apple jam	Dried prunes, dried apples, prune jam, apple jam, dried pears	Dried prunes, dried apples, prune jam, apple jam, dried pears, dried cherries without stones	Dried prunes, dried apples, prune jam, apple jam	Dried prunes, dried apples, prune jam, apple jam, organic dried cherries without stones	Organic and traditional apple and prune jam, organic dried prunes without stones, organic dried cherries without stones
Total Revenue (€)	82,926	202,615	290,599	301,250	477,515	504,100	574,254	625,412	501,420	572,128
Export Revenue (€)	25,686	173,181	253,175	270,035	442,515	466,465	551,942	525,289	479,420	560,768
Key Export Markets	Czech Republic, Ukraine, Romania			Germany, Austria, Lithuania, Czech Republic, Ukraine, Romania				Germany, Austria, Lithuania, Czech Republic, Romania, Slovak Republic		
Investment (€)	10,000	50,000	40,000	20,000	100,000	100,000	62,500	11,560	0	0

Nonetheless, it was a different story for Tamara. Several factors played a crucial role in deciding on the direction of internationalization. From her experience, Tamara had learned that Russian partners are not trustworthy and are unwilling to cooperate on payment and delivery terms, sometimes even refusing to pay while insinuating various motives. Moreover, the trading relationship between the two countries was quite politicized, exposing the Moldovan companies to a high political risk. Apart from the above, there were also market-related factors that influenced Tamara's decision. Not all of the company's products had a market in Russia. For example, apple jam and apple juice concentrate were not in demand, although dried fruit, especially dried prunes, were in demand, as they are even today.

The road to the west was not easy either, though the situation was different. In those days, "Made in Moldova" did not evoke a lot of trust. So Tamara had to earn the trust of the EU partners, and at the same time prove and maintain the quality of the products. To mitigate this risk, in addition to her efforts to sell directly, Tamara exported indirectly to the EU customers via Romanian trading agents. VM-Plumcom Ltd. lost quite substantially on pricing, but that was the price Tamara was willing to pay to earn the trust of the key players in the market and keep the company going.

The first international market was the Czech Republic. Tamara knew one buyer from the Czech Republic from her previous experience as Executive Director. At the same time, VM-Plumcom Ltd. entered the nearby markets of Romania and Ukraine. The Czech partner later introduced VM-Plumcom Ltd. to a large buyer in Austria, while the Romanian partner introduced VM-Plumcom Ltd. to another large buyer in Germany. As the company grew, VM-Plumcom Ltd. was also approached by a large buyer from Lithuania.

VM-Plumcom Ltd. started exporting dried prunes to begin with, and now also focuses on organic food, having been certified as an organic food producer. Apart from exporting, Tamara has had plans to open a sales subsidiary in Germany; however, the financial constraints over the last few years due to the global economic crisis and recession have put this vision on hold. From the company's inception, the sales from exports grew at a high rate, almost 120% per year, with the ratio of revenue coming from international sales growing from 31% in 2001 to 96% in 2007 and reaching 98% in 2010 (Table 1).

To continue expanding into the EU market, VM-Plumcom Ltd. had to enhance its compliance with the safety and quality requirements of the EU market. In 2007, the Hazard Analysis and Critical Control Points (HACCP) framework was implemented at VM-Plumcom Ltd., with support from the Citizens Network for Foreign Affairs (CNFA), in order to comply with food safety requirements. In 2009, the key company products — dried prunes, dried cherries, and jam products — received organic certification, "BIO," demonstrating compliance with a set of production standards for growing, storage, processing, packaging, and shipping. The company's own agricultural land was also certified to make possible the growth of ecological products.

The internationalization efforts were also facilitated by the EU's European Neighbourhood Policy, which was developed in 2004 with the aim of avoiding the emergence of new dividing lines between the enlarged EU and EU neighbors (European Commission, 2010). In 2005, based on this policy initiative, the EU–Moldova Action Plan was adopted. On the basis of this plan, Moldova, *inter alia*, benefited in 2006 from the new EU Generalized System of Preferences (GSP+)[2] that made duty-free (zero-tariff) access to the EU market possible for 6,400 products covered by GSP+ (European Commission, 2008a). In the process, the EU introduced autonomous trade preferences to Moldova by removing all remaining tariff ceilings for industrial

---

[2]The eligibility of countries placed in the GSP+ incentive scheme is confirmed by an assessment of their effective implementation of core human and labor rights, good governance, and environmental conventions (European Commission, 2005).

products and by improving access to the European Community market for agricultural products (European Commission, 2008b).

The EU Market

The consumption of dried fruit in the EU is valued at €2.3 billion or 871,000 tons (CBI, 2008). Being a net importer of dried fruit, EU production of dried fruit amounts to approximately €1.7 billion or 428,000 tons, and mainly consists of dried grapes, dates, figs, and prunes. Total EU imports increased on average by 9.1% annually in value between 2003 and 2007. Developing countries account for approximately 55% of the total imported value of selected dried fruit to the EU (CBI, 2005, 2008). Overall, the EU market absorbs approximately 80% of the Moldovan sector's output of dried fruit, with the remainder going to CIS markets, primarily Russia, Belarus, and Ukraine. Being a net exporter of dried fruit despite the fact that the sector is operating under its capacity (CNFA, 2008), Moldova is among the leading suppliers of selected dried fruit (from developing countries) to the EU with a total share of 1.3% (see Table 2).

There are three market segments for dried fruit: the food processing market, the retail market, and the catering market. The food processing market is the largest market, accounting for approximately 80% of EU imports of dried fruit; retail-sector sales are dominated by the supermarket sector, but health stores are increasingly gaining market share; while the catering market is the smallest of the three markets (CBI, 2008). Dried fruit is used as raw material input for further applications in breakfast cereals, baked goods, desserts, and confectionery products. Dried fruit is usually imported to a centrally located EU country, often the Netherlands or Germany, and from there distributed to other EU member states (see Figure 1).

According to FoodAndDrinkEurope.com, one of the key factors boosting the consumption of dried fruit is the need for convenient, on-the-go snack food, which is related to innovative packaging design

Table 2. Leading developing country suppliers of selected dried fruit (in €1,000).

Country	Dried Prunes	Dried Apples	Other Dried Fruit
Chile	18,314	7,578	8,070
China	265	4,226	3,587
Argentina	5,043	291	0
Turkey	1,062	2,040	598
Serbia and Montenegro	1,062	146	0
Moldova	265	146	299
Iran	0	0	598
Tunisia	531	0	0
South Africa	0	0	448
Albania	0	73	299
Philippines	0	0	149
Georgia	0	73	0
Total	**26,542**	**14,573**	**14,048**

Source: CBI (2005).

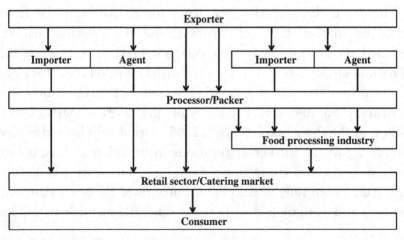

Figure 1. Distribution channels for dried fruit entering the EU market (source: CBI, 2008).

and marketing. Recent research conducted by EHI Retail Institute showed that despite the substantial progress made in reducing the costs of packaging for retailers, the main retail requirements relevant to packaging are still a challenge, with marketing and cost being the other two top priorities (FoodAndDrinkEurope.com, 2011). The consumption of various (organic) dried-fruit products is forecasted to continue to increase as consumers become more and more aware of the contribution of dried fruit to a healthy diet (CBI, 2008).

The dried fruit market is characterized by high prices but low margins, with prices being determined (but not "set") by importers and wholesalers (CBI, 2008). There are several factors that affect the high level of pricing. One of the main factors relates to the expensive and rather difficult production process, which requires large quantities of fresh fruit and tight quality control, as well as to the drying/processing method. The other factors affecting prices of dried fruit include the quantities and the type of dried fruit in question, the harvest output in the supplying countries in relation to demand, negotiations between the different chain partners and the number of intermediaries buying and selling, the quality of fresh fruit (and vegetables) aimed at the consumer markets, and exchange rates. Overall, changes in supply due to wide variations in availability, caused by fluctuating harvests, weather conditions, or disasters, have a much larger effect on price levels than changes in demand (CBI, 2008).

Successful access to the EU market is also determined by compliance with the EU requirements for dried fruit that are based on environmental, consumer health and safety, and social concerns, as well as with the legislated requirements concerning labels, codes, and management systems (CBI, 2008). Two of the most important EU regulations are the Regulation on Maximum Residue Limits (European Commission, 2011) and the Regulation on Food Additives, Food Enzymes, and Flavourings (European Commission, 2009).

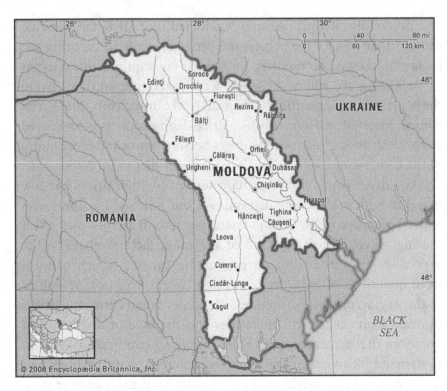

Figure 2. Map of Moldova (source: *Encyclopædia Britannica*, 2008).

Local Market

VM-Plumcom Ltd. is located in Ungheni city, just over 100 km northwest of the capital of Moldova, Chisinau (see Figure 2). Ungheni is a district center, located at the border with Romania, and has an international railroad hub. Moldova is a country landlocked between Romania and Ukraine; it became independent in 1991 as a result of the collapse of the USSR. Moldova stretches just under 450 km from north to south, and less than 250 km from east to west, having just over 3.5 million citizens (Eurostat, 2009).

Historically, the agricultural sector has been considered as one of the main pillars of the national economy, accounting for over 16% of the country's GDP and contributing approximately 50% to

Moldova's total exports. The production of dried fruit per year is somewhere between 2,000 and 3,500 tons, subject to the quality and growing conditions of the raw material. A few large and medium companies dominate the dried fruit market in Moldova, accounting for about 67% of the total turnover; the remainder is generated by a large number of small companies (CNFA, 2008). Some of the key players in the sector include the following:

- *Inmark* (www.inmark.md). Inmark was founded in 1998 to produce dried fruit and vegetables, such as cherries, peaches, apricots, prunes, tomatoes, peppers, eggplants, and zucchini, and to process and sell walnuts. The initial export markets were Russia and other CIS countries. In 2008, Inmark started implementing the HACCP framework, with a view to start producing organic food. It invested in its own supply base: in 2008, the company planted 120 ha of orchards, which would allow it, from 2010 to 2012 inclusive, to harvest approximately 800 tons of apples, 100 tons of prunes, 200 tons of cherries, and 300 tons of peaches. These efforts have made it possible for Inmark to extend its export markets to EU countries and beyond.
- *Monicol* (www.monicol.md). Monicol was founded in 2001 with the aim of producing and exporting walnut kernels and dried fruit. It has 10 employees as permanent staff, and during the harvest season it employs somewhere between 200 and 250 people. With the help of CNFA under a United States Agency for International Development (USAID) project, Monicol invested USD 1.9 million in a fruit-drying facility upgrade. The fruit drying facility has an annual production capacity of 200 tons of dried apples and 300 tons of dried prunes. The company attained a revenue of USD 0.67 million in 2004, and more than USD 3.5 million in 2007. It purchases its raw material from over 50 farmers and 50 small-scale processors. Monicol exports mainly to the EU. The company is ISO 9001:2000-certified, and has implemented the HACCP system.

- *Prometeu-T* (PT) (www.walnut.md). PT was established in 1995 to grow/acquire, process, and sell walnut kernels and in-shell walnuts. In 2008, it started to produce dried fruit, such as prunes, cherries, and apples. It has grown rapidly over the years, approximately 25% per year, reaching an annual revenue of up to USD 10 million. PT is a medium-sized company with less than 500 employees. PT exports between 91% and 100% of its products to the EU, Turkey, and the Middle East. PT owns approximately 110 ha of agricultural land, of which 35 ha are planted with walnut trees, 50 ha with prune trees, 15 ha with almond trees, 5 ha with peach trees, and 5 ha with sour cherry trees. In 2009, PT passed ISO 22000:2005 certification for the processing of walnut kernels and dried fruit.
- *Reforma Natural Nuts & Fruits* (RNNF) (www.reforma.eu). RNNF is a subsidiary of Reforma-Werk, a European enterprise with a long tradition in the natural and organic food business. With an initial investment of about DEM 18 million, the company was established in 1996 with the sole aim of producing organic food. It has grown rapidly over the years to about 1,000 employees today. The company has a wide product range, e.g., animal feed, dried fruit and vegetables, nuts, and seeds, with 99% of its output being exported. The range of dried fruit includes apples (rings and cubes), apricots, cherries (sweet and sour), melons, peaches, and pears. It has over 3,250 small farms as suppliers. All organic products are certified according to EU Regulation 2092/91.

There are also a large number of small exporters that are focused on the Russian market and/or the markets of other CIS countries. These exporters could be described as those that do not have the necessary capabilities to meet the safety and quality requirements of the EU market, and that are unable to ensure proper communications with EU customers (CNFA, 2008).

Growth Challenges and Opportunities

Given that changes in supply have a much larger effect on price levels than do changes in demand, the quantity and quality of raw material are of paramount importance to the success of the venture. The poor raw material production base in Moldova is considered to be the major constraint to further expansion of the dried fruit sector (CNFA, 2008). This is due chiefly to the aging and decreasing of orchards, the lack of varieties suitable for drying, and inefficient growing technologies. In addition, Tamara factors in the human factor in making the supply of raw material unreliable. For example, local suppliers often do not know what a contract means. As Tamara explained, "Today they, the suppliers, deliver you a loaded truck; tomorrow they will not, saying they have a delivery for somebody else, for their relatives, etc."

Tamara has faced all of these issues as the company has grown. To mitigate these risks, in 2006 Tamara bought 100 ha of agricultural land, with the aim of planting plum and cherry trees in 2007.[3] However, this did not happen for several reasons. The soil was in a very deplorable state and required time to be prepared and ready for new orchards. At the same time, the planting trees and seeds had to be imported as there was no local production base for such planting material. But an import tax of 15% and a Value-Added Tax (VAT) of 20% were levied on such planting material, which made such imports unattractive. Only in 2008/2009 did the local production base for planting trees and seeds start to emerge, which made it possible for VM-Plumcom Ltd. to buy the necessary planting material locally.

---

[3]This backward integration trend can also be witnessed in other sectors of the economy, e.g., sugar and wine. The author had the opportunity to work as a consultant within a USAID project to one of the local sugar producers that was supporting sugar beet growers financially, logistically, and technologically (sometimes taking a stake in the ownership). Wine makers started buying land and growing their own vineyards in early 2000.

In 2010, VM-Plumcom Ltd. started planting its own orchards of plums and cherries.

This kind of backward integration has required VM-Plumcom Ltd. to acquire additional and considerable expertise in the management of physical resources such as land and water/irrigation; production systems such as crop rotation, varieties, operating costs, technology, and husbandry; related human resources such as family labor, permanent employees, and fruit-picking labor; related capital items such as debt management and depreciation; and off-farm interests (RMCG, 2004). To this end, VM-Plumcom Ltd. has had to implement best business practices directed towards the protection of the environment.

When VM-Plumcom Ltd. bought the industrial land, there was no access (distribution pipes) to gas and there was no proper road. Tamara approached the local gas company to ask them to build a distribution pipe to the company's premises. She was told to use her own resources to build the pipe with later reimbursement. Tamara spent approximately €65,000 to build this pipeline. After the pipe was built and became functional, many other residential and small commercial customers "hooked" onto the pipeline. To this day, the local gas company refuses to record the pipe onto their balance sheet and reimburse the money. The same thing happened with the road. Tamara invested in the construction of the road that connects VM-Plumcom Ltd. to the main road. When Tamara asked the mayor to record the road onto the balance sheet, she was refused on the grounds that such a road had not been budgeted by the mayor's office.

Another enduring challenge is access to credit. The local financial market is not sophisticated[4] and is dominated by local banks, with foreign banks only being granted access to the market in 2008. The

---

[4]In 2009, Moldova was ranked as the fifth most stable economy in the world, with the main reasons being its primitive financial system, its low level of credit issuing, and its agriculture- rather than real-based economy. Thus, Moldova was less vulnerable to the global financial and economic crisis (www.thebanker.com).

issue, however, is not so much the amount; it is about the cost and time. Interest rates are very high, 14% to 16% for the USD or Euro, and over 20% for Moldovan leu. The settlement period for a loan is somewhere between 1 and 3 years. From 2006 to 2008 inclusive, VM-Plumcom Ltd. benefited from a better loan from CNFA to support its capital investment in new equipment. The issue here is further amplified by the reluctance of banks to extend credit to the agricultural sector due to perceived high risks (CNFA, 2009).

A related challenge is the exchange rate. For political reasons (namely the general elections in the spring of 2009), the Moldovan leu was artificially strengthened in 2008 against the U.S. dollar (see Figure 3). Due to this artificial strengthening of the leu, VM-Plumcom Ltd. suffered a loss of approximately 4 million lei.

Another growth challenge for VM-Plumcom Ltd., which is related to the variable costs of production, is labor. It is estimated that somewhere between 500,000 and 1 million citizens have left Moldova to work abroad since its independence in 1991 (U.S. Department of State, 2006). Such scarcity of labor poses a real threat to the operations of VM-Plumcom Ltd., given the company's rural location, far away from the capital and district centers. The scarcity of labor in numbers

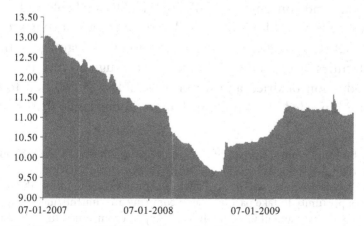

Figure 3. Evolution of Moldovan leu against USD, 2007–2009 (source: National Bank of Moldova (www.bnm.md)).

is further compounded by the scarcity of high-quality labor. For example, VM-Plumcom Ltd. needs plumbers and electricians, as well as shift engineers/managers. However, vocational education has been nearly destroyed since the country's independence in 1991, and the extant university graduates are of low quality.[5] The company internships are only on paper, with students coming only to ask for attendance sheets to be signed without any real interest to learn from hands-on experience.

Yet another challenge is to cope with the disloyal competition in the market that comes from small dried fruit producers. Their products are of low quality and are unofficial (bypassing the tax authorities), making them "low-cost/low-price" producers/exporters. To deal with this problem, VM-Plumcom Ltd. joined the Association of Canned Producers. Through this association, VM-Plumcom Ltd. has also received support in finding potential investors and making its voice heard at the government and parliament levels.

The Vision

There is an increasing interest in different (organic) products in the EU, addressing key consumer demands such as health, wellness, enjoyment, and convenience (CBI, 2008). With a reliable and high-quality supply base, Moldova could double or triple its exports to the EU market (CNFA, 2008). Tamara wants to take advantage of these opportunities by expanding her business through an investment in the production of dried and frozen vegetables. In addition to the quest for a needed US$3 million, Tamara understands that there is

---

[5] Again, this trend is not sector-specific. As an Executive Director of IABP-Moldova (the International Association of Business and Parliament, an NGO that facilitates dialogue between members of the parliament and business community), the author had the opportunity to take part in several company attachments/internships for members of the parliament in several ICT and apparel companies. In both sectors, high turnover of employees and low quality of graduates were among the main concerns of the entrepreneurs.

another equally challenging quest for suitable, reliable suppliers of needed vegetables with whom Tamara can sign long-term contracts.

Another growth path Tamara is currently considering is an international joint venture. She was recently introduced to one of the largest German wholesalers of dried fruit products, who expressed an interest in such a venture. Both parties have taken some time off to learn more about each other and prepare for the negotiations. The quest for funding could end if the deal is successful. However, the quest for a quality and reliable raw material base remains a challenge. With this in mind, the question is: How much further should VM-Plumcom Ltd. integrate backwards or horizontally? Will VM-Plumcom Ltd. be able then to preserve its mission to produce and sell dried fruit products?

Bibliography

CBI (2005). "EU Market Brief: Dried Fruit." CBI Market Information Database, http://www.cbi.eu/ [accessed May 19, 2011].

CBI (2008). "Preserved Fruit and Vegetables: The EU Market for Dried Fruit." CBI Market Information Database, http://www.cbi.eu/ [accessed May 19, 2011].

CNFA (2008). "Moldova's Dried Fruit Sector Assessment." http://www.cnfa.md/ [accessed May 16, 2011].

CNFA (2009). "Moldovan Agricultural Risk Evaluation System." http://www.cnfa.md/ [accessed May 16, 2011].

Encyclopædia Britannica (2008). "Moldova." http://www.britannica.com/EBchecked/media/62193/ [accessed May 30, 2011].

European Commission (2005). "EU Member States Back New EU Generalised System of Preferences." http://www.europa-eu-un.org/articles/en/article_4827_en.htm/ [accessed May 31, 2011].

European Commission (2008a). "EU Gives Developing Countries Duty-Free Access with GSP+." http://ec.europa.eu/trade/wider-agenda/development/generalised-system-of-preferences/index_en.htm/ [accessed May 31, 2011].

European Commission (2008b). "European Communities — Request for a Waiver for the Application of Autonomous Preferential Treatment to Moldova." http://trade.ec.europa. eu/doclib/docs/2008/september/tradoc_140567.pdf/ [accessed May 31, 2011].

European Commission (2009). "Food Additives — New Regulations on Food Additives, Food Enzymes and Flavourings." http:// ec.europa.eu/food/food/chemicalsafety/additives/new_regul_en. htm/ [accessed June 6, 2011].

European Commission (2010). "The Policy: What Is the European Neighbourhood Policy?" http://ec.europa.eu/world/enp/policy_ en.htm/ [accessed May 26, 2011].

European Commission (2011). "Medicinal Products for Veterinary Use — Regulation on Maximum Residue Limits." http:// ec.europa.eu / health / veterinary-use / maximum-residue-limits/ regulations_en.htm/ [accessed June 6, 2011].

Eurostat (2009). *European Neighbourhood: A Statistical Overview.* Luxembourg: Office for Official Publications of the European Communities.

FoodAndDrinkEurope.com (2011). "Research Points to Retail Value of Investment in Packaging." http://www.foodanddrinkeurope. com / Retail / Research-points-to-retail-value-of-investment-in-packaging/ [accessed June 6, 2011].

RMCG (2004). "Business Analysis of Dried Fruit Growers." http:// www.rmcg.com.au/web/RID_-_P4_files/Dried%20Grape%20 Benchmarking%20-%20final%20report%20v1.1.pdf/ [accessed May 23, 2011].

U.S. Department of State (2006). "Moldova — International Religious Freedom Report 2006." http://www.state.gov/g/drl/ rls/irf/2006/71396.htm/ [accessed June 6, 2011].

Case 15

Winery Startup within a Wine-Producing Cluster*

This case study examines the financial aspects of starting a new winery within a wine cluster in the southern Moravian region of the Czech Republic. This region has great economic potential. The geography of the region is rather favorable, as it lies on a historical connection between Southern and Northern Europe. Its traditional industries were mechanical engineering and processing, but the arrival of foreign high-tech companies with new technologies has been changing the economic profile of the region. Although engineering is still the most important sector, other industries such as food processing, textile, and printing are now also important parts of the region's economy.

Background

Changing lifestyles are creating challenges and opportunities for several industries in Central Europe that in the past were considered to be hobbies or, in some cases, preoccupations of members of

---

*Hamid Moini, of the University of Wisconsin-Whitewater (USA), on leave at Aalborg University (Denmark), developed this case for educational purposes only to illustrate financial issues in the formation and management of industrial clusters. Information on which this case is based has been collected by the author from primary sources; however, the characters and wineries described in the case are fictitious and are made up by the author solely for educational purposes.

collective farms. Wine production in southern Moravia is one of those industries. Under the previous regime which ended in the fall of 1989, wine production was the presumed responsibility of collective farms operated under the dubious leadership of the local communist party. Wine production then had three quasi-markets: the first consisted of all the stakeholders in the farm cooperative; the second market was reserved for special clients that would economically, politically, and socially facilitate the cooperative's production operations or justify the lack of production; and the third represented personal consumption.

Although southern Moravian wines had an excellent reputation in Central Europe and the several varieties of grapes that were grown in the region were special, the wine was not well known outside of the region. Most of the wine production was distributed in bulk and was consumed as quickly as it was produced. During that time, some individuals were able to maintain their own cellars and occasionally invited family members or special friends to "sample" their wines. Although the nearby Austrian wine industry had been producing high-quality wines using advanced technology for many years, southern Moravian producers lacked the necessary resources to purchase the necessary equipment to produce wines of comparable quality.

Late 1989 changed all of that. Collective farms were privatized; some individuals whose land had been collectivized after 1948 and some aspiring wine producers returned to the region. A large number of small vineyards started growing traditional varieties of grapes that were unique to the region, and several varieties of wine were again produced for commercial purposes. A number of entrepreneurs invested in acquiring larger vineyards and winemaking facilities.

There has always been a tradition of wine production in Central Europe. Wine production in southern Moravia has had a long tradition going back to the Romans in the third century. Over the centuries, several successful wine-growing clusters formed and were most successful in the mid-1930s, just before the Second World War. Moreover, southern Moravia was not unique in the region. Successful wine-producing clusters were found in northwestern Bohemia to the west; in parts of southern Slovakia north of the Danube; and in parts of Hungary, Romania, and Bulgaria. Even a small cluster in Moldova produced excellent wine. After the Second World War and after the countries became subject to communist domination and subsequent collectivization, wine production was decimated. Some of the wines produced in Romania, Bulgaria, and Moldova were sold in Central Europe as a part of the Eastern European Common Market.

Wine-growing regions in Central Europe are typically located in remote agricultural areas, kilometers away from the main cities. Some vineyards are located in clusters just under or on the foothills of the Carpathian Mountains. Others, such as the vineyards in southern Moravia, are located on rolling hills closely coexisting with each other. The actual production facilities and cellars, dating back hundreds of years, are maintained in small villages strategically positioned among the rolling hills. Moravia is located approximately 350 kilometers southeast of Prague, the capital of the Czech Republic (see Figure 1). Brno is the largest city in Moravia, about 100 kilometers away from the center of the wine-producing clusters. There are three major clusters: Mikulov, Město Hustopeče, and Znojmo.

The wine-producing clusters are relatively small. Several wine growers neighbor each other, borrow each other's pressing and crushing equipments, and customarily help each other during the grape-harvesting season. When necessary, they buy each other grapes and even mix their wines. All of these practices changed, however, when the Czech Republic joined the European Union (EU); new production standards were introduced, commercial opportunities materialized, and friendly competition emerged. Some of the wine growers quickly became entrepreneurial in their activities and started bottling and labeling their production. Now, they are competing with their neighbors. Because much of the production consisted

Figure 1. Map of the Czech Republic.

of small batches, cooperative clusters started forming to increase the members' commercial potential; however, in order to succeed, some of the cluster members need to make significant marketing and financial decisions.

Importance of Clusters

The concept of industry cluster has been used by a number of researchers in economic development studies (Porter, 1990). It refers to geographic concentrations of firms in related industries that benefit not only from close proximity but also from the increased competition amongst members of the cluster. Over the years, policy makers have used industry clusters to identify local industries with high employment concentration and to promote regional competitive advantage.

Agricultural regions have always represented an important part in the overall economies of Central European countries. Hungary, Romania, Bulgaria, and even Moldova were highly productive agricultural countries. Moravia, as a part of Czechoslovakia in the 1930s, was considered to be the "bread basket" of Central Europe. Although Poland was also heavily agricultural, it also had a strong reputation, along with Czechoslovakia, for production of agricultural equipment. Since all of these countries, with the exception of Moldova, became members of the EU, agricultural production as well as wine production have been closely monitored, but grape cultivation and wine production are encouraged in the region.

The region's agricultural industry is also of a high standard. About 60% of the region is made up of agricultural land, of which 83% is arable land. A particular specialty of the region is wine growing. The Danube River provides the warmth and the moisture that add up to an excellent grape production. The region has a number of small wineries with more than 11,000 hectares under cultivation. While this region is known for its white wines, lately red wines have become popular.

During the last 10 years, the quality of wines from the region has improved and today they are popular in Europe and even the United States. The production of wine in the region almost doubled in 2008 and reached a record output of 820,000 hectoliters. This is almost double the 434,000 hectoliters of wine produced in 2007, according to a report released by the Czech Republic's Ministry of Agriculture and Union of Winegrowers. The increase in wine production is expected to continue as the number of wineries is increasing. Also, wine exports, mostly to neighboring countries, have increased, reaching more than 175,000 hectoliters in 2009.

In an increasingly competitive market, wine producers in the region have decided to join forces in restructuring their vineyards and improving their performance. This cooperation is usually in the form of improvement in irrigation systems and support to wine producers to attend international exhibitions. These initiatives are financed through a Wine Fund, with half of its revenue coming from the government and the other half funded by contributions from wine producers themselves.

With encouragement from the EU, availability of capital from the Wine Fund, and growing interest in the consumption of regional wines, growing grapes in places such as southern Moravia is beginning to be considered as a potentially good investment. The members of wine-producing clusters are starting to experience financial pressures from international investors. However, many of the local wine producers have little, if any, financial skills to determine what their commercial opportunities are and how to financially evaluate them.

Most of the wine-producing entrepreneurs are marginally coping with the new market realities and marketing activities such as developing their brand identities and designing labels for bottles. Few of them have had any experience with marketing or management consultants. The fact that outside investors are now interested in investing in their activities and are ready to develop custom business models is overwhelming for them. Some of the potential investors, aside from occasional trips to the region, are not even closely familiar with the nature and dynamics of the region.

Entrepreneurial Activities in the Cluster

Recently, Mr. Jeff Smith, an international investor with a special personal interest in wines, hired Mr. Milos Karel as a consultant. Mr. Smith discovered this wine-growing region about a year ago while on a family vacation to the area. He has asked Mr. Karel to assess the feasibility of setting up a new winery in the region. This winery will be located in a small village near Brno, the main city in the region. Mr. Smith plans to produce quality wines from grapes harvested from a 24-hectare plot of land that he wants to acquire. The winery's main specialty wines will be Riesling and Pinot varieties, and it will be called Brno Winery. Mr. Smith hopes to produce organic and eco-friendly wines through the minimum use of chemicals in the cultivation of the grapevines. This will create suitable living conditions for many different species of plants and animals. It will also ensure the emergence of natural biodiversity balance in the vineyard ecosystem. He argues that the results of this work will be sound-quality grapes that can mature until late fall.

Brno Winery will be the largest acreage under cultivation in the region. The whole area is surrounded by hills. Due to the fact that this area is in the northern region of Central Europe, grapes are ripened under the influence of coastal and inland climate conditions. Moist and fresh air flowing from the Atlantic slows the ripening of grapes, but it contributes to creating spicy and aromatic substances. On the other hand, the hot continental air increases the effective temperature, which contributes to the reduction of some phenological growth stage. This allows these areas to grow the quality and variety with a longer growing season.

Financial Issues

Mr. Karel, a recent MBA graduate (with a specialization in marketing) from a major university in the region, has limited financial knowledge. During his MBA program, Mr. Karel learned a number of techniques that can be used to evaluate this project. For example, he wants to use Bayesian analysis in which the results are continually revised in light of new evidence on the basis of Bayes' theorem. He also wants to use linear programming, which is the process of taking various linear inequalities relating to this project, such as the size of the winery, and finding the "best" value obtainable under those conditions. However, before he uses the above techniques, he wants to use financial analysis, such as capital budgeting, in order to determine if this project is feasible or not.

In a recent visit to the wineries in order to gather information on investment and operating costs of wineries in the region, Mr. Karel discovered that many of these wineries have limited financial resources and poor knowledge of proper pricing of their wines. He found out that the main sources of financing for most of these wineries are self-financing and limited access to bank loans. Since these wineries are small and anchored in an agricultural tradition, the financing choice is more often the first of the two possibilities. This is mainly because many of these wineries are afraid to lose control of their business in case they cannot generate enough cash flow, due to slow demand, to pay the interest and the principal of their loans. Mr. Karel knows that this lack of financial resources can constitute a serious obstacle to the expansion of these wineries.

Mr. Karel has already gathered information on investment and operating costs from wineries in the region with annual production of 1,000, 2,000, and 4,000 cases (each case contains 12 bottles of 750-ml capacity). He believes that these are three alternative sizes Mr. Smith should consider for the startup production size. This information would allow him to create a generic cash flow model with common characteristics to most wineries in the region. He believes that these characteristics, along with many others, influence the capital requirements, investment, and operating costs of the wineries in the region. In developing his financial analysis, Mr. Karel is asking you to consider a number of assumptions about the quality, production, and marketing practices of the wineries before you start your financial analysis.

Financial Analysis

After lengthy discussions with wineries in the region, Mr. Karel found that, although an increasing number of wineries in the region are introducing red wines into their product mix, the great majority of them still produce mostly white wines. This would fit Mr. Smith's plan in producing Riesling and Pinot wines. Table 1 provides details of the wine production in the region.

Table 1. Production mix (as a percentage of total wine production).

Wines	1,000 Cases	2,000 Cases	4,000 Cases
White			
Müller-Thurgau	14.8	15.3	16.0
Grüner Veltliner	13.0	15.0	14.8
Welschriesling	10.5	12.0	13.5
Riesling	9.5	7.2	7.8
Sauvignon blanc	6.5	6.4	5.6
Chardonnay	6.0	5.8	4.8
Pinot gris	5.0	4.8	4.5
Gewürztraminer	5.7	4.8	4.0
Total White	71.0	71.0	71.0
Red			
Saint Laurent	9.0	10.5	9.5
Blaufränkisch	5.7	6.0	6.7
Zweigelt	5.6	4.6	4.2
Pinot noir	5.0	4.4	6.0
Cabernet Sauvignon	3.7	3.5	2.6
Total Red	29.0	29.0	29.0

Mr. Karel estimated that total investment for the wineries ranges from €250,000 for a 1,000-case winery to €550,000 for a 4,000-case winery. This includes investment in land and equipment. As shown in Table 2, the required investment increases as the size of wine production increases. Also, the land as well as plant and office expenses account for a large portion of total required investment.

Mr. Karel has decided to seek your help to conduct a detailed financial analysis for presentation to Mr. Smith. He has provided you with information about the revenue and costs associated with wine production (see Table 3). The winery is not expected to generate any revenue in the first year, as wines would not be ready for sale yet. In order to determine the components of the production cost, Mr. Karel made a number of assumptions. He calculated the cost of grapes using a three-year average by variety of grapes used in the wine

Table 2. Required investment for proposed Brno Winery.

	1,000 Cases	2,000 Cases	4,000 Cases
Receiving equipment	€30,000	€45,000	€55,000
Cellar equipment	€8,000	€10,000	€15,000
Handling equipment	€20,000	€25,000	€35,000
Refrigeration equipment	€15,000	€25,000	€40,000
Fermentation equipment	€25,000	€40,000	€60,000
Wine barrels	€22,000	€45,000	€65,000
Plant and office	€80,000	€110,000	€130,000
Land for cultivation	€50,000	€100,000	€150,000
Total investment	€250,000	€400,000	€550,000

production in the region. Generally, wineries which mostly produce white wines are expected to have a lower cost for the grapes used, as the grapes used in white wines such as Riesling cost less than the grapes used in red wines such as Cabernet Sauvignon.

Another major cost of production is the new barrels used for wine storage. Most barrels are replaced frequently. This is a major part of the production cost. Mr. Karel assumes that about three quarters of barrels are replaced every year, except for the first three years of production when the winery needs to add additional barrels. Therefore, he assumes that the initial barrel purchases are part of the required investment for the winery.

The packaging expenses — which include the costs of bottles, corks, labels, etc. — are also a major component of the production cost. Mr. Karel examined the packaging cost for a number of wineries in the region, and has decided that the lowest cost quoted by the region's wineries should be used for this analysis.

Like other industries, wineries are also subject to taxation. The regional government taxes wineries for their properties and the number of wine cases produced. At the moment, the regional government taxes wineries at a rate of 1% of the assessed value of the property. The regional production tax is €2 per case for wineries with production of

Table 3. First-year cash flow projection for proposed Brno Winery.

	Size of Winery		
	1,000 Cases	2,000 Cases	4,000 Cases
Sales revenue	€0	€0	€0
Operating expenses			
Variable costs			
Grapes	€15,000	€28,000	€50,000
Barrels	€0	€0	€0
Packaging	€10,000	€17,000	€25,000
Bottling	€0	€0	€0
Excise taxes (federal and regional)	€0	€0	€0
Full-time labor	€10,000	€16,000	€25,000
Part-time labor	€3,000	€7,000	€10,000
Marketing	€0	€0	€0
Utilities	€2,000	€3,000	€5,000
Office	€2,000	€3,000	€5,000
Total variable costs	€42,000	€74,000	€120,000
Fixed costs			
Property taxes	€2,000	€3,000	€4,000
Depreciation	€20,000	€30,000	€40,000
Maintenance	€2,000	€4,000	€8,000
Insurance	€2,000	€4,000	€8,000
Interest costs	€4,000	€6,400	€8,800
Total fixed costs	€30,000	€47,400	€68,800
Total cost	€72,000	€121,400	€188,800

less than 5,000 cases per year. However, the federal government also taxes wineries for their income and the number of cases produced. The federal income tax is 30% of taxable income. The government also allows wineries to apply their carryover losses to future earnings. The federal production tax is €1 per case for all wineries.

In recent years, most of the region's wineries have discovered that in order to sell their wines they need to have a marketing plan. Mr. Karel found that most wineries in the region spend around

€2 per case for marketing their wines to national distributors. Other production cost information, such as labor, insurance, depreciation, and interest costs, is provided in Table 3.

Potential Markets

There are several potential markets for southern Moravian wines. According to the wine producers in the cluster, the major market for their wines is the Czech Republic. Most of the major hypermarket chains, including Tesco, Kaufland, and Lidl, sell southern Moravian wine. Many restaurants in the Czech Republic offer good-quality wines, including some vintage varieties. And, as the interest in wines increases, individuals purchase their own cellars in the cluster and stock them with local wines for personal consumption. Moreover, a number of international wine experts believe that wines from the southern Moravian cluster have an international market potential. Distributors in Chicago, New York, and Washington, D.C. are starting to import wines from Moravia.

To determine the project feasibility of an investment in each winery size, Mr. Karel is asking you to conduct a capital budgeting analysis using both net present value (NPV) and internal rate of return (IRR) by using the following additional assumptions:

1. Use a 10-year investment horizon for your analysis.
2. Sales revenues are expected to grow at an annual rate of 7% in years 2 through 5 (super growth period), and 5% in years 6 through 10 (stable growth period). Remember, the winery will not have any revenue in the first year.
3. All expense items, including the depreciation (but excluding the excise taxes and interest costs), will grow at 3% per year — the average rate of inflation — throughout the life of the project.
4. All initial capital investment and those beyond the initial year are 80% financed by equity. The remaining amount is financed by debt.

5. The risk-free rate is 5.4%, the market risk premium is 5.5%, and the beta of the winery is expected to be 1.2. He believes this is the average beta for wineries operating in the region.
6. The cost of debt is 8% and is fixed for the duration of the loan. Assume that the debt has a 10-year maturity and the bank has agreed on equal annual installments of principal repayments.
7. Use straight-line depreciation over a 10-year project life.
8. All sales are to national distributors. There are no tasting room sales.

To help you with your project, Mr. Karel has offered you his cash flow projections for the first year. Your tasks are as follows:

1. Develop a forecast of free cash flows for Brno Winery (for each alternative winery size) covering the next 10 years (including the first year provided by Mr. Karel in Table 3).
2. Calculate the weighted average cost of capital (WACC) for Brno Winery.
3. Perform a capital budgeting analysis using both NPV and IRR analyses to determine which winery size you would recommend Mr. Smith should start his wine business with.

After you made your recommendation to Mr. Smith, he asks you some questions about your assumptions. For example, he wants to know if there are differences in a financial analysis of a winery versus other industries. If there are any differences, then he wants to know how that affected your recommendations. Furthermore, Mr. Smith is wondering if there are some inherent risks that were not incorporated in your analysis.

Bibliography

Porter, Michael (1990). *The Competitive Advantage of Nations*. New York: The Free Press.

Case 16

Convergence and Differentiation in Regional Know-How — The Case of Central Otago Pinot Noir*

The Case of Central Otago

Central Otago is a young wine region in New Zealand's South Island, the southernmost wine region in the world, with characteristic hot, dry summers and snowy winters. There are over 80 wineries, with differences in geology, soil, and even climate within the vineyard properties themselves. Growing of vines for wine in the modern era[1] began in the 1970s, but picked up pace only in the 1990s. Most vineyards are owner-operated and the average size is less than 20 ha. From slow beginnings, Pinot noir has become the main variety grown, and success with this variety accounts for the popularity of the region both domestically and internationally. Other grapes grown include Riesling and Pinot gris. Most of the established wineries have full-time or part-time vintners, but some achieve a premium-quality product using local wine production companies.

---

*David Ballantyne, Sue Caple, and Maree Thyne, all at the University of Otago (New Zealand), developed this case for educational purposes only.
[1]The first winemaker attracted to Central Otago was John Desiré Feraud, who came to the area during the Central Otago gold rush and planted grapes in 1864. However, the cultivation of grapes for wine petered out after 20 years or so (Cull, 2001).

Central Otago wine and the diversity of its wine brands has boomed over the last 20 years, as new growers and winemakers have decided to try their luck. The early pioneers recognized that they were too small to develop individual market clout, so developing a premium image for the region as a whole was a crucial first step. Pinot noir is notoriously difficult to grow and make into premium-quality wine, but this has been achieved from the beginning through a network of collaborative relationships within the region that has facilitated the circulation and growth of viticulture and winery knowledge (Caple *et al.*, 2010). In other words, the growers and winemakers have successfully developed regional awareness by working together in building their knowledge, even though they were competitors.

The Central Otago wine region is more than 280 km by road to Dunedin in the southeast, the nearest major regional city (see Figure 1). There are good links, however, to Queenstown, 30 km to the west. Both cities have an international airport. Queenstown is the "adventure capital" of New Zealand, catering for skiers and mountain climbers, canoeists and bungee jumpers. Dunedin is a pioneer town with light industry and a large university.

The global recession in 2008–2010 impacted on international sales volumes for New Zealand wine products overall. There are 700 wineries and 4,000 wines. Some wines are currently selling on the domestic market at below cost (Cooper, 2011). For example, premium grapes that had fetched NZ$3,500–$4,000 per ton before the recession fetched only NZ$2,500 per ton in 2010 (van Kempen, 2010). Some small growers have failed and sold out to their winery customers. The situation in Central Otago has not followed the market downturn, although customers on winery subscriber lists have experienced some especially favorable price discounts on case lot purchases. Also, some Central Otago growers have responded by introducing second- and third-tier labels at cheaper prices to protect their premium brands. Others have introduced ultra-premium labels

Figure 1. Location of Central Otago region (near Cromwell) relative to Dunedin.

at ultra-premium prices (van Kempen, 2010). Coinciding with the current recession, vintages in 2008, 2009, and 2010 were at record volume levels with high-quality grapes, leading to a need for some reappraisal of competitive strategies.

Terroir as an Elusive Quality Marker

Central Otago has a higher proportion of premium wines with claims to distinctive terroir than any other major growing area in New Zealand. This is due in part to the intentions and determination of the early wine growers and winemakers to succeed with Pinot noir and to do so at a cooperative regional level, benchmarking themselves against the wines of Burgundy, adopting or adapting their methods of viticulture and winery practices. The region has been recognized as one of the top Pinot noir wine-producing regions in the world (*Decanter*, 2011). The reputation of the *region* is arguably the primary quality indicator, notwithstanding the excellence of many individual vineyards and winery skills.

Central Otago claims to have a unique *terroir*, much prized in France and other Old World countries as a quality marker. Terroir is usually taken to mean the combination of well-draining soils for viticulture, a favorable climate which is warm in summer but frost-free in winter, and grape clones that match these requirements. The subject of terroir is much debated as to whether it is an historical association with French viticulture or whether it is of much use in the New World as a quality marker. Nonetheless, it is a popular idea among many vignerons and wine lovers, and as a consequence plays an important role in communicating brand value at both individual vineyard and regional brand levels. One issue in Central Otago is that the topographical land mass under cultivation for wine is by no means uniform in type across the region (see Figure 2), so various nuances in the terroir and consequently the quality of the wine product might be expected from site to site, and from winemaker to winemaker, even if the overall regional quality is high. The challenge for the region as a whole is to lift its quality standards internationally, given the variations among different winemakers in terms of their approaches and vineyard properties, and to cooperate in doing this while competing from firm to firm at the same time.

The region's solution to this conundrum involves up-skilling, as rapidly as possible, across the region. But how can knowledge in the form of business competencies or *know-how* be achieved through collaborating with competing businesses?

How Knowledge Works

Knowledge, including specialized skills, is an important resource in any business; according to some, it is the fundamental source of

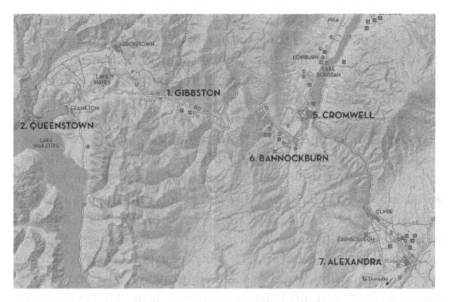

Figure 2. Snapshot of the Central Otago wine region with major subregions.

competitive advantage (Vargo and Lusch, 2008). It may seem unusual, but the need to protect knowledge from competitors has seldom existed in the emerging and developing Central Otago wine region. Knowledge has been shared across the region and modified *in use* at each winery, thus improving regional standards but maintaining the diversity (differentiation) of each winery's skills, methods, and output (Caple *et al.*, 2010). This knowledge sharing has allowed the Central Otago region to emerge rapidly over the last 10 years as the leading producer of Pinot noir wines in New Zealand.

The *prisoner's dilemma* is often thought to constrain such reciprocal knowledge transfer between firms operating in close proximity. While the existence of this paradox is known, there has been little investigation of how it might be resolved (Zhang *et al.*, 2008). We see this as an under-examined factor in business today, and it is particularly relevant to wine marketing in gaining a preeminent global status for wines from small regions.

The idea that knowledge underlies the economic development of physical assets has a long history, associated with the dynamics of competitive innovation (Schumpeter, 1934). An important contribution to the understanding of the workings of knowledge was the theoretical distinction made between a person's know-how (sometimes called *tacit* knowledge) and *explicit* knowledge (see, for example, Nonaka (1991) and Nonaka and Takeuchi (1995); these are based in part on work by Polanyi (1967)). Explicit knowledge is easily expressed in speech or text, and hence is transferable; an example would be knowledge stored in customer relationship management (CRM) databases. However, tacit knowledge is difficult to explain or codify, and so is harder to pass on to others. We have to either be shown *how* to do such things or experiment in a cycle of trial and error, with corrections and adjustments. Tacit knowledge, then, is individual competency or *know-how*. Instead of transferring knowledge by reading "how-to" books or accessing databases, tacit knowledge is transferred in more collaborative ways — by instruction, observation, and doing, and through communities of practice. Also to note is that through obsolescence and competitive innovations elsewhere, knowledge can "wear out." Of relevance to any New World wine region, competing in a world market, is the need to gain and leverage Old World knowledge and combine it with a deep understanding of the local *terroir*. We will return to this tacit/explicit distinction and its relevance to Central Otago terroir later.

Collaborative and Competing Knowledge Networks

A wine region has the general characteristics of a business cluster — a geographically bounded network of actor firms who both compete and cooperate (Porter, 1990). The variety of desirable but unevenly distributed resources (including know-how) that exist across a closely proximate network of competitors helps explain why individual business actors might develop collaborative relationships with each other. According to Bengtsson and Kock (2000, p. 421), it is this *heterogeneity* of resources that fosters collaborative relationships among competitors, because the actor firms seek to gain access to what they do not have and may succeed if there is perceived mutual benefit. Another important network conceptualization involving knowledge transfer is *social capital*, which refers to the relationship ties operating in a social context that facilitate the willingness of individuals to share their knowledge at a social exchange level (Tsai and Ghoshal, 1998). Strong (close) social ties and the interdependencies that they create also facilitate knowledge transfer and learning in a network setting (Granovetter, 1973). Also of note, Håkansson and Johanson (1992) and Håkansson and Snehota (1995) — in a seminal work known as the *AAR model* — describe business networks from three interconnected perspectives: the interaction of *resources* that are tied to each other, that are exchanged through *activities* which are linked to one another, and which in turn are performed by various *actors* who are connected through relationship bonds that affect their propensity to act in a certain way. Later, we will examine the underlying processes at work in these three dimensions (following Håkansson *et al.*, 2009, p. 224).

A case study research approach was adopted as our research strategy, which involved the collection and analysis of in-depth information in the Central Otago wine region. As the main aim of this research was to understand how competing wineries collaborate, the logical approach was to study the region as a whole. A *focal net* framework (Halinen and Törnroos, 2005) was adopted to assist in choosing reliable key informants within the region, chosen because they were able to respond authoritatively to the central questions of the study. In the end, 12 wineries with 25 respondents representing the elite and knowledgeable wine people were chosen as our focal net.

We found that wineries exchange knowledge with their counterparts, trial it at their own site, and make needed adaptations as they see fit. Networks of collaborative relationships within the region facilitate the circulation of such knowledge. This knowledge (explicit, oral- and text-based) becomes know-how (tacit, skills and competencies) only when it is put into practice (Nonaka, 1991). The degree of knowledge exchange is by no means routine, uniform, or consistent, as will be described next, using the AAR categories of network analysis (actors, activities, and resource ties) provided by Håkansson and Johanson (1992) and Håkansson and Snehota (1995).

Actor Bonds

Initial collaboration between wineries included the pooling of winemaking facilities and information exchange, as during the early days there were few expert winemakers in the region. This approach worked well for the early pioneers, with the catalyst being Rolf Mills, the founder of Rippon Wines (see Figure 3). His vision in the 1980s was to develop a collaborative approach for the future success of the region.

Figure 3.   Rippon Wines vineyard, 2010 (photograph supplied by J. Ballantyne).

From the beginning, all wineries marketed their wines under the Central Otago regional brand, with their individual winery labels usually in a subordinate position. Collaboration between winery staff was facilitated by the *proximity* of wineries in the region. This follows what might be expected from the literature on regional firm clusters (Porter, 1990). Formal and informal activities (both business and social) have sustained the interaction and collaboration, and the development of relationships within the region. Moreover, this is not just confined to the wineries; many trade and distribution firms are also regionally interdependent, relying on personal relationships to ensure their continued success and growth. An interesting development is that the vintners interface frequently with contract vintners. The contractors work with grapes from all of the subregions and have much knowledge about the wines of the region. The contractors' relationships with other vintners ensure knowledge retention specific to the region. The interaction between the vintners and contractors also provides constant knowledge renewal within the region as they exchange new ideas.

Porter (1990) indicates that business relationships within a region often become inseparable with social relationships. Porter (1990) also suggested that proximity leads to frequent contacts; therefore, social relationships develop more quickly. Indeed, many positive statements concerning socialization emerged during the interviews. As one owner stated: "We socialize with a number of the wine people, yeah. But we're not out there, we're not out there sort of sitting in their back pocket all the time. But, I mean, we'll ring them and say 'come and have a meal,' and they ring us and say 'come and have a meal' [Owner 10]."

The influence of new, young vintners arose in the interviews. In probing this issue further, attracting young, enthusiastic vintners to the region was seen as a source of pride by the existing vintners. It provides continual evidence to them that Central Otago is a region to be taken seriously. There is a sort of nurturing effect occurring in that the established vintners want to ensure the success of the new vintners: "So, we are just in this wave of, you know, young ones who left New Zealand and came back with more knowledge and the ambition to do a good job. The knowledge base here is extremely good [Vintner 11]."

The new vintners come into the region with previous contacts, and develop contacts and networks with their neighbors. Also, the young vintners themselves group together socially and rely on each other. There is concern that this may lead to a departure from the cohesiveness on the part of some of the wineries. Many see it as being a detriment to future growth: "I mean, I have a strong belief that you should contribute to the [wine] community in which you belong, which is — And I'm not sure that everybody believes that now. At the beginning, everybody did [Viticulturalist-owner 7]."

Activity Links

There are associations supporting marketing and viticulture. The Central Otago Winegrowers Association (COWA) was established in 1982; and Central Otago Pinot Noir Ltd. (COPNL, 2011) was set up in 2002 under the umbrella of COWA, exclusively to provide marketing assistance with exporting. It is at the discretion of the owner to join or not to join. For example, COPNL brings wine writers to the region and the vintners facilitate tastings and attend dinners associated with these events. Also, although the activities of COWA are mainly aimed at the needs of viticulturalists, many vintners attend their events. COPNL sponsors 16–20 events each year, held in Central Otago and internationally, in which member vintners participate. All of these events, such as the annual Central Otago Pinot Noir Celebration (2011), are well attended by members. The more members participate in joint activities, the more new relationships develop or the closer existing relationships become. Seeing many others doing the same thing supports a positive attitude about collaboration. Success instills pride in the members as individuals, and perpetuates cohesiveness within the region. If someone was previously employed at a winery and has moved to a new one, they still maintain contact with the first winery and meet at informal gatherings.

Viticulturalists are likewise keen to maintain open communication. They are aware that the quality of their grapes impacts the region as much as individual winemaking skills. Sharing viticultural resources across the region is critical to keep costs low. They also want to learn from each other about new techniques that could benefit vineyard management. Sustainability and organic certification are current areas of interest.

Resource Ties

Resource sharing occurs in a variety of ways. These include information exchanges, borrowed equipment and personnel, or shared marketing costs and activities. In the words of one vintner: "I suppose the thing about Central is like, let's say I have a problem that I could ring up another winemaker and ask them, 'Hey, I've got this problem. . . . Can you give me any advice on it?' [Vintner 4]"

This collaborative information exchange raises the quality level of output across the region. The winemakers can take quite small snippets of information from each other and apply it to their particular environment, or they can work collaboratively to solve a problem. Of special interest to us is the fact that seemingly insignificant information is taken seriously: "On the one hand, we are such a young region. The daily learning curve, even if you think it's not important — Like if someone says, 'Ah, it's much drier out there than I thought.' Maybe I think about irrigation because I thought, 'It's fine.' So you think about it and you say, 'Well, let's have a look. . . . Well, that's true, it is very dry' [Vintner 12]."

The fact that they are growing Pinot noir grapes in a marginal climatic region for top-end world markets means that they are still learning, so they need to use each other as a resource: "I struggled with the ferments this year. Okay, what can I do to not get blocked there in the first place? You know, there's no small talk, but you always pick up something that alerts you and something else. . . . I might hear something and say, 'Hey, I need to look at this,' and I think that's the good part. And we're all learning [Vintner 6]."

Viticulturalists worry about the costs associated with vineyard production. They source products in bulk for discounted prices by purchasing together. They also face battles in finding casual workers for the vineyards, particularly during the harvest season, and they frequently telephone each other to try to access new workers. Viticulturalists are seen more as farmers involved with day-to-day decisions rather than strategic decision makers. We found this odd, as terroir starts in the vineyard and is dependent on exemplary vineyard management. Some viticulturalists have academic degrees, some at the master's level, so their relative status is gradually changing.

Certainly, the dominant view in Central Otago is that sharing information to solve problems builds common knowledge and this is to the region's benefit. But some owners expressed the view that the need to share information has lessened over time. Many of them stated that they were beginning to know every small space in their vineyards and the quality and taste of grapes grown there. With this specialized knowledge and experience, confidence has grown: "I'm getting recognition for the way I'm working and the way that we're making our wine, and the wines themselves. So I'm getting more and more confidence about what we're doing, which is good [Owner 1]."

Is the Pioneer Ethos Changing?

The atmosphere of the region has changed since the early pioneer winemaking days. The fact that the owners said they collaborate but do it less seems to be a contradiction. Our interpretation is that they can still call on virtually anyone in the region if they need help, but they tend to need help on more specific topics such as organic or subregional production, which means the group of people with whom they collaborate has become more specific or more localized.

The majority of current vintners travel to premier Pinot noir wineries in California, Oregon, and Burgundy, and help them harvest and make wines. Several mentioned that it was "mandatory that their assistant winemakers participate in vintages elsewhere." Many of the vintners stated that Central Otago probably would not be as advanced today without outside knowledge introduced from other Pinot noir-producing areas: "With some friends of mine in Burgundy, we started up a cultural exchange between Central Otago and Burgundy. So we sent three people over there, they sent three people over here, for each harvest, and that's been going on for a year and a half now. It's been doing really well [Vintner 1]."

The concept of knowledge circulating in a network or region is not new (see, for example, Bathelt *et al.*, 2004; Nonaka, 1991; Nonaka and Takeuchi, 1995). This conventionally requires high levels of trust to protect the interests of the knowledge giver. However, the need for know-how is also a motive, as has been discussed (Bengtsson and Kock, 2000). A surprising discovery in this study was that wineries are willing to share their knowledge across the region because each winery *uses* that knowledge differently. In other words, new knowledge has to be adapted to individual environments to be of *value in use*, and this can only happen when it becomes part of the *know-how* particular to that winery. Different vineyard terroir and different approaches to winemaking have protected the knowledge giver from loss of competitive advantage, because information exchanges are less risky when they require practical adaptation at the next winery. Such knowledge transfer cycles occur in both winemaking skills and vineyard management: "But the exchange of information is quite amazing, really. People with Pinot are willing to give that information because they realize what works from their side may not work for someone else [Owner 3]."

Looking to the Future

Terroir is an emerging concern for many wine lovers of Pinot noir, as it *differentiates* Central Otago wines from the wines of other domestic and global Pinot noir-producing areas. The Pinot noir consumer as a global archetype is very discerning and develops preferences for wines from specific regions with different nuances. This being so, and given the high production costs and the boutique size of most vineyards, Central Otago wines necessarily claim quality distinctiveness because of their terroir. This is not, of course, to downgrade the skills of various winemakers. Distinctive terroir and skillful winery handling have so far succeeded in supporting a regional brand strategy for gaining and growing international consumer recognition. Most wineries have their own Internet sales sites, and this has enhanced the status of the region as much as that of individual wine products and wineries. Cellar door sales in the region are highly developed, as many visitors can combine Queenstown "adventure capital" experiences with visits to the wineries. But can a strategy of "collaborate and compete" hold into the future?

Bibliography

Bathelt, H., A. Malmberg, and P. Maskell (2004). "Clusters and Knowledge: Local Buzz, Global Pipelines and the Process of Knowledge Creation." *Progress in Human Geography*, 28, 31–56.

Bengtsson, Maria and Sören Kock (2000). "Coopetition in Business Networks — To Cooperate and Compete Simultaneously." *Industrial Marketing Management*, 29, 411–426.

Caple, S., D. Ballantyne, and M. Thyne (2010). "Diversity and Convergence in Regional Know-How: The Case of Central Otago Pinot Noir." Paper presented at the 5th International Academy of Wine Business Research Conference, University of Auckland, New Zealand, February 8–10.

Central Otago Pinot Noir Celebration (2011). http://www.pinot-celebration.co.nz/ [accessed September 2011].

Cooper, Michael (2011). "Culley's Creed." *New Zealand Listener*, January 29, p. 58.

COPNL (2011). "Central Otago Pinot Noir Ltd." http://www.centralotagopinot.co.nz/ [accessed September 2011].

Cull, D. (2001). *Vineyards on the Edge*. Dunedin: Longacre Press.

Decanter (2011). "Decanter World Wine Awards 2011." http://www.decanter.com / dwwa / 2011 / dwwa_search.php/ [accessed September 2011].

Granovetter, M. (1973). "The Strength of Weak Ties." *American Journal of Sociology*, 78, 1360–1380.

Håkansson, H., D. Ford, L.-E. Gadde, I. Snehota, and A. Waluszewski (2009). *Business in Networks*. Chichester, West Sussex: Wiley.

Håkansson, H. and J. Johanson (1992). "A Model of Industrial Networks." In Axelsson, B. and G. Easton (eds.), *Industrial Networks: A New View of Reality*, London: Routledge.

Håkansson, H. and I. Snehota (eds.) (1995). *Developing Relationships in Business Networks*. London: Routledge.

Halinen, A. and J.-Å. Törnroos (2005). "Using Case Methods in the Study of Contemporary Business Networks." *Journal of Business Research*, 58, 1285–1297.

Lawson, C. and E. Lorenz (1999). "Collective Learning, Tacit Knowledge and Regional Innovative Capacity." *Regional Studies*, 33, 305–337.

Nonaka, I. (1991). "The Knowledge-Creating Company." *Harvard Business Review*, November–December, 96–104.

Nonaka, I. and H. Takeuchi (1995). *The Knowledge-Creating Company: How Japanese Companies Create the Dynamics of Innovation*. New York: Oxford University Press.

Polanyi, M. (1967). *The Tacit Dimension*. New York: Doubleday.

Porter, Michael E. (1990). *The Competitive Advantage of Nations*. London: Macmillan.

Schumpeter, J.A. (1934). *The Theory of Economic Development.* Cambridge, MA: Harvard University Press.

Tsai, W. and S. Ghoshal (1998). "Social Capital and Value Creation: The Role of Intra-Firm Networks." *Academy of Management Journal,* 41(4), 464–476.

van Kempen, Lynda (2010). "Pinot Noir Sets Growers Apart." *Otago Daily Times,* Regions Section, May 8, p. 19.

Vargo, S.L. and R.F. Lusch (2008). "Service-Dominant Logic: Continuing the Evolution." *Journal of the Academy of Marketing Science,* 36, 1–10.

Zhang, L., X. Zheng, J. Li, G. Nie, G. Huo, and Y. Shi (2008). "A Way to Improve Knowledge Sharing: From the Perspective of Knowledge Potential." *Journal of Service Science and Management,* 1, 226–232.

Part IV

Information Technology Issues and Geographically Remote Industrial Clusters

Entrepreneurs, startup ventures, and smaller manufacturing enterprises interested in information technology are also instrumental in forming geographically remote industrial clusters (GRICs). Such GRICs are somewhat different in terms of their operations and strategies. The information technology industry tends to be somewhat fragmented and less cooperative in joining GRICs. Each enterprise member has its own objectives and market specializations that generally deviate from the overall central focus of an individual GRIC. Nevertheless, information technology-focused enterprises may have strong market and technological interest in operating within a GRIC. It is important to understand the underlying conditions that motivate information technology enterprises to become active members of GRICs.

Case 17

Software Development in a Remote Geographic Location — The Case of TextFlow*

Nordic River Software AB was founded in Umeå in northern Sweden in 2006. Their product is a web-based word processor named "TextFlow," compatible with Microsoft Word. The unique feature of this product is that more than one person can work in parallel, and at the same time, with the same document. All parties have an overview of the document and can see how the document has been changed and by whom. A text document can be sent to multiple individuals, who suggest changes and text to add. When the document is returned to the sender, the software automatically combines all suggested changes in one original document. Based on color codes and layers, it is possible to continuously trace all changes and compare versions of the same document.

The company's mission is to "deliver tools for Visual Version Management, VVM, that allows our users to take full advantage of a distributed workflow, over the Internet and on the desktop"

*Jan Bodin, of the Umeå School of Business and Economics, Umeå University (Sweden), developed this case for educational purposes only. The author wants to thank Tomer Shalit for making it possible to write this case by giving the required access to his company.

(InfoTech Umeå, 2010). Its vision is to become the leading actor within co-produced word processing. The challenge is how to achieve that vision.

Geographic Location and Community Actors

Umeå is a town approximately 700 km north of Stockholm, located on the coast of the Gulf of Bothnia. It is a youthful town with 115,000 inhabitants averaging 38 years of age. One of the key drivers of the region's development is the local university. Umeå University is one of Sweden's comprehensive universities and was founded in 1965. It currently boasts more than 36,000 students and is responsible for a large number of distance/blended learning courses throughout the northern part of Sweden. As a fairly young university, cross-disciplinary research groups and clusters have been reasonably easy to establish. Some noticeable examples are the Center for Biomedical Engineering and Physics (CMTF), the Center for Regional Science at Umeå University (CERUM), the High Performance Computing Center North (HPC2N), the Umeå Plant Science Center (UPSC), Biotech Umeå, the Computational Life Science Cluster (CLiC), and the Forest Engineering Cluster.

The Umeå Institute of Design (UID) at Umeå University was founded in 1989. It has had, since day one, the ambition to educate industrial designers ready to work in industry from the first day they are hired. This ambition has had many strategic implications, like close cooperation with industry throughout its educational program, as well as close linkages with other departments within Umeå University regarding both teaching and research. Besides its bachelor's program, UID offers three different master's programs in advanced product design, interaction design, and transportation design. UID is today internationally recognized and considered as one of the best design schools in the world (*Businessweek*, 2009).

Industrial design is a young academic discipline and UID's research has, as a consequence, been fairly applied. Lengthy research projects have been carried out together with Volvo Trucks, Ericsson, and ABB, to name a few. Close cooperation with other parts of the university, like the Umeå School of Business and Economics, the Department of Psychology, and the Department of Informatics, is evident through recruitment of researchers and research leaders who divide their time between the different departments.

The Entrepreneur

Tomer Shalit is the founder and CEO of Nordic River AB. Born in Israel to a Scottish mother and an Israeli father, he moved with his parents to Sweden at 4 years of age. During his Swedish upper secondary school years where he chose a science program, he helped his father with some advanced extracurricular activities. His father was working at the time as a statistical analyst at the former National Defense Research Establishment (*Försvarets Forskningsanstalt* or FOA), today known as the Swedish Defense Research Agency. Tomer helped his father with transforming statistical results into presentable graphics. At the time it involved some serious programming, since the computers had no dedicated graphics hardware cards. The knowledge he gained from this was solid knowledge of how computers operated and were programmed. He noted: "I learned the foundation for computer programming very early. I understand how a computer works on processor-stack level — after that, it is all about adding and overlaying other information on that."

He also founded his first company with some friends during the same period (in his late teens). They built specialized computerized boxes based on Amiga computers with the objective to present commercials on television screens at airports. It was a technically fairly advanced product using something called "Ratex" for communication between the Amiga box and the TV screens. Ratex utilized overlaying signals on the Swedish TV broadcast system via specialized modems. The phenomenon of commercials at airports was at the time still at infancy, but the company managed to survive and was still operating when Tomer left for his mandatory military service.

After completing his military service, Tomer's interest in the new area of interaction design emerged. He moved to Umeå in 1995/1996 with the intention of studying the newly formed program in cognitive psychology at Umeå University. However, once in Umeå, he was rather surprised to learn that the program was actually only at the planning stage, so he decided to study mathematics in the meantime. In a random turn of events, Tomer decided to visit the Umeå Institute of Design (UID) to see what they were doing. As he phrased it:

> I literally knocked on the door of the design school. I met with the Dean and told him that I had some ideas about a new type of computer mouse. I was wondering if there was any student that might be interested in working on it as a degree project, and how I should go about getting someone interested in the project.
>
> We started to talk, and I showed him my business card I had before as a computer technician in the municipality of Karlstad. He gave me an offer — "If you work here as a computer technician half of the time, you can do whatever you like in the other half. Then you can do this project yourself."

As Tomer laughingly noted, "That was extremely far-sighted of this man who had never met me before!"

Tomer started work as an information technology (IT) technician at UID, and was free to do what he wanted the rest of the time. He became involved in creating a new master's program in interaction design at UID, as well as being a teacher and project manager at UID's Interaction Design Lab. One thing led to another, and soon he was involved in different projects with people in both Singapore and Australia concerning haptic technology,[1] 3D technology, and virtual reality. It should be noted that Tomer has also developed new

---

[1] The word "haptic" has its roots from the Greek *haptesthai*, meaning "to touch" (*Encyclopædia Britannica*, 2011).

products that have resulted in his own patents, one of which has been sold to an American software company.

Reachin Technologies AB

In 1997/1998, during the emerging phase of what later became the era of "dot-com" companies, Tomer formed the company Reachin Technologies AB (www.reachin.se) together with people from UID and with the contacts that had been established in Australia and Singapore. Tomer and his business partners moved to Stockholm and set up an office at the fashionable address of Stureplan. Tomer acted as both product manager and executive vice president during his years at Reachin. For a short while, he was even the acting CEO before he left the company in 2001. In retrospect, he noted: "When I left, we had gone through a number of venture capital injections and I had probably made all of the mistakes one can make as an entrepreneur. I was fairly young and realized quite early that I did not have that much influence on the development of the company. Fortunately, I realized that I could not do anything more and decided to leave the company."

His analysis of the situation was that there was so much venture capital available at the time. What the company did was to adjust its mission statement to fit the venture capitalist that it was presently courting, or to fit the "story" that was easiest for it to market. The fit with what it might have considered best for the company's long-term survival and competitive advantage was, in other words, rather low. Tomer stated:

> It is considerably much easier to come up with a good story that is easy to sell to venture capitalists than present a really good business idea. As an example — I can say I want to be like Dropbox but better, and define some reasons for being better and receive a lot of venture capital for it. That does not mean that I think it would be the right thing to do. ... The best situation is if they are overlapping; they do that sometimes, but they don't have to [laughter].

After the Reachin experience, Tomer decided to take a break for about six months and not only focus on work all the time. He rejoined UID in Umeå and divided his free time between Stockholm and Umeå. After spending some additional time to think about his life, goals, etc., he decided to carry out his long-lasting desire of being a student. He wanted to try the "student experience" before he became so old that he could not pass as a student anymore. He then studied applied mathematics for a while. After finishing his studies, he felt it was time to start thinking about founding his next company. He stated: "I knew very well that regardless of what I would start working on, it would involve a lot of work and time, so it was very important to decide what project to start working on. So I waited and worked as a consultant for the time being."

Tomer's way of distinguishing between consulting firms and other types of firms is interesting. He noted:

> Consulting, well — people will hang me for saying this, but consulting firms and especially small consulting firms where you sell your time and try to create a profit margin on that and maybe on the sales process itself can be fun, but... it will not change the world. You will not change the big things. I have not found it challenging in any way. I know many who become very upset when I say this. I have on occasion said that I don't want to fall into the "consulting swamp" and received scolding for it.

An Idea Emerges

Even though Tomer did not want to become a consultant for the rest of his life, he established Pado Metaware AB with the business idea to help other companies write business plans. While doing this, Tomer realized that there were no suitable tools to facilitate writing this type of document. There were a number of tools for collaboration when producing text, such as Google Docs as well as a number of project and document management systems. However, the main problem with these types of software was that they could not help Tomer sufficiently as a professional writer, for example, in collecting and obtaining feedback from many people and then summarizing the essence of it. In other words, he lacked a good tool for visualizing text changes in a document.

The idea emerged in 2006, and during the summer of that year he sat down and wrote the basic strategies for his new venture. He then contacted two people he had worked with at Reachin Technologies AB, who later became his co-founders: Tim Poston as the chief scientist, and Mark Dixon as the chief technology officer. They flew in from Bangalore, India and Stockholm, respectively. Tim Poston is a mathematician and academic best known for his work on catastrophe theory.[2] Mark Dixon is an engineer, software developer, and inventor with seven patents of his own.[3] They all worked together for a few intense weeks, where they decided on the main structure for the interface and technical solutions. They then went ahead and started the company, Nordic River AB, during the autumn of 2006 with the ambition to develop and market the product, TextFlow, as a cloud-based service.

Starting a company when the co-founders are not present in the same city, or even in the same country for that matter, is a challenge. The three of them decided that — due to the distance, and because Tim is an academic (not an entrepreneur) and Mark did not want to be the entrepreneur/manager of this project — this task would fall to Tomer. In retrospect, Tomer noted: "I don't think I would dare to attempt this task when being geographically separated one more time. You need at least one person in your vicinity, one who you can discuss business development with — that is not possible to do on your own. On the other hand, there was no one else to speak to at that time. I cannot say it is an advantage to be spread out like this. I have tried to find positive aspects of it, but …."

---

[2]For further information on Professor Poston, please see LinkedIn (2011b).
[3]For further information about Mark Dixon, please see LinkedIn (2011a).

The reason for contacting Tim and Mark and asking them to be partners in his project was based on his previous experiences of cooperating with them at Reachin Technologies. Tomer stated: "We have been through hell and high water together. We know each other very well and know where we stand, which is an absolute prerequisite in this situation. Being geographically spread out like we are, it is extraordinary that we have managed to keep it together and pursue this project despite our geographically challenged position."

Financing the Development

Mark was responsible for developing the technical solutions. When it was time to hire more people for the actual development, Tomer scanned through his personal network for competence in interaction design and programming. He then hired Anna (who followed him from his former company Pado) and Oscar, who worked at UID. Due to very early seed money financed from a regional source, the startup phase was fast. Finding seed money was fairly easy due to Tomer's previous consulting activities where he had helped other firms write business plans and find venture capital. He had, in other words, already built a well-established financial network, ready to utilize for himself this time.

They went through a number of seed money injections in incremental steps — first to provide financing for a few months while a proper business plan was constructed, and then to apply for patents. After that, they continued in the same way with different steps in the actual development as goals. At the same time, each new infusion of venture capital was growing in size.

A Key Financier — Polarrenen AB

Polarbröd is located in Älvsbyn. It started as the mother company of Polarbageriet AB, Polarbröd Försäljnings AB, Omnebröd AB, and Gene Bageri AB, all located in the north of Sweden. It is a family-owned company with a history of more than 100 years of baking bread. It has good market coverage in Sweden, and has had partial successes with exporting. Due to changes in the company structure, Polarrenen AB was the mother company of Polarbröd between 2002 and 2006. After 2006, changes were made once again and the mother company's name today is Polinova AB. Since 2004, Polarrenen AB (www.polarrenen.se) has acted as an investor in small emerging companies in northern Sweden with a good potential to expand. It is an equity investor, with the strategy being to invest in unlisted companies as a minority owner (maximum 49% ownership). It invests between 1 and 15 million SEK (approximately 110,000–1,650,000 EUR). Loans in addition to the equity investment can be granted, and exit should be possible within a period of 5–10 years.

Polarrenen AB is currently involved as an investor in seven different companies (a complete list is found on http://www.polarrenen. se/?p=2). A majority of them are IT-based firms located in Umeå, and one of them is Nordic River AB. Polarrenen AB invested in Nordic River AB in November 2008, in the middle of the Lehman Brothers crisis. Tomer perceived that their attitude had a clearly regional perspective, which went along the lines of, "Well, this is something that we will overcome, and therefore there is no reason for us to change our investment strategies." Raising venture capital in Stockholm would have been impossible during the same time period.

The importance of local venture capital (VC) of this nature is obvious in this case, but there are also noticeable differences in priorities from the VC firm's side. Tomer noted that the local VC's priority is sales, and that they tend to downgrade the importance of technology. He found this attitude different from, for example, that in the U.S., where the technology is the first thing they focus on. A comment from a U.S. venture capitalist he once met was, "If you solve the technical side, I'll fix the rest!" Tomer became almost frustrated when discussing the Swedish cultural attitude of underestimating the importance of technology and how it is closely connected today to the user experience. He stated:

> It is a great responsibility to receive this capital and I want to manage it well, but I cannot expect any support for our business development. They come from a world where common sense is extremely important. Common sense is important, but it does not help me solve the complex equations I need to solve. We are talking about people that ask me, "But Google is free of charge, so how can we really earn any money?"
>
> It is important to gain access to capital at an early stage, but it does not help in assessing if I did the right or wrong things market- and business-wise. The money is there to help us survive. We cannot expect to gain competence as well from the venture capitalists.

The Product Evolves

TextFlow is built for multiple users spread via the Internet. It utilizes Adobe Flash and the Adobe AIR platform for seamless integration with Windows, OS X, and Linux in what is known as cloud computing. All files are stored on the Internet in the cloud, and not on local hard drives or servers. It is made possible via Nordic River's own developed (patent-pending) technique named "WeaveSync." Originally, the idea was to launch TextFlow as a "parallel word processor" software and to generate revenue by selling directly to companies and other professional organizations via a yearly subscription fee. An option to license the software to other producers of document and project management software was also considered. After a while, the company realized that to get customers to buy into this solution, they needed to build not only a complete word processor but also a document management system. Since there were only three engineers, they decided to find an alternative solution by integrating TextFlow with other products instead.

The original positioning of TextFlow as an alternative word processor was a challenge. It was attractive since "everyone loves an underdog," and here was someone that wanted to challenge Microsoft Word. The problem was to deliver a product meeting these expectations. Over time, the product has been repositioned as a component and complement to a word processor and document management system, and the repositioning is now more in line with what the product delivers. This repositioning has had consequences for how to market the product as well. Instead of a classical product focus, the emphasis is now on sales, where the company acts as a consultant that helps the customer integrate products to obtain an improved solution to the customer's problem.

As part of the public relations (PR) and to help with the market exposure, the company launched a website called www.compare mydocs.com (which today contains a link to www.nordicriver.com). It runs on the actual TextFlow software and acts as a market window for the company's integrative module to the word processor. The website www.textflow.com (which today also has a link to www.nordicriver.com) was launched on May 15, 2008. During the first four weeks, 4,000 out of the 10,000 visitors to the website ordered the beta version of TextFlow. International media have been more willing to write about the company than the local and national media. As Tomer noted, "In the U.S., if I meet someone, I am an Israeli living in the North Pole. The response is often, 'Cool, tell me more!'" The exposure was so successful that one day he received a telephone call from the marketing director of one of the world's largest computer companies who said, "I like your website." The marketing director then asked, "Will you be in the vicinity anytime soon?" Tomer gave the only viable response regardless of the situation: "Yes, what about next week?" Tomer admitted that this contact was an ego boost, but since the product was still not up to par with the expectations created in the media, nothing more came out of it. He realized that the

447

company's product was not correctly positioned and the large U.S.-based company was not waiting for them.

Even if no business deal came out of the meeting with the large U.S.-based company, Nordic River's main market is in the U.S. Currently, they have only one customer in Sweden, in Luleå. It is a small but very important client. It fits Nordic River's customer profile very well, and the geographical closeness probably impacted its decision to use TextFlow in a positive way.

In total, Nordic River applied for seven different patents at first. Today, Tomer has reassessed the situation and is thinking of canceling two of them due to changes in the development of the project. His attitude towards patents is that they are helpful, but that they cannot be considered fool-proof protection. As he stated, "At least the patent applications make it more probable that they contact us than just start making copies."

Tomer has not experienced any difficulties in convincing people to invest in his venture. His analysis is that he knows how to sell a story, but that this also has its downsides. The result is frequently that he either receives inquiries on things he finds irrelevant, or receives no questions at all by people who just say, "This is fantastic!" None of this is helpful to him. He would actually like to be challenged with relevant questions more often. The problem is to find people with that competence.

The last venture capital infusion in June 2010 was different. He managed to get two experienced entrepreneurs, one from Stockholm and one from Malmö, to invest in his company. Both of them had built their own companies within the same type of industry from scratch and subsequently sold them. These two investors were the first to infuse competence into the company. It served as a wake-up call for Tomer. For the first time, he realized what he had been missing out on all those years. He also realized that he could not expect board members to invest as much time as was needed for the business development. In addition, both of them helped Tomer to get in contact with others in their network. This has resulted in the hiring of a new colleague from Malmö, who will focus on the business development side together with Tomer. After a joint customer visit with his new colleague, the limitations of sitting alone trying to plan the business development became even more obvious to him. Aspects of the product and the business offer that he thought had been clearly thought out suddenly became vague when the colleague from Malmö started to probe with his questions. Tomer sees this as an immense help, and pointed out that it has also made him reflect on what he has been missing until now. In some aspects, the actual business development has not started until this point in time.

Time to Decide

Tomer is sitting in his office gathering his thoughts. Tomorrow will be the first serious meeting with the new colleague. They have booked the whole day tomorrow to sit and discuss the business development plan, and it is time to prepare.

The industry for this type of product has a tendency to create complex business models. It is a world in which some market their products by giving parts of the product away for free, by existing on multiple platforms, by helping to create and shape new behavior, and by adjusting to others. The number of parameters is numerous.

Nordic River's current business model is to commercialize TextFlow towards two target markets: towards companies as "software as a service" through yearly user fees, and towards distributors of other applications (partners) through licensing. When focusing on distributors, the question is how that part of the market should be handled. At present, the focus is on the legal and financial sector. Should the company expand into more sectors? Should the mobile market be included with, for example, an iPad application? Should they concentrate on earning money via the end user, or should they give the product away to gain a solid traffic flow to their website and as a result be able to sell their solution to other actors?

Table 1. Financial information on Nordic River Software AB.

	2010	2009	2008	2007
Results (in tSEK)				
Turnover	2,128	2,456	1,321	16
Results before tax	−3,043	−2,226	−831	
Results after tax	−3,043	−2,226	−831	−415
Balance sheet (in tSEK)				
Total assets	13,359	6,968	3,568	1,842
Current assets	5,234	1,143	486	
Own capital	9,000	3,208	1,395	

There are many questions to resolve. Looking at the information in Table 1, what should Tomer's opening position be tomorrow?

Bibliography

Businessweek (2009). "World's Best Design Schools — Umeå University." http://images.businessweek.com/ss/09/09/0930_worlds_best_design_schools/27.htm/ [accessed October 10, 2011].

Encyclopædia Britannica (2011). "Haptic." http://www.britannica.com/bps/dictionary?query=haptic/ [accessed October 10, 2011].

InfoTech Umeå (2010). "Nordic River." http://www.infotechumea.com/en/nordic-river/ [accessed October 10, 2011].

LinkedIn (2011a). "Dixon, Mark." http://se.linkedin.com/pub/mark-dixon/1/371/411/ [accessed October 10, 2011].

LinkedIn (2011b). "Poston, Tim." http://in.linkedin.com/in/tim-poston/ [accessed October 10, 2011].

Nordic River AB (2011). http://www.nordicriver.com/ [accessed October 10, 2011].

National Computer Services, Inc. — Market Options for a Small Middle Eastern IT Company*

Introduction

Geographically remote industrial clusters (GRICs) are customarily defined as groups of smaller manufacturing enterprises (SMEs) with similar market objectives. In an effort to increase efficiency, these clusters share resources, knowledge, productive capabilities, and other inputs. They are typically located 150 miles (240 kilometers) or more from major metropolitan areas or administrative centers. SMEs located in areas of the Middle East outside Cairo and Dubai metropolitan areas fit this definition primarily because of transportation infrastructure and environmental difficulties within the region. Regional automobile and rail transportation networks are relatively underdeveloped, obsolete, or non-existent, particularly outside of capital cities. Extreme weather conditions often make travel by land dangerous or impossible. These difficulties are usually amplified by administrative problems, such as visa requirements and customs duties, which increase the isolation of individual countries rather than promote regional integration.

In this case, I will present the efforts of Al-Babtain Group, located in Kuwait, to grow their information technology (IT)

---

*Tom Bramorski, of the University of Wisconsin-Whitewater (USA), developed this case for educational purposes only.

solutions in business-to-business (B2B) and business-to-consumer (B2C) environments. Marketing and operations management issues at Al-Babtain will be examined. The role of local governments in stimulating industrial development, creating jobs, and promoting sustainable economic growth will also be discussed.

A series of 2010 and 2011 upheavals labeled the "Arab Spring" have shaken up major countries of the Middle East, including Algeria, Egypt, Tunisia, Morocco, Libya, Syria, Bahrain, and Kuwait. Optimists argue that democratic transitions in the Middle East and North Africa could quickly transform the region's economies, which experienced only 0.5% annual growth in per capita GDP over the period 1980–2010 (*The Economist*, 2011b). Others argue that the region's transition to a market economy will be long and turbulent.

Countries such as Egypt and Tunisia do not have to build a market system from scratch. Their state-dominated economies swiftly need a major overhaul, but accomplishing this task will be difficult. The necessary market reforms include eliminating the system of subsidies, fostering private enterprise, breaking up monopolies, reducing the size of the state, and rewriting regulations so that they support rather than suffocate competition. The economies of the Middle East and North Africa require economic cooperation from Europe and the United States in order to establish business partnerships and promote bilateral trade. The Arab countries (those with oil wealth and those without) have capitalist economies, in which prices and private enterprise play a big role. Yet it is a distorted, patriarchal capitalism, characterized by dominant state monopolies, heavy regulation, and massive subsidies. This has fueled corruption, stunted growth, and left millions without jobs. High oil prices give petro-economies the ability to counter discontent by generously dispensing assistance. Those without such wealth face a growing fiscal mess. In Egypt, for example, over 40% of the economy outside agriculture is in state hands, with a hefty chunk controlled by the army. Private firms are strangled with red tape. Subsidies for food and fuel, worth some 10% of GDP, are busting the budget. The result is that the country is facing a fiscal crunch as well as an urgent need to overhaul its economic model.

Popular anger at corruption and high joblessness in the region has not produced fundamental economic reforms. For example, in Egypt the transitional government has expanded subsidies and increased employment in state firms. Economic liberalization has a poor reputation throughout the Middle East, largely thanks to reforms earlier this decade whose fruits flowed mostly to the well-connected (*The Economist*, 2011b).

The Economic Issues in Kuwait

Kuwait has fared relatively well in coping with the Arab Spring challenges, largely because of its oil wealth. Its corruption rating is rated average and the likelihood of unrest is considered low. However, in a recent analysis, the country received low ratings on democracy and freedom of the press (*The Economist*, 2011a). Moreover, continued instability in Iraq and the threat of Islamic radicals from Iran have adversely influenced the economy of Kuwait. The government has directed oil profits toward safer investments abroad rather than channeling them to develop the national economy. As a result, domestic manufacturing and service sectors are not developed and funded as well as they should be.

Kuwait officially promotes openness and advocates the benefits of market competition while restricting and/or eliminating monopolies. For example, market monopolies have recently been eliminated in telecommunications and Internet service provider (ISP) sectors. Currently, there are three telecom companies and four ISPs operating in the country. Sectors such as electricity generation and distribution, gasoline distribution, and wired telephone network services await privatization.

Businesses and individuals frequently complain of excessive bureaucracy that has a crippling effect on daily business operations. For example, business decisions such as facility expansion and hiring of personnel require government permits, which may take a long time to obtain. Implementing these actions without the needed permits exposes a business or an individual to hefty penalties.

Kuwait has passed legislation that requires businesses and government agencies to give hiring priority to citizens of the country. Such a policy may be beneficial in agriculture and construction, where the labor supply is relatively high. However, it restricts the supply of highly skilled labor in sectors such as IT, where the local talent pool is not sufficiently large to meet the growing demand. The official "Kuwaitization" policy aims at keeping a high level of employment for the citizen population. The policy requires private organizations to hire a certain percentage of citizens in order to be eligible to bid on government projects, either as a main contractor or as a subcontractor. This produces an inflated government-imposed wage rate that applies only to the citizens of Kuwait, while compensation packages for expatriate labor are determined by the market. Such labor policy restrictions not only produce unfairness accusations, but also significantly increase the cost of labor and result in uneven resource utilization. In addition, the government provides direct monetary incentives to private businesses to encourage them to employ citizens. Private-sector businesses complain that they are forced to hire local labor with poor or questionable credentials just to meet the quota.

Public-sector employees in Kuwait enjoy very generous compensation packages including high salaries and comprehensive benefits packages (such as free medical, dental, and life insurance and generous retirement benefits). The private sector faces major challenges in attracting the best and the brightest.

An analysis of labor and capital factors for the IT sector is presented below.

Labor

The Middle Eastern countries are either exporters or importers of labor. Due to the lack of a local skilled workforce, Kuwait is an importer of IT-sector employees primarily from Egypt, Syria, Jordan, and Palestine. Although English is commonly spoken in Kuwait, proficiency in Arabic is required particularly in customer and technical support positions. The IT sector in Kuwait employs less than 10% of expatriate specialists, mostly in middle-level management areas. Recruitment and selection processes are based on a network of formal and informal contacts. Employee compensation and benefits packages are kept competitive and flexible to prevent critical employees from leaving. Employee loyalty tends to be low, leading to a high turnover even in cases where compensation and benefits differences are marginal.

Labor contracts for all employees in Kuwait are controlled by the Ministry of Social Affairs and Labor, and must be approved by the Ministry on a case-by-case basis. Businesses often employ specialized staff to facilitate the lengthy government approval process for existing and new hires.

Membership in the labor unions in Kuwait is restricted only to professional employees, including engineers, medical doctors, and government- and oil-sector workers who are citizens of Kuwait. Foreign employees are not covered by these agreements. The unions have been successful at renegotiating employment contracts for medical doctors and professional engineers. These modifications have focused on salary increases and minimum wage adjustments rather than developing a compensation program covering wages, benefits, and work safety. Other categories of workers are currently not unionized. The minimum wage rate is set competitively in the market, and there are no restrictions on workers regarding the ability to switch employers.

Hiring new staff in the IT sector is a complex procedure that requires elaborate justification documenting to the higher organizational echelons and to the government as to why a new employee is needed. Such documentation for a position must include a description of work scope, statement of the minimum salary grade required, value analysis, as well as analysis of costing and budgeting implications. Employers systematically update their IT hardware and software and provide training opportunities for their staff in new technologies in order to ensure high-quality technical support for their customers.

Capital

The commercial and private banking infrastructure in Kuwait is very well developed. Major European and North American banks have branches operating in the country. A variety of traditional business financial instruments, from unsecured loans to confirmed irrevocable letters of credit, are available to finance business trans-actions in an accurate and timely manner. In Kuwait, business is conducted using a combination of traditional and modern approaches. The traditional tools rely on family/clan relation-ships and word of mouth. Modern tools involve a less biased determination of client creditworthiness using financial quanti-tative decision support tools, such as cash flow and profitability projections.

Actual financial performance of a business in terms of payables and receivables is usually closely monitored by a bank on a weekly basis to prevent financial disasters. Detailed monthly product/service performance reports, covering cash in hand, payables and receivables performance, and sales expectations, are customarily prepared and submitted to corporate management and to creditors for analysis. Aggregate financial reports are generated for all product/service lines on a quarterly basis. These reports create a sound foundation for factual marketing and operations strategy decisions, including phasing out declining or unprofitable lines and approving new business development projects.

The NCS Company History

National Computer Services (NCS) is part of the Middle Eastern Al-Babtain conglomerate, which consists of 10 companies in Kuwait and many more companies outside Kuwait. The company was founded in 1948 and is headquartered in Safat, Kuwait. The group engages in automotive (Nissan, Citroen, Dunlop) and computer (NCS, Compaq, Hewlett-Packard) trading, paint and plastic manufacturing, real estate, and tourism activities. Its Automotive Products Division imports and distributes cars, heavy-duty vehicles, and construction equipment, as well as provides car rental and leasing services. The company's Computer and Allied Products Division offers computers, computer software and allied equipment, accessories, and services. Al-Babtain's Manufacturing Division manufactures paints for marine, industrial, and decorative applications. Other products include plastics (polyethylene rolls and bags) and automotive (vehicle body parts, trailers, tippers, tankers) (Bloomberg, 2011).

The closely held group is fully owned by the Al-Babtain family. Since its inception as a used car business, the company has diversified and has developed a solid business reputation. In 2010, the annual volume of business was estimated at US$35 million. The group is managed by a board of directors consisting of nine family members.

The IT Business

NCS started operations as an exclusive trade representative of Digital, Inc. in Kuwait. As an exclusive agent for mainframe computers, NCS realized healthy IT annual systems profits of approximately 35–40% with long-term maintenance contracts providing another steady profit stream. At the time, the IT market was classified as monopolistic competition with manufacturers offering often incompatible platforms. After the merger between Digital and Compaq, NCS became a Compaq agent and eventually became a Hewlett-Packard business partner in Kuwait. NCS offers a complete line of IT products, including a full range of HP and Compaq computer systems, networking solutions, accessories, and consumables. Access to HP technology solutions has enabled NCS to bid on turnkey projects in Kuwait and throughout the region. Today there are common IT specifications for all products, allowing connectivity across different software and hardware platforms. With IT products becoming commodities, profit margins have also narrowed down.

With the projected double-digit growth in Dubai, NCS owners decided to open a branch in this market in 2000. Currently, the United Arab Emirates (Dubai) branch continues to be the most profitable branch for NCS, doubling its volume of business every two years. The financial crisis of 2008–2009 significantly slowed down UAE business, but the volume and profit have since returned to healthy 2007 levels.

An Egypt branch was also established in 2000 to take advantage of the incentives offered by the government to businesses entering the market. However, frequent changes in policies, taxes, and licenses, combined with the elimination of subsidies to NCS, quickly made Egyptian operations unprofitable. A high annual inflation rate reaching 50%, a low annual growth rate of less than 2%, and a high unemployment rate of 25% all contributed to the 2004 decision by NCS to suspend operations in Egypt. Fearing social unrest, the Egyptian government swiftly lifted all restrictions in 2006 and offered a new schedule of taxes and a low rate of investment to encourage businesses to continue investing in the country. As inflation was brought under control, NCS decided to reopen operations in Egypt in late 2006. Between 2006 and 2010, NCS business in Egypt remained marginally profitable. Because of the market potential, NCS owners have decided to continue to maintain a presence in Egypt even though the exact impact of the social upheaval and the resulting regime change of 2011 on NCS business in Egypt, which is expected to be significant, remains to be quantified (*The Economist*, 2011a).

Although the market potential in Qatar and Bahrain is significantly smaller than that of Egypt, the problems faced by businesses there as well as social unrest risks are quite similar. Despite economic and political instabilities, NCS continues to operate in these markets.

Currently, NCS does business in five Middle Eastern countries: Kuwait, Qatar, Bahrain, UAE (Dubai), and Egypt. It has plans to expand in other countries of the region, such as Oman. Each country branch has an identical organizational structure and consists of the following functional departments: Business Intelligence, Systems, Sites, Computer Services, and Finance. Each division is headed by a country operations manager, who reports to an executive manager, who in turn reports to the President of IT Group and Vice Chief Executive Officer of Planning and Business Development. Formally, collaboration between divisions is encouraged; however, at the present time there are no formal channels, such as corporate symposia and training workshops, to encourage activities such as sharing of experiences, identification of best practices, and benchmarking. NCS is an agent for 20 companies in the global computer business, and vigorously pursues new market opportunities to increase market penetration and enhance the product portfolio.

The upper management committees (board of directors) control the strategic planning and budgeting processes, and supervise their implementation. The General Manager of the NCS group serves as a liaison between the board of directors and operations managers. Operations managers are responsible for implementing the decisions taken by the board of directors. Control at all levels is maintained by customary business reporting on monthly and quarterly bases. However, progress in new ventures and key projects is monitored on a weekly basis. The organizational structure at the country branch level follows a multidivisional form (M-form), while the division is organized as a unitary form (U-form).

The group operates a central website (Al-Babtain Group of Companies, 2011) for all branches, and has IT division control of the stores and accounting for all operations. Customary IT services, such as email, are available for all employees.

The Cost and Pricing Policy

In general, the global IT industry grows quickly as a result of shortening product life cycles and new technology development. Largely due to a high obsolescence risk, the IT products tend to be price-sensitive, build-to-stock commodities. IT manufacturers continuously strive to minimize the product cost, leading to rapid outsourcing of manufacturing and product support tasks. The outsourcing drivers include lower cost of inputs (labor, energy, raw materials, land, etc.), less government regulation (specifically with respect to union contracts and labor laws), and availability of incentives (tax exemptions, free access to infrastructure, etc.). A major competitive threat for European and North American companies which outsource their operations is the risk of technology transfer to locations that offer little or no intellectual property protection.

Regions tend to erect bureaucratic and administrative barriers based on a system of homologation/compliance requirements, import quotas, and duties that restrict access to markets. For example, fiber optic cables sold in Europe must be manufactured there in order for the product to be considered domestic. Similarly, in order to qualify for export subsidies, a portion of the manufacturing task must be completed within the European Union. In order to meet the domestic content requirement, manufacturers often produce bulk fibers in one country but cover them with insulation, cut them to size, and install connectors in another country where manufacturing costs are lower. In the Middle Eastern fiber optic cable market, such finishing plants have been established in Oman, Saudi Arabia, Egypt, and Kuwait. Indeed, shipping the unfinished product packed in bulk packaging (drums) is cheaper than shipping the finished product bundles. This is because bulk product weighs less and takes up less volume compared to the finished product. The benefit of a postponement strategy is that cables are customized locally to best meet the needs and preferences of local customers in sensitive areas, such as color palette selection. Local customization encourages efficient use of bulk material and minimizes product and inventory-related costs.

In the IT business, various products require an individual pricing policy. For example, personal computers in typical configurations need to be in stock at all times. On the other hand, excessive stock levels of these products are not desirable due to a low profit margin and high perishability risk. Sometimes, prices for computer products are set at or below cost in order to gain and maintain market share. The intent of such a policy is to offset the initial loss from a sale of a product over the technology's lifetime. This is operationalized by providing customers with long-term service and maintenance contracts as well as special offers (discounts, coupons, etc.) on service items and consumables.

Typically, government tender regulations require that a contract be awarded to the lowest bidder — a procedure that uses price as an order-qualifying criterion. But IT vendors know that at system delivery time, the actual price to be paid by the customer will often be higher than the bid price. This allows the vendor to make sound profit on a complete contract because of modifications and new technology updates. Such comprehensive solutions allow the vendor to build and maintain relations with customers for a long time through providing technical support and training contracts, maintenance contracts, and updates or replacements. Under such a system, product pricing covers all costs and ensures a reasonable margin to cover all business expenses. The pricing policy changes frequently in response to the actions of competitors, the emergence of new market entrants, or new technology introductions.

In 2008, NCS launched a vigorous advertising campaign in Kuwait that materially affected their business, producing an increase in the number and complexity of big projects. The company used a combination of channels including newspapers, professional publications, and television commercials. Customers were offered discount certificates and gifts of free products and/or services. The company developed and implemented a formal system of maintaining contacts for the potential sales leads, hence allowing systematic pre-sale follow-ups.

In the volatile IT field, the inventory turnover ratio ranges from 30 to 50 per year. NCS has consistently generated US$15–$20 million in annual revenue per year, with US$250,000–$300,000 in cash. The cash is typically obtained from a bank as a short-term (1–2 weeks) high-interest loan. A more attractive long-term financing arrangement in the form of a revolving credit line would significantly improve NCS' profitability.

The Growth Strategy

In the fiber optic communications infrastructure business, NCS has adopted a growth strategy based on the following principles: market penetration, new product development, market development, and diversification. For example, in order to avoid competing on price with cheaper Chinese CAT5 fiber optic cables, the European and American companies developed next-generation and faster CAT6 cables. Currently, the Chinese offer CAT6 cables while European and American businesses offer higher-quality CAT7 cables. Since NCS carries various types of fiber optic cables at various price levels, its customers in Kuwait benefit. Business and government customers who demand faster speeds and higher signal quality purchase CAT6 and CAT7 cables. Individual customers, who are more price-sensitive, purchase CAT5 cables for less demanding applications. The rapidly increasing installed product base generates demand for other advanced network hardware, which is also supplied by NCS. Such derived demand enhances market penetration and stimulates new product development.

Strategic Considerations

Organizations operating in the Middle East find themselves in a highly volatile environment that is expected to continue for several years. Therefore, their strategies must be designed to be robust in order to be able to quickly respond to a set of complex political, social, financial, regulatory, and competitive challenges that may occur in the market on very short notice. The key elements of such a flexible strategy include the following:

- An organizational structure that eliminates or significantly reduces bureaucracy, minimizes reporting and control, encourages multidirectional communication, and enables timely exchange of information. The structure may take a matrix form or even move toward a neural network characteristic of a virtual corporation;
- The creation of a strategic alignment between organizational and personal strategies of the employees, as well as between strategies of organizations that are part of the extended supply chain;
- A highly capable, cross-trained workforce that is able and willing to change physical location on short notice as the business climate changes. Companies should develop and implement recruitment, retention, training, professional development, and compensation policies to create growth opportunities and increase job satisfaction;
- The development and maintenance of long-term, trust-based business partnerships with suppliers and equipment vendors. This requires providing corporate payment guarantees for product and service deliveries irrespective of the branch's geographic location;
- The development and maintenance of close relationships with customers based on the principle of value added. Organizational capabilities must be geared toward offering customers quick

response, high product/service quality, and competitive price (low cost and low overhead);

- The development and maintenance of political connections and investments in business intelligence in order to better anticipate future political, competitive, and new technology developments; and
- The availability of a state-of-the-art, secure IT network to support the exchange of information.

Addressing these priorities will allow a business to quickly move to a new location and continue operations with minimum setup.

Case Questions

1. Prepare a timeline showing the major political and social changes that have occurred in Kuwait since Operation Desert Shield in 1990. What impact did these events have on the IT sector in Kuwait in general and on Al-Babtain Group's Kuwait operations in particular?

2. Analyze the risks and potential benefits to the Al-Babtain business in Kuwait related to the Arab Spring of 2011. What specific strategic recommendations would you give to the owners of the company regarding future operations in Kuwait and throughout the Middle East? Support your analysis with relevant facts and data.

3. Do you think that the organizational structure and operational procedures of Al-Babtain Group are appropriate for the volatile social, political, and market situation in Kuwait and the Middle East? What strategic changes would you recommend? Be specific and justify your answers.

4. Using a clean-slate approach, develop a model for business–government–university partnership to support business development in an oil-rich country like Kuwait. Focus specifically on how universities and the government can assist a small IT business

like the Al-Babtain Group. How would your recommendations differ for a country with more modest oil deposits (e.g., Oman)?

Bibliography

Al-Babtain Group of Companies (2011). http://www.albabtaingroup. com.kw/en/index.shtml/.

Bloomberg (2011). http://www.bloomberg.com/.

Businessweek (2011). "Trading Companies and Distributors — Company Overview of Al-Babtain Group." http://investing. businessweek.com/research/stocks/private/snapshot.asp?privcap Id=6478743/.

The Economist (2011a). "Arab League." http://media.economist.com/ sites/default/files/media/2011InfoG/Interactive/ArabLeague_Jan 16/Arab6.swf/.

The Economist (2011b). "Open for Business? Economic Reform in the Middle East Could Prove Harder than in Eastern Europe." June 23.

Case 19

Golf Goes Virtual with GOLFZON*

A Virtual Golf Business Is Established

Back when Young-chan Kim was head of Samsung Electronics' Operations Division, he often had no time to play golf, his favorite sport. He had tried to play indoor golf with business associates and friends, but it was not challenging enough and he soon lost interest in it. However, on one business trip abroad, he was introduced to virtual golf, and it was far more realistic than just hitting a golf ball towards a screen and not knowing how good the swing was. With the virtual golf system, you actually had a feeling of being on the golf course yourself.

With all his knowledge from the electronics industry and the opportunities available in developing virtual golf to outstanding heights, Young-chan Kim decided to establish a company with the aim of producing high-end golf simulators. Golf had for many years been a growing sport in Korea, and a very prestigious one too. But it was also incredibly expensive to play golf, and golf courses were already crowded.

Koreans have always been keen on being with friends in small rooms. Many restaurants, bars, and cafés in Korea have rooms where people can be with their friends in private. For decades, Korea has

---

*Jens Graff, of the SolBridge International School of Business, Woosong University (South Korea), developed this case for educational purposes only.

also been enthusiastic about karaoke, where one typically sings in a small room with friends.

After debating the idea with friends and business peers in 2000, GOLFZON was established in 2002 with five founding partners and has now become a USD 250 million business. Let us look at the GOLFZON virtual golf system in more detail.

GOLFZON is a virtual golf system based on hardware and software. The system uses real clubs and balls to generate an authentic, three-dimensional (3D) golfing experience. The advanced technology enables accurate game physics simulation. GOLFZON-patented swing plates automatically adjust to simulate field slope, giving players a realistic in-game feeling. Players can select the swing plate's range.

GOLFZON's patented analysis system consists of 170 infrared sensors that instantly and accurately measure ball speed, trajectory, launch angle, flight time, club head speed, club face angle, and club path. The system measures slice, hook, draw, and fade, making the system very accurate.

The system reproduces the results in 3D graphics. The aim is to give practitioners real swing practice and accurate feedback to improve their game. Accurate infrared club and ball tracking lets players see true strike results, improving consistency and lowering handicaps.

GOLFZON's information technology (IT) system is based on real, international golf courses recreated through aerial photography and geographical surveying. One can even see clouds blow by and hear birds chirp. As of August 2011, more than 160 international golf courses had been displayed in realistic and officially licensed 3D graphics, and two or three new courses are added each month. Also included are fantasy courses with realistic virtual city courses at, for example, Seoul City Hall, Incheon International Airport, and Seoul World Cup Stadium. The system is illustrated in Figure 1. As seen in Figure 1, GOLFZON gives a quite realistic image of a natural golf course.

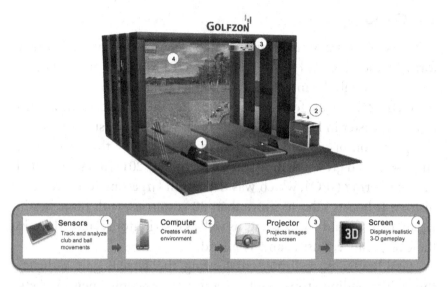

Figure 1. How the system works (source: GOLFZON).

There are online services, such as GOLFZON Live online tournaments, player records, swing analysis, online shopping, and golf equipment information. This software really gives GOLFZON a competitive edge. Based on this system, the golfer can track scores and progress, adjust club recommendations, and compare one's performance with other players. GOLFZON also holds GOLFZON Live Tournaments and GOLFZON Live Festivals, where players can compete against each other in real time.

GOLFZON has established golf sites where a new indoor golf culture concept has been created. These sites have luxurious interiors, specialized services, and GOLFZON simulators. People pay by the hour. In Korea alone, GOLFZON has sold more than 4,000 systems. They have all been sold to independent owners, except for four in Seoul which are owned by GOLFZON. GOLFZON provides after-sales service and hardware and software upgrades to these systems. The system itself requires $28\,\mathrm{m}^2$; including space for chairs/sofas, about $40\,\mathrm{m}^2$ of area is needed.

The Company

GOLFZON's mission is to promote golf culture and provide a new form of pleasure and convenience by creating new products and services through the integration of golf, IT, and culture.

GOLFZON was founded in 2002 in the Daedeok Innopolis research cluster in Daejeon, South Korea. When first established, the company comprised only five people, but by 2011 the number of employees had grown to more than 400. In May 2011, it had its initial public offering (IPO), which was the eighth largest in South Korean history. It boasts sales to more than 30 countries, with branches in Japan, Beijing, and Hong Kong, as well as distributor relationships in the U.K., France, Russia, and Thailand.

GOLFZON is dedicated to leading the virtual golf industry through providing a top-quality experience, developing new markets, and furthering its vision of a new golf culture for everyone to enjoy. There are 50 million people in South Korea, of which about 200,000 people a day use the GOLFZON system. GOLFZON analyzes game data and customer feedback to constantly improve system performance and stability, and to ensure that players have fun. Parameters such as ball speed, club angle, and time are registered, and scores appear immediately.

Sales have been impressive for GOLFZON (see Figure 2). Since its establishment in 2002, it has grown to a USD 250 million business in 2011 (see Appendices A and B at the end of this chapter for a brief review of GOLFZON's economic development).

The steady growth of the golf industry and an increase in leisure time are popularizing golf worldwide; however, the notion that golf is a luxury sport for the rich is still prevalent. Since its foundation in 2002, GOLFZON has consistently worked to popularize golf by cultivating its cultural value. GOLFZON's vision and mission are to promote golf to a wider audience and to create a GOLFZON culture that is enjoyable and accessible to everyone, regardless of

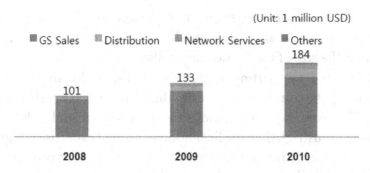

Figure 2.   Sales progress (source: GOLFZON).

time or location. It is advancing as a global network-establishing IT corporation, integrating online and offline products and services.

GOLFZON's simulators commanded tremendous industry attention by taking the majority share of the South Korean market in its first year. Manufactured with South Korean technology, GOLFZON has sustained rapid and steady growth. GOLFZON is currently the biggest player in the international golf simulation market, earning worldwide recognition and having exported simulation systems to over 30 countries.

Clusters

Michael Porter (1998) has defined clusters as "geographic concentrations of interconnected companies and institutions in a particular field." This geographical nearness to each other is usually advantageous for the companies in the cluster and makes them more competitive. In his diamond model, Michael Porter (1990) explained how companies could profit from the following factors:

- Factor conditions — The presence of skillful workers and specialists in the field of business when the startup company needs them is, of course, a necessity.
- Demand conditions — On the demand side, it is important to have consumers as close to one's location as possible. This means that

one's home market matters, as supply chains are easier to manage and, most importantly, the founder understands the culture. Of course, the size of the home market also matters.

- Related and supporting industries — Especially in a startup situation, the company needs everything and every expertise it can get. Therefore, supporting industries are essential; and if there are related industries, then the likelihood of needed expertise is higher.
- Firm strategy, structure, and rivalry — The founder is of crucial importance for the upstart, establishment, and growth of his business. That he has a story he wants to tell, as expressed in the business mission and vision, is fundamental for his ability to motivate employees to aim toward growth with him.
- Government — Visionary governments are important, especially if they put money behind their ambitions to support the fields of business the company is involved in.
- Chance — An idea or innovation may take off in the area and become the trigger for new growth and development. This has in many cases given birth to the establishment of a cluster, because research shows that new companies often appear close to where the founder is located (Stuart and Sorenson, 2003).

All of these factors complement each other and also often create synergy.

Remote Geographical Clusters

After the end of the Korean War between North and South Korea in 1953, South Korea was devastated and people suffered. Technically, the two countries are still at war, as there is only an armistice and not a genuine peace treaty between them. North Korea has a communist, centrally governed political system; whereas South Korea has a capitalist, democratic system. At present, the two Koreas are not on very friendly terms with each other, and the border between North and South Korea is heavily guarded by both parties with a demilitarized zone between them.

This political reality has existed for nearly 60 years now, and the geography of Korea as a peninsula has made South Korea a relatively isolated state. Korea used to be remote to big Western markets such as the USA and Western Europe, but advancements in transportation systems and communications have reduced these distances.

South Korea is made up of 50 million inhabitants on an area of about 100,000 km^2. South Korea is a mountainous region, with its population concentrated in low areas. This makes it one of the most densely populated countries in the world. Its capital, Seoul, has about 10 million inhabitants, but during the day this number goes up to about 13 million. In fact, about half of Korea's population live in Seoul and nearby municipalities.

Daejeon is located in the middle of South Korea, 153 km south of Seoul and 283 km northwest from Busan, the largest harbor in South Korea. It is Korea's fifth-largest city with 1.5 million inhabitants. It is a hub for railway traffic, and Korea Railroad has its headquarters in Daejeon. There is a high-speed train service between Seoul through Daejeon to Busan. The train ride from Seoul to Daejeon takes less than an hour; and to Busan, less than two hours. South Korea also has a well-developed highway system. Korea's international airport is located in Incheon, west of Seoul. From there to Daejeon, the airport bus ride takes three hours. In 2009, Incheon International Airport was ranked as the best international airport in the world, ahead of Hong Kong International Airport and Singapore Changi Airport. It ranked highest on criteria such as "easiest international transit airport," "best security processing," and "best terminal cleanliness."

Daejeon is regarded as the Silicon Valley of Korea, with its Daedeok Innopolis research cluster. This area hosts research institutions for information technology, biotechnology, nanotechnology, aerospace, energy, and robotics. Daedeok Innopolis is home to a cluster of firms that represent a cross-section of cutting-edge industries, including information technology, biotechnology, and nanotechnology. Daedeok Innopolis consists of representatives of

473

top-tier venture and research firms from diverse fields. Most of them have a proven track record in the commercialization of DRAM and SRAM chips, LCD modules, cellular phone technology, and wireless broadband technologies. Tens of companies at Daedeok Innopolis have already been listed on KOSDAQ, the Korean stock exchange. There were about 1,200 high-tech resident industries in Daedeok Innopolis in the middle of 2011, and this number is forecasted to double by 2015. In 2011, there were more than 20,000 researchers working in the area, of which about 7,000 had PhDs.

The area is now part of a bigger research cluster called Daedeok Science Belt, with a 2011 government donation of about USD 3.2 billion to the area broadening from Daejeon into neighboring regions. Daedeok will be home to the project's two major research facilities: the National Basic Science Institute, which will employ up to 3,000 elite scientists, and a KRW 410 billion (about USD 400 million) state-of-the-art particle accelerator. The Ministry of Education, Science, and Technology expects that the selection of Daedeok and other locations will create a national science belt, which will play a role in getting South Korea to carry out key experiments in such fields as chemistry, physics, and other applied sciences. In other words, the area will form an innovation ecosystem.

An important institution in the Daedeok Science Belt is the Korea Advanced Institute of Science and Technology (KAIST). KAIST was established in 1971 as the nation's first graduate school specializing in science and engineering education and research. The school's founding was a catalyst for Korea's rapid rise from a producer of light industry goods to a world leader in high-technology industries.

GOLFZON's golf simulation systems and other products require advanced IT. When it established its headquarters in Daejeon, GOLFZON received technological support from KAIST and other research institutions. That was an important reason for setting up its headquarters in Daejeon. It was not difficult for the company to find talented employees, because the area contains so many people who are well trained in technology.

Given that the Daedeok area is gifted with research and development people primarily within science, and not so much within sales and marketing, GOLFZON established a branch office in Seoul, where the number of sales and marketing people is bigger, and because it is the capital of South Korea and is closer to Incheon International Airport. GOLFZON felt that if it wanted to globalize, it simply had to have a presence in Seoul, where the people network functions on a larger scale and where the big foreign companies have their Korean subsidiaries. Besides, the majority of GOLFZON systems were sold in Seoul from the very beginning, so the company had to build a branch there. It was also necessary to be in the Seoul area to source people for GOLFZON's expansion, because the company could not find enough people with different specialties in Daejeon.

The coordination of activities between the Daejeon and Seoul branches is not a problem for GOLFZON, as they perform different tasks. In Daejeon, GOLFZON carries out its hardware research and development, production, and shipping; whereas software research and development, marketing, sales, human resources, legal, and other business functions are handled by the larger Seoul branch.

The founder and current CEO of GOLFZON, Young-chan Kim, is the former head of Samsung Electronics' Operations Division. He has a profound understanding of electronics and IT, and also has access to a large network within this industry. He was aware of KAIST's expertise in Daejeon, and wanted to be part of this research and development cluster. There were also government tax incentives to be gained by establishing there. Moreover, the founder himself is from Daejeon.

GOLFZON profited widely from its KAIST link, and later from the unique cluster of research companies in Daedeok Innopolis. All along during its incubation period, GOLFZON was protected by the government and government-supported venture companies, and benefited from its nearness to chipmakers and hydraulic expertise. As neighbors, they were also able to support each other.

Today, it is difficult to get new GOLFZON people to reside in Daejeon. New employees typically have spouses who work in Seoul, and the Seoul area has all the perks of a big metropolis.

If GOLFZON were to grow out of Daedeok Innopolis and lose its government subsidies there, this could pose a threat for the company. Korean companies are very nationalistic and have a tendency to do everything in the Korean way. For example, websites can only be used with Microsoft Internet Explorer software. So when Korean companies go international, they often fail because they do not pay attention to other ways of doing things. Everything has to be done in the Korean formatted way.

South Korea's Golf Market

The golf market in Korea has developed quickly over the last few years, and it now consists of over two million players, as is shown in Figure 3. Figure 3 also shows that the virtual golf market has grown even faster and now makes up 60% of South Korea's total golf market. In terms of value, the total golf market — comprising field, driving range, and simulation golf — was worth nearly USD 5 billion in 2009 (see Figure 4).

Compared with other developed countries, there is room for growth in South Korea's golfing population. Of GOLFZON's sales, only 4% came from overseas in 2010, although this figure increased to 8% in 2011.

The Virtual Golf Market in Korea

Golf is the fastest-growing sport in Korea, but it is expensive. For example, membership at a South Korean country club costs, on average, over USD 7,000 for one year. At luxurious clubs, it costs

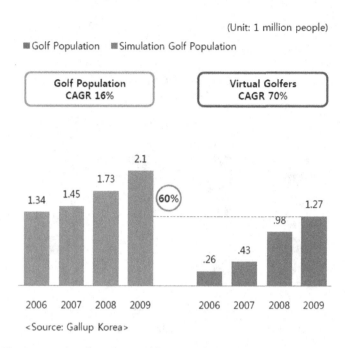

(Unit: 1 million people)

■ Golf Population ■ Simulation Golf Population

| Golf Population
CAGR 16% | Virtual Golfers
CAGR 70% |

<Source: Gallup Korea>

Figure 3.   South Korean golfing population (source: GOLFZON). *Note*: CAGR = compound annual growth rate.

over USD 30,000 per year. Without a membership, it is very hard for people to book their play.

As of August 2011, GOLFZON had sold more than 22,000 systems in Korea alone. Korea is the biggest market in the world for virtual golf. In Seoul, one can take a walk and see quite a few indoor golf venues.

Why do people go to indoor venues to play golf instead of going to real golf courses? "The main reason is that I can save money and time. Whenever I want to play golf, I can go there with my friends, and then enjoy playing golf," Ki-mun Choi said. "However, when I have a round of golf in natural surroundings, it is very expensive and I have to book for the play. Indoor golf only costs me about USD 20–30. Also, it usually takes me at least five to six hours for a regular round of golf, while playing indoor golf takes only one hour per person for 18 holes."

(Unit: 1 million USD)

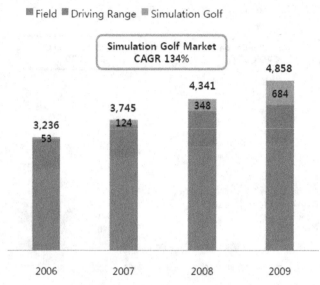

■ Field ■ Driving Range ■ Simulation Golf

Figure 4. South Korean golf market (source: GOLFZON).
Note: CAGR = compound annual growth rate.

"People playing indoor golf practice their golf skills, but the main reason is just for fun," the manager of one indoor golf site said. He continued, "They enjoy competing with their friends by playing indoor golf. Also, when it rains or is very hot, they go to indoor golf places for entertainment." The biggest seasons for indoor golf are winter, spring, and autumn. In springtime, serious golfers want to train before they enter the natural golf courses. Most natural golf courses in Korea are closed during winter due to the cold weather and snow. Because golf has become such a popular sport, golf courses are often crowded, and this is another reason why indoor golf has become an attractive alternative to the real golf courses.

With the many indoor golf sites around in cities of Korea, they are easily accessible for people. Going to a natural golf site requires planning and often driving long distances, and sometimes involves hotel nights. People save time by going to indoor golf sites. They have also become a new place to meet friends. Koreans have a penchant for being with friends in rooms; one can find rooms in restaurants, cafes, and karaoke bars. Indoor golf sites are typically arranged in rooms as well, so they have become something new for people to entertain themselves with.

"Koreans in general are embarking on a healthier lifestyle," said Mi-ju Lee, who continued: "They don't smoke as much as before, they eat healthier, and they drink less than before. Spending time at a virtual golf course keeps them out of the usual eating and drinking places. Learning to play golf is difficult. It is a tough sport. Meeting with your friends in a virtual golf room does not put so much pressure on you. You can be more relaxed in privacy with your friends. And there is no dress code, although some people like to dress golf-like."

"Instead of going to a pub with my friends after work, I come to golf-practicing places," said Eun-joo Bae, a salesman. He continued: "This is a new culture among people, especially salesmen. Nowadays, people are very interested in playing golf. There are many people who want to learn how to play golf. Also, some people want to learn playing golf as a tool for their social life. Therefore, people come to golf-practicing places and practice with their friends after work." Won-yeop Kim supplemented: "Now, people are accustomed to playing golf in their daily lives, and they think playing golf is a good way to take care of their health. There is an increasing reluctance among Korean business people to participate in the very common after-work drinking gatherings, which many Koreans do to please their bosses. They simply feel they eat and drink too much at these frequent gatherings." "I typically go to indoor golf two or three times per month," said Ki-mun Choi, who continued: "People go to indoor golf much more than having a round of golf at golf courses."

Jae-un Ahn, the owner of a small-medium enterprise, likes playing golf indoors on golf simulators: "It's the ultimate indoor experience. It is truly a virtual world, because you can get an experience indoors as if you were at a natural golf course. It is more realistic and exciting for me to play than just hitting golf balls at a wall, like other indoor golfing facilities."

GOLFZON Marketing

These days, the number of people who want to learn how to play golf is increasing. However, having a round of golf is relatively expensive, and Korean golf courses are very busy. Although demand for playing golf is increasing, supply is not enough to handle the demand. Therefore, people think about alternatives instead of going out to the field. When GOLFZON introduced its virtual golf system to Korean golfers, it was instantly popular. It was cheap, and people could enjoy playing golf by playing virtual golf. Moreover, Korea has a special culture where people like to gather in a room to play some game or talk with their friends. Since people can play virtual golf with their friends in a room, GOLFZON quickly became popular among players.

GOLFZON's *selling propositions* include the following:

- Each site offers 5–15 golf simulators.
- Entertainment is provided; some sites also provide golf lessons by professional teachers.
- Most sites offer food and beverages.
- Beginning golfers can learn in privacy and without investing in golf equipment.

As of August 2011, approximately 4,000 virtual golf sites had been established in South Korea.

GOLFZON has segmented the market into four main segments:

- Corporate buildings:
  - Provides a space for entertaining guests where everybody can be informal.
  - Allows employees to improve their game without having to spend time away from the office.

- Is a healthy break from work stress.
- Creates a progressive, creative work atmosphere.
- Promotes office morale.

- Hotels and resorts:

  - Is a unique marketing tool.
  - Encourages family leisure.
  - Draws in business guests.
  - Keeps visitors spending money at the location.
  - Can be used for business meetings and socializing.

- Condominiums and residential developments:

  - Increases property value.
  - Creates a feeling of community by helping neighbors socialize.
  - Promotes physical activity.
  - Allows residents golf access without having to travel to and from golf courses.

- Private installations:

  - Is a great addition to a home.
  - Allows owners to host golf parties for friends and neighbors.
  - Is an easy way to get the kids to learn golf.
  - Allows golfers to play without sacrificing family time.

GOLFZON markets golf tournaments where players can compete through online registration. In this way, a golfer can play against any player in the world, as long as they are also registered in GOLFZON's database. Golfers can be imaged by signing up to GOLFZON's Facebook page, thus enabling Facebook users to follow friends and their achievements through the statistics of the GOLFZON online service. They can see videos of their swings, which is very popular among Korean virtual golf players. Through the online system, they can retrieve YouTube-like videos and comment on each other's swings. It is a highly social platform, in addition to being a tool for instructors to improve the individuals' playing technique.

The biggest unique selling proposition for GOLFZON is the entertainment value of the play. There are competing systems on the market that are more advanced in the physical product setup and that focus on more parameters than the GOLFZON system does, but GOLFZON delivers play results earlier so that the player has a more intense feeling of being at the golf course and not participating in a video game. Competing systems use the hardware to do the calculations, whereas GOLFZON uses the software to do the calculations. Therefore, GOLFZON can incorporate more variety in different models, for example, adjusting swing parameters for beginners so that the golf ball stays on the field. This makes the play more enjoyable for some segments of players.

Managers of GOLFZON sites consistently point out the big advantage which GOLFZON possesses in the sense of the reality it delivers. For example, the board where players stand on can be tilted or moved according to geographic conditions in the real field. Such realistic factors make players enjoy the GOLFZON virtual golf.

GOLFZON develops its equipment all the time so that, for instance, the cameras become more and more precise. Most of the development is on the software side, with new games and new golf courses being added. But room furnishings are also updated periodically, besides offering new accessories such as clothes, jewelry, and pottery.

GOLFZON has not spent much money on marketing communication until now. Most business has been generated by references. GOLFZON does, however, carry out in-game advertising. In Korea, GOLFZON co-markets with, for example, Samsung Card, Hyundai Capital, and Jinro/Ballantine.

In terms of overseas sales, most of them have been due to requests from overseas customers. In some cases, these requests have come from technical companies which are familiar with GOLFZON; in other cases, they have come from exhibitions that GOLFZON has participated in. In Canada, GOLFZON got its start through a Canadian-Korean person who opened a GOLFZON shop there and experienced success with it; GOLFZON has since made him a Canadian agent.

GOLFZON Competition

There are many indoor golf system companies competing with GOLFZON, both domestically and internationally. The most common business format is a space with room for 5–10 golf simulation systems, about 5 meters wide and 7 meters deep. Players hit golf balls towards a screen on the wall.

"We are dominating the simulation golf market 10 years after our establishment with a market share of 84% as of 2011," GOLFZON's Public Relations Manager Seungmyo Seo said. He continued: "A good part of its success is that the company aims to make golf enjoyable and accessible to everyone. GOLFZON is just more fun to play. You can have more fun with your friends. The scores of your play appear instantly on the screen, whereas the scores for competing systems appear with a time lag. This means a lot for the motivation of players."

A GOLFZON system costs USD 35,000–45,000, dependent on features. The cheapest systems are targeted more at customers who play for fun with their friends, whereas the costlier systems are meant for serious golfers who want to build and train their skills. With GOLFZON, players can upload their results, including videos of their swing motion, to a central GOLFZON database. This makes it educational, motivational, and entertaining when playing with others.

Innovation is an important part of technological competition. Here again, GOLFZON has an advantage over its competition, holding 75 intellectual patents while its nearest four domestic competitors hold a total of only 15. GOLFZON achieves most of its revenue growth from its software and service activities; the service part of its turnover is currently bigger than the equipment part. GOLFZON intends to expand its GOLFZON Academy, where people can be trained by professional instructors, to several big city centers.

"Internationally, our competitors are HD Golf, aboutGolf, and Full Swing," said GOLFZON's Marketing Manager, Jason Allenberg, who continued: "There are also smaller players, like Holiday Golf, Sports Coach in England, and P3ProSwing." He added that the virtual golf systems market worldwide is quite fragmented and no single company poses a specific threat to GOLFZON. According to GOLFZON's Senior Research Engineer, Lee Mi Sun, the company has a first-mover advantage and other competitors are just following GOLFZON.

GOLFZON Business Strategies

GOLFZON's competitive strategy is to maintain its lead in Korea through unique competitiveness. Its market share rose from 62% in 2008, to 77% in 2009, to 84% in 2010, hence creating a new golf culture in Korea with more than one million people who play simulation golf. This way, GOLFZON has raised the entry barrier into the virtual golf market in terms of technology and brand awareness.

GOLFZON wants to continue improving its core technology through continuous R&D investment. It aims to develop and refine its hardware and software to the highest standards. The three decisive components in this area are the vision sensor (creating a 99% accuracy of the virtual play), the game design (storytelling with several game modes), and the graphics (expressing exact colors). To achieve these goals, GOLFZON maintains a focus on its R&D workforce, with 188 of its 408 employees being R&D engineers.

GOLFZON provides distinguished services that are delivered through network technology and an established infrastructure. For site owners, GOLFZON offers store management support services, enabling them to have efficient and comprehensive golf system management, member management, and golf room reservation services.

For users, GOLFZON organizes Korea's biggest virtual golf tournaments and broadcasts them on the Korean cable TV's golf channel. It also gives support to site owners and club competitions. It offers a real-time ranking service, online reservations, Internet-uploadable videos of players' swing motions, detailed game result analyses, and tracking of players' progress.

GOLFZON's network services sales have developed rapidly over the last few years, from under USD 1 million in 2007 to more than USD 11 million in 2010. More than 30 million rounds were played with GOLFZON simulation systems in 2010 (see Appendix C at the end of this chapter).

GOLFZON Internationalization

Currently, GOLFZON has branch offices in Japan (established in 2009) and China (established in May 2011). It plans to set up branch offices in North America (second half of 2011), Europe (2012), and Southeast Asia (2012). The concrete status as of August 2011 is as follows:

- Japan
  - Has directly managed stores in Tokyo and Osaka.
  - Is currently expanding its local distribution network for sales expansion.
  - Enjoys good response to products used in the driving range.
- China
  - Has five distributors.
  - Is reviewing the establishment of a joint venture with local companies.
- North America
  - Is expected to expand in Canada in the second half of 2011.
  - Has high marketability due to long winters.

- Will be the first to establish the virtual golf culture in major cities.
- Europe
  - Is expected in 2012.
  - Already has distributors to cover Europe and Russia.
  - Is planning to directly enter the region with marketability.
- Southeast Asia
  - Is expected in Taiwan in 2012.
  - Already has distributors in Taiwan and Thailand.
  - Has high regional marketability in Southeast Asia and the Middle East, due to geographical and seasonal restrictions.

Some Issues for GOLFZON

GOLFZON's vision is to establish a diverse virtual golf business focused on golfers worldwide. GOLFZON is focused on becoming the global golf industry leader by 2013, as it is already the No. 1 domestic simulation golf company. This is expected to occur through a combination of its virtual golf system, GOLFZON Academy (driving range), distribution, media, golf course images, games, and directly managed golf sites.

The GOLFZON organization today is very Korean. Of its roughly 400 employees, only one is foreign — the Marketing Manager, Jason Allenberg, who is American. As he sees it, it is a challenge for GOLFZON to adapt to foreign market cultures, because cultures are so different around the globe and the reasons for playing golf vary too.

GOLFZON has a different business model in mind for the future. GOLFZON realizes that the Korean virtual golf market is nearly saturated in its present form. When it was first introduced to the Korean market, it was a new phenomenon and people were excited about it. There are still opportunities to grow in Korea, but the offering has to be developed and expanded. Therefore, GOLFZON has plans to set up wholly owned GOLFZON sites, where they can experiment with new services such as food and beverages.

At the present stage, GOLFZON is still relatively new to the global market and the vastness of the global market seems a little bit scary. GOLFZON has, for example, only entered the Russian market with two GOLFZON sites. Golf is still in its infancy in Russia and a big surge in playing golf can be expected in the future. How should the company handle this market?

GOLFZON has about 50% of the global market share for virtual golf systems. GOLFZON sells to more than 30 countries and is not completely new to the international market, but there are competitors who are more internationally established. GOLFZON believes that it has to do a lot of marketing internationally in order to have a global presence. At the moment, the Korean market is becoming saturated, so GOLFZON has to go international to maintain its sales and grow. The challenge is to be able to adapt to the international environment because, until now, GOLFZON has been very Korean in its approach to marketing and sales. As of August 2011, GOLFZON had entirely Korean employees in an organization of 400 people, except for one foreigner who was hired 14 months ago to do overseas marketing and sales.

Natural golf courses worldwide are coming under pressure. The increasing demand for resources, created by the increasing world population, is influencing the golf market. Natural golf courses require a lot of water, but water prices are rising in most places in the world. Global warming has changed the climate profoundly in many places too. Additionally, the maintenance of golf courses requires a lot of chemicals, which creates environmental concerns.

Future developments for GOLFZON involve satisfying different segments in the market, from the more entertainment-prone people to the most advanced golfers. There are also GOLFZON systems for the more price-sensitive, developing golf markets like Russia, India, and other countries.

Case Questions

1. How can GOLFZON ascribe its success to its location in the Daedeok Innopolis research and production cluster in the remote geographical area of Daejeon in the middle of South Korea? Porter's diamond model might be used in your analysis.
2. What can challenge GOLFZON in its further growth? Porter's five-forces model might be used in your analysis.
3. Which options do you see for GOLFZON in the context of Ansoff's market growth matrix?
4. GOLFZON is at the very beginning of its global expansion. What global strategies would you propose for GOLFZON (in terms of market selection, entry mode, and decision variables)?

Bibliography

Birkinshaw, Julian and Neil Hood (2000). "Characteristics of Foreign Subsidiaries in Industry Clusters." *Journal of International Business Studies*, 31(1), 141–154.

Daedeok Innopolis (2011). http://www.ddi.or.kr/eng/.

GOLFZON (2011). http://www.golfzon.com/.

KAIST (2011). "Korea Advanced Institute of Science and Technology." http://www.kaist.edu/edu.html/.

Mattsson, Henrik (2009). "Innovating in Cluster/Cluster as Innovation: The Case of the Biotechvalley Cluster Initiative." *European Planning Studies*, 17(11), 1625–1643.

Porter, Michael (1990). *The Competitive Advantage of Nations.* New York: The Free Press.

Porter, Michael (1998). "Clusters and the New Economics of Competition." *Harvard Business Review*, November–December, 77–90.

Sorenson, Olav (2003). "Social Networks and Industrial Geography." *Journal of Evolutionary Economics*, 13, 513–527.

Stuart, Toby and Olav Sorenson (2003). "The Geography of Opportunity: Spatial Heterogeneity in Founding Rates and the Performance of Biotechnology Firms." *Research Policy*, 32, 229–253.

Acknowledgments: The author would like to thank the GOLFZON staff, especially the Marketing Manager Jason Allenberg, the Public Relations Manager Seungmyo Seo, and the Senior Research Engineer Lee Mi Sun. They were my primary source of information about GOLFZON and the virtual golf market in general. Jason Allenberg in particular was very committed to the case at any moment I needed him. I would also like to thank my Teaching Assistant, Hee-Seung Lee, who is Korean and who linked me to golf sites in Korea for observation and interview purposes and assisted me in many ways.

Appendix A: Revenue History

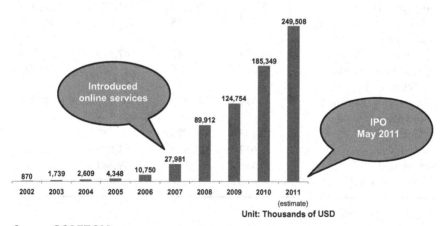

Source: GOLFZON.

Appendix B: Summarized Financial Statements

Balance Sheet

Title of Account	2007	2008	2009	2010
Current assets	3,052	52,938	62,035	124,542
Non-current assets	13,344	13,271	28,460	43,054
Total assets	**16,397**	**66,209**	**90,495**	**167,596**
Current liabilities	4,430	10,992	10,336	17,136
Non-current liabilities	356	1,258	2,538	3,166
Total liabilities	**4,785**	**12,250**	**12,874**	**20,302**
Capital	460	940	4,658	4,728
Retained earnings	11,150	49,010	95,593	134,401
Total equity	**11,612**	**53,959**	**77,620**	**147,293**

Income Statement

Title of Account	2007	2008	2009	2010
Sales	28,912	92,819	122,370	169,453
Cost of goods sold	11,036	36,027	50,596	75,246
Gross profit	17,877	56,792	71,774	94,206
Selling and administrative expenses	6,106	14,945	23,851	36,934
Operating profit	11,771	41,847	47,923	57,272
Operating profit-to-sales ratio (%)	41%	45%	39%	34%
Non-operating profit and loss	371	−1,119	3,223	7,601
Ordinary profit	12,143	40,729	51,145	64,873
Company tax	1,652	2,868	1,804	3,174
Net income	10,490	37,861	49,341	61,700
Net profit ratio (%)	36%	41%	40%	36%

Source: GOLFZON.
Note: Units are in thousands of USD.

Appendix C: Network Services Sales Progress

(Unit: 1 thousand USD / 1,000 Rounds)

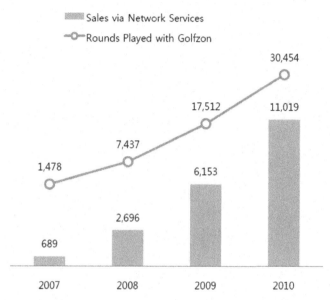

■ Sales via Network Services
─○─Rounds Played with Golfzon

Source: GOLFZON.

Selected Bibliography

[no date] "What Are Industrial Clusters?" San Diego Regional Technology Alliance, San Diego Association of Governments, pp. 1–18. http://www.sandag.org/rta/transfer/industrial_clusters.pdf/.

Aaker, David A. (1995). *Strategic Market Management*, 4th ed. New York: John Wiley & Sons, Inc.

Adams, David and Michael Hess (2010). "Social Innovation and Why It Has Policy Significance." *The Economic and Labour Relations Review*, 21(2), 139–156.

Ante, Spencer E. (2008). *Creative Capital: Georges Doriot and the Birth of Venture Capital*. Boston: Harvard Business Press.

Baptista, Rui and Peter Swann (1998). "Do Firms in Clusters Innovate More?" *Research Policy*, 27, 525–540.

Barabba, Vincent P. (1995). *Meeting of the Minds: Creating the Market-Based Enterprise*. Boston, MA: Harvard Business School Press.

Bathelt, Harald (2005). "Geographies of Production: Growth Regimes in Spatial Perspective (II) — Knowledge Creation and Growth in Clusters." *Progress in Human Geography*, 29(2), 204–216.

Bell, Geoffrey G. (2005). "Clusters, Networks, and Firm Innovativeness." *Strategic Management Journal*, 26, 287–295.

Beveridge, W.I.B. (1950). *The Art of Scientific Investigation*. New York: Vintage Books.

Bilkey, Warren J. (1970). *Industrial Stimulation*. Lexington, MA: Heath Lexington Books.

Bilkey, Warren J. and George Tesar (1977). "The Export Behavior of Smaller-Sized Wisconsin Manufacturing Firms." *Journal of International Business Studies*, 8(1), Spring/Summer, 93–98.

Blair, John M. (1972). *Economic Concentration: Structure, Behavior, and Public Policy*. New York: Harcourt Brace Jovanovich, Inc., pp. 85–133.

Brenner, Thomas (2004). *Local Industrial Clusters: Existence, Emergence, and Evolution*. London: Routledge.

Christensen, C. Ronald (1987). *Teaching and the Case Method*. Boston: Harvard Business School Press.

Cooke, Philip (2001). "Regional Innovation Systems, Clusters, and the Knowledge Economy." *Industrial and Corporate Change*, 10(4), 945–974.

Cortright, Joseph (2006). "Making Sense of Clusters: Regional Competitiveness and Economic Development." A discussion paper prepared for the Brookings Institution Metropolitan Policy Program, Washington, D.C., March.

Engel, Jerome S. and Itxaso Del-Palacio (2011). "Global Clusters of Innovation: The Case of Israel and Silicon Valley." *California Management Review*, 53(2), Winter, 27–49.

Feldman, Maryann P., Johanna Francis, and Janet Bercovitz (2005). "Creating a Cluster While Building a Firm: Entrepreneurs and the Formation of Industrial Clusters." *Regional Studies*, 39(1), February, 129–141.

Felzensztein, Christian and Eli Gimmon (2009). "Social Networks and Marketing Cooperation in Entrepreneurial Clusters: An International Comparative Study." *Journal of International Entrepreneurship*, 7, 281–291.

Feser, Edward J. and Edward M. Bergman (2000). "National Industry Cluster Templates: A Framework for Applied Regional Cluster Analysis." *Regional Studies*, 34(1), February, 1–19.

Feser, Edward J., Kyojun Koo, Henry C. Renski, and Stewart H. Sweeney (2001). "Incorporating Spatial Analysis in Applied Industry Cluster Studies." Document prepared for *Economic Development Quarterly*, Department of City and Regional Planning, University of North Carolina, Chapel Hill, North Carolina, March.

Florida, Richard (2010). *The Great Reset: How New Ways of Living and Working Drive Post-Crash Prosperity*. New York: Harper Collins Publishers.

Frank, Ronald E., William F. Massy, and Yoram Wind (1972). *Market Segmentation*. Englewood Cliffs, NJ: Prentice-Hall, Inc.

Galbraith, John Kenneth (1964). *Economic Development*. Boston: Houghton Mifflin Company, Sentry Edition.

Gordon, Ian R. and Philip McCann (2000). "Industrial Clusters: Complexes, Agglomeration and/or Social Networks?" *Urban Studies*, 37(3), 513–532.

Guliani, Elisa (2005). "Cluster Absorptive Capacity: Why Do Some Clusters Forge Ahead and Others Lag Behind?" *European Urban and Regional Studies*, 12(3), July, 269–288.

Harwood, Tracy, Tony Garry, and Anne Broderick (2008). *Relationship Marketing: Perspectives, Dimensions and Contexts*. New York: McGraw-Hill.

Hutt, Michael D. and Thomas W. Speh (2007). *Business Marketing Management: B2B*. Mason, OH: Thomson Higher Education.

Iammarino, Simona and Philip McCann (2006). "The Structure and Evolution of Industrial Clusters: Transactions, Technology and Knowledge Spillover." *Research Policy*, 35, 1018–1036.

Kotler, Philip (1967). *Marketing Management: Analysis, Planning, and Control*. Englewood Cliffs, NJ: Prentice-Hall, Inc.

Kotter, John P. (1996). *Leading Change*. Boston: Harvard Business School Press.

Kukalis, Sal (2010). "Agglomeration Economies and Firm Performance: The Case of Industry Clusters." *Journal of Management*, 36(2), March, 453–481.

Lazer, William and Eugene J. Kelley (1962). *Managerial Marketing: Perspectives and Viewpoints — A Source Book*. Homewood, IL: Richard D. Irwin, Inc.

Mattsson, Henrik (2009). "Innovating in Cluster/Cluster as Innovation: The Case of the Biotechvalley Cluster Initiative." *European Planning Studies*, 17(11), November, 1625–1643.

McCraw, Thomas K. (2007). *Prophet of Innovation: Joseph Schumpeter and Creative Destruction*. Cambridge, MA: The Belknap Press of Harvard University Press.

Medawar, P.B. (1984). *The Limits of Science*. London: Harper & Row.

Meier, Gerald M. and Robert E. Baldwin (1957). *Economic Development: Theory, History, and Policy*. New York: John Wiley & Sons, Inc.

Messinger, Paul R. (1995). *The Marketing Paradigm: A Guide for General Managers*. Cincinnati, OH: South-Western College Press.

Mohr, Jakki (2001). *Marketing of High-Technology Products and Innovations*. Upper Saddle River, NJ: Prentice Hall.

Molina-Morales, F. Xavier and M. Teresa Martinez-Fernandez (2009). "Too Much Love in the Neighborhood Can Hurt: How an Excess of Intensity and Trust in Relationships May Produce Negative Effects on Firms." *Strategic Management Journal*, 30, 1013–1023.

Morosini, Piero (2004). "Industrial Clusters, Knowledge Integration and Performance." *World Development*, 32(2), 305–326.

Mytelka, Lynn and Fulvia Farinelli (2000). "Local Clusters, Innovation Systems and Sustained Competitiveness." Discussion Paper Series #2005, United Nations University–Institute for New Technologies, Maastricht, The Netherlands, October.

Niu, Kuei-Hsien (2010). "Organizational Trust and Knowledge Obtaining in Industrial Clusters." *Journal of Knowledge Management*, 14(1), 141–155.

Penzias, Arno (1989). *Ideas and Information: Managing in a High-Tech World*. London: W.W. Norton & Company.

Porter, Michael (1980). *Competitive Strategy: Techniques for Analyzing Industries and Competitors*. New York: The Free Press.

Porter, Michael (1998a). "Clusters and the New Economics of Competition." *Harvard Business Review*, November–December, 77–90.

Porter, Michael (1998b). "The Adam Smith Address: Location, Clusters, and the 'New' Microeconomics of Competition." *Business Economics*, 33, January, 7–13.

Porter, Michael (2000). "Location, Competition, and Economic Development: Local Clusters in a Global Economy." *Economic Development Quarterly*, 14(1), February, 15–34.

Prahalad, C.K. and M.S. Krishnan (2008). *The New Age of Innovation*. New York: McGraw-Hill.

Russo, Margherita and Federica Rossi (2009). "Cooperation Networks and Innovation: A Complex Systems Perspective to the Analysis and Evaluation of a Regional Innovation Policy Programme." *Evaluation*, 15(1), January, 75–99.

Schiele, Holger (2008). "Location, Location: The Geography of Industry Clusters." *Journal of Business Strategy*, 29(3), 29–36.

Schnaars, Steven (1991). *Marketing Strategy: A Customer-Driven Approach*. New York: The Free Press.

Smith, Madeline and Ross Brown (2009). "Exploratory Techniques for Examining Cluster Dynamics: A Systems Thinking Approach." *Local Economy*, 24(4), June, 283–298.

Snow, C.P. (1963). *Two Cultures: And a Second Look*. New York: A Mentor Book.

Sölvell, Örjan, Göran Lindqvist, and Christian Ketels (2003). *The Cluster Initiative Greenbook*. Stockholm: Ivory Tower AB/European Cluster Observatory.

Sorenson, Olav (2003). "Social Networks and Industrial Geography." *Journal of Evolutionary Economics*, 13, 513–527.

Sparrow, John (2001). "Case Study: Knowledge Management in Small Firms." *Knowledge and Process Management*, 8(1), 3–16.

Staber, Udo (2007). "The Competitive Advantage of Regional Clusters: An Organizational–Evolutionary Perspective." *Competition & Change*, 11(1), March, 3–18.

Steinle, C. and Holger Schiele (2002). "When Do Industries Cluster? A Proposal on How to Assess an Industry's Propensity to Concentrate at a Single Region or Nation." *Research Policy*, 31, 849–858.

Stuart, Toby and Olav Sorenson (2003). "The Geography of Opportunity: Spatial Heterogeneity in Founding Rates and the Performance of Biotechnology Firms." *Research Policy*, 32, 229–253.

Tesar, George, Steven W. Anderson, Sibdas Ghosh, and Tom Bramorski (2008). *Strategic Technology Management: Building Bridges between Sciences, Engineering and Business Management*, 2nd ed. London: Imperial College Press.

Tesar, George, Hamid Moini, John Kuada, and Olav Jull Sørensen (2010). *Smaller Manufacturing Enterprises in an International Context: A Longitudinal Exploration.* London: Imperial College Press.

Tillväxtverket (2010). "Nationell Klusterutveckling i Andra Länder: Tyskland, Finland, Japan och EU." Dnr: 2010/124 [in Swedish].

Ulrich, Dave and Norm Smallwood (2007). *Leadership Brand: Developing Customer-Focused Leaders to Drive Performance and Build Lasting Value.* Boston: Harvard Business School Press.

van der Linde, C. (2003). "The Demography of Clusters — Findings from the Cluster Meta-Study." In Bröcker, Johannes, Dirk Dohse, and Rüdiger Soltwedel (eds.), *Innovation Clusters and Interregional Competition*, Berlin: Springer.

vom Hofe, Rainer and Ke Chen (2006). "Whither or Not Industrial Cluster: Conclusions or Confusions?" *The Industrial Geographer*, 4(1), 2–28.

Waits, Mary Jo (2000). "The Added Value of the Industry Cluster Approach to Economic Analysis, Strategy Development, and Service Delivery." *Economic Development Quarterly*, 14(1), February, 35–50.

Whitford, Josh and Cuz Potter (2007). "The State of the Art: Regional Economies, Open Networks and the Spatial Fragmentation of Production." *Socio-Economic Review*, 5, 497–526.

Wu, L., X. Yue, and T. Sim (2006). "Supply Clusters: A Key to China's Cost Advantage." *Supply Chain Management Review*, 10(2), 46–51.

Zinsser, William (1976). *On Writing Well: An Informal Guide to Writing Nonfiction.* London: Harper & Row.

Cluster Marketing Management-Related

Czerniawski, Richard D. (1986). "Cluster Marketing: An Alternative Approach to Marketing Planning and Implementation." *Journal of Consumer Marketing*, 3(2), Spring, 81–86.

European Clusters

Dahl Fitjar, Rune and Andrés Rodríguez-Pose (2011). "Innovating in the Periphery: Firms, Values, and Innovation in Southwest Norway." *European Planning Studies*, 19(4), 555–574.

Hervas-Oliver, Jose-Luis and Jose Albors-Garrigos (2009). "The Role of the Firm's Internal and Relational Capabilities in Clusters: When Distance and Embeddedness Are Not Enough to Explain Innovation." *Journal of Economic Geography*, 9(2), 263–283.

Jagger, Anna (2010). "Mega Clusters." *ICIS Chemical Business*, 278(4), August 9–15, 26–27.

Karaev, Aleksandar, S.C. Lenny Koh, and Leslie T. Szamosi (2007). "The Cluster Approach and SME Competitiveness: A Review." *Journal of Manufacturing Technology Management*, 18(7), 818–835.

Ketels, Christian (2007, reprint). "European Clusters." In *Structural Change in Europe 3 — Innovative City and Business Regions*, Bollschweil, Germany: Hagbarth Publications.

Madsen, Erik Strøjer, Valdemar Smith, and Mogens Dilling-Hansen (2003). "Industrial Clusters, Firm Location and Productivity — Some Empirical Evidence for Danish Firms." Working Paper 03-26, Department of Economics, Aarhus School of Business, Denmark.

Mattsson, Henrik (2009). "Innovating in Cluster/Cluster as Innovation: The Case of the Biotechvalley Cluster Initiative." *European Planning Studies*, 17(11), November, 1625–1643.

Nadabán, Márta Völgyiné and Ágnes Barbara Berde (2009). "Clusters: Definition, Typology and Characteristics of Some Clusters in the Észak-Alföld Region — Case Study." In *Proceedings of the 4th Aspects and Visions of Applied Economics and Informatics Conference, Debrecen, Hungary, March 26–27, 2009*, pp. 772–779.

Australian Clusters

Adams, David and Michael Hess (2010). "Social Innovation and Why It Has Policy Significance." *The Economic and Labour Relations Review*, 21(2), 139–156.

Enright, Michael J. and Brian H. Roberts (2001). "Regional Clustering in Australia." *Australian Journal of Management*, 26, August, 65–85.

Asian and Indian Clusters

Arita, Tomokazu, Masahisa Fujita, and Yoshihiro Kameyama (2006). "Effects of Regional Cooperation among Small and Medium-Sized Firms on Their Growth in Japanese Industrial Clusters." *Review of Urban & Regional Development Studies*, 18(3), November, 209–228.

Dayasindhu, N. (2002). "Embeddedness, Knowledge Transfer, Industry Clusters and Global Competitiveness: A Case Study of the Indian Software Industry." *Technovation*, 22, 551–560.

Resources on the Internet

Website Name	Website Address
Adobe's Buzzword	https://www.acrobat.com/main/en/online-document-sharing.html/
Apple's iCloud	www.apple.com/icloud
Athelia Entreprendre (only in French)	www.atheliaentreprendre.fr
Autoblog: "GM to cut number of vehicle platforms, engines in half"	http://www.autoblog.com/2011/08/09/gm-to-cut-number-of-vehicle-platforms-engines-in-half/
Be Green Umeå	en.greencit.se, www.begreenumea.se
BioEthanol for Sustainable Transport (BEST)	www.best-europe.org
BioFuel Region	www.biofuelregion.se
Biorefinery of the Future	www.bioraffinaderi.se
Cardvdstore.com's Blog: "Daimler, Renault are set to share vehicle platforms and engines"	http://blog.cardvdstore.com/uncategorized/daimler-renault-are-set-to-share-vehicle-platforms-and-engines.html/
Centre for the Promotion of Imports from Developing Countries	www.cbi.eu
Citizens Network for Foreign Affairs (CNFA) Moldova	www.cnfa.md
Clean Clothes Campaign	www.cleanclothes.org
Cluster Offensive Bavaria	http://bayern-innovativ.de/1f1d267a-e8d7-7b95-259a-3dc6be3597ab/
Council on Competitiveness: "Clusters of Innovation Initiative: Regional Foundations of U.S. Competitiveness"	http://www.compete.org/publications/detail/220/clusters-of-innovation-initiative-regional-foundations-of-us-competitiveness/
Ecologie Industrielle (only in French)	www.france-ecologieindustrielle.fr
Europe INNOVA	www.europe-innova.eu
European Cluster Alliance	www.proinno-europe.eu/eca
European Cluster Collaboration Platform	www.clustercollaboration.eu

(*Continued*)

(Continued)

Website Name	Website Address
European Cluster Observatory's free educational video series	http://www.clusterobservatory.eu/index.html#!view=classroom;url=/classroom/OnClusters/
European Cluster Policy Group: "Final Recommendations — A Call for Policy Action"	http://www.clusterobservatory.eu/common/galleries/downloads/ECPG_Final_Report_web-low1.pdf/
Excellence for Cluster Management	www.cluster-excellence.eu
FältCom	www.faltcom.se
Food & Drink Europe	www.foodanddrinkeurope.com
Frost & Sullivan: "30 per cent reduction in vehicle platforms by 2020: OEMs to ride on platform standardization and modular strategy"	http://www.frost.com/prod/servlet/market-insight-top.pag?Src=RSS&docid=240652140/
General Motors	www.gm.com
Google Docs	docs.google.com
H&M's CSR reporting	http://about.hm.com/csr/
International Society for Industrial Ecology (ISIE)	www.is4ie.org
Invest in Med	www.invest-in-med.eu/en
Japanese Ministry of Economy, Trade, and Industry: "Industrial Clusters"	http://www.cluster.gr.jp/en/relation/data/brochure_e.html/
Kompetenznetze Deutschland: "Clusters in Germany: An Empirical Based Insight View on Emergence, Financing, Management and Competitiveness of the Most Innovative Clusters in Germany"	http://www.kompetenznetze.de/service/bestellservice/medien/broschure-clusters-in-germany_online.pdf/
Marine Stewardship Council	www.msc.org
National Bank of Moldova	www.bnm.md/en/home
Natura 2000 Networking Progamme	www.natura.org
Nordic River AB	www.nordicriver.com
Pang Da	www.pdqmjt.com/EN
Polarrenen AB	www.polarrenen.se

(Continued)

(Continued)

Website Name	Website Address
Processum Biorefinery Initiative	www.processum.se
Reachin Technologies AB	www.reachin.se
redQ	redq.se
Republic of Moldova	www.moldova.md/en/start
Saab	www.saab.com
Scania	www.scania.com
Spyker	www.spykerworld.com
STICS	www.facebook.com/SticsResearch
Strategic Centres for Science, Technology and Innovation, Finland	www.tekes.fi/en/community/Strategic_Centres_for_Science__Technology_and_Innovation_(SHOK)/360/Strategic_Centres_for_Science__Technology_and_Innovation_(SHOK)/1296
Swedish Waste Management	www.avfallsverige.se/in-english
Technology Strategy Board — Low Carbon Vehicles	http://www.innovateuk.org/ourstrategy/innovationplatforms/lowcarbon vehicles.ashx/
ThinkFree	www.thinkfree.com
Umeå Institute of Design	www.dh.umu.se
University of Cambridge's Institute for Manufacturing — Sustainable Manufacturing Group	http://www.ifm.eng.cam.ac.uk/sustainability/
U.S. EDA's Regional Innovation Cluster	http://www.eda.gov/AboutEDA/RIC/
U.S. SBA — Innovative Economy Clusters	http://www.sba.gov/about-sba-info/24931/11574/
Vinnova's Vinnväxt competition	http://www.vinnova.se/sv/Verksamhet/VINNVAXT/
Windows Live Mesh	explore.live.com
Youngman	www.young-man.cn/eng/index.aspx
Zoho Writer	writer.zoho.com

Index